THE THOUSAND AND ONE DAYS

THE THOUSAND AND ONE DAYS

WILLI FEHSE

Translated by
ANTHEA BELL

Illustrated by
ERICH HOLLE

ABELARD-SCHUMAN
London   New York   Toronto

I.S.B.N. 0.200.71724.3

LONDON
Abelard – Schuman
Limited
8 King Street
WC2

NEW YORK
Abelard – Schuman
Limited
257 Park Avenue South
NY 10010

TORONTO
Abelard – Schuman
Limited
228 Yorkland Boulevard
425

CONTENTS

THE PRINCE OF THE FLOWERY MEADOW   7

ABDALLAH THE UNGRATEFUL   15

ABDUL KASIM THE RICH   24

PRINCE MONKEY   66

KING SOLOMON'S RING   79

HARCHAND THE JUST   98

THE WICKED SANKHASHURNI   104

THE NINE-HEADED BIRD   107

TURANDOT   115

SEMRUDE THE FAIR AND THE CADI   154

THE THREE DOOMS   177

THE PRINCE OF THE FLOWERY MEADOW   188
(continued)

About THE THOUSAND AND ONE DAYS   210

THE PRINCE OF THE FLOWERY MEADOW

Long, long ago a beautiful princess called Faruknas lived in Kashmir. She loved to walk in the rose garden of her father's palace. This rose garden was surrounded by high walls.

One day, as she was wandering among the lawns and flower beds, a wind suddenly arose. The princess shut her eyes for a moment, and when she opened them again she found that the palace and the rose garden had disappeared. She was standing all alone in a broad, flowery meadow.

"What can this mean?" asked the king's daughter.

But there was not a living soul in sight to answer her question.

Suddenly Faruknas heard a man's voice behind her. "Who are you, beautiful maiden? And how did you come here?"

The princess turned around, raising her hand in alarm. Two paces away from her, behind a tall thistle, stood a young man. He was tall and handsome, and he wore princely robes. There was a buttercup in the jewelled clasp of his turban, and he held a bunch of fresh wild flowers in his right hand.

The young stranger smiled at Faruknas, bowed, and offered her the bunch of flowers.

The princess thanked him. She had fallen deeply in love with this young man at first sight, and was eager to know who he really was. So, fastening the flowers to her dress, she asked, "Who are you? Tell me your name!"

"I am a prince . . . " the young man began. But before he could say anything more, a gentle wind arose again. Faruknas shut her eyes for the space of a heartbeat, and when she opened them again she was back where she had been before, in the walled rose garden of her father's palace. There was no sign of the flowery meadow, the tall thistle or the prince.

Faruknas went straight to her nurse and told her about this wonderful adventure.

"Your mind must be wandering child!" cried the old nurse Sutlumene. "Or were you dreaming in broad daylight?"

The princess shook her head. "What do you mean, Sutlumene?" she replied. "I was not dreaming, and my mind is not wandering either. Do you see this bunch of wild flowers? The prince gave it to me! And have you noticed all these thistles clinging to my dress?"

Since there were no thistles or wild flowers growing anywhere in the king's well-kept garden, Sutlumene had to agree that what the princess told her must have happened; some mysterious power seemed to have spirited her away briefly from the palace grounds and then brought her back again. But what kind of power could it have been, and why had she been carried off?

No one could answer these questions — neither the nurse, nor the king or the queen, least of all the wise men of the land with their long beards, although they were kept at court and paid to solve just such problems.

"Have no fear, dear daughter!" said the queen at last. "Six men of the bodyguard have been chosen to keep watch over you. From now on they will follow wherever you go, and take care that no one comes too near you again."

Faruknas felt like interrupting her mother. What did she want with guards? She was not afraid of another meeting with the young man — quite the opposite. What she feared was that she might never see him again! But since she dared not say as much, she merely nodded and kept her thoughts to herself.

Time passed by. The bunch of wild flowers had withered long ago, but the princess still wore it on her dress. When she went walking in the garden little gusts of wind would arise now and then, but they never brought back the young man who had smiled at the princess and called her "beautiful maiden". Faruknas longed for him all the time; she could not eat or sleep for thinking of him, and her nurse and her parents grieved to see her growing paler day by day, as her health failed.

One day her mother took her aside. "Tell me what the matter is, my child!" said she. "Perhaps I can help you."

"I would not tell you," Faruknas replied. "Even if I wanted to, I could not do so. You would think me a fool!"

And much as the queen pressed her, and tried to persuade her to change her mind, Faruknas remained silent.

"Perhaps we ought to find you a husband!" suggested the king. "Yesterday the Prince of Bokhara sent me word that he would be happy to welcome you as his son's wife. Shall I give him your consent?"

"In heaven's name, Father!" cried the princess. "I will never marry anyone but that young man!"

"What young man?" inquired her father.

9

Now that she had betrayed herself, Faruknas was obliged to come out with the whole story. Her parents listened quietly, but then they voiced their doubts.

"How can we be sure," they asked, "that the prince of the flowery meadow was not just a vision? A phantom creature? A lovely apparition that will never return again? However, we will not force you to do anything, dear Faruknas. You need never become the wife of the Prince of Bokhara against your wish. We will be patient with you, and — forgive us — with your whims and fancies, too!"

And the king concluded, "Of course, you may go walking alone in the rose garden again, without your guards, if you wish. Then, perhaps, your beloved may appear to you again!" he added in tones of gentle mockery, as he embraced Faruknas.

The princess was deeply touched by all this kindness and tolerance. She thanked her father for his suggestion, and sure enough, from that day on she would walk in the palace grounds and gardens alone again. Whenever a gentle breeze blew through the flowers and the rose bushes, lifting the veil from her face, she would close her eyes at once, and her face was transfigured with hope, not just for the space of a heartbeat, but long enough for her heart to beat a hundred times, and yet a hundred more, against the faded bunch of wild flowers she still wore on her dress.

But when she opened her eyes again she saw only the rose garden, and her father's palace in its usual place, as solid as ever. There was never a sign of the flowery meadow, the tall thistle or the princely young man. Soon the princess was heart-broken with the continual disappointment of her hopes. Even though she scarcely dared to expect that she would see her beloved prince again, she was waiting for him all the time. Although her parents did not take her account of the strange meeting in the meadow very seriously, they encouraged Faruknas to hope. They did not want her to despair, and they may have thought to themselves that time would cure all their daughter's troubles.

However, just the opposite happened. One day the princess said, "I see that the young man is not returning for me."

"Does that not prove that he is only a creature of your imagination?" said her father.

"Oh, no!" said Faruknas. "It can only mean that some misfortune has befallen him, and that is why he cannot come. It is my duty to go in search of him and help him."

"This is madness!" cried the king. "Why, you are only a weak girl!"

"Love will make me strong!" Faruknas said.

"But have you any idea where to search for him?" her father objected. "The world is very wide!"

"I am sure to find my way to him!" replied Faruknas firmly. "Fortune will not forsake me."

"I will never agree to such a thing! Never!" declared the king, and the queen agreed. "From now on your bodyguard will go with you wherever you go, to keep you from doing anything foolish. They will pay with their lives if you escape. Please, Faruknas, my dear daughter, you must be reasonable!"

But the princess refused to answer, and her anxious parents left her in tears — tears that soon ran dry, since no one can weep all day and night. However, day and night the princess thought of nothing but the strange prince. She would imagine his fate over and over again as she lay on her couch, never moving. If her parents spoke to her, she would only move her head slightly, and she seemed not to feel it when anyone touched her.

The king and queen consulted all the wise doctors in the land, but in vain — they could not cure the sick girl. Sometimes the jesters would try to cheer her up, or her friends would dance and sing for her. Faruknas was inconsolable, and inconsolable she remained.

One day the nurse, Sutlumene, flung herself at the king's feet. "O my lord!" said she, "I am only a simple old woman, but I have had an idea. Will you hear it?"

"Tell me your idea, good Sutlumene," replied the king. "You are a faithful creature, and I am deeply moved that you take the fate of Faruknas so much to heart. Speak, and I will hear you!"

"Perhaps we could make the princess happy again and bring her back to life by telling her stories."

"Stories?" said the king. "Do you know any stories?"

"Indeed I do!" answered Sutlumene. "I know any number of stories, almost more than I can count. Tales of good and evil spirits, dragons and monsters, mysterious treasures, treasure seekers, journeys and enchantments, beautiful and clever maidens, enchanted princes and wicked stepsisters, tales of poor folk made rich and sad folk made happy, and many other things! See how old I am now, my lord! I have seen and known many things, and turned many of them into stories. For I must confess to you, your Majesty, that many of the tales I tell are of my own making!"

"How many of these stories do you know?" asked the king.

"I must not exaggerate," replied Sutlumene, "but there are certainly enough to last a thousand and one days."

"And do you think you could cure my daughter with your tales?" inquired the king.

"There is a strange power in such stories, my lord," replied the old woman. "They do more than banish boredom, sadness and despondency. They give strength to the weak, calm the distressed, and give clear answers to all questions, even those that no one has ever asked before. Then, think — a thousand and one days is a long time. During that time the princess may forget her grief. Perhaps — who can tell — the wonderful prince of the flowery meadow may send some message meanwhile. Let me see what I can do!"

The king did not really believe that the nurse could do what she suggested, but since he could think of nothing better, he nodded his consent.

"I agree, Sutlumene!" said he. "You may try your cure."

Sutlumene thanked him, and hurried straight to the princess's

rooms. As usual, Faruknas was lying on her couch. She was neither asleep nor properly awake; she looked as if she were really somewhere else as she lay there, staring straight ahead of her, her eyes wide open.

"Little one, can you hear me?" the old nurse coaxed her.

Faruknas did not reply. Sutlumene stroked her forehead gently, but the princess did not move. Then the nurse turned to the girls who had been dancing and singing around the couch of the sick princess, and were now sitting quietly at her feet.

"Shall I tell you a story, fair maidens?" asked Sutlumene.

"Oh yes!" cried the girls, jumping up and clapping their hands. "Do tell us a story!"

Some of them wanted to hear a tale of dangerous adventures, mysterious treasures and cunning plots. Others demanded a story to make them laugh, or a tale where the wicked were punished and the good rewarded.

"Patience, patience!" said the old woman. "I will tell you all kinds of stories, and so each of you will have her wish!"

And with that, sitting down on the divan at the princess's feet, and asking no leave of Faruknas, Sutlumene began to tell a story.

ABDALLAH THE UNGRATEFUL

Once upon a time a venerable old dervish, or begging monk, named Abu Nadar, lodged for the night at the house of a widow in Basra. This widow was so hospitable and gave him such a warm welcome that he wished to repay her kindness.

"I can see that you are poor, dear sister," said the dervish as he took his leave. "You will find it hard to bring up your son Abdallah and have him educated as you would wish. Will you entrust the boy to me? I will be a father to him and look after him well."

The widow had known this dervish as a holy man for many years; no one could ever think ill of him. So she was happy to agree to this suggestion, and sent her son away with him.

The dervish came from Maghrebi. Taking Abdallah with him, he travelled through all the fairest lands and the greatest cities of Asia, yet he always took great care to avoid his native city. The old man treated the boy like his own son. He gave him lessons, taught him much wisdom and many skills, and once, when Abdallah was sick, the dervish risked his life to nurse him until he was well again. It was no wonder the boy kept assuring Abu Nadar of his gratitude!

But the dervish would not listen to his protestations. "Gratitude, my son, springs from the heart, not the lips," said he. "It shows itself in deeds, not words. You may yet be able to prove your gratitude to me."

As they journeyed on they came one day to a desert place, where a great rock barred their way.

"There is treasure inside this rock," the dervish told Abdallah. "It is ours if you will obey me. This is the time for you to prove your gratitude and love, if you so wish!"

Abdallah promised to do everything his kind benefactor said.

"Good," replied the dervish, and raising his staff, he struck the rock with it. Next moment the stone opened like a door.

"Go in, my son!" said the dervish. "Inside this cave you will find an iron candlestick. It is this candlestick that I want. Take it! But you must not touch any of the gold and silver treasure lying around. Remember what I say — you are to take only that candlestick. The rest is not for us. Can I rely on your obedience?"

"Why, of course you can, dear Father," Abdallah promised. "I know what I owe you!" So saying, he climbed into the opening in the rock.

However, as soon as he set eyes on the gold and silver coins, the jewels and the gems lying around the candlestick, he was dazzled, and his heart turned over. He could not resist the temptation. Forgetting the monk's command, he filled his pockets with the gleaming treasure. As he did so the rock closed again. Suddenly it was pitch dark all around him. Grasping the candlestick, Abdallah groped back and forth, hoping to find a way out.

At last he saw a faint gleam of light in the distance. He went toward it, and to his astonishment the depths of the cave suddenly seemed to open, and there he was outside. He looked around in amazement. The dervish was nowhere to be seen, and, to his great surprise, the desert and the rock had vanished too. Instead, he found himself near Basra, where his mother lived.

"Never mind the dervish, wherever he may be," thought Abdallah. "I'm rich enough to do without him now."

His mother, of course, asked after the holy man. Abdallah described what had happened in the desert, and ended by saying that he no longer needed the old man's help.

With that, he emptied his pockets, pouring out the gold and silver and jewels on the table, and they both feasted their eyes upon their riches. They counted the money out, coin by coin, laid plans, and were just deciding what to do with it when suddenly the treasure disappeared as if it had been blown clean away. Only the candlestick was left on the table.

"Alas, what does this mean?" the widow wailed. "We have made the holy man angry, Abdallah! He was only testing us, and now all our wealth has been taken away because we forgot him. Take him the candlestick, to please me! Perhaps that will soften his heart. You're sure to find him somewhere!"

But Abdallah, who had inherited none of his mother's timid and pious nature, sat down in a corner and cursed the old man, contemptuously kicking the candlestick aside.

"A fine thing this is that the old skinflint's left me!" said he angrily. "I risk my life climbing into that rock, and he takes away what I brought out without so much as a by your leave! Say what you like, Mother, I don't want to be ungrateful, but that dervish is no holy man! I believe he's a magician and a sorcerer!"

While Abdallah was venting his anger this way, night fell. His mother lit a small oil lamp and put it on the table. Abdallah did not think it looked quite right there, so he hung it from one branch of the great iron candlestick. Suddenly a dervish in a long brown robe appeared. He twirled around like a top, threw a copper coin — an asper — on the table and vanished without a word.

"What can this mean?" said Abdallah, and he brooded about the strange apparition all night.

The following evening he had an idea. The iron candlestick had twelve branches; he put a candle in each, and lit them all. At once twelve dervishes, dressed in brown, appeared. They whirled around and around for a good quarter of an hour, and finally disappeared, each of them throwing down an asper.

The next evening Abdallah repeated his experiment, and they came again. But they would not appear more than once each day.

So now Abdallah and his mother had a little money — twelve copper coins a day. It was not much, but it was enough for them to live on. However, the wealth they had lost preyed on their minds. The gift of these few small coins was nothing in comparison! What could they do with twelve aspers? Would it not be better for

Abdallah to take the candlestick and look for the dervish? Then perhaps the holy man might return the riches that had once filled Abdallah's pockets. The boy's mind was soon made up. He talked it over with his mother, and since she approved of his decision, in the morning he set off with the candlestick for Maghrebi, where he expected to find the dervish. Sure enough, he was directed to the house where Abu Nadar, the holy man, lived. House? It was a vast palace! Ten doorkeepers guarded the gates, and the courtyard was swarming with slaves and servants. Abdallah hardly dared set foot on the threshold. Could this be where the poor begging monk lived? As he was still hesitating, wondering what to do, he suddenly heard the voice of a slave at his side.

"Welcome, Abdallah! My master has been expecting you for some time. I will take you to him."

18

The slave led Abdullah to a magnificent hall of marble and jasper, where the dervish, wearing his simple brown robe, was lying on an ottoman. Abdallah, as if dazzled by the magnificence of the hall, threw himself at the dervish's feet and offered him the candlestick.

"Forgive me for keeping you waiting so long for this token of my love and gratitude," said he.

"You are trying to deceive me, my son," Abu Nadar told him. "I can see into your heart. You have not come out of gratitude. All you want is to win me over with your gift, and what is more, you would never have brought me this candlestick at all if you had known all its secret powers. I will show you the right way to use it, for the twelve aspers it has been giving you daily will not go far."

The dervish placed a candle in each of the twelve branches, and then lit them. The twelve dervishes Abdallah already knew appeared again. They whirled around like tops, and after a while, Abu Nadar took a stick and struck each of them a violent blow. The next moment they stopped whirling and collapsed. Twelve great piles of gold pieces, diamonds and other jewels lay in their place.

"You see, my son," said Abu Nadar, "this is the way to use the candlestick properly! Not that this was the real reason I wished you to fetch it out of the rock. It is the work of a skilled artist, whom I respect deeply, and since such masterpieces as this candlestick give me pleasure, I collect them. Here, take the key to my treasure chamber. See what it contains, and then tell me whether it would not satisfy any mortal man!"

Abdallah did as he was told. There were six great vaults in Abu Nadar's treasury, all filled with so many rare treasures of gold and gems that he hardly knew what to marvel at first, or what to admire most.

"Fool that I am!" said he to himself. "Why did I give the candlestick away? Now I must look at another man's riches, while I might have been just as rich myself had I been cleverer! I might even have stumbled on the secret by chance! Oh, what a fool I am!"

When Abdallah came back, Abu Nadar could read his thoughts in his face. But he acted as if he had noticed nothing; instead, he treated the young man as kindly as ever. He entertained him as his guest for several days, as though he were his best friend.

After seven days, however, he called for Abdallah, and said, "Half of the treasures you saw in my vaults I inherited from my father. I acquired the rest myself. I was not miserly, but I needed only a fraction of my income to support myself. I realized at an early age that wealth does not make men either better or happier, and that it would be foolish to squander the riches I had accumulated, and so I let it appear that I was a poor man. I wore the shabby robes of a dervish, went on my travels, and tried to grow wiser by observing the follies of mankind.

"I made the pilgrimage to Mecca on foot three times, kissed the stone in the Kaaba reverently, and lived like the humblest of pilgrims. I gave the unfortunate folk I met only as much as they really needed to relieve their distress, since I believe that earning a living by one's own efforts makes one happier than idleness.

"Years passed by, and the time was coming when I must leave the world as empty-handed as I came into it. I had no children, and I wished for an heir who could manage my property with wisdom and moderation. My choice fell upon you, Abdallah, and as Allah is my witness, I have shown you as much love and kindness as any father could! Your ingratitude has dashed my hopes. All I can wish for is that the frankness with which I have told you all this may cure you of ingratitude. I will not keep you here any longer. Go home to your mother in Basra!

"However, since you brought me the candlestick I wanted so much, as a token of my gratitude you will find my best horse saddled for you when you leave tomorrow. It is yours, and so is the slave who leads it out to you! I will also give you two camels. You may load them with as much of the gold and jewels from my treasury as they can carry. Here are the keys again!"

Abdallah thanked him for his trust, and went to bed full of hope. But he hardly slept a wink all night; he could not get the iron candlestick out of his mind.

"Abu Nadar would never have had it at all but for me!" said he to himself. "It was I who risked my life to fetch it out of the rock and, once I had it, I made the long journey to Maghrebi to give it to him. And what thanks do I get for that? A horse — and I don't even know what kind of a horse it will turn out to be — and two camels laden with some gold and a few jewels! It's Abu Nadar who is ungrateful! Why, that candlestick can produce more than six camels could carry every single day! Why shouldn't I take back my own property, if I'm to be so poorly rewarded for all my trouble?"

This was the way Abdallah reasoned with himself, and by next morning he had made up his mind. He was going to take back the

21

candlestick. Everything went more smoothly that he had expected. Abu Nadar left him to make his choice in the treasury, and while he was filling his sacks with gems, he popped the candlestick into one of them. Then he gave the key back to Abu Nadar, said a brief farewell, and set off with his horse, the slave and the two loaded camels.

Before he arrived in Basra he sold the slave, and bought another in the market to replace him. He did not want anyone in his native city to know where his wealth came from.

His mother came to meet him when he arrived, happy to see him and eager to know what had happened, but Abdallah was so busy unloading his treasures that he gave only brief answers to all her questions.

Abdallah's chief concern was for the candlestick, and when no one was looking he took it into a secluded room. He was burning with impatience to try the secret, and turn the dancing dervishes to heaps of treasure. As soon as it was dark he went back to the room and lit candles on all the twelve branches of the candlestick. Just as he had expected, the twelve dervishes appeared in their brown robes and twirled around like whipping tops.

Abdallah had a stick ready and, believing that the magic lay in the strength of the blow, he hit each of the twelve dervishes with all his might.

Unfortunately, however, he had not noticed that Abu Nadar held the stick in his left hand when he struck the dervishes. Abdallah was holding his stick in his right hand, and so the dervishes did not change into gold and jewels, as he had hoped. Instead, they took out cudgels from under their long brown robes and beat the faithless and ungrateful Abdallah until he fell to the floor half-dead, groaning and wailing.

That was how his mother found him. She helped him get up and led him to the room where he had put the sacks of treasure. What a sight met their eyes! All the treasures they had left lying on the table, sparkling and glittering, had disappeared, and so had the horse, the slave and the candlestick.

22

Worst of all was the fact that the story soon spread around the whole city, and the miserable young man became known until his dying day as Abdallah the Ungrateful.

ABDUL KASIM THE RICH

One warm spring evening, Caliph Haroun al Raschid — or to call him by his full name, Abu Mohammed Haroun Ibn al Mahdi al Raschid — was sitting in his palace garden with his Grand Vizier, Jaffar the Barmecide, listening to the splashing of the fountains, the song of the nightingales, and the beating of their own contented hearts.

"All my life," said Haroun al Raschid, "I have tried to be a just, magnanimous and generous ruler. Tell me now, Jaffar, have I succeeded in my aim?"

The Grand Vizier stroked his white beard, and bowed as he sat. "O my lord, you are a great king," said he, "the greatest of all kings! The people already speak of your reign as a Golden Age, for you are kind and just, generous and merciful. In your whole kingdom there is not a soul who would disagree."

"Your words are pleasing to my ear," replied Haroun al Raschid, "for I know that your tongue never utters flattery."

"True, great Caliph," replied Jaffar. "Nothing but the exact truth ever passes my lips!"

"Tell me then, upon your conscience, my faithful Grand Vizier, do you know of anyone in the world who surpasses me in princely virtues?"

Jaffar scratched his head under his turban. He did indeed love truth more than anything on earth, but at the same time he knew that the Caliph was extremely vain, and could never bear to take second place. And so the Grand Vizier did not answer immediately.

"Why don't you speak?" asked Haroun al Raschid suspiciously. "Is it so difficult to answer my question?"

Overcoming his doubts, Jaffar said, "I do not find it easy, my lord! However, you despise flatterers and love frankness, and you know that I am always frank and open. So do not be angry with me if I do not offer you smooth words now!"

"No beating about the bush, my friend!" said Haroun al Raschid, with an inscrutable glance.

"Then I must admit, O King of Kings, Commander of the Faithful," said the Vizier, bowing even lower, "I must admit that I do indeed know of a man whose generosity and munificence far surpass your own!"

"What is this?" cried the Caliph, leaping up. "Do you really dare to say there is any man alive more generous and munificent than I am."

Realizing that his words had wounded the Caliph deeply, and knowing Haroun's touchy nature, Jaffar added, as he rose, "Of course, I may be wrong. Remember that I am an old man; my eyes and ears are failing me . . . ."

"Nonsense!" said the Caliph. "Now tell me this man's name. What country does he rule?"

"He is not a king, O Caliph," stammered the Grand Vizier, "only a commoner."

"And what is his name?"

"Abdul Kasim."

"Where does this — this Abdul Kasim live?"

"In the city of Basra, my lord!"

"How can a commoner give so generously?" asked Haroun al Raschid. "Where does he get enough money? Why, what with all the feasts and the gifts I give to poets and wise men, so that they will spread word of my fame, my own treasury sometimes stands quite empty!" The Caliph went closer to his Vizier. "Surely you do not mean to say," he went on, frowning, "that this — this Abdul Kasim is richer than I am?"

Jaffar was in a difficult predicament. He shrugged his shoulders and cast down his eyes, but then his natural love of truth prevailed.

"I cannot tell a lie, my lord," said he. "Abdul Kasim *is* richer than you are."

The Caliph's face turned as red as the sun that was just setting behind a distant grove of palm trees, and without another word he turned angrily on his heel and clapped his hands three times. The next moment, the captain of his bodyguard was standing there, sword drawn, followed by four gigantic Moors who had been concealed nearby, ready to leap to their master's bidding.

"What is your command, my lord and king?" asked the captain.

"Put this man in irons!" cried Haroun al Raschid, pointing to Jaffar.

"O great Caliph!" wailed the Grand Vizier. "Did you not charge

26

me by my love of truth — "

"Love of truth!" laughed Haroun al Raschid. "Why, what you told me cannot possibly be true. Allah alone knows why you should tell such lies!"

In vain did the Barmecide protest that he was not lying. In vain did he plead for mercy and forgiveness. The Caliph would not listen.

"Take him away!" he ordered the bodyguard.

The Moors seized Jaffar and dragged him off. But on their way to the dungeons they had to go through a rose garden, and they passed a bower where the Caliph's wife, the beautiful Queen Zobeide, was enjoying the cool evening air. The noise startled her. She told the slave girl who had been playing the lute to stop, and stepped out of the bower. To her amazement, she saw the old Grand Vizier Jaffar in the hands of the Moorish guards.

Zobeide went to the Caliph at once. "What does this mean, my lord and master?" she asked. "Why have you ordered your bodyguard to take old Jaffar prisoner — Jaffar, who has served us faithfully so long?"

"He is a traitor!" said Haroun al Raschid grimly.

"Who would have believed it!" cried the queen.

"Listen to this, then!" said the Caliph, and he told her what had happened.

Zobeide listened carefully, and she soon realized that her husband's hot temper had made him act hastily again. But knowing how touchy he was, she thought of a clever ruse.

"I would never have believed it!" said she, when Haroun al Raschid had finished his tale. "How could Jaffar even compare the noble lord of all the Muslim peoples to a common man? This is incredible!"

"I could forgive him that," said Haroun al Raschid. "But the worst of it is that he tried to belittle my princely virtues — Allah alone knows why!"

"He deserves to be well punished!" said the queen. "I hope you

27

will show no mercy — once you have made sure of his guilt, of course."

"Made sure of his guilt?" asked the Caliph.

"Well, speaking for myself, I am sure of Jaffar's guilt," explained Zobeide. "I was thinking of you. You always have to be convinced yourself before you will pass judgement! The people have good reason to call you Haroun the Just!"

As Zobeide spoke, the Caliph became more and more thoughtful.

"If you want to be certain of the full extent of Jaffar's guilt," said she, "you will have to send an envoy to Basra. Myself, I imagine there can't be a grain of truth in what the Grand Vizier says!"

Haroun al Raschid shook his head. "An envoy?" he repeated. "By no means!"

"Why not?" asked Zobeide.

"Because I am going to Basra myself," decided the Caliph. "It would be ridiculous to think I might find a man who is kinder, more generous, more magnanimous and richer than the Commander of the Faithful! I want to convince myself in person that Jaffar was lying!"

Zobeide breathed a sigh of relief. "Very well, my lord," said she. "Ride to Basra yourself, make inquiries about this Abdul Kasim, and satisfy your sense of justice! But then hurry home to Zobeide, who loves and respects you so deeply because you are so tireless in the search for truth!"

Haroun al Raschid's Ride to Basra

The Caliph set off the very next morning. He was wearing a simple robe that made him look like a travelling merchant, and in this disguise he mounted his horse. He rode alone, as was his custom when he went out among his subjects to conduct his own inquiries, and he did not reveal his name or rank to anyone he met.

On the second day, after a tiring ride, he came to a caravanserai. Here he refreshed himself, slept briefly, and then asked the man who kept the caravanserai the quickest way to Basra.

The man told him all the fords and mountain passes he would have to cross. "Have you never been to Basra before, then?" he asked the supposed merchant.

"Many years ago," replied Haroun al Raschid, evasively.

"Then I suppose you don't know Abdul Kasim's magnificent palace?"

"No — how could I? Is it finer than the palace of the Sultan of Basra?"

"Oh, yes!" replied his host. "It's even more magnificent than the palace of our high and mighty king, Haroun al Raschid, and I am sure there is no palace like Haroun's anywhere in Baghdad!"

The Caliph was annoyed, and secretly he decided to have this man thrown into prison along with the Grand Vizier Jaffar when he returned from Basra. What barefaced lies people would tell! Haroun al Raschid did not stay in the caravanserai any longer; he took his leave abruptly, and spurred on his horse, eager to reach Basra and see Abdul Kasim's palace. He rode over the mountain passes, waded the fords, trotted along broad paths and dangerous tracks, hardly stopping to rest, and so, after a journey of seven days, he came to the place where the two great rivers of the Tigris and Euphrates flow into one another. Here he found a large village standing on a hill, and far away in the distance he could see the towers and minarets of Basra.

Haroun al Raschid rode into the village, and stopped to break his journey. His cloak had been torn by thorns, and he wanted to get it mended.

There was a tailor's workshop in the very first street he came to, and the tailor was sitting on his doorstep, sewing. The Caliph dismounted and told him what he wanted. Without a word, the tailor took the cloak and set to work.

"Tell me, have you ever heard of a man called Abdul Kasim?"

29

asked the Caliph, approaching the subject cautiously. "He is said to live in Basra."

The tailor roared with laughter. "Do you come from the moon, stranger? What a ridiculous question!"

"What do you mean? Is Abdul Kasim so famous?"

"My dear sir," replied the tailor, "you won't find a soul around here who doesn't know that name! Lord Abdul Kasim is more respected in these parts than Haroun al Raschid himself, the Commander of the Faithful, and that's saying something!"

The Caliph smiled wryly at these double-edged words of praise, deciding to throw the tailor into prision along with Jaffar and the keeper of the caravanserai when he returned from Basra. Taking his cloak, which the tailor had finished mending, he paid what he owed, said good-bye and remounted his horse.

"Remember to visit Abdul Kasim as soon as you get to Basra!" the tailor called after him. "No one ever leaves his house empty-handed. There's not a kinder, more generous man in the whole world . . ."

"To Shaitan with you!" thought Haroun al Raschid, spurring on his horse.

It was getting dark by the time he rode into Basra. The streets were thronged with people, all of whom seemed to be hurrying in the same direction.

There was only one young man who did not appear to be joining the crowd. He was standing at the door of his house, with a tall, slender woman beside him. Her face was veiled, according to the custom of the country.

The Caliph stopped and leaned down from his horse. "Excuse me," said he, "I am a stranger in this city. Can you tell me where all these people are going?"

"To the house of Abdul Kasim!" replied the young man.

"And what do they want there?" asked the Caliph.

"Every day, at this time, Abul Kasim's treasurer throws a sack of silver pieces to the people from one of the palace windows. And if

30

one sack isn't enough, then the master of the house has a second sack
brought and thrown out."

"Why don't you go too?" asked the Caliph. "Are you so rich that
you can afford to despise such a gift?"

"By no means," the young man told him. "To tell you the truth, I
live in very humble circumstances. I work as one of the Sultan's
gardeners from early morning until late in the evening, and I have to
share everything I earn by the sweat of my brow with my old parents
and my unmarried sisters. I have only one reason for keeping away
from Abdul Kasim's palace — I owe him far too much already. If you
would like to hear what I owe Abdul Kasim, and why I shall praise
his name until my dying day, why, sir, I will be glad to tell you my
story!"

"Go on!" said the Caliph, dismounting. "I would like to hear it."

By now the street was empty. The people were crowding around Abdul Kasim's palace, and a ringing noise could be heard in the distance. It sounded like hundreds of little silver bells chiming, but it was not bells; the sound was the chinking and ringing of the silver pieces falling on the paving stones as they were thrown to the people from Abdul Kasim's window.

The Tale of the Gardener's Boy

"My name is Ali," the young man began, "and, as I told you, I am a poor gardener's boy. I was rich only in one thing – my love for a girl called Balkis, since she loved me in return. There was no more beautiful girl in the world than my Balkis. She lost her parents when she was young, and a miserly uncle brought her up. I begged the hard-hearted old man to give me Balkis for my wife, but all in vain – he showed me the door. I thought he had picked a suitor for Balkis, and was going to force her into marriage with my rival, but I was wrong. I soon discovered that the only reason he had brought Balkis up was to get a good price for her in the slave market. Before I found this out, the wicked old man had sold her to a wealthy Hindu merchant, a sea captain, who had the girl smuggled aboard his ship. The crew hoisted sail, and away they went.

I learned about this when I came home from work that day. I ran to the quayside as fast as my legs would carry me, but the ship was already out of sight. In desperation, I plunged into the water, intending to swim after the ship and catch up with it, never giving thought to the crocodiles that infested the waters. I thought only of Balkis – I had to reach her! Luckily for me a sloop came by, the sailors threw me a rope and pulled me on board.

The master of this sloop, as you will have guessed, stranger, was

Abdul Kasim. He was sitting under a canopy in the stern. He called me to him and questioned me, and then made a sign to his men. The sloop turned, and before sunset it had caught up with the Hindu merchant's ship. Abdul Kasim offered the merchant double the price he had paid for Balkis if he would let her go. But the rich sea captain only laughed scornfully at this offer. Abdul Kasim raised it to three, four and five times the price. The Indian would have nothing to do with it. Finally, Abdul Kasim took a gold chain set with diamonds from his neck, removed a garnet the size of a clenched fist from his turban, pulled the ruby, sapphire and emerald rings from his fingers and gave them to the Hindu captain, together with his purse. The Hindu could have bought hundreds of slave girls with so much treasure, and so, tempted by the jewels, he finally agreed. The sailors let down the gangplank, and Balkis was free.

We both fell at Abdul Kasim's feet, while the sloop turned to go back to Basra.

"Rise! You owe me no thanks," said Lord Abdul Kasim. "I acted as I did purely for the sake of justice — for it is unjust to force apart two loving souls who belong together!"

So saying, he gave me Balkis, and now she is my wife. Look, sir, here she is! She will tell you that everything happened just as I say!"

This was the tale of the gardener's boy, and Haroun Al Raschid listened to it thoughtfully.

"If this tale is true," said he, "Abdul Kasim is indeed a remarkably just and generous man!"

However, he was still suspicious, and he thought to himself, "If your tale should turn out to be lies, my good Ali, you will make a fourth in my dungeon, along with Jaffar, the keeper of the caravanserai and the tailor!"

Saying good-bye to Ali and his wife, Haroun al Raschid mounted his horse and rode to Abdul Kasim's palace. The vast, magnificent building was made of marble, with silver gratings all around it, and decked with countless turrets and cupolas. The white walls were illuminated by many torches. From an upper window, Abdul Kasim's treasurer was scattering a final shower of gold and silver to the people below.

The gates were open and the Caliph rode right into the courtyard. "Announce me to your master, if you please," said he to the servant who hurried to meet him. "I am a merchant from Baghdad, and I would like to speak to him."

"There is no need to announce your arrival, sir," replied the servant. "Dismount from your horse, and follow me, Abdul Kasim will be happy to welcome you."

"How do you know that?" asked Haroun al Raschid. "Why, your master doesn't even know me!"

"Anyone who sets foot over the threshold of this house, whoever he may be, is a welcome guest," replied the servant quietly. The Caliph looped his horse's reins around one of the silver gateposts, and followed the servant into the entrance hall of the palace, where other servants, bowing low, opened the door of a banqueting hall.

Haroun al Raschid's eyes were blinded by the magnificence of the room. The walls, ceiling and pillars were covered with pure gold, richly set with jewels of every kind. On the costly carpets stood tables covered with white damask cloths, bearing dishes of irridescent crystal and agate. As Haroun al Raschid entered the room, a man rose from the cushions where he had been sitting. He was a fine, impressive figure; kindness and goodness of heart shone out of his face. Placing his hand on his forehead, he greeted his new guest with respect.

"I am Abdul Kasim!" said he. "Sit down here at my table, stranger! I hope my food and wine may be to your liking!"

Haroun al Raschid sat down beside the master of the house, and looked around the room as he raised a goblet of palm wine to his lips. His suspicions that Abdul Kasim and his household might have recognized him in his merchant's disguise, and were paying him so much attention on that account, were gradually receding. He saw that the other guests eating and drinking in the room were of all ranks of life. Magnificently robed noblemen sat beside poor folk in rags and tatters; there were cheerful young men and silent dervishes, high officials of the Sultan wearing their seals of office, pilgrims with the dust of the road still on their feet, merchants and porters, even a Bedouin sheikh. And an old camel driver was squatting beside Abdul

Kasim himself. The servants were offering food and drink to everyone present with equal respect.

After a while, twelve boys dressed in white and twelve girls in long silken robes entered the banqueting hall, and began to play music. The boys played flutes, the girls harps. Haroun al Raschid listened, enraptured. Then one of the harp players began to sing.

The Caliph was so entranced by her song that he did not notice his host get up and leave the room. He did not realize that Abdul Kasim had gone until he came back and stood in front of him.

Abdul Kasim had an ebony stick in one hand, and a little golden tree with emerald leaves and fruits of red topaz in the other. A glittering peacock perched in the branches at the top of the tree.

The master of the house placed the little tree at Haroun al Raschid's feet, with a gesture that seemed to indicate he was giving it to his guest. Then he touched the peacock with the ebony stick. At once, the bird began to move, spreading its tail feathers to form a sparkling fan of jewels, while its head nodded up and down, spraying the aromatic scent of amber and aloes through its beak.

"How do you like this work of art?" Abdul Kasim asked the Caliph.

"Wonderful!" cried his guest. "I never saw anything so charming in my life!"

"A skilled Arabian goldsmith spent fifty years contriving it," Abdul Kasim said. "No one really knows how the peacock comes to life; the secret of the goldsmith's masterpiece was buried with him."

So saying, he picked up the little tree and took it away, although, judging by the way it had been presented to him, his guest might well have thought it was a gift.

"These are strange manners!" thought the Caliph. "So this Abdul Kasim is supposed to be generous? He parades his wealth and boasts of it, which is not the way to behave at all! My Grand Vizier deserves his punishment, sure enough!"

The Caliph was still engrossed in such thoughts when Abdul Kasim returned. This time he had a wonderfully cut opal goblet filled with red wine in his right hand. He offered the goblet to his guest, saying, "Consider this goblet yours!"

The Caliph emptied it to the dregs, and was about to put it down when, to his amazement, he realized that the goblet was full again. He raised it to his lips once more, and once more he drained it — that is to say, he tried to drain it, for when Haroun al Raschid looked, he saw that the goblet was full of wine again.

"What is this?" cried the Caliph, and Abdul Kasim smiled.

"This goblet was made by a wise and holy man, who understood the laws of nature better than any man alive, so he was able to make use of his great knowledge." With these words, Abdul Kasim took the goblet from his guest's hand and went out of the room, leaving the Caliph sunk in thought.

But before long Abdul Kasim was back, this time carrying a simple lute made of sandalwood. He laid it on the Caliph's knees, despite

Haroun's attempts to refuse it and push it away. Instantly, the lute began to play sweet music, although no hand had touched it. Haroun al Raschid had never before heard melodies of such unearthly sweetness.

"How can this be possible?" he asked, bewildered.

"Only one man ever knew the secret of this instrument," said Abdul Kasim. "He lived in Egypt about a hundred years ago. No one has ever been able to make such a lute since, and no one knows how this lute plays and makes music of its own accord."

So saying, he took the instrument away and left the room again. The Caliph stared after him, shaking his head and wondering whether to reproach the master of this house for his strange and discourteous manners, when he came back.

But when Abdul Kasim returned – empty-handed – and sat down on the divan beside his guest, Haroun al Raschid swallowed his annoyance. Instead he stood up, ready to leave this place where people were treated so strangely.

"Why, sir, what is this?" cried Abdul Kasim. "You do not mean to start out in the middle of the night? It's pitch-dark outside by now, and you will never find an inn in the city. Stay here and be my guest until morning. You will lack for nothing, and your horse will be cared for, too."

The Caliph bit back a sharp remark that was on the tip of his tongue, and accepted the invitation, knowing very well that no one would take him in at this time of night.

"You are tired," said Abdul Kasim. "You have a long journey behind you. Follow me to the room that has been made ready for you!"

Taking his guest by the hand, he led him along long corridors, up flights of steps and through great halls until they came to a bedroom. The doorway was draped with heavy crimson velvet. Abdul Kasim pushed the drapery aside and invited the stranger to go in.

Haroun al Raschid gasped with astonishment. The room was lit by many candles. On a table, beside a broad ottoman strewn with silken cushions and covers, lay rich clothes and weapons, sparkling jewels, chains and rings, and in the midst of all these treasures stood the golden tree with the peacock, the opal goblet and the lute that played by itself.

Haroun al Raschid saw a piece of parchment on the table, bearing the words, in large letters, "A gift for my respected guest!"

"I ask you not to despise these small gifts," said Abdul Kasim. "Take them to remind you of me, as a token of my thanks to you for accepting my hospitality."

With some difficulty, the Caliph struggled to control himself. At last he managed to say, "Your generosity is unparalleled! But I need nothing to remind me of this day — I shall never forget it! Nor do you owe me thanks! Rather, *I* am in *your* debt. I cannot accept such princely gifts."

"That would grieve me deeply, sir," replied Abdul Kasim. "I was sure that you liked the tree, the goblet and the lute when I showed them to you. It is the custom in my house for my guests to keep whatever pleases them. So do not refuse these small things, to which I might add a few more, or I would be forced to think that something in my house had displeased you and made you angry!"

"How could I be angry, noble Abdul Kasim!" cried the Caliph. "You speak of small things — but you offer me treasures more precious than any that could be found in the whole wide world! If I glanced covetously at them for a moment, I must now say in all seriousness that no one should give away such things! Do not squander your treasures thoughtlessly!"

Abdul Kasim smiled. "You come from far away, or you would know that my treasure is inexhaustible. Shall I tell you the strange story of my life? Then, perhaps, you will believe me."

The Caliph nodded, and they both sat down on the ottoman, taking turns to drink from the goblet that was never empty, while Abdul Kasim the Rich began his story.

"As a lad I was a cabin boy, and I went to sea on a ship owned by a merchant from the Yemen.

We crossed many oceans, put in at many ports, and one day we came to Basra in the Persian Gulf. While our ship lay at anchor, I went to see the city, since I had often heard of its beauty. I stayed longest outside the Sultan's palace, which made a great impression upon me. Its walls were built of great squared stones, each of its many windows had a carved frame, and the carvings were wonderfully beautiful.

Suddenly I saw a girl at an upper window. She was as beautiful as the day; no veil hid her lovely face, nor did she cast down her eyes when our glances met. Fair as her face was, however, it wore an expression of deep grief.

I came closer, raised my head and asked her, "Who are you? And what is the cause of your sorrow?"

The girl put a finger to her lips in alarm, and I realized that she wanted me to speak more quietly. Then she replied, "My name is Derdane, young man, and I am a slave girl. My father was a doctor. The Sultan had a false accusation brought against him and threw him into prison, so that he could take me to his palace as a slave. I have every reason to be sad. There is no hope that I will ever see my father and be free again!"

Glancing around, she lowered her voice, and went on, "If the Sultan's guards see you under my window, you will perish! Go away at once and leave me to my fate!"

"I will do no such thing, fair maiden!" said I. "I am going to set you free. I will leave now, but only to come back tonight when the moon sets behind the hill. Wait for me at your window!"

I waved to Derdane, and at that very moment I heard the footsteps of the guards who were constantly patrolling the palace. The next minute I had disappeared around the corner.

That evening I went back to the palace and secretly examined the wall. Luckily, there were plenty of chinks and cracks between the blocks of stone, deep enough to give me footholds and handholds to climb the wall, which was what I proposed to do. I was only waiting for the moon to set, so that the palace would be wrapped in darkness.

When the night watchmen had finished their rounds, I took off my shoes, and quietly began my climb. It went more smoothly than I had expected.

Derdane was waiting for me at the open window. Helping me over the sill and into the room, she whispered, "Not a word! There are guards outside!"

I made her understand that we had to escape together, the way I had just come. She nodded, clinging to me and trembling. It was dark in the room, and I did not see a little table with a porcelain vase on it standing by the window. As I was carefully groping my way back, I collided with this table. The vase fell and crashed to the ground. Instantly, there was noise and shouting outside the room.

"Save yourself!" cried Derdane, letting go of me.

"Not without you!" I replied.

But it was too late. The door was flung open, light flooded the room, and we were seized by several armed men. They dragged us before the Sultan.

"This girl is innocent!" I told the Sultan. "I climbed up to her room to steal her away — she knew nothing about it."

"That is not true!" Derdane interrupted me. "I begged this young man to rescue me, and he had no idea he was entering the Sultan's palace."

We both tried to take all the blame, and soon the Sultan lost his patience. "Throw this lying couple into the river!" he ordered.

This meant certain death for us, for we knew that the waters of the Satt-el-Arab, which flowed past the palace, were infested with hundreds of voracious crocodiles. Weeping and wailing would do us

no good; the guards seized us again and dragged us up a spiral staircase to the top of a tower. The waters of the river washed around its foot. I whispered a few last words — "Forgive me, Derdane! Forgive me for being the cause of your misfortune!" Then I was pushed over the parapet, and the water closed over my head. When I came up again I heard a splash nearby. It must have been the beautiful slave girl, who had been thrown in after me. I moved my hands about — being a sailor, I knew how to swim — and called out to Derdane in the dark.

No answer. I called louder; still nothing. Had the river already swallowed her up?

Something cold and scaly brushed my knee, and I gave it a mighty kick. Ahead of me gleamed the murderous, shining teeth in a

crocodile's gaping jaws. I swam aside, flailing the water frantically, and tried to reach the bank.

Quite soon I felt solid ground underfoot. But before I fell upon the bank, I shouted again and again, "Derdane! Derdane!" There was no answer, only the echo of my own voice. I gave up. Weeping, I threw myself on the ground; finally exhaustion overcame me, and I fell fast asleep.

When day began to dawn, I found that the river had cast me up on land far from the palace and the city. I climbed a sand dune; from its top I could look down on the port of Basra. Where was my ship? There was no sign of her among the boats and sailing ships moored by the quayside. Most likely she had weighed anchor by this time and sailed away.

Where was I to turn now? What was I to do?

I dared not return to Basra for fear of the Sultan's guards. I thought they would recognize me and take me prisoner. So I set out along a path that went around the city, and at last led me to a fishing village by the sea. I entered the first inn I came to, and found a crowd of people from all countries gathered there. A bottle was being passed around, full of strong barley beer mixed with red-currant juice. They offered it to me too, but I refused it. I did not feel like drinking — I could not get Derdane out of my mind.

As I was about to leave, I caught sight of an old man in the corner of the room. He had obviously seen better days, and did not feel at home here. He made room for me, and I sat down beside him.

"Something is troubling you, my son," said he, after watching me for some time.

I merely nodded sadly.

"Let me share your grief," said the old man. "Perhaps I can help you. The ways of Allah are wonderful!"

"No one can help me," I replied. "I am guilty of the death of a girl I loved more than anything in the world."

"Tell me about it!" said the old man, and, touched by his kind and friendly manner, I told him what had happened that night.

"Can you tell me the name of the young slave girl you hoped to rescue?" asked the old man. I was deeply moved to hear his voice tremble suddenly as he asked this question.

"She was called Derdane," I replied.

"Derdane!" the old man sobbed aloud. Tears ran down his wrinkled face, and at first I could hardly understand what he was saying, he was so shaken by sobs. The noisy company fell silent for a moment and stared at us.

Finally, I realized that this old man must be Derdane's father. Gradually he pulled himself together.

"I," said he, "am the doctor who was thrown into prison by the Sultan of Basra! May Shaitan take him! This Sultan is the cause of all our misfortunes — not you, my son, however much you may blame yourself. You had the best of intentions when you went to my daughter's aid!"

Again his voice was interrupted by a flood of scalding tears. The old man leaned against my shoulder and wept and wept. At last he regained his self-control, and told me his story. He had recently escaped from the same tower from which the guards had thrown Derdane and me into the river. Since then he had been living in this village, near Basra, trying to think of some way to set his daughter free.

"Now," the old doctor went on in a whisper, "now that I have heard from your lips that Derdane was drowned in the river, I do not wish to live any longer. I am old and sick, and all my hopes have died with my daughter."

He put his mouth close to my ear, not wishing any of the company, who had resumed their riotous merrymaking, to hear a word of what he was whispering to me.

"I am going to tell you a secret, my son," he said, "one that I would otherwise have taken to the grave with me. My father told it to me on his deathbed, and it was told to him by my grandfather when he lay dying. I know a place where treasure is buried, so vast and inexhaustible a treasure that it far surpasses the wealth of Haroun al Raschid himself . . ."

The old man's voice was so low that I had to strain my ears to hear where the treasure was buried, and how a man might come by it.

"And now you must take my purse," went on the old man, somewhat louder. "I need nothing more in this world. No, do not refuse it! Buy yourself rich clothes, get a horse and weapons and hire servants. Then you must go back to Basra, where, as you now know, the treasure is hidden. If you ride in looking like a lord, no one will recognize you as the cabin boy of yesterday. The hour of my death is not far off . . ."

I stood up to go and find a doctor.

"Why?" asked the old man. "I am a doctor myself; I know what I know! Take me to my room."

I helped him as he got up, with difficulty, and led him to one of the miserable rooms in the inn. Here he grasped my hands, and said, "Let me give you one last word of advice, my son! I have told you where the treasure is hidden, because you were the last to see my beloved Derdane, and you intended to rescue her. But do not squander the riches you will find there! They will surely last longer than your lifetime— but I am afraid that you might attract the attention of the Sultan of Basra. The Sultan is a grasping, suspicious scoundrel, and he will do everything he can to take away your wealth. So keep what I have told you a secret, and be moderate in your enjoyment of the riches that will be at your disposal . . ."

The old man looked keenly at me for the last time, and then sank back. His last hour had come.

I had him buried with all due ceremony. Then I went to the bazaar, bought myself magnificent robes, fine weapons and a noble horse, and went straight back to Basra. My heart beat fast when I set eyes upon the tower where Derdane had died. Outside the Sultan's palace stood the guards who had seized me and punished me. They glanced indifferently at the distinguished stranger passing them, and no one recognized me in my fine clothes.

The Sultan, sitting at the window and looking out into the street, did not bat an eyelash at the sight of me.

I cursed the tyrant in my heart. "No," said I to myself, "I will not do as the old doctor advised me. All those who are oppressed by the wicked Sultan's taxes and unjust punishments will share my wealth! I will give generously to these poor folk."

I found the place Derdane's father had described without any difficulty. The treasurer was far, far greater than I expected. I soon realized that I could not possibly spend it all, not if I lived a thousand years.

And so I settled in Basra and built this palace. My doors and gates stand open to all comers. As you see, stranger, I live in comfort and luxury, but I have not forgotten Derdane — not for an instant. My grief for her is lightened a little only when I can help other lovers who are the victims of cruelty or injustice. Quite recently, I was able to help a gardener's boy named Ali. He was trying to swim after a ship on which a Hindu merchant was taking away his beloved, whose name was Balkis. I was able to ransom her, and I know that I did as Derdane would have wished if she had been alive . . ."

"But does no one envy you your riches?" asked Haroun al Rashid. "Has not the Sultan of Basra, who, you say, is cruel, grasping and wicked, tried to seize your treasure?"

"He has indeed!" replied Abdul Kasim. "Many times, at that! First I was called before the *daroga*, the leading citizen of Basra, then before the Vizier, and then the Sultan himself. Each time they asked me where I got my riches. Somehow or other the Sultan knew that I possessed a treasure, and he kept asking where it was hidden. But I swore a thousand times that I would never tell him, not if he tortured me on the rack! Since then, he has contented himself with the high taxes and the yearly tribute I pay him. He may still be trying to discover my secret, but my lips are sealed."

"It is just as well that you do not tell anyone where your treasure is hidden," said the Caliph. "I can see that it is in the best of hands."

"Thank you," replied Abdul Kasim. He pointed to the gifts lying on the table with the tree and the peacock, the goblet and the lute. "Now, please do not hesitate to accept these things. They are for you, as my guest, and I shall be no poorer without them."

Haroun al Raschid smiled. "What a fool I was," he thought, "to have my Grand Vizier Jaffar thrown into prison! He was telling nothing but the truth when he praised the generosity of Abdul Kasim. So were the gardener's boy, the keeper of the caravanserai and the tailor! When I get home I will make up to my faithful servant for his imprisonment."

The Underground Treasure Chamber

Abdul Kasim rose to his feet.

"It is late," said he, "and you must be tired. I will leave you to your rest now."

"No, do not go yet, Abdul Kasim!" begged the Caliph. "Your tale was so thrilling that it has banished my weariness. May I ask for one thing more?"

"Certainly," replied his host. "I will grant all your wishes."

"I have only one," said the Caliph. "I believe every word of the tale you have just told me . . ."

"And what is your wish?"

"Show me your treasure! I swear by the Beard of the Prophet and all that is holy to me that I will never abuse your confidence."

A shadow passed over Abdul Kasim's face. He hesitated, and then said, "I can grant this wish only on one condition. I am sure you will understand, sir!"

"What condition?"

"I will blindfold you with a scarf, which you must not remove until I have led you through all my secret vaults and corridors, and give you the word to take it off. And you must leave your weapons here. I will go beside you with my sword drawn, ready to kill you if you try to break your promise. Will you agree to this?"

"Let us go at once," said Haroun al Raschid, putting his weapons aside.

Abdul Kasim blindfolded his guest, drew his sword, and took him by the hand. The Caliph could tell that many tapestries were being drawn aside, and they were passing through long halls. He heard trapdoors open and shut behind them. They climbed down slippery stairways where the air smelled musty. Then gravel crunched

underfoot. They made their way down a long passage; a key grated in a lock, a bolt was drawn back.

At last they stopped. "You may remove the scarf!" said Abdul Kasim, replacing his sword in its sheath.

The Caliph obeyed his instructions. He opened his eyes, but immediately closed them again, so dazzlingly bright was the vault in which he stood. Diamonds and jewels reflected the light of the

49

torches on the walls, refracting it a thousand times. Tall pillars of pure gold held up the jasper ceiling. In the middle of the hall stood a great marble basin filled to the brim with silver coins.

"This basin is thirty feet deep," Abdul Kasim told the Caliph. "Deeper than the Satt-el-Arab where I fought the crocodiles and lost Derdane. I have been taking out pieces of silver for years, baskets and sacks full of them, but, as you can see, the treasure in this basin has scarcely sunk by a finger's breadth."

"Astonishing!" said the Caliph, walking around the marble basin several times. "What is the wealth of the great Caliph of Baghdad compared to this? And yet, if you are too lavish with it, even this basin will be empty in the end."

Abdul Kasim shook his head and smiled. "Unlikely!" he said. "But supposing such a thing did happen, I would not be at a loss . . ." and he led the Caliph into the next room, which was even bigger. Here the vaulted ceiling was of gold, and it, too, was held up by golden pillars. Around the walls on shelves, there were all kinds of wonderful vessels and cups of precious metal. In the middle of the hall there were two marble basins, much broader and deeper than the first. One held gold pieces, and the other jewels — sparkling white diamonds, grass-green emeralds, yellow topaz, blue sapphires, blood-red rubies, tourmalines, turquoise, beryl, milk-white pearls and iridescent opals.

"Would you believe that I have been taking treasure constantly from this basin, too?" said Abdul Kasim. "Yet it is as if everything I take out is instantly replaced."

The Caliph felt as though he were dreaming. "Who can have amassed this vast treasure?" he asked.

"Follow me!" replied Abdul Kasim, and he led his guest into a third hall. Its walls, ceiling and floor were made of black agate. The huge room was lit only by a few oil lamps, so that there were deep shadows and shafts of light. The Caliph could make out two marble statues of a king and queen on their thrones at the back of the room, and, in the flickering lamplight, he deciphered the following inscription at the base of the king's statue:

> "Stand here, good friend, and think of me
> If you should chance to pass this way.
> I was a living man like you,
> And you, like me, must die some day.
>
> I was a king, I wore a crown,
> I put my enemies to flight.
> Now I lie here, the prey of death,
> Forever dumb in endless night.
>
> Silver and gold I had in plenty,
> Though I was always wanting more,
> But to my grave I went a beggar,
> Tell me, then, what are riches for?
>
> Listen, good friend, and heed my story.
> Whatever riches Fate may send,
> Give them away, and thus enjoy,
> A happy life, a peaceful end."

Haroun al Raschid read the last two lines out loud, in a soft voice, and then repeated them. He turned to Abdul Kasim.

"How wise of you to take this king's advice, rather than that of the old doctor!" said he.

After a while he approached the queen's statue, bent down to see the inscription, and read:

> "I was a queen; men called me fair.
> I spent my days in idle pleasure.
> I dressed in satin, silks and jewels,
> And cared for nothing but such treasure.

Heartless I was, cruel and vain.
I did not like the old or poor.
The sins within my heart were many,
As were the jewels in my store.

My beauty, life and riches faded,
The flower bloomed once and now is gone,
Even my name has been forgotten,
For only good deeds will live on."

Haroun al Raschid looked up, a question in his eyes. Abdul Kasim shrugged his shoulders.

"No," said he, "no one knows who these statues are. This king and queen must have lived very long ago; all that is left of them is this treasure deep below the earth. And now, since no doubt it was once

stolen from the poor people of this land, I am giving it back to them. But forgive me, sir!" he interrupted himself. "Day must be dawning outside. It is time for us to leave my treasury."

The Caliph allowed Abdul Kasim to blindfold him with the silken scarf. Abdul Kasim again drew his sword and took his guest's hand, and they returned to the palace through the halls and corridors, the doors and archways, over gravel paths and up slippery stairways.

When the master of the house took off the scarf, the Caliph found himself beside the ottoman in the room behind the crimson drapery. The torches on the wall had burned down, and daylight was shining into the room.

"O fortunate Abdul Kasim!" cried the Caliph. "By Allah, your treasure has no equal anywhere!"

"Do not call me fortunate!" replied the master of the house. "I would be fortunate if I had Derdane with me, but now I can never be happy again."

"Forgive me!" said Haroun al Raschid gently, and he pressed his host's hand in silence. He decided he would not waste time by sleeping now.

"I am going back to Baghdad, to put right certain wrongs," said he, and Abdul Kasim understood him. He sent for his guest's horse, and ordered his servants to load a pack-horse as well. Finally, he gave the parting guest one of his best slaves to accompany him on his journey and serve him as a page.

The two men took leave of one another at the palace gates, and Haroun al Raschid and his companion trotted briskly through the awakening city.

As soon as the Caliph got back to his palace in Baghdad he went straight to Queen Zobeide's rooms. Before he began telling his tale, however, he ordered the guards to set the Grand Vizier free and bring him to the palace. Zobeide's face lit up when she heard these words.

"Did you met Abdul Kasim?" she asked.

"I have been his guest," replied the Caliph. "He is a man of humble origin, who was once a sailor, but no man alive could be juster, richer or more generous! His possessions are far greater than mine."

"Then old Jaffar was not lying?" said Zobeide gladly.

"If he had claimed twice as much for Abdul Kasim as he did, he would still have been far behind the truth."

As the Caliph spoke, the Grand Vizier entered, threw himself at the foot of the throne and looked up at his sovereign with a tear-stained face.

"You — you are not going to punish me?" he stammered.

Haroun al Raschid raised his old servant. "Forgive me for what I did!" he said. "Do not mention punishment again! I will make amends for the injuries you have suffered. I will reward you too, Zobeide," he said, turning to his wife. "It was you who urged me to convince myself of the truth before I passed judgement."

So saying, the Caliph beckoned to the young slave that Abdul Kasim had given him. The slave brought out the gifts from Basra; the golden tree with the silver peacock perching at the top, the never-empty goblet and the lute that played by itself.

"The tree is yours!" said the Caliph to Zobeide, when he had described the secret powers of the gifts. Then he turned to Jaffar the Barmecide.

"I will give you the goblet, my faithful Vizier! May you live long to refresh yourself with the wine it holds! As for the lute," the Caliph went on, "that I will keep for myself, to remind me always of

Abdul Kasim and the night I spent in his palace!"

"And what did you give Abdul Kasim in return for these wonderful gifts?" asked Zobeide.

The Caliph was taken aback. "In return? Yes, to be sure, I should have thought of that! He does deserve a reward. But what can I give a man who is many times richer than I am myself?"

"Now that you are no longer angry with me, may I offer you a piece of advice, O mighty king?" asked the Grand Vizier.

"Speak!" said Haroun al Raschid. "Speak, and I will hear you!"

"You should make Abdul Kasim Sultan of Basra," replied Jaffar. "Appoint him your governor, my lord! The present Sultan is a wicked man who oppresses the people in every way he can. There is no end to the complaints we hear about him."

"You have spoken wisely, Grand Vizier!" cried the Caliph. "I will entrust you with the task of carrying out your own suggestion. Go to Basra at once and make the Sultan give Abdul Kasim his crown!"

That same day old Jaffar set off to carry out his master's orders. Mounted on a camel, he rode to Basra at the head of two hundred armed men. When he started out the moon was new; when he arrived it was at the full. He went at once to the Caliph's governor, the Sultan of the city, and told him Haroun al Raschid's commands.

The Sultan turned pale when he heard the news, but he hid his dismay very cunningly, and acted as though he were quite resigned to his master's wishes.

"I will go and tell Abdul Kasim the news myself," said he craftily. "My house is at your disposal while I am gone, noble Grand Vizier! Pray refresh yourself after your long journey!"

Suspecting nothing, Jaffar agreed.

Abdul Kasim received the Sultan as a guest, and the Sultan acted as though he were only paying the rich man a visit. He sat down on the divan where Haroun al Raschid himself had sat, and praised the girls whom the master of the house called in to play the flute and harp, saying not a word about Jaffar's message. He emptied one goblet of wine after another, apparently without a care in the world. But when Abdul Kasim turned his back for a moment, the Sultan secretly put a strong sleeping powder in his host's goblet.

Suspecting nothing, Abdul Kasim drank to his guest's health, emptying the goblet right down to the dregs. The very next moment the powder began to work. Abdul Kasim passed his hand over his forehead and collapsed.

The horrified servants tried in vain to revive their master, casting cold glances at the Sultan. Before long they were all convinced that Adbul Kasim had suffered a stroke and was dead, and they began to weep and wail.

The Sultan joined in their lamentations. "I have lost one of my most faithful subjects!" he cried. "O mourners of Basra, do not

touch the corpse! It shall lie in state in my palace, and then I will bury it under the palm trees in the palace grounds."

He would not listen to any objections, and ordered the unconscious body to be taken to his palace. Once the gates were closed and the crowd had gone home, the Sultan had Abdul Kasim placed in a secluded little summerhouse, while he himself returned to the room where the Grand Vizier was waiting.

"Alas, your journey to Basra was wasted!" he told Jaffar, with pretended grief. "Listen to what has happened! Our friend Abdul Kasim is dead. His joy at the Caliph's message was so overwhelming that he suffered a stroke."

If at first Jaffar had his doubts of the truth of this tale, he was forced to believe the Sultan when the story was borne out by others. Sadly, he took his leave, to go and tell his master of the new state of affairs in Basra, and so he rode back at the head of his two hundred armed men, having achieved nothing. As for the wicked Sultan, he rubbed his hands with glee, and went to the summerhouse alone to visit the unconscious Abdul Kasim. With a gloating smile, he bent over him and trickled several reviving drops into his mouth from a little bottle.

Abdul Kasim came back to life, stretched his arms, rubbed his eyes and sat up. "Where am I?" he asked, looking around in surprise.

"You are in my power — where else?" the Sultan jeered.

"In your power? What have I done to harm you?"

"You ask that? You have hidden your treasure from me, and you still keep its hiding place a secret. Yet you know that half of every man's goods belong to Allah, and Allah's deputy is the Commander of the Faithful, Haroun al Raschid, and I am *his* deputy in Basra! Therefore, half of your treasure belongs to me. You kept it from me, so now you will lose it all!"

"This treasure you speak of is not mine, Sultan," replied Abdul Kasim. "It belongs to the poor people of Basra. It is my duty to look after it for them, and distribute it wisely and well. Torture me as

57

much as you like — I will never tell you where to find the treasure!"

"We'll see about that! I am going to leave you alone now, but I will come back with the executioner tomorrow and tear your secret out of you·with red-hot pincers."

"You can kill me, but you can never force me to talk!" Abdul Kasim called after the wicked Sultan. Then the door grated as the Sultan locked it from outside.

Abdul Kasim struggled to his feet and tried the doors and windows. They were all barred by strong iron gratings. It was impossible to escape, and since he was determined never to betray the hiding place of his treasure, Abdul Kasim prepared to die.

Lying down on the floor, he closed his eyes, and his whole life seemed to pass before him. His thoughts lingered long on Derdane as he reflected that he, too, was about to die at the hands of the Sultan of Basra, and there was nothing he could do to prevent it.

Or was there a way to escape after all? Abdul Kasim started up in alarm when he suddenly heard a soft noise at the door, as if someone were fitting a key into the lock. Then the door swung open.

"Who's there?" asked Abdul Kasim.

"Hush sir!" came a whisper. "I am Ali, the gardener, whom you saved from the crocodiles, and whose wife you ransomed from slavery. Get up, sir, and follow me!"

It so happened that Ali had been digging in the garden when the Sultan's men carried the unconscious Abdul Kasim into the summerhouse.

"I thought it was strange," he whispered to his benefactor as the two of them stole along the dark garden paths. "So I peeped through the window and recognized you, sir. I hid behind a bush until the Sultan came back. Then I overheard you talking, and learned what that scoundrel intends to do. I knew at once that I must set you free." He stopped, and pressed Abdul Kasim's hand. "Now you must climb this wall," said he. "You will find a saddled horse ready on the other side. Make haste to escape before the Sultan finds you are gone!"

"How can I ever thank you?" asked Abdul Kasim, deeply moved.

"It is nothing!" said Ali, the gardener. "After all, I am only paying back a little of what I owe you, sir."

Early next morning the Sultan, accompanied by his executioner, entered the summerhouse. He went pale when he found it empty.

"What a fool I am!" he cried. "I should have killed him at once! Now no doubt, he has fled to Baghdad to see the Caliph and accuse me!"

He beat his forehead with his fist in terror, but at last he calmed down. "Never mind," said he. "I am sure to think up some story to tell the Caliph — and after all, Haroun al Raschid ought to believe his governor, the Sultan of Basra, rather than that wretched Abdul Kasim."

Meanwhile, the Commander of the Faithful and his Grand Vizier were discussing what was to be done in Basra.

"I don't understand how Abdul Kasim can be dead," the Caliph kept saying. "If he *is* dead, it was no natural death he died. I'd believe anything of the Sultan. Perhaps he had a hand in it — perhaps he has had Abdul Kasim murdered."

"That was my first thought too," replied Jaffar. "But how could we prove his guilt?"

"I'll tell you what!" went on the Caliph. "Ride to Basra again and bring the Sultan to me! But take at least a thousand armed horsemen. I will get the truth out of that villain!"

Jaffar was just riding out of the city gates with his troops when Abdul Kasim himself arrived at Baghdad on his tired horse. The Grand Vizier saw the lonely rider, but he would never have recognized him as the rich lord of Basra.

First Abdul Kasim stabled his weary mount at a caravanserai. Then he wandered aimlessly through the streets of the Caliph's capital city. He was reluctant to trouble Haroun al Raschid with his case against the Sultan of Basra. "Perhaps," he thought, "I might meet the merchant who was my guest. He would help me."

He kept walking through the bazaars, stopping to look at the display of wares here and there, but he could not find the merchant anywhere. At last his wanderings brought him to the palace of the Commander of the Faithful.

As it happened, the young slave he had given his guest, the supposed merchant, in Basra, was looking out of the window at that very moment.

"What is this?" cried the slave. "May I lose all my hopes of Paradise if that isn't my former master down there! By the Beard of the Prophet, it *is* Abdul Kasim!"

"What do you mean?" asked the Caliph. "Haven't you heard that Abdul Kasim is dead?"

"But I can see him with my own eyes!" replied the slave. "I can see he's alive."

Haroun al Raschid stepped over to the window.

"It's true!" he cried. "It *is* Abdul Kasim, dressed as a poor beggar. Quick, bring him up to me!"

The slave hurried off, and arrived at the spot just as Abdul Kasim was about to move away.

"Wait, sir!" cried the slave breathlessly. "Come with me to Haroun al Raschid! He is waiting for you."

The slave led the bewildered Abdul Kasim through the ranks of the bodyguard and up the golden stairway that led directly to the Caliph's throne. In amazement, Abdul Kasim recognized the Caliph as his recent guest. He prostrated himself and touched the ground with his forehead.

However, the Caliph raised him, welcomed him warmly, and made him sit at his side. At his command, Abdul Kasim told the Caliph everything that had happened — how the Sultan of Basra had taken him prisoner, and how the grateful gardener's boy had rescued him.

"That villainous Sultan!" raged the Caliph. "But my Grand Vizier is already on his way to Basra with a thousand horsemen. He will bring him back, and by Allah, he shall not escape punishment! But now you must refresh yourself, Abdul Kasim. I feel privileged to be able to return the hospitality you extended to me in Basra."

So saying, Haroun al Raschid led his guest to the baths. He ordered his servants to take away Abdul Kasim's tattered clothes and provide him with gorgeous robes. When that was done, the Caliph took Abdul Kasim by the hand and led him to a great hall, where a richly laid table awaited them. The servants brought in the choicest delicacies; soups, dishes of spiced meat, golden honeycakes, pomegranates from Amlah and Siri, grapes from Melach and pears that had ripened in the Shah's gardens in Isfahan. Serving maids and slave girls poured sweet, heavy wine and sherbet from golden pitchers. Suddenly, as they were eating, there was a slight disturbance in the room: a pitcher of wine fell clattering on the flagstones. One of the serving maids had dropped it. She stood beside the pitcher, frightened to death and nearly fainting.

The Caliph cast an angry glance at the unfortunate girl, but Abdul Kasim gazed at her wide-eyed. The next moment he jumped up from the cushions where he had been sitting.

"Derdane!" he cried. "Derdane, you are alive!"

He was just in time to catch the serving maid in his arms.

The Judgement of the Caliph

At a sign from the Caliph, the court doctor soon revived the girl. Haroun al Raschid made her sit down beside him and his guest.

"How did you manage to escape the voracious crocodiles in the Satt-el-Arab?" he asked.

"My story is a simple one," replied Derdane. "When I was thrown into the water a fisherman happened to be rowing past that very spot. The current swept me into his net, and he pulled me up, unconscious, on board his boat. When I came to he had brought me to land. I stayed with his family for a little while, but I still had to escape from the wicked Sultan, and I dared not stay there long. I dressed myself in men's clothes, and came to Baghdad with a caravan as a camel driver. Here I dressed as a girl again and took service at your court, great king. Your people were kind to me, but my heart was eaten away by grief. Day and night I thought of the sailor who had given his life for me — or so I believed!" Her glance rested gratefully on Abdul Kasim.

At that moment the clip-clop of horses' hooves was heard outside the palace. It was the Grand Vizier Jaffar returning with his horsemen, and who should be riding at his side but the Sultan of

Basra? The Sultan was in fetters, and the Vizier brought him before Haroun al Raschid, who had signalled to Abdul Kasim and Derdane to hide in the next room.

Jaffar briefly told his master that he had met the Sultan on the way to Basra. The Sultan himself was coming to see Haroun al Raschid, hoping to get his word in first before Abdul Kasim could accuse him.

At this point the Sultan boldly interrupted Jaffar. "Punish your Vizier, my lord!" he cried. "See how he dares to treat me! He accuses me of killing Abdul Kasim, when all I did was to have him carried to my summerhouse to be nursed back to life again!"

"You lie!" cried a voice. And it was Ali, the gardener's boy, who pushed his way through the ranks of soldiers and courtiers. "I joined the Sultan secretly as he rode to Baghdad," he explained, "suspecting that he would go to our noble Caliph to give false evidence against Abdul Kasim. And so here I am, the bearer of the truth!"

He told everything he knew and had heard. The Sultan, listening, grew paler and paler. Then he flung himself to the floor in front of the throne, begging for mercy.

Haroun al Raschid made a sign. A door swung open, and Abdul Kasim and Derdane, arms closely entwined, entered the room.

"Here lies the evil-doer!" said the Caliph, pointing disdainfully to the Sultan. "He has harmed you two more than anyone — it is for you, therefore, to decide what is to become of him."

"Then I will ask for his life, O King!" replied Abdul Kasim, and Derdane said the same. "But order him to give away all his treasures," Abdul Kasim went on, "for he has stolen them from his people. Let him earn a living with his own hands!"

"Very well," replied the Caliph. "It shall be as you wish, O Sultan of Basra!"

"Do you really mean to lay the heavy burden of ruling upon me?" asked Abdul Kasim, as his enemy was taken away.

"That is my will!" replied the Caliph. "With Derdane at your side, you will rule more justly than that wicked man, since both of you have known so much injustice and misery yourselves!"

With these words, he beckoned to his wife Zobeide, and they went up to the happy couple and decked them with the insignia of their new rank. The very next day Abdul Kasim and Derdane were married, and for a whole week the royal palace was full of sounds of rejoicing, music, and the cheerful clink of goblets. The sandalwood lute played more sweetly than ever before, and the Grand Vizier Jaffar led the wedding dance. The old man was happy to be in his master's good graces again — he was to come to a sad end a few years later, but that is another story, which you can read in many books.

As for the Sultan Abdul, he went back to Basra with his

wife. He made Ali, the faithful gardener's boy, his chief counsellor, and he gave orders for his treasurer to scatter not one or two sacks of silver pieces to the people every evening, but three or four. However, no one ever heard that this treasure was exhausted.

Abdul Kasim the Rich reigned long and peacefully. If the people called Haroun al Raschid, Commander of the Faithful, Haroun the Just, they named the Sultan of Basra Abdul the Generous, and by this name he lived on for many, many hundreds of years after his death.

Once upon a time there was a Rajah called Jabihu living in India. He married seven wives one after another, but none of them presented him with a son and heir. This grieved Jabihu so deeply that he resolved to die, and he went out to a swamp to take his own life.

On the way he met a fakir, who said good day and asked what was troubling him.

"I am a withered tree," replied the Rajah, "a tree fit only to be cut down and burned, and not a trace of it left behind. I have married seven wives, and not one of them has given me a son to whom I could leave my kingdom. Why should I live any longer? I am going to the jungle to drown myself."

"Stop!" cried the fakir. "If you will take my advice, your troubles will soon be over."

"And what is your advice, wise man?" asked Jabihu.

"Take this staff," replied the fakir, "and walk eastward for seven hours. You will come to a mango tree of remarkable size and beauty, covered all over with ripe fruit. When you are standing under this tree, take the staff in your right hand and knock down seven of the mangoes, catching them with your left hand before they touch the ground. Then go home and give each of your wives one of the mangoes to eat!"

The Rajah thanked the wise man for his advice, and followed his instructions to the letter. When he got home, however, and was about to share out the fruit between his wives, they fell upon the mangoes, tearing them from each other's hands. The mangoes were gone in an instant — but only the six eldest wives of the Rajah ate any of the fruit; the youngest, whose name was Rani, had to go without. Sadly, she picked up the mango stones which were scattered on the ground, cracked them open and ate the kernels.

Lo and behold, the following year each of the six eldest wives gave birth to a baby boy! But the seventh, the beautiful young Rani, had a baby who looked just like a monkey, although he soon learned to think and speak like a man.

As this creature grew up, getting uglier all the time, people called him "Prince Monkey", in mockery. His brothers hated him, and treated him worse than the lowest of their servants. The Rajah, after taking just one look at the monster, gave orders that he was never to set eyes on it again. He sent the poor young Rani and her son to live in a house by themselves, some way away from the Palace.

Monkey grew up in this lonely spot, running wild in the forest while his brothers were learning their lessons.

His mother would say sadly, "My son is indeed a monkey – he spends all day climbing trees." And the poor Rani wept bitterly as she spoke.

But Monkey was not really wasting his time, as she supposed. He learned more out in the world of nature than his brothers got from all their teachers, for the forest fairies took care of him and taught him their magic arts.

However, Monkey was careful not to reveal to anyone the skill and knowledge he had learned from the fairies.

Some twenty years passed by and the six young princes grew up to be fine young men. Monkey was rather smaller than his brothers, but had just as slender and athletic a figure as they did, although his body was still covered by ugly, brown monkey's fur and his face had the features of an animal.

At that time, another mighty prince or Rajah ruled a land ninety days' journey away from Jabihu's kingdom. His name was Jamarsa, and he had an only daughter called Jahuran, a girl of such wonderful beauty that princes came from far and near to seek her hand in marriage. But Jahuran found it difficult to decide which of these kings' sons she preferred. She was determined to give her heart only to the strongest and bravest.

So her father, old Jamarsa, had a heavy iron ball made, and let it be known that whichever of the princely suitors could lift this ball would win his daughter's hand in marriage.

This news came to Jabihu's court too, and his six sons decided to try their luck and test their strength. The old Rajah had no objection, and sent off his sons equipped with fine horses and gleaming weapons.

Sadly, Monkey watched his brothers ride away. Then he slipped off to the forest, and told his teacher, the good fairy, how much he, too, would like to go and woo the fair Jahuran. The forest fairy took pity on him. She pulled off his brown monkey skin, and, lo and behold, underneath it Prince Monkey had the finest, smoothest skin imaginable! His complexion was like milk and roses, and masses of dark curls framed his face.

The fairy gave him princely clothes and weapons, and a magnificent horse besides. This horse was so swift and fiery that

Prince Monkey caught up with his brothers in two hours although they were a full day's journey ahead of him.

"Who is that handsome young man riding up, I wonder?" one of the brothers asked.

"His robes are so rich and magnificent that he can only be a rajah or a king," replied the others.

The stranger approached them with a friendly greeting, and went along with them for the rest of the journey. His saddlebags seemed to be inexhaustible, for he entertained his travelling companions with a ceaseless supply of food and wine every evening. In the daytime he talked so wisely and cleverly that as the journey continued the brothers were more and more impressed with his knowledge.

When they came to the capital city of the land, Monkey dropped behind his brothers, dismounted from his horse in a wood, took off his fine clothes, and put on his monkey skin. He tied his clothes and weapons to the saddle of his stallion; the horse rose in the air with them and vanished.

The princes were very much surprised to see their brother Monkey as they were about to pitch their tents outside the city gates. He had hurried along a footpath and arrived ahead of them.

"How did you get here, Prince Monkey?" one of the brothers snapped at him.

"What do *you* want in this country?" asked another.

And without waiting for an answer, the third added, "Why, what do you suppose? Prince Monkey followed us out of curiosity, and caught up with our horses on his long legs!"

"Well, Monkey, since you're here, you can take care of our meals," said the fourth brother. "We're just riding off to the Rajah's palace. When we come back we want a good meal waiting for us. If it's not ready you'll get a beating — and you know we mean what we say!"

Then the six princes put on their best clothes and galloped away. As soon as they had left Monkey went to the nearest inn, where he told the innkeeper to serve a good supper in the princes' tent. He paid fifty pieces of gold for it, and the innkeeper promised to provide the best of everything.

Monkey went back to the tent and clapped his hands three times. A loud neigh told him that his horse had heard and was on its way. The next moment it was standing outside the tent, laden with magnificent clothes and weapons. Monkey took off his skin again, put on his royal robes, mounted his horse and went after his brothers.

There was a beautiful garden outside the Rajah's palace, and the huge iron ball was lying on the grass. A crowd of young princes were trying to lift it, one after another, but not one of them could move it a fraction of an inch.

The princess was standing on a rose-covered verandah, wearing robes of white silk. Her gleaming, golden hair fell loose like a cloak around her slender form. She was watching her suitors' vain attempts with indifference.

Suddenly Jahuran gave a start of surprise, and her cheeks blushed rosy-red.

"Father," she cried, trembling, "Father, who is that rider galloping up on the black horse?"

"I do not know him," replied the Rajah, "but judging by his appearance, he must certainly be among the noblest of the kings' sons."

Monkey stopped at the bottom of the steps leading up to the verandah, dismounted swiftly and hurried up to the princess with a bunch of flowers.

"O Queen of the Spring," said he, bowing deeply, "accept these messengers of Spring who come to greet you!"

Jahuran took the gift, thanking him, and bent her face over the lovely flowers. When she raised her eyes again, she found that the young man was back in the saddle. He exchanged one last word and glance with the princess and then rode away.

"Who was that?"

"Who was the young horseman?"

"Did anyone recognize him?"

Questions flew fast among the bystanders when he left, but no one knew anything at all about the mysterious horseman.

Soon afterward, the six sons of Jabihu rode dejectedly away. They, like all the other suitors, had failed to move the iron ball.

When they reached their tent, Prince Monkey had a supper of the very choicest dishes waiting for them. He himself was allowed to eat some scraps in a corner after his brothers had finished their meal.

The next day the princes decided to try their luck once more. Again, they ordered Monkey to provide a good supper, and again he followed them on horseback as soon as he had carried out their orders.

Jahuran, standing on her verandah, was not as calm as usual. Her beautiful eyes searched the bustling crowd on the grass, but did not rest long on anyone there. Not until the horse with its rider appeared in the distance again did her eyes light up. Catching the king by the arm, she cried, "Father, here comes the stranger again! Put an end to this foolish game! He and no other shall be my husband, whether he can lift the iron ball or not!"

By this time, Prince Monkey had ridden past her, with a respectful greeting, dismounted from his horse, and was now standing on the grass with the other young men.

"Step back a little, good friends!" said he. "I don't want to hurt anyone!"

The princes and rajahs drew back, with mocking smiles. Monkey bent down, picked up the ball as if it were a child's toy, and threw it so far that it landed at the princess's feet, just in front of the verandah.

It was an unheard-of feat of strength! Fear and astonishment showed on the faces of all the onlookers. But before they could pull themselves together, the mysterious stranger had disappeared.

Jahuran, however, was flushed with love and admiration for this bold young man.

"I want to know who he is!" she cried. "Next time make sure he does not get away without telling me his name!"

The following day, Monkey came again. He jumped down from his horse at the foot of the verandah, bowed low before Jahuran and went up to the iron ball, which had been dragged back to its old place on the grass. Without a moment's hesitation, he flung the ball over the heads of the crowd to land on the ground in front of the princess. The next moment Monkey was in the saddle again.

But Jahuran reached swiftly for a little golden bow that lay ready beside her. She put an arrow to the bow; it whirred through the air and struck the heel of the rider's right foot as he galloped away.

Monkey winced with pain, but in a moment he had disappeared from sight.

"Dear Father," begged Jahuran, "send your servants and tell them to look for a trail of blood left by a horseman with a fresh arrow wound in his right heel. When we find him, he shall be my husband!"

The Rajah's servants searched every palace, hut and tent in the vicinity of the royal court and the city.

"We found only one man with a fresh wound in his right heel," they told Jahuran when they returned. "However, this creature, O Princess, is more like a monkey than a man. His body is covered with shaggy fur, and his face is nothing like that of the handsome stranger you love."

"Bring this monkey man here!" the princess ordered. "I want to see him."

Monkey was fetched from the corner of the tent where the servants found him. Jahuran gazed at him for a long time, and at last said firmly, "This is the man I was looking for. I know him by his eyes. He and no other shall be my husband!"

The old Rajah, naturally, made objections, and all the princes who had come to seek the princess's hand declared themselves his enemies — including the six brothers.

"She has refused all of us, only to marry an ugly ape!" they cried. "Down with him!"

However, Jahuran said, "My heart tells me he is a rajah's son. He alone could lift the iron ball, and so he shall be my husband."

The foreign princes went away, their feelings wounded. As for Jahuran and Prince Monkey, they were married.

When the young couple were alone, Monkey asked, "Jahuran, do you truly love me with all your heart?"

"Yes, Monkey, I love you because of your eyes," she replied.

Then the prince took off his ugly skin and showed himself to his wife in his true form. Now Jahuran recognized the handsome young man whom she had loved at first sight. The next morning, however, her husband put on his ugly monkey's skin again, and, in reply to Jahuran's questions, he said, "The day of my release from the spell has not yet come. Be patient for a little while, beloved. The time will certainly come."

Jahuran was content, and asked no more questions. Her servants were all assembled in the great hall to say good-bye, and she came in on her husband's arm. They were all sorry for the beautiful young princess, and none of them could understand why she seemed so gay and happy.

The young couple were to travel home by sea. Monkey's brothers had bought a ship too, so as to accompany the newly married pair. Jahuran watched all the six brothers very closely. Love can be quick to notice things, and though her brothers-in-law acted in a very friendly way, the envious looks they kept secretly casting at the young couple did not escape her. Just before they set off, the princess said to her father, "Dear Father, I would like to have six bolsters for the bed in our ship."

"Six?" asked King Jamarsa. "Why do you need so many?"

"I want my bed to be comfortable," replied Jahuran. "It will be a long journey, and Monkey's country lies far away, even though it is quicker to get there by sea than by land."

So the six bolsters were taken on board the princess's ship, and she and her husband embarked. Monkey's brothers followed in their own ship. When they had been sailing for a day, the first brother called across the water to Monkey, "Brother, we are running out of salt. Will you give us some of yours?"

The ships were alongside, and Monkey swung himself over to his brothers with a jar of salt in his hand. This was what the eldest brother was waiting for. When Monkey gave him the salt, he pushed him into the sea. But Jahuran saw, and immediately she threw one of the bolsters into the water. Her husband caught it, and so saved himself and clambered back on board.

On the second day it was the second brother's turn.

"Dear Monkey," said he, "we did not bring any bread with us, and you have plenty. Will you give us some of yours?"

Monkey willingly let down a plank from his ship across to his brothers' ship. But when he set foot on it the treacherous brothers pulled it away; he fell into the sea again, and would certainly have drowned if Jahuran had not thrown him the second bolster at once.

"We have finished all our betel nuts, dear Monkey," said the brothers on the third day. On the fourth they asked for wine, on the fifth for some fruit. Each time they managed to make Monkey fall in the water just as he was about to give them what they wanted, and each time Jahuran saved him from the waves. On the sixth day, they reached Monkey's country, which was just as well, since Jahuran had only one bolster left.

Meanwhile, news had reached the Rajah Jabihu that one of his sons had won the great contest for Jahuran's hand, and was bringing his young wife home.

"It must by *my* son who has won the victory," said the eldest of the Rajah's wives. "None of his brothers is a match for him in skill and strength."

She was so certain she was right that, when the ships drew near, she got into her gorgeous palanquin and had herself carried down to the shore, to welcome the young couple and take them home.

She was astonished, however, to see the princess climb out of the ship on Monkey's arm!

"I will never give that ugly ape a place in my palanquin, never!" she cried. Then, as soon as her own son had climbed in, she gave her bearers the signal to turn back.

The other five brothers were also met by their servants and carried away in magnificent litters, but no one bothered about Monkey and his beautiful young wife.

"As you see, beloved," said Prince Monkey, "we must go on foot."

He took Jahuran's arm, and they went together to his mother's pavilion, away from the other palace buildings.

75

The good Rani could scarcely believe her eyes when her son appeared with his lovely wife. She welcomed Jahuran a thousand times, and could hardly stop gazing at her beauty. So the three of them lived happily together. Jahuran often asked her husband to tell his mother his secret, but he always answered, "Be patient, my love. It is not yet time."

Now it happened that there was a great feast at the old Rajah's court, and Monkey wanted to be present at the festivities. He went to his bedroom, took off his monkey skin and put on his fine robes. As for the skin, he put it behind his wife's pillows (she had already gone to bed). He said a loving farewell to her, and went to mingle with his father's guests.

Everyone in the Rajah's hall was asking who the handsome stranger might be. No one knew him, and yet he acted as if he were quite at home at the Rajah's court. However, Monkey avoided all questions, and after a few hours he disappeared as quickly as he had come. This went on for several days, and there was more and more discussion at court about the stranger – what might his name be, where did he come from? However, no one could solve the riddle.

A year passed, and one evening Monkey again left his house to go to a magnificent feast at court. That very night Jahuran gave birth to a fine, well-formed baby boy. Monkey's mother was there to help her with the birth, and she placed the newborn child in the young woman's arms. In so doing, she discovered the skin, which Monkey had hidden under Jahuran's pillows.

"What is that ugly brown skin you have there, my child?" asked the Rani.

"I cannot tell you, dear mother," replied Jahuran, reaching out her hands for the skin.

But the Rani, guessing what it was, threw it into the fire. "My son's wife deserves a better pillow!" said she. "She need not lay her fair head on such a shaggy skin!"

Jahuran uttered a loud cry as the flames caught the monkey skin.

At that moment Monkey, sitting at his father's table, started violently, sprang up and hurried out of the hall. What was the Rani's amazement when the door of her pavilion suddenly opened, and a strange young man, magnificently dressed, came in!

"Jahuran," he cried, "has the time come at last? Where is our child — the child whose birth was to set me free?"

In silent joy, his wife held the newborn baby out to him, and

Monkey took Jahuran and her son in his arms. Then he told his faithful mother everything.

The wonderful news soon reached the old Rajah. He and his sons went to Monkey's house at once. When they entered and the monkey prince in all the glory of his beauty and good fortune approached them, the brothers were so dazzled that they fell on their knees before him and promised to mend their ways.

But Monkey raised them and embraced them lovingly; badly as they had treated him, his heart had remained pure. From that time on, nothing marred the brothers' peace and happiness. Monkey lived on the best of terms with them, and since none of the six married, he and his son became the sole heirs to the throne.

One day, many, many years ago, Prince Muluk, the eldest son of the
Sultan of Egypt, went to visit his father's treasury. There he found a
black ebony casket lying in a corner full of cobwebs. The dust lay
thick on this casket, so it was obvious that it was a long time since
anyone had opened it.

The prince was very curious. What could be inside?

Blowing away the dust, he took the wooden box in his hand. The
lid was inlaid with pearls, diamonds and emeralds. It was easy to see
that this was no ordinary casket. Without a shadow of doubt, there
was something strange about it . . .

Muluk shifted it back and forth. In so doing, he discovered a small spring on the side of the box. When he pressed it, the lid flew open. Inside the casket lay a precious ring set with rubies, the fiery red jewels sparkling brightly, and by the ring lay a roll of parchment. Prince Muluk unrolled it, went over to the window to get a better light, and read:

"Friend, you who find this casket here,
Take up the ring and put it on.
Saddle your horse without delay,
The time has come — you must be gone.

Cross land and sea, deserts and crags,
Press on, whatever Fate may send.
For know that someone far away
Awaits you at your journey's end.

Be not faint-hearted in your search,
Only the bold can win the prize.
Go forward ever, undismayed.
As for the way, follow your eyes!

Let nothing hold you back; go on,
Whatever other folk may say,
For now you never can forget
Someone awaits you far away."

Prince Muluk did not know what to make of these verses. Taking the casket under his arm, he went to the throne room and showed it to his father.

The Sultan examined the beautiful ring, and read the puzzling verses several times, but he could not solve the riddle.

"I don't know what to make of it, nor can I think how the casket with this ring came to be in my treasury," said he at last. "Perhaps it was taken in some war, or maybe one of my vassals gave it to me as tribute. Possibly some guest brought it as a gift — I'm afraid I cannot tell you anything about it!"

"And what do you think of the parchment?" asked Muluk.

"Heaven knows who wrote that!" replied the Sultan. "Probably the writer has long been underground. However, this much is certain: this mysterious command is no concern of yours. You had better forget about it, my son! You are welcome to keep the ring. Wear it, if it pleases you."

Prince Muluk thanked his father, and placed the gift on his finger. He tried to forget the verses, as his father advised him. But it was a strange thing — no matter how he tried to think of something else, his thoughts kept returning to the mysterious words on the parchment. Then Muluk would say quietly to himself:

"Friend, you who find this casket here,
Take up the ring and put it on.
Saddle your horse without delay,
The time has come — you must be gone."

The prince sought amusement and company wherever he could, but all in vain. In his heart he kept hearing the words:

"Let nothing hold you back; go on,
Whatever other folk may say,
For now you never can forget
Someone awaits you far away."

Muluk told himself a hundred times and more that he had come upon this old manuscript quite by chance . . . however, what was chance? The question tormented him. Who could the 'someone' be who was waiting for him far away? He could not help puzzling over it all the time. Soon, he was in such a distracted state of mind that neither books nor music, hunting nor the exercise of arms gave him any pleasure. One day he went to his father again. The Sultan was in the midst of discussing matters of policy with his highest officers of state.

"Noble Lord and Father," said Prince Muluk, "I can stay here at court no longer. Certainly you may be right to say that the man who wrote these verses on the parchment has been dead many years. Perhaps the message does not mean anything now — and yet, dear Father, I cannot get it out of my mind. My heart tells me to go out into the wide world and look for the one who awaits me somewhere far away . . ."

"This is nonsense, my son!" objected the Sultan.

But Prince Muluk would not be put off. "Let me go, Father," he begged, "or my mind will never be at rest again!"

The Sultan hesitated for a moment. Then he replied, "Very well, if you wish to go, I will not stand in your way. It will do you no harm to see something of the world — you're at the right age for it. After all, you will succeed me on the throne some day, and it will be useful for you to come to know the people while you are young, so that you can understand their cares and troubles later on!"

The Grand Vizier and the other counsellors agreed.

Muluk was about to say good-bye when his father asked, "Have you any idea where this 'far away' place to which you feel so drawn lies — north, south, east or west?"

The prince was taken aback. "I never thought of that," said he.

"Well then, ask the wise men of this land to advise you," said the Sultan. "Luckily, they are all assembled here. Begin with my Grand Vizier — ask him your question."

Muluk handed the Grand Vizier the parchment, and he studied it closely for a long time. Finally he said, "The meaning of these words seems clear to me:

'Go forward ever, undismayed.
As for the way, follow your eyes.'

"It's perfectly simple. We must discover which way the prince was facing when he read these lines, and that is the way he has to go."

Prince Muluk tried to remember which way he had been facing. "I was standing at the window when I opened the casket," said he, "and the window faces north. That means I ought to go north."

"But the sea lies to the north," said the Sultan. "Are you to go out to sea?"

"By no means, my lord!" interrupted the Imam, the high priest of the land. "We do not need to know where the prince was standing, but which way he was looking. Since he was reading at the moment in question, it goes without saying that he was looking at the writing — in other words, downward."

"Downward?" cried the Sultan. "Do you mean to say he is to burrow into the earth?"

"That cannot be the meaning," objected one of the counsellors. "True enough, the prince was looking downwards. But he was in the treasury, which is on the upper floor of the palace. So these words can only mean that he has to go downstairs. However, this does not tell us which way he is to go when he starts out on his journey!"

"But think!" cried another officer of state. "Think — if a man stands by a window facing north, he must turn to the side to read so that his shadow will not fall upon the writing."

"It therefore follows that he should set out towards the east or west," mused the Imam.

"But he may just as well have been standing with his back to the window," suggested the Grand Vizier. "In that case he would have to go neither east nor west, but south."

And so the wise men disputed for many hours. It was enough to drive anyone to distraction.

Prince Muluk's Departure

Finally the prince became exasperated with all these arguments. He cut them short, saying, "Many thanks, gentlemen! My father will pardon me if I now consult someone else. I can see from the way all of you disagree that there are many ways of interpreting this writing.

I think it will be best for me to seek out Omar, the wise man of Baghdad. He will know the answer — so forgive me if I go in search of him."

The Sultan was not at all angry with his son for breaking off the discussion so abruptly. "I understand your displeasure," he said. "I, too, am disappointed in my counsellors! Go to Omar!"

The prince set off the next day, taking only one companion, a young man called Saïd who was a close friend of his. On his finger Muluk wore the gold ring set with rubies, as the parchment instructed him. He journeyed to Baghdad by the shortest way, and then he and his friend sought out the learned Omar. The wise man's fame had spread far and wide, and they hoped that he would be able to help them.

Omar paid little attention to the ring, but he examined the parchment very closely. He turned it over, held it up to the sun, held it in the shadow again and then shook his head. "I am sorry, my young friends," he said at last, "I cannot understand it. But I have one suggestion. You may have heard that a man who knows everything lives in Basra. He is over a hundred and seventy years old. If anyone alive can solve the riddle of these verses, he is the man!"

Muluk and Saïd thanked him, made haste to Basra and sought out the man who knew everything.

But he, too, failed to live up to his reputation; he could not help them. "Alas, I cannot tell where this far away place is, or who it is that awaits the wearer of the ring," said he to Saïd and Muluk.

Almost at their wits' end, the two Egyptians strolled down to the sea, for the day was getting hotter. In a secluded bay they both took off their clothes, intending to bathe. Prince Muluk removed the ring from his finger, so as not to lose it in the water, and laid the jewel on top of his clothes. There was not a soul in sight, and the beach could easily be seen from the water.

A small bird with bright feathers, a silver head and a golden beak fluttered above their heads, singing. Enraptured, Muluk and Saïd listened to its song. Suddenly, they realized that the bird was circling lower and closer. Swift as lightning, it darted down on their clothes on the shore. They saw something glittering in its beak; the next moment it was rising in the air again.

"By the Omnipotence of Allah! The ring!" cried Muluk. He leaped out of the water to find his fears confirmed — the ruby ring had gone.

The prince tried in vain to lure the brightly-feathered bird down to earth again, stretching out his hand as if he wanted to feed it, but the bird climbed higher and higher, then turned southward and vanished into the distance. Muluk, downcast, watched it go. Suddenly he struck his forehead.

"Do you know what that bird wanted?" he cried to Saïd. "It came to show us the way — that is why it took the ring . . ."

Whether his friend was right or not, Saïd agreed. They put on their clothes and set off southward, the same way as the bird had gone. To the south lay the great Arabian Gulf. Muluk and Saïd sold their horses and went on board a ship that was about to set sail. Two or three weeks later they reached the coast of India. The ship put in at the port of Goa to land her cargo and take new merchandise on board. Prince Muluk and his friend went on shore.

"Where shall we go now?" asked Saïd, as they looked around at the busy, bustling streets.

At that moment they heared twittering and singing overhead. They looked up, and what should they see but the bird — the brightly-feathered bird with the silver head and the golden beak. If they narrowed their eyes against the glare of the sun, they could even make out the ruby ring it was carrying.

The bird circled above them a couple of times, then flew off southward again. It seemed to look back several times as it flew, until at last it disappeared into the distance.

The two friends had had quite enough of the sea, but there was nothing for it. They looked around the port for a ship going further south that was about to sail soon. Why, you may ask, had they had enough of the sea? Well, on the voyage to Goa, they had met with a storm, and barely escaped a shipwreck. This time things turned out even worse. During their second week at sea they encountered a hurricane such as they had never known before. The mainmast snapped, the sails ripped, and the rudder was torn from its place. The ship drove helplessly before the storm.

That night she ran aground on a sandbank, waves breaking high above her decks. When morning came, the crew tried to save themselves by swimming, since in the distance, scarcely visible to the naked eye, they could make out land. But the current was so strong that only Muluk and Saïd managed to reach the shore. The two shipwrecked travellers flung themselves on the ground, exhausted. It was a long time before they regained consciousness, sat up and looked around.

Not far away, beyond the bushes and brushwood, they saw a wooded mountain. They decided to climb up it, hoping that from its summit they might be able to determine where they were. They clambered up through the bushes with difficulty; great ferns grew under the trees. Once at the mountain top, the friends discovered that Fate had cast them up on an island. Whichever way they looked, there was nothing but the waves of the sea.

The island was very fertile. Yellow bananas, brown dates and red pomegranates gleamed among the leaves of the trees. They had only to reach out to pluck the fruit with their hands. Springs and brooks gushed up in the shade of huge palm trees.

Nowhere, however, was there any sign of a living creature.

They were not happy about the place, for they felt as if some mysterious danger were lying in wait for them. Since Muluk was very tired, Saïd offered to explore the island. The prince warned his friend not to go too far, and soon he fell asleep in the shade of a tree.

When he awakened, the sun was low in the west. He looked around, wondering where Saïd could be. He had not come back! The prince jumped up, put his hand to his mouth and shouted Saïd's name.

His friend did not answer. There was no sound except for a strange, deep snarling and snorting. The nearer it came, the more menacing the noise sounded. There were crashing, snapping sounds in the bushes and undergrowth, and in a moment Muluk saw two — no, three, four, five dragon-like creatures making their way toward him. Their jaws were full of pointed teeth. They were hissing, and their wicked little eyes were fixed on Muluk.

What was he to do? There was only one way to escape — he would have to climb to the top of the tree under which he had been resting. He clambered up into the branches at lightning speed, looking down in alarm as he climbed. The dreadful monsters were tearing the bark from the tree with their sharp claws, as if they intended to follow and get him.

At that moment, there was a singing and twittering in the leaves above Muluk's head, and lo and behold, the silver-headed bird with the golden beak was sitting on a branch quite near Muluk's own perch, looking at him in such a friendly way that all his fears vanished. Then the bird flew down on to the prince's hand and — suddenly the ruby ring was on his finger. There were more rustling sounds in the leaves, and the little bird vanished but the ring shone and sparkled brightly, and it seemed as though it were casting most of its rays downward.

Immediately a strange change came over the dragon-like monsters. Their angry growling and hissing turned to wails and whimpers, and when Muluk looked down he saw that the creatures were retreating. One by one, their scaly bodies disappeared into the thick undergrowth. For a while, their growling could still be heard, but it was no longer alarming. Then all was quiet in the wood.

Prince Muluk scanned the ground over and over again before he decided to climb down, very cautiously. It was a full hour before he set foot on the ground again.

He called in vain for his friend — "Saïd, Saïd! Where are you?" Only the echo answered him.

At last, the prince plucked up his courage and struck out into the wilderness where the monsters had disappeared. His friend must be somewhere on the island! He did find the monsters' tracks, but the creatures themselves had gone, and did not come back. The rays of light from the ruby ring had chased them away — perhaps even wounded or killed them.

While Muluk was searching for his friend, he came out into a large clearing, where he saw a huge block of black basalt. As the prince came hesitantly closer, the rock suddenly opened, revealing a cave with walls of snow-white marble. Invisible lamps seemed to be lighting it. Muluk entered the cave, and realized that it was not a cave at all. He had set foot in a vast hall. A door flew open, and Muluk saw a broad, richly carpeted stairway beyond it, leading downward. He went down the stairs, which brought him to a door that opened by itself as he reached it.

Now Muluk found himself in a hall even larger than the first. Its walls were of pure gold and silver. Although there seemed to be no lamps or candles here either, the room was as light as day.

In the middle of this hall stood a wide divan, covered with satin. A young girl was lying on it, asleep. She was beautiful beyond compare. Her long, golden hair spread over the cushions on either side of her lovely face.

Prince Muluk stared in silence at this beautiful sight. At first he dared not move, but finally he went quietly up to the divan and leaned over the sleeping girl, like a man in a dream. Carefully, he put out his hand to awaken her.

However, before he could touch her a door flew open at the end of the hall, and a giant with a mighty club in his right hand strode over the threshold.

"What do you seek here, son of the earth?" he roared in a terrible voice. The prince stepped back in alarm. The giant repeated his question, but, strange to say, his loud shouts did not awaken the girl. Brandishing his club threateningly, the giant made for the prince, and

the blow would certainly have struck him to the ground and broken him to pieces.

Muluk raised his hand to defend himself — the hand upon which the ruby ring sparkled. As soon as its rays shone on the giant, he fell at the prince's feet, touching the marble floor with his forehead, while he stammered out excuses.

"O my master!" said the giant. ' I did not know you were the owner of the jewel! Take me as your servant! Command, and I will obey!"

"Do you know this ring?" asked Muluk.

"Who would not know King Solomon's ring?" replied the giant. "He who wears it has power over everything on earth. No creature can withstand him — as you see, I myself am at your feet!" Again he touched the marble floor with his forehead.

"Who are you?" asked Prince Muluk.

"I am the spirit Thousandform," replied the giant. "If it pleases you, I can change myself into a bird, a fish or a snake — even into a cloud, a wind or waves . . ."

"I am glad for your sake," replied the prince. "You must see a great deal of the world — and since that is so, perhaps you can tell me what has become of my friend Saïd?"

"To be sure!" replied the giant. "He is a prisoner of the dragons."

"Those monsters?"

"Yes — they are guarding him in their den in the rock!"

"Then change into whatever shape you will — a cloud or a wind — and set him free. That is my first command to you."

No sooner had he uttered these words than the giant rose to his feet, whirled around and vanished, but only for a moment. Then the hall was filled with a rushing, roaring sound, and there stood Saïd at the prince's side. The spirit, back in his own form again, stepped back submissively. The two friends embraced and, speaking quietly, briefly told each other their adventures. Suddenly Saïd broke off, as his gaze fell on the divan.

"Who is this beautiful maiden?" he exclaimed.

"Who is she, Thousandform?" the prince asked the giant.

"That is Princess Selika," replied the spirit obediently, "the daughter of King Kabal."

"And how does she come to be here?"

"I will tell you," replied Thousandform. "I brought her here myself. You must know that I came to her father's court as a knight to seek her hand in marriage, but King Kabal refused me. So I changed my shape and carried her away. But as soon as Selika set foot upon my island she fell into a deep swoon. I could do nothing to awaken her, and I am skilled in many magic arts. But none of them were of any use; my power was at an end . . ."

Prince Muluk bent over the divan and stroked Selika's forehead, breathing on her face and calling her name. However, nothing happened; not even the eyelashes of the fair princess flickered.

Awakened from a Thousand Years of Sleep

Saïd came closer. "Perhaps," said he, "we should have Selika taken back to her father's court. After all, if she does not come back to life there at once, his physicians will have some kind of medicine to help her."

Muluk thanked his friend for his advice. "Did you hear what we want you to do, Thousandform?" he asked, turning to the spirit.

Thousandform did not move. "I am sorry," said he, "but this wish of yours cannot be granted."

"Why not?" asked the Egyptian prince, frowning.

"King Kabal has been dead a thousand years," replied the giant. "His kingdom is long forgotten, and his palace is in ruins."

"O monster!" cried Muluk. "Do you mean to say you have kept the princess prisoner on your island for a thousand years?"

The spirit nodded. "But she has not grown a day older," said he. "Inside this room, time stands still."

"Well, I will accept that what you say is true," replied Muluk, "even though it is beyond the understanding of mortal men! If I did not have to continue my journey, I would say that we should take Selika to Egypt, to my father's court . . ."

"But why must you travel on?" asked Saïd.

"Have you forgotten the reason for my journey?" replied Prince Muluk. "Surely you know that there is someone awaiting us far away!"

"But suppose that 'far away' is here? And suppose Princess Selika were the 'someone'?"

"What was that you said, Saïd?" cried Muluk, striking his forehead with the palm of his hand. "Yes, that's it — that must be it! Did I not feel it, deep in my heart?"

Without delay he gave Thousandform the necessary instructions, and soon they were sailing through the air on a great cloud. The princess lay on her divan beside them. They went as fast as the storm wind, and within an hour they saw Egypt and its capital city lying below them. Muluk pointed out his father's palace among the clustered houses.

"Take us there!" he ordered Thousandform, indicating the marble terrace of the palace. The next moment, the friends landed before the palace with the divan and its precious burden.

Thousandform, back in his own gigantic shape again, folded his arms and bowed humbly before Muluk, the bearer of King Solomon's ring.

"I await your orders, master!" he said.

"I have nothing else to ask of you," answered Prince Muluk. "I know the limits of your power. You cannot help Selika! Go home to your island, and never leave it again! If any shipwrecked sailors should be washed up on your shores, give them a kindly welcome, and let them go in peace, if they wish to leave. This is my last command to you, Thousandform!"

The spirit bowed once more — then the air was full of rushing and roaring, and he was gone.

While Saïd stayed on the terrace with the unconscious Selika, Muluk went to find his father, who embraced him joyfully. When the Sultan and his counsellors and physicians had heard the whole story, they followed Muluk to the terrace. One by one they went up to the beautiful sleeping girl. One suggested a brew of herbs to bring her back to life; another recommended the use of essences; a third wanted to let the princess's blood; a fourth suggested incense; but whatever they tried, nothing worked. The fair Selika never moved.

The Sultan commanded her to be carried into the finest room in the palace and there she lay, sleeping and sleeping. Day after day Prince Muluk stood at her bedside, and day after day his love for the beautiful sleeping princess increased. He tormented himself, wondering what he could do.

Remembering the power of King Solomon's ring with its fiery rubies, he summoned spirits and djinns to the princess's bedside. They tried all manner of magic arts, but in vain. None of them could break the spell that held the princess unconscious. In despair, Prince Muluk abandoned himself to grief. One day he rose and took his dagger in his hand.

"What is life to me without Selika?" he said, turning its point against his heart.

At that moment he heard the beat of wings, and a twittering and singing outside the open window. The brightly-feathered little bird with the silver head flew into the room, and circled around him.

"You have come just at the right moment," cried Prince Muluk, letting his dagger fall. Taking the ring from his finger, he threw it to the bird, who caught it delicately in one of its claws. "What good is such a jewel to me if it cannot bring Selika back to life?"

"Would you throw away King Solomon's ring?" twittered the bird, settling on one of the window sills. "It could give you power over the whole world — have you thought of that?"

"I have thought of it indeed," replied the prince, "but a world without Selika is no world for me! I renounce all its glories, if the princess cannot be mine!" And he put the dagger to his heart again.

"Stop!" commanded the bird. "If your love is so great, it shall be rewarded. Look at the divan!"

The prince turned around, and what a sight met his eyes! Selika was beginning to move. She took a deep breath, rubbed a thousand years of sleep from her eyes, and sat up.

"Where am I?" she asked in amazement. "And who are you, young man?"

Prince Muluk knelt before her, took both her hands, and told her, with tears of joy, how he had found her and freed her from the spirit that could take a thousand forms.

"Then you are the man I have been awaiting, from far away!" said she, in the words of the verse. "Oh, thank you, thank you, my rescuer!"

"It is not me you have to thank, Selika," replied the prince, "but the brightly-feathered little bird there on the window sill. He showed me the way and led me to you."

"That was nothing!" twittered the little bird, as Selika turned to it. "I was only a messenger, and all I did was my duty. But now I will take away King Solomon's ring again."

"Yes, take it!" cried the prince, putting his arm around the princess's slender waist. "I do not need it any more."

"I will carry it away to the great desert," said the bird. "In the desert there stands a palm grove, in the palm grove stands a great marble palace, and in the palace there is a room of gold. In this room there stands a golden table, and on the table lies a casket made of ebony, just like the one you found in your father's treasury, Prince Muluk. This casket stands open. I will drop the ring into it, and as soon as that is done, the lid will close. A winged dragon will guard the ring, so that no one can touch it until a mortal man has need of it again."

"Why was I the one to find the ring?" asked Muluk. "Why was I chosen to free Princess Selika from her prison on the spirit Thousandform's island, and wake her from her thousand years of sleep?"

"Every man," replied the brightly-feathered bird, "has his own task on this earth, a task he can perform if he musters his strength and finds the means to do it."

"And if he does not find the means?"

"Remember that you made the greater part of your journey by your own efforts," said the bird. "Courage and determination will often work miracles."

95

"But who wrote those verses on the parchment?" asked Muluk. "The message that made me venture out? And how did the ebony casket come into my father's treasury?"

"That I do not know myself," replied the bird, "but if you must know the answer, it can easily be done! I will give you back King Solomon's ring, and with its aid you may conjure up the most ancient spirits; that which happened many, many years ago is no secret to them. Of course, Selika will fall asleep again . . ."

"No, keep your ring!" cried the prince. "In the name of Allah! I would rather the mystery remained a mystery for ever!"

The little bird gave such a cry of joy that the hall re-echoed. Who would ever have thought that its little throat could utter such a sound? The brightly-feathered bird twittered and sang louder and

sweeter than ever before. Then it spread its wings, circled around the young couple, and flew out of the window with King Solomon's ring.

Muluk and Selika never saw the little bird again. Soon they were married, and the prince was very happy with his fate. It was a strange fate, too, by the Beard of the Prophet — not every man can bring home a woman a thousand years old as his wife, and still live happily ever after!

No one will be surprised to hear that the couple often thought of the little bird who brought them happiness as they walked in the Sultan's gardens, listening to the rustling and twittering in the leaves near by. Yet, there were only ordinary birds in those gardens — not one of them had a silver head or a golden beak. They were no one's messengers, and none of them carried a jewel like King Solomon's ruby ring, which has never been heard of again. The little birds in the garden of the Sultan, to whose throne Prince Muluk succeeded some years later, fluttered through the bushes and the leaves of the tall trees only at their own pleasure.

However, they sang sweetly, for all that!

HARCHAND THE JUST

Like Job, the man of the land of Uz, the great Maharajah Harchand was known far and wide for his piety. He was one of the fortunate of this world; he had power and authority, a beautiful young wife called Hiraldi, and a son named Marikhand whom he loved more than himself. He owned much land and great riches, too.

When the Maharajah went to say his prayers early in the morning, all he had to do was to put his hand into his wallet, and there was always so much money inside that it was his custom to give two and a half pounds of gold to the poor every day.

Shiva, the Lord of Heaven, loved this devout man for his virtues. But perhaps he thought, "It is not hard for this great man to live piously and act justly. It is not difficult for a man who is the darling of fortune to be generous. The owner of boundless riches can afford to act magnanimously. But let us see whether his virtues will hold out in adversity. If we make him poor and unhappy for the next twelve years, will he be able to pass the test?"

So Shiva sent a huge boar into Harchand's fields and gardens, and in one night that boar uprooted all the plantations and destroyed every growing thing.

When the Maharajah came out of his bedroom in the morning, he found his gardener weeping and wailing at the door.

"My lord!" the man sobbed. "Your garden is no longer a pleasant place — it has become a wilderness!"

"What is all this foolishness?" replied the Maharajah. "How can my beautiful garden have been laid waste overnight?"

"But it has been!" wailed the gardener. "Come and see for yourself what has happened."

Unwillingly, Harchand followed him, and saw that everything his faithful servant had said was true. His beautiful garden was destroyed

and laid waste. This misfortune deprived the Maharajah of speech. Silent and downcast, he returned to his rooms, where it was his custom every morning to take a bath before going to the temple to pray. His eyes lowered sadly to the ground, he walked on until the voice of a beggar made him glance up. An old fakir was asking for alms.

"Come with me to my palace," said the Maharajah kindly, "and I will have two and a half pounds of gold given to you."

"You must be jesting, noble sir!" replied the beggar. "Whoever heard of such rich alms?"

"It is no jest," replied Harchand the Just. "It is my custom to give that amount to the poor every morning."

The fakir bowed and followed the Rajah, who told his treasurer to count out the sum he had promised.

The treasurer went away, but soon he came back in consternation. "My lord!" he cried. "All the gold and jewels in your treasury have been turned to charcoal overnight!"

"Nonsense!" said Harchand. "How could such a thing come about?"

"Come and see for yourself!" replied the treasurer, and when the Rajah followed him he found, to his horror, that his servant had spoken all too truly. His entire treasure, all the glittering gems and jewels, the vessels full of gold and silver — everything had turned to blackened coals.

Harchand the Just reflected for a moment.

"Well," said he, "I have promised this holy man two and a half pounds of gold, and I will keep my word."

Without pausing for further thought, he went to a merchant and pledged him his beautiful wife Hiraldi for one pound of gold. Then he fetched his son Marikhand and sold him for half a pound of gold; and since he still had not accumulated all of the sum he had promised, he decided to sell himself into slavery for the remainder. Accordingly, he went down to the river to the overseer of the dead. People brought this man corpses to be buried by being thrown into the water. Harchand sold himself to the overseer of the dead for a pound of gold, and then gave the fakir the gift he had promised.

"What must I do?" Harchand asked his new master.

"You can sit here by the water for a while," replied the man. "I am going away on business. People will bring you bodies of the dead, and you must throw them into the water. If it is the body of a man or a woman, you must ask one rupee, and for the body of a child eight annas. But if anyone should come with a corpse, bringing no money, keep a piece of clothing as a pledge. Do not forget to do

100

that! When I return I will look closely into everything you have done and demand a reckoning!"

The Rajah promised to do as his master told him, and the overseer of the dead went his way.

When evening came, Harchand caught a fish and cooked it. Then he took off his clothes.

"I will bathe first," he thought, "and then eat my fish."

But, lo and behold, when the unfortunate Rajah came out of the water and looked into his pan, he found it empty. The fish had jumped out before it was cooked.

"It is Shiva's will that I should go hungry to bed," said the devout Harchand. He said his prayers and lay down to sleep, uncomplaining. And Shiva, the Lord of Heaven, was well pleased to see how patiently and submissively Harchand bore all his trials. But the hardest of all was still in store for him.

Every day many dead bodies were brought to the waterside, and Harchand always followed his master's orders. He asked one rupee for a man or a woman, eight annas for a child, and if someone came who had no money, he kept a piece of clothing.

One day, however, a beautiful woman came sobbing to the waterside carrying a dead boy in her arms. To his horror, Harchand recognized his wife Hiraldi, and the little corpse in her arms was their beloved son Marikhand.

Harchand began to weep bitterly. Before he threw the boy into the water, however, he called out to the god of the river, "Take good care of this body; be sure that no harm comes to it."

"I will do so," said the lord of the water, who was a great crocodile, and, taking the dead boy on his back, he carried him away.

"Now you must pay me eight annas," said Harchand.

"Alas, you know that I have no money," sobbed the unhappy mother. "I am a slave. Is it not enough that your piety and faith in Shiva have brought us to such misery? Would you take money for the burial of your only child?"

"I must!" replied Harchand the Just. "I promised my master to do so. If you have no money, give me your scarf in payment."

Hiraldi shed hot tears, but she took off her scarf and gave it to her husband. In silence, he placed it with the other clothes he had been given. Then they both sat down by the waterside and mourned.

But the body of little Marikhand had not sunk. It was floating gently on the water, and the boy's face looked as happy and peaceful as if he were asleep.

"Is it not cruel," said the unhappy mother, "that Shiva has heaped grief and misfortunes on us so long? Twelve years must have passed in this way!"

"It is sad indeed," said Harchand, resigned as ever, "but since it is Shiva's will, we must endure our fate."

At that moment, a handsome man in magnificent robes approached the couple. He was accompanied by a younger man. Harchand and Hiraldi did not see where the two men came from, nor did they guess that this was Shiva himself, with one of his companions.

"Harchand," said the god to the Rajah, "would you like to have your wife and your son back and return to your kingdom?"

"Why not, if it pleases Shiva?" replied Harchand.

Then the stranger stretched out his hand over the water, and, lo and behold, Marikhand's body came slowly floating along. When it reached the bank the boy stood up, climbed out of the water, and went up to his parents. Harchand and Hiraldi embraced him with joy; then they fell on their knees and thanked the unknown miracle worker.

However, the stranger said, "Come with me!" And he went with them to the place where the overseer of the dead was.

"What will you take for this man?" asked the stranger, pointing to Harchand.

"I bought him for one pound of gold," replied the overseer, "but as he is very faithful and a good worker, I will not sell him now for less than four pounds."

"Here are the four pounds of gold," said the stranger, and Harchand was freed from slavery.

Then they went to the merchant to whom the Rani had been pledged.

"What do you want for this woman?" asked the stranger.

"I gave one pound of gold for her," said the merchant, "but since she is a good woman, I will not take less than six pounds for her now."

"Here are your six pounds of gold," replied Harchand's unknown benefactor, and so the Rani, too, was free. The stranger would not listen to Harchand's attempts to thank him; he waved his hand to them for the last time, and then he and his companion had vanished.

But as for the Maharajah Harchand, his wife Hiraldi and his son Marikhand, they went home to their palace.

When they entered the garden they found to their surprise that it was in full bloom. The lumps of charcoal in the treasury had changed back to gold, silver and jewels, and the servants were awaiting their master's orders, just as usual. And when he saw them, Harchand's first words were, "Treasurer, give another two and a half pounds of gold to the poor, and then let us thank Shiva for his boundless mercies!"

THE WICKED SANKHASHURNI

In the Indian province of Bengal, folk believed that people who had done evil deeds during their lifetime had to haunt the earth after death before they could find peace. The men became ghosts called Sankchinis, and the women ghosts were called Sankhashurnis.

One day, while she was fetching water from the pond, the wife of a Brahman struck one of these Sankhashurnis with her bucket by mistake. The ghost was angry. She shut the poor woman up in a hollow tree, dressed in her clothes and went to the Brahman's house, carrying the bucket of water. So absorbed was he in his prayers that at first he did not notice the change, nor did his old mother.

The one thing that struck them both was that the young woman's character had suddenly altered. She used to be rather lazy, but now she would get through the work of the house at an amazing speed.

At first this pleased the mother and son, but soon they realized that it was rather strange. It took less and less time every day for the meals to be cooked, and when the Brahman's mother asked her daughter-in-law for something that was out in the yard, or in another room in the house, the Sankhashurni would bring it to her in less time than she could have taken to reach the place, let alone get back again.

One day, both women were working in the garden. The mother was kneeling on the ground planting vegetables, while her daughter-in-law stood behind her.

The old woman said, "We'll need a jug of water when we have finished. If we don't water the seedlings they won't grow."

As she spoke she glanced up secretly, and what do you think she saw?

Her daughter-in-law made her right arm so long that it reached right across the garden and into the kitchen. There she took a jug from the shelf and, without filling it, handed it to her mother-in-law full of water.

Of course, the old woman was frightened to death, but she said nothing, and gave no sign of having noticed anything uncanny.

That evening, she told her son about her strange discovery, and they both decided to watch the weird creature closely. For this purpose, the man bored a small hole in the kitchen door and peeped through it. The fire in the stove was just dying down, and was in danger of going out. Suddenly he saw that his wife was not putting wood on the embers; instead she thrust her right foot into the stove. The next moment, the flames shot up again, and the dinner was cooked in a trice.

Now the Brahman knew for sure that this creature was not his wife, but a Sankhashurni. So he hurried off to getch an Ojha, a man who could cast out demons.

First of all, the Ojha put some turmeric on the embers in the stove — for you must know that no spirit, whatever he may be, can bear the smell of burning turmeric. And so it proved. No sooner did the smoke begin to rise to the nostrils of the Brahman's supposed wife than she let out a dreadful screech and ran to the door to escape. But the Ojha had foreseen that she would try to get away. Not only had he barricaded the door, he had even stopped up the keyhole. So he was able to catch the fugitive by the hair and shake her back and forth. Then he took off one of his slippers and beat the Sankhashurni's back until it was black and blue.

The ghost gave up. "I am a Sankhashurni!" she wailed. "I admit it. I lived in a tree on the bank of the pond . . ."

And the Sankhashurni told them that in order to revenge herself on the Brahman's wife, she had shut her up inside the hollow tree. While the Ojha held the ghost tight, the Brahman and his mother hurried away to the place she had described. Sure enough, they found the poor woman inside the tree, more dead than alive. However, she had been lucky, for there was a swarm of bees nesting

in the hollow trunk, and she had lived on the honey all this time,
despite the stings which the bees inflicted upon her.

Weeping with joy, she fell into her husband's arms. But when they
got back home, the Ojha once again made his slipper dance on the
spiteful Sankhashurni's back until she sang a fine tune! Then he
made her swear a dreadful oath before he let her go free. She
promised never to touch a human being again, and she kept her
word. As for the Brahman and his wife, they lived happily and in
peace, and later, if what the folk of Bengal say is true, Shiva gave
them many sons and daughters.

Once upon a time, in China, there lived a king and queen who had an only daughter.

One day she was walking in the garden, when all of a sudden a great storm arose, wrapped her around as if in a cloak, and carried her away. Now this storm was caused by the nine-headed bird. The princess had taken his fancy, and so he stole her away and carried her off to his cave.

As for the king, he had no idea where his daughter had gone. He

had it proclaimed throughout the land that the man who brought the princess back should have her for his bride.

As it happened, a young man had seen the great bird carrying the king's daughter to its home, a cave high up in a steep mountain side. No one could climb up to it from below or reach it from above.

While the young man was looking at the precipice, wondering what to do, a man came along that way.

"Why do you keep looking up?" said he.

The young man told him what he had seen, and how the nine-headed bird had stolen away the king's daughter and vanished into his mountain cave with her. "I wonder how I could get up there?" he mused.

Well, his new acquaintance knew what to do. He sent for some of his friends, and they all went up to the mountain top. The young man climbed into a basket, and they let him down from the top of the precipice on a long rope. Sure enough, he succeeded in finding a foothold on a ledge of rock outside the cave. When he entered the cave, the king's daughter was sitting beside the nine-headed bird, washing his wounds, for the Hound of Heaven had bitten off his tenth head and it would not stop bleeding.

The princess secretly signalled to the intruder to hide, and he did as she told him. He waited until the great bird had fallen asleep, one head after another hanging down in slumber. Then the young man came out of his hiding place, drew his sword, and chopped off all nine of the monster's heads, one by one.

When that was done, he said to the king's daughter, "Follow me!" and they both went out on to the ledge, where he showed her the basket.

"Climb in and you will be hauled up," said the brave young man.

But the princess, fearing some evil plot, replied, "It would be better for you to climb into the basket first. I will wait until they let it down again."

However, the young man would not hear of it. "Certainly not!" he said. "How could I possibly have myself brought to safety first? That would not be right."

At last the king's daughter let him overrule her. Taking one of her hairpins set with jewels, she broke it in half and gave her rescuer one of the halves, while she kept the other one herself. In the same way, she cut her silken veil in two.

"Keep both these tokens safe!" she said, before climbing into the basket. As soon as she was inside it, the rope was stretched taut and the basket rose in the air. The young man watched for a long time. When the princess reached the mountain top, the man up there took her by the hand, and, in spite of her struggles, she was forced to go with him. The treacherous man left her young rescuer in the cave, despite his shouts and entreaties.

The young man looked around in vain for some means of escape from his plight. There was nothing at all. The rocks were far too steep for him to climb. Finally he went back into the cave and searched it. He found it full of human bones and skeletons, the remains of all the maidens the nine-headed bird had carried away, who had died of starvation here.

Suddenly the young man came upon a dried fish nailed to the wall of the cave. Curious to know what it was, he came closer and touched it with his hand. Thereupon, the fish turned into a youth who knelt down before the young man and thanked him. "You have set me free!" he cried. "Let us be friends!"

They swore to be brothers, but no sooner had they done so than the young man's new friend disappeared. It was all a riddle to him. He went out on the ledge outside the cave, but there was no sign of the vanished youth.

Soon the deserted young man began to feel the pangs of hunger, and looked around for something to eat, but he could find nothing. Suddenly, he caught sight of a dragon close to the cave mouth, clinging to the rock wall with its claws and licking at a stone. The young man did the same, and, lo and behold, he was not hungry any longer!

The dragon had made room for him willingly when he leaned over the stone, and seemed quite disposed to be friendly, so the young man asked the creature's advice. "Do you know how I can get away from here?" said he.

The dragon jerked its head toward its tail, indicating that his questioner was to sit on it. At first, it seemed rather an unsafe place to sit, but at last the young man plucked up his courage and did as the dragon told him, and the creature glided gently down to the ground.

The young man climbed off its back, but just as he was about to thank the dragon it disappeared, exactly as his new friend had done. He looked around for his rescuer again and again, but there was no sign of him, so he set off to leave the wilderness and return to inhabited parts.

On the way, he found a tortoise shell full of gleaming pearls, and stuffed both his pockets full of them. He soon discovered that these were magic pearls. If he threw one of them into fire, the flames were extinguished, and if he threw one into water, the water parted to let him through dry-shod.

The pearls came in very useful, for soon he came to the sea. He threw a pearl into it, and at once the waves parted and towered up like walls on either side.

Without delay, the young man went along the path that opened up in front of him. When he had gone some way the path grew wider, and led him to an open space where he saw a sea dragon.

"Who disturbs me here in my realm?" roared the monster.

"I found some pearls in a tortoise shell," replied the young man, "and I threw one of them into the sea. Then the water parted, and a path opened up in front of me."

"If that is so, come here!" said the dragon. "We will live together and be happy."

Then the young man saw that this was the same dragon who had rescued him from the cave. The youth, too, suddenly appeared — the friend with whom he had sworn brotherhood. And now many things he had not understood before were clear to him. His new friend was the son of the dragon, who was a mighty prince of the sea, and lived and ruled in the ocean depths.

"When you touched the fish you saved my child," the dragon prince told the young man, "and now you will fare as well as he! From this day on, I will be *your* father too!"

So saying, he led his guest to his crystal palace in the sea, and set a banquet of the choicest dishes before him.

The young man was content, and for a long time he lived happily with his friend in the crystal palace. At last, however, he began to yearn for the world of men. He would often look forlornly into space, or gaze at the two halves of the hairpin and the veil that the king's daughter had given him when they parted. One day, he confided his troubles to his friend.

"Well, I will speak to my father!" said the son of the prince of the sea. "But remember, if he wishes to reward you for saving me from the power of the nine-headed bird, do not take any money! And you must refuse any jewels he may offer you too. Out of all his riches, you must choose only a small bottle made of a gourd. It does not look very valuable, but if you rub it, you can do whatever you like by magic."

The young man remembered what he had been told. Sure enough, the dragon led him to his treasure chamber and asked what he would like as a reward for rescuing his son.

The treasure chamber shone and glittered with beautiful things, but the young man refused all the rich gifts that the prince of the sea offered him. He had seen a little gourd in one corner of the chamber, and he asked for this gourd as his reward.

At first, the dragon was taken aback, but he recovered and gave his

111

guest the little gourd. The young man thanked him and set off home to the land of men.

He walked a considerable distance, but long after he had left the sea behind him, there was no town or village in sight. The young man was beginning to feel hungry.

"Oh, if only I had something to eat!" he cried.

As he spoke he accidentally happened to touch the gourd, which was hanging over his shoulder on a strap. The next moment, a table appeared before him, covered with choice food and wine.

The hungry man ate his fill, and went on his way. After a while, however, he began to feel tired.

"Oh, if only I had a donkey to carry me!" he said, and again he touched the gourd.

Instantly, a donkey stood beside him, and carried him until he was tired of riding. He touched his gourd and wished for a cart; and again his wish was granted.

When a man can have anything, soon it seems that nothing will suit him, for such is the way of the world! So the owner of the gourd, who had always been able to withstand weariness before, now found that the cart jolted too much, and touching the gourd with his fingers, he wished for a litter.

The litter appeared. He sat in it, and sure enough, it was better than the donkey and cart. There was no more jolting or rattling, shaking or jarring! So the traveller arrived in the capital city of China, from which the nine-headed bird had carried off the king's daughter, in the most comfortable way possible.

Meanwhile the king's daughter had come home to her father's court, along with the faithless man who had left her rescuer to his fate in the cave. On the way, this wicked man had made her swear a solemn oath not to betray his evil deeds to anyone. So preparations were now being made for their wedding, but everyone wondered why the king's daughter was so sad at the thought of it.

"Wait one more day!" she kept saying, for secretly she still hoped that the man she really loved might have been saved, and would turn up.

However, as she put off the wedding from day to day, and then from week to week, her father lost patience, especially as his prospective son-in-law kept complaining to him.

"You are treating your rescuer badly when you keep looking for excuses," the princess's father told her. "The wedding will be to-morrow, and that's that!"

Sadder than ever, the king's daughter went walking through the city streets, looking to left and right, her eyes searching for her lover.

It was on this very day that the young man arrived in the capital city in his litter, with the half of the veil the princess had given him drifting idly in his hand. The moment the king's daughter set eyes on the litter, she told the bearers to take it straight to her father's court. Nothing could have suited the young man better. He had to produce the half hairpin before the king's eyes, and when it was placed against the half that the princess herself still had, they fitted together as if they had never been broken apart!

Now the king was forced to believe that this young man was the true bridegroom. As for the princess, she would say nothing against the traitor, since she was bound by her oath, but it was not necessary. The villian gave up and confessed his guilt when he was faced with the princess's true rescuer. The king had him thrown into prison, where neither sun nor moon ever shone.

As for the young man, he was married to the princess, and given the title of 'Conqueror of the Nine-Headed Bird' — which, in China, was as good as saying that he was the king's chief minister.

He lived happily with his beloved wife for many years, and they had many children. When the old king died, the Conqueror of the Nine-Headed Bird succeeded to the throne. He sent for his friend, the son of the sea dragon, and made him his chief counsellor. Now he was allied to supernatural as well as to earthly powers, and he reigned so well that his people were happy and content.

As for the time when he and his lovely wife lived and reigned in China, it came to be known as the Epoch of the Wonderful Gourd.

Why?

You can answer that question for yourselves!

TURANDOT

Timurtas, ruler of the Nogai Tartars, had a brave and handsome son called Kalaf. No one in all Astrakhan was as bold and skilful in the use of arms as this prince, and he was a great scholar too, which is not very common among princes. When he was scarcely eighteen years old, he was commander of his country's army, and his royal father also appointed him one of his counsellors. Even the oldest and wisest ministers of state would listen to what Kalaf had to say.

The Khan of the Nogai Tartars and his people lived on the shores of the Caspian Sea. Peace and quiet would have reigned long in their land, but for the powerful Sultan of Chosrem. One day, the Sultan sent messengers demanding tribute from Timurtas, threatening to invade the land of the Nogai Tartars with two hundred thousand men if he refused to pay.

"What are we to do?" Khan Timurtas asked his son and his other counsellors.

One said this, another that, and last of all Kalaf spoke.

"I advise you to refuse the tribute," said he. "If we pay it once, the Sultan's demands will never cease. To be sure, the men of Chosrem are more numerous than we are, but perhaps we can enlist the Circassians, who live near our land, as our allies. Then we could easily march against the Sultan."

This was Kalaf's advice, and so it was decided.

Timurtas sent the Sultan of Chosrem a reply, saying, "We are not afraid of your threats!" At the same time, he sent envoys to the Prince of the Circassians, who realized that the suggested alliance might be useful to him.

"If Chosrem conquers the Nogai Tartars," said the Prince of the Circassians to himself, "the Sultan will attack me and my people next. A powerful nation can always find some reason to invade a country."

115

So the Lord of the Circassians mustered his troops at once, and hurried to the aid of the Nogai Tartars.

When they arrived, the battle was already in progress, and the Tartars were getting the worst of it. But once their allies joined them, the tide began to turn. It seemed as if the troops led by Kalaf would win the day — but before the outcome of the battle could be decided, night fell, and the men laid down their weapons.

The Sultan of Chosrem was not only a man of violence, but crafty too, and if he could not win by force, he would try cunning. Under cover of darkness he sent a secret envoy to the Circassian camp, carrying all kinds of promises, as well as a big sack of gold pieces for the Prince, and asking him in return to betray his allies and to withdraw from the battle.

Sure enough, the Prince of the Circassians was taken in by the honeyed words of the envoy, and decided to do as the Sultan asked. He struck camp and withdrew with his entire army that very night, abandoning the Nogai Tartars. The Sultan's men took up their positions where the Circassians had been encamped.

At daybreak, Kalaf saw that he had been betrayed, but by then it was too late for him to break through the enemy lines with his army. However, with the courage of despair, he gave the signal to charge. Drawing his sword, he placed himself at the head of his horsemen, and broke through the surrounding enemy with a thousand men.

Kalaf galloped straight from the battlefield to the capital city. He knew that the army of Chosrem would follow him, which they did, but he was just in time to fetch his father and mother and snatch up the most precious of their treasures. Then, with a small troop of followers, they eluded their pursuers and escaped to the forest.

However, what were they to do now?

At last Prince Kalaf, his parents and a few faithful followers decided to pass through the land of the Osmans, in search of some refuge. Somewhere, they thought, they would be sure to find a ruler

116

who would give them shelter until they could go back to their own country, arouse the people and drive out the invaders.

Their journey led them through deserts and stony mountain ranges. Often they had to clamber over steep rocks and cross deep chasms. Half their horses perished on the way, and many of their faithful companions died. At last, Kalaf allowed his little group of men to rest for a while in a valley. The Sultan's warriors could never catch up with them there . . . .

But that night, when their camp fires were out, robbers crept out of the woods and took the fugitives by surprise. There were so many robbers in this band that they found Kalaf's little troop easy prey, and the Tartars were struck down, one by one.

Prince Kalaf barely managed to save himself and his parents, and hide in a cave. They waited until the robbers tired of looking for them, divided the spoils and went back to their den.

Kalaf's father, Khan Timurtas, abandoned himself to despair. It was a source of great sorrow and grief to him to think that he must go begging through the land with his wife and son, and eat the bread of strangers.

Kalaf, however, did not lose heart. "Fortune is fickle," said he. "To be sure, our present situation is not exactly rosy! But things may take a turn for the better, and I feel sure I can see us through."

He consoled his parents with such words, and they went on their way. When they could go no further, Kalaf would take his father or mother on his back, like a precious burden, although he himself was so exhausted that he often had difficulty in staying on his feet. They satisfied their hunger with berries and mushrooms that they picked by the wayside, but this poor fare did not last long.

Khan Timurtas suffered most from his privations, and after a few days he collapsed.

"I am resigned to my fate!" he groaned. "Leave me here! This is the end of my wanderings."

"I can go no farther, either," lamented Elmazen, Kalaf's mother.

117

"Embrace us for the last time, my son, and go your way! You at least must be saved — you are young, and will avenge our deaths."

"I will never go on without you!" replied the prince. "Rest here in the sun until I come back. I am going to see if I can find a drink of fresh water or a morsel of food for you somewhere."

While the Khan and his wife lay down to rest in the shade of a tree, the prince climbed to the top of a rock. But he looked in vain for a spring of water, and there was nothing edible to be seen anywhere, far or near. There seemed to be no way at all leading out of this stony desert. Were they all to perish miserably here?

Just as Kalaf gave up hope, and was about to turn back, he suddenly heard the splashing of a little stream. He found a spring of water, and a tree laden with fruit growing beside it. The fruit tasted bitter, but refreshing. However, Kalaf did not stop to satisfy his own hunger and thirst, but went straight back to his parents.

"We are saved!" he cried breathlessly. "Follow me, dear Father and Mother! You will want for nothing now!"

The two old people rose, groaning, and staggered on behind their son. Their legs trembled, but their spirits were revived by new hope.

What was their delight when they saw the spring of water and the tree of fruit! They quenched their thirst and satisfied their hunger, then bathed their weary bodies in the cool water and lay down to sleep.

The next day, refreshed and stronger, they filled their pockets with fruit and climbed down a rocky hillside to the plain below. At the foot of the mountain they came to the walls of a city. Prince Kalaf and his parents sat down under a tree outside the city gate. They were ashamed of their ragged, dirty clothes, and did not want strangers to see them in this state in broad daylight.

Dusk was falling when a dignified old man passed the three travellers. He seemed surprised to see them, looked more closely and stopped.

"What city is this?" Timurtas asked him.

"This is the capital city of Khan Ileng's kingdom," replied the old man. "Your question amazes me! Have you never heard of Khan Ileng? You must come from very far away!"

Kalaf was about to reply, but Timurtas interrupted him; he did not want to reveal who they were, not knowing what the old man's attitude to them might be. He feared treachery everywhere, and so he told only part of the truth.

"We come from the other side of the mountains," said he, evading the question. "Alas, a robber band fell upon us, as we were on our way. They killed our companions and stole all our possessions."

119

"And where are you going now?" asked the old man.

"We are looking for some place of refuge," replied Khan Timurtas. "But where will we find a man noble enough to take in three innocent folk who have fallen on hard times?"

"Must it be a noble man?" replied the old man. "I myself am not a man of high rank, but I would be more than happy to receive you as my guests. I live quite near here."

Timurtas, Elmazen and Kalaf put out their hands in protest. "That was not what we meant!" said they as one. "You must think us very importunate!"

But the old man reassured them, and when he had swept aside their scruples they finally accepted his invitation.

By now it was evening, and they followed their new friend through the city gates. He led them to his house, which was small but charming. First, he gave them new clothes — silken trousers, caftans and Indian turbans for Prince Kalaf and his father, and an intricately embroidered white lined robe for Elmazen. When they had all bathed and changed their clothes, the old man invited his guests to eat. Fine porcelain dishes stood on a table lit by candles. The perfume of ambergris drifted from rose-red coral bowls, and servants hurried busily back and forth, bringing in first a delicious soup, then black caviar. These were followed by venison pies and little dishes of pilaf — rice cooked with meat. Next came exquisitely cooked partridges, roast meat and sturgeon. The feast ended with spiced honeycakes.

The servants kept the guests' goblets filled with sour *kumys* and date wine, so that they were never empty.

The old man drank to the health of his guests, and kept urging them to eat their fill — which was not really necessary; they had gone hungry long enough on their wanderings.

"How is it that you are able to keep such a good table in this little house of yours?" Timurtas asked his host. "Forgive my curiosity!"

"I was once a prosperous merchant," replied the old man, "but I have given up trading now. Since my wife's death, I have lived quietly and in seclusion. The only pleasure I occasionally allow myself is to entertain guests as I used to do in the old days. I can see from your faces that you are content, and I am glad of it!"

After this explanation, the master of the house rose from the table. When it was time to go to bed, he signalled to his servants, and, carrying sweetly perfumed candles, they led Timurtas, Elmazen and Kalaf to their rooms. As soon as the three were left alone, they fell into a deep, refreshing sleep.

In the morning, the old man came to their rooms and awakened them.

"Yesterday you told me of your misfortunes," said he, "but it seems there are folk even unhappier than you — let that thought comfort you! I have just heard that a messenger from Chosrem was sent to Khan Ileng, bringing word from the Sultan that his enemy King Timurtas, with his wife and son, have probably fled here. He asks our ruler to take the Khan of the Nogai Tartars and his family prisoner, and deliver them to him. Now, tell me, are not these poor folk much worse off than you yourselves?"

Timurtas and Kalaf went pale at this news, and Elmazen almost fainted.

This did not escape the notice of their host. "Why do you take the misfortunes of these Nogai Tartars so much to heart?" he asked. "Are you from Astrakhan, too?"

"I will be frank with you," replied Timurtas. "You have heaped kindness upon us, and won our trust. I must tell you that I am the unfortunate Khan Timurtas! This is my son, Kalaf, and this is my wife Elmazen. Forgive us for not telling you the truth at once — we did not know if we could trust you."

The old man waved his apology aside. "I can understand that well enough," said he. "But now, what are we to do? I would like to shelter you in my house, but you will not be safe anywhere in this city. Your presence will surely become known. I know that Khan

Ileng fears the wrath of the Sultan of Chosrem, and he will have the whole city searched for you."

"Then what do you advise us to do, in these circumstances?" asked Khan Timurtas.

"Leave the city at once!" replied the old man. "It grieves me to have to suggest it, but you are in great danger. You must travel westward, and try to reach the land of the Berla tribe as quickly as possible. You can hope for a friendly welcome in the kingdom of Khan Alinger, for he fears nothing and depends on no one."

The old man went to his stables and had three horses saddled. Food and warm blankets for the journey were tied to the saddles, and he gave Timurtas a bag of silver coins besides. The Nogai Khan thanked his host for his kindness and generosity. He and his family mounted their horses, and left the city at a fast trot.

After a good day's journey, they came to a river, found a ford and crossed the water. Once on the opposite bank, they were in the land of the Berla tribe, where no immediate danger threatened them.

Not far from the border, they came to a city of tents. Here they settled down, sold their horses, and lived for half a year on the proceeds, and the silver coins the old man had given them. But when six months were up, their money was gone, and all Kalaf's attempts to earn a living had failed. They were starving, and ashamed of their poverty.

Then Prince Kalaf said, "We might have better luck in the chief settlement of this land, where the tent of Khan Alinger is pitched. Let us go there!"

They did as he suggested.

The Khan's Hawk

The Khan's tent was pitched some two or three day's journey from the city of tents where they had been living, on a gently sloping hillside among woods and meadows.

The three travellers were in luck; they found shelter at once. At the edge of the settlement a roomy hut stood ready for any poor travellers whose journey brought them that way. The Khan of the Nogai Tartars and his family settled down in this hut. But what were they to live on?

"I will go to the market place," said Kalaf. "Porters are always needed there. Honest work is no disgrace, and I am sure to find someone ready to hire me. I will earn enough to keep us from starving to death."

Kalaf, a king's son, a common porter? Timurtas and Elmazen were horrified, but hunger is painful, and necessity knows no law — so, at last, they let their son go.

However, Prince Kalaf was wrong; he offered his services in the market place in vain. There was not a soul who needed him here either.

Toward evening, when the place was becoming quieter, Kalaf had had enough of waiting. He felt oppressed by his troubles. How was he to support his old parents if he could earn no money?

He wandered past the tents, came to the outskirts of a wood and sat down under a tree. There sat Prince Kalaf, racking his brains, and, as he sat, he gazed up at the pale clouds in the sky.

Suddenly he caught sight of a hawk hovering in the branches of the tree above his head. It came down upon a bough, wings outspread. Kalaf could see in the light of the setting sun that the bird had a hood with a bright plume of feathers on its head, and around its neck hung a thin gold chain set with topaz, diamonds and rubies.

"This hawk must certainly belong to some chieftain or prince," thought Kalaf. "I will catch it and return it to its master. Perhaps he may reward me, or take me into his service."

No sooner said than done. Kalaf knew how to manage falcons — he often used to go out hawking at home. Slowly, the young man rose from the ground, avoiding any sudden movement. Then he called to lure the bird, reaching out his arm to it. The hawk came down on his wrist and settled there. Kalaf spoke to it gently, until it felt quite secure, and then carried it back to the tents. There was a great uproar when he arrived.

"There he is! There's the Khan's best-loved hawk!" all the people cried. "Our master has sent men out in search of him everywhere! Follow us, stranger!"

They led the young man to their ruler's tent. The Khan was delighted to have his hawk back, and embraced Kalaf. Then he asked the young man where he found the bird, and how he managed to catch him.

When Kalaf had finished telling his story, the Khan said, "You do not speak exactly as we do — I have been listening to the tone of

124

your voice. Where are you from, and how did you come to us?"

Kalaf resorted to the same subterfuge his father had used when he first spoke to the old merchant outside Khan Ileng's city; he told no lies, but neither did he tell the whole truth.

"I came from far away, with my father and mother," he replied. "We are from the other side of the mountains. When we started out, we had great treasures with us, but we arrived here in dire poverty, for we fell into the hands of robbers who killed our companions and robbed us of everything we had."

"I am glad, then, that it was you who brought back my hawk!" replied the Lord of the Berla Tartars. "You must know that I have sworn to grant three wishes to whoever returned him. Now, let me hear what you wish for!"

"My parents are living in the hut reserved for poor travellers at the edge of the encampment," said Kalaf. "Give them a tent to live in near your own, O Khan, and give them food and drink, and whatever clothes they need during the brief time they still have to live. This is my first wish."

"It is granted!" the Khan nodded. "What else do you wish for?"

"A good horse, saddled and bridled, my lord," replied Kalaf. "And thirdly, I would like a fine robe, a sword and a bag of gold."

"You shall have what you ask," replied Khan Alinger. "My hawk is worth as much and more to me."

Kalaf thanked the Khan with all his heart, and then hurried back to the hut on the outskirts of the encampment, where his parents were waiting anxiously for him.

"Good news!" he cried out when he was within hearing distance.

Then Kalaf told the two old people everything that had happened to him, and took them to the Khan without delay. Khan Alinger provided a magnificent tent for them to live in, close to his own. Light at heart, Timurtas and Elmazen lay down on the soft Kashmir and Persian carpets.

"And now, dear Mother and Father," said Kalaf, "since Khan

Alinger has taken you under his protection, I will ask you one thing! Let me go my own way — you do not need me any more. I long to go to China, to the Middle Kingdom. I would like to see its capital city, Peking, and I believe our luck will not turn until I have won the friendship of the mighty Emperor of China by some great deed. I have a strange foreboding that tells me so."

At first, Timurtas and Elmazen were very sad to learn of their son's plans, but soon they realized that they could not hold him back.

"Go, my son!" said Timurtas, and Kalaf's mother took him in her arms. "Go, and Got be with you! You are a brave and wise young man, and I am confident you will achieve whatever you undertake. My blessing goes with you!"

Next morning the Khan's servants dressed Kalaf in costly robes. Then, as he had promised, the ruler of the Berla Tartars gave him a splendid horse, a sword set with diamonds and a heavy bag of gold.

The prince put the bag of gold in the pocket of his caftan, mounted his horse and pulled on the reins. His steed reared up at the touch of his thighs. Once more he waved to the Khan and his parents, who were smiling through their tears. Then he galloped away into the bright morning.

At the Court of China

Kalaf's journey lasted for ever and a day, as the saying goes. He rode through great expanses of hot and sandy deserts, climbed mountain passes to reach dizzy heights and crossed marshes and steppes. Often he had to fight wild beasts and robbers on his way. But the prince rode boldly on, ever eastward.

After some six months he reached a great city, surrounded by a high stone wall. Roofs of yellow, blue and green tiles decked the palaces, and the temples were built of milk-white stone. Bell towers with curved porcelain roofs rose above the walls.

To his right, Kalaf saw a little house with a small garden, where an old woman was weeding. He stopped to wish her good day and to ask if this was the capital city of China, since that was where he was bound.

"Well," said she, "if you wanted to go to Peking you have reached your journey's end! This is the capital city of the Great Khan Altun, Emperor of China. What brings you here?"

"I have come to place myself and my sword at the Emperor's service," replied the young man, "if I can be of any use to him, and if he values the faithfulness of one who comes from distant lands."

"Why should he not?" cried the old woman. "Altun is a wise and kindly ruler. He loves his people, and his people love him."

"I have heard this many times along my way," replied the prince.

Kalaf and the old woman took a liking to each other. She told the prince she had been a widow for several years, and she let lodgings; one of her rooms happened to be free at the moment, and it was at his disposal if he cared to have it.

Nothing could have been more welcome to Kalaf. He found a place to stable his horse, and went with the widow to her house.

Soon she had a meal on the table — soup, and meat cooked with fruit in the Chinese fashion. It was about midday, and Prince Kalaf had a good appetite for his meal. But suddenly he raised his head. In the distance he heard trumpets blowing, drums rolling and the clash of cymbals.

"What does that music mean?" Kalaf asked the widow.

"A new suitor has arrived," replied the old woman.

"A new suitor?"

"Yes — another young man come to woo Turandot."

"And who is Turandot?" the prince inquired.

"Turandot is the Emperor's daughter, and the court musicians are playing to announce her suitor. If they play again in a quarter of an

127

hour, and play a sad tune, that means that another unhappy young
man is lost, and is being taken to the place of execution in chains."

Prince Kalaf put down the chopsticks he had been using to carry
his food to his mouth, in the Chinese manner. "What do you mean?
What is this?" he asked in astonishment. "Is it the custom here to
execute suitors?"

The widow sighed. "It is easy to see you are a stranger! Have you
never heard of Turandot? And of her beauty and her cruelty, and the
fate of those who come to seek her hand in marriage? Well, I will tell
you the story."

And she began: "If I am not mistaken, young man, you must have
seen plenty of beautiful maidens in your life. But however many you
have seen, or may see in days to come, there was never a maiden like
Turandot among them. The whole world praises her beauty, and the

128

whole world says she is not only beautiful as the day, but wise beyond compare. She knows the teachings of Confucius, and has studied all the knowledge there is in the world. She herself writes the most exquisite verses, so it is no wonder that the most famous kings' sons come to Peking to seek her hand in marriage. And that is where the trouble lies!

"About two years ago, the son of the King of Tibet sought her hand, and Emperor Altun promised to give her to him as his wife. As for the princess, however, she was so proud of herself and all her learning that she did not think her suitor good enough, and she refused the Crown Prince of Tibet. The Emperor had tired of her constant fault-finding with her suitors, and he commanded her to marry the young man. Thereupon, Turandot pretended to be ill, and said she would die if she were forced into this marriage. The Emperor

129

was alarmed, and granted his daughter's wish — after all, what father would willingly be guilty of his child's death?

" 'That is not enough,' said Turandot. 'If you want me to live, swear that you will never give me to a man who cannot answer the three riddles I ask him.'

" 'I swear it!' replied the anxious Emperor, no doubt thinking that his daughter would see reason sooner or later, or a suitor who could satisfy her condition would soon turn up.

"Now the princess had the upper hand. 'Swear, too,' she added, 'that you will put every man who fails to answer all three questions in chains, and have him led to the place of execution!'

"The Emperor swore, though reluctantly. Then Turandot recovered from her sickness, and Khan Altun was delighted with her speedy return to health. But soon he realized that his daughter had tricked him. However, he was now bound by his oath, and ever since then, he has been forced to send one suitor after another to the place of execution, for Turandot's riddles are so difficult and cunningly contrived that no one has yet been able to answer them. Ah — do you hear that?" the widow asked Kalaf. "The trumpets, drums and cymbals have stopped playing. Now the new suitor is going before the princess, the Emperor, the mandarins and the entire court to undergo the test."

"How I would like to see this!" said Kalaf. "Is it possible to do so?"

"Certainly," replied the widow. "Anyone is allowed in, and if you hurry, you will be just in time. But guard yourself against wishing to imitate this unfortunate young man! Any attempt to try Turandot's test means certain death."

Kalaf reassured the widow, telling her that he would never dream of doing any such thing, and the old woman told her guest the way to the Emperor's palace. He set off, and had just reached the gates when music began to play in the palace courtyard. The test had come to an end . . . It was easy to guess what that end was from the melancholy tones now being played.

A strong bodyguard appeared, swords and halberds in their hands. They were followed by twenty mandarins, and as many white-bearded judges, all wearing long cloaks hanging in folds from their shoulders. Behind them walked the ushers with the suitor in chains, and close on his heels followed the executioner, in a red robe, a drawn sword in his hand. A second troop of guards brought up the rear of the procession, which was going toward the place of execution, a gloomy spot surrounded by dark walls.

Prince Kalaf looked compassionately at the unfortunate young suitor, and thought angrily of Turandot, whose pride and vanity sent so many brave young men to their deaths.

And just a little curiosity stirred within him. Suppose, said he to himself, suppose I, too, were to go before her some day, and pit my wits against hers in front of the imperial court? Am I not known to be wise and clear-headed too?

By now, the sad procession had passed him, and the crowd, eager to see the sight, was slowly dispersing. Kalaf noticed an old man leaning against a doorpost, weeping bitterly, and went up to him.

"What is the matter?" he asked. "Can I help you?"

"No one can help me, sir!" replied the old man. "I was the teacher and friend of that young man who is now being led to the place of execution by the Emperor's soldiers. He might be living happily today in his native land of Samarkhand, but for an Indian painter who happened to come to our country some months ago. This painter showed him Turandot's picture, and as soon as he saw that picture, the Prince of Samarkhand fell in love with the Emperor of China's lovely daughter. He decided to go to Peking. I tried to stop him, but in vain; nothing I said could induce him to give up his plan. He set out with a company of horsemen to undergo the test that the princess sets her suitors. However, he could not answer the three riddles, and now he must pay for his ambition with his life. That, stranger, is the cause of my grief. I weep for the Prince of Samarkhand, and all the other young men who have trodden this dreadful path before him, as well as those who are yet to follow."

"Is the princess really so beautiful?" asked Kalaf. "I cannot imagine how anyone could fall so desperately in love at the mere sight of her picture! People tell strange tales!"

"Judge for yourself, sir!" replied the old man, and, taking a picture from the pocket of his caftan, he handed it to the prince. "Look — this is Turandot!"

Kalaf looked at the picture, and at once his heart began to beat fast. The widow in whose house he was lodging had indeed told the truth. He had never seen a more enchanting girl in his life, nor could

he imagine one. Turandot's beauty left the wildest flights of fancy far behind. But it was not only the princess's beauty that dazzled Kalaf; in this picture he saw a certain light in Turandot's eyes, a light that no one else, perhaps, had ever seen before. He felt that Turandot could not only hate and despise her suitors, but that once she met the right man, she would also be capable of loving with all her heart. And perhaps, thought the Prince, he, Kalaf, was the right man. Perhaps Fate had been reserving her for him. Should he not try to woo her, conquer her in a battle of wits and tame her cruel nature?

Looking at Kalaf in alarm, the old man snatched back the picture. "Alas, my lord, what have I done?" he cried. "Why did I ever show you this picture? I see in your face what you intend to do! Change your mind! You will meet with the same fate as my unhappy master, the Prince of Samarkhand, and those who went before him."

Kalaf laid a hand on the old man's shoulder. "You are wrong, good old man," said he. "Princess Turandot will soon demand no more cruel sacrifices. Give me the picture!"

And as the old man still hesitated, he took it from his hand and walked swiftly into the palace.

Twenty elephants stood harnessed together in the courtyard, and behind them, drawn up in line, waited at least a hundred palace guards in silver coats of mail. A captain wearing a golden helmet came out to meet Kalaf.

"What do you want here, stranger?" he asked.

"Tell your master," replied Kalaf in a steady voice, "that a king's son from far away has come to his court, to ask for the hand of Princess Turandot!"

A few minutes later, a chamberlain appeared in a doorway leading to the inner rooms of the palace, and bowed low before Kalaf, saying, "Follow me!"

He led the prince through magnificent rooms, wide halls and passageways, to a golden door, guarded by pages on either side. The door opened, and Kalaf found himself on the threshold of a great hall. Its walls were covered with soft silk, shimmering with a thousand hues. At the end of the hall he saw a throne shaped like a dragon. It was made of pure silver, and on it sat the Emperor, the Great Khan Altun, surrounded by his counsellors and mandarins.

The chamberlain led Prince Kalaf up to the throne, saying, "Your Imperial Majesty, here is a king's son from far away who asks for the hand of the Princess Turandot!"

The Emperor looked kindly at the young man. "What is your name, my son?" he asked.

"Allow me to keep my name to myself a little longer, your Majesty," replied Kalaf.

The Emperor nodded his consent. Then his wrinkled face clouded over, and he sighed. "Anyone can see that you are of noble birth," said he. "Do you know the fate that threatens those who seek my daughter's hand in marriage? Do you know that your way may lead you from this throne-room straight to the place of execution?"

"I know that well enough, my lord," replied Kalaf. "I know of the harsh law that has been the death of so many young men. But I am not afraid of the danger. I will do what I have to do! Allow me, your Majesty, to submit myself of my own free will to the test that no one has yet passed!"

"Then you believe you can answer Turandot's three riddles?" asked the Emperor. "They are not easy riddles, young man! Do you think you are clever enough to solve them?"

"I hope I am," replied Kalaf. "I am not quite without learning, and some believe I may lay claim to a certain amount of wisdom."

The Emperor shook his grey head. "Most of those who made the attempt before you spoke just as you do. The Prince of Samarkhand, who was taken to the place of execution just now, said the same! I am afraid you will fare no better. Give more thought to what you are about to do, bold young man! Consider it all wisely and soberly before you come to any decision. Be my guest to-night, and then, if you still wish it, you can take the test at midday tomorrow, in front of the princess, the mandarins and the whole court."

The Great Khan Altun waved his hand, and the prince was dismissed.

A chamberlain led him to a magnificent room, where a crowd of servants were awaiting his orders. But the prince had only one wish — to be left in peace. As soon as he was alone he took off his clothes and lay down on the bed. Since it was now evening, he would have liked to go to sleep at once, so as to conserve all his strength — for he knew very well that great demands would be made upon him the next day.

However, Kalaf passed a restless night; again and again he started up out of sleep. Once his old parents came into his mind, another time he reflected that if their exiled ruler did not set them free, the Nogai Tartars might remain slaves of the Sultan of Chosrem for ever. Kalaf asked himself time and again whether it was right for him to risk his life on the riddle test, when the happiness of his parents and his people depended on him? At daybreak, he had almost decided to take heed of the Emperor's warnings. It seemed better and wiser to give up the idea of the test.

But when he opened his eyes and his glance fell on the princess's picture, which he had placed on a table beside his bed, his original decision came uppermost in his mind. In the rosy light of dawn, Turandot's face looked even lovelier than it had the day before, and again some mysterious promise seemed to shine out of it, dispelling all his doubts.

The door opened, and the chamberlain came in. He bowed to the Emperor's guest, and said, "His Imperial Majesty, the Great Khan of China, sends me to ask if you have now reflected upon your intentions and reconsidered them."

"Tell the Emperor," replied Kalaf, "that I was never so certain of my decision as I am now. I will take the test!"

The chamberlain bowed and went away. Servants came in and helped the young man to dress. They led him to the bath, rubbed him with nard and precious ointments, and dressed him in splendid robes of white silk. Over these they cast a cloak embroidered with golden flowers. They put stockings and sandals on his feet, set a white hat on his head. Then they brought him a delicious meal.

When the sun was at its height, the Emperor's messenger presented himself again, and told the prince to follow him to the throne-room.

The whole imperial court was already assembled there, with the counsellors, mandarins and ministers of state. A great crowd had poured in, and the armed bodyguards formed a wall in front of the people. The executioner, sword in hand, stood ready by the door. Only the throne was still empty; the Emperor and Princess Turandot were not yet present.

Kalaf went to the middle of the hall, and a dignified old man, the Emperor's chief minister of state, approached him.

"Young man," said he in a clear voice, "answer me this question: have you considered that your path from here leads directly to the place of execution, if you cannot answer the princess's riddles?"

"Yes, I have considered it."

"Do you acknowledge that his Majesty, our noble Emperor Altun, has taken great pains to make you change your mind?"

"I acknowledge it freely!"

"Then do you realize that you can hold no one but yourself responsible for your fate?"

"I do."

"And in spite of all this, are you ready to undergo this test before the Emperor, the princess, the learned mandarins, the court and the people?"

"That is my wish."

"Then let the test begin!" cried the chief minister.

The musicians started to play in the palace courtyard. Horns blared, trumpets sounded, drums rolled. The two halves of the golden door swung open, and the Emperor entered the room with Princess Turandot, heavily veiled, on his arm. Both of them took their places on the throne. The music stopped suddenly.

"Young man," said the Emperor, "I wish to point out to you for the last time that your life is at stake. You can still reconsider your decision. No one will accuse you of cowardice if, after all, you would like to withdraw now."

Prince Kalaf did not move.

Then the Emperor turned to Turandot. "My daughter," said he, "now do your part. My only wish is that Fortune may smile on this suitor, as she has frowned on all others."

"I wish him neither good fortune nor ill," replied Turandot. "His fate is in his own hands. Now let him try his wits!"

Prince Kalaf bowed. "I await your questions, Princess!"

Turandot rose from the throne. "Listen to the first riddle, then!" said she.

"I know a picture fair to see,
A picture full of fire and light,
This picture changes hourly,
Yet it is ever fresh and bright.

A narrow frame contains it all,
Yet all great things that move the heart —
Although this picture is so small —
They reach us only by its art.

Come, can you tell this crystal's name?
No jewel can approach its worth.

A gem that burns without a flame,
And drinks in everything on earth.

The heaven itself is painted here,
Within this picture's little space.
And yet its own beams, shining clear,
Are fairer far than heaven's grace."

138

Prince Kalaf thought for a moment. Then he smiled, bowed to the princess, and replied, in verse.

"The riddle's cunning, I admit!
And yet to solve it I will try.
Say, Princess, does my answer fit?
Your little picture is — the eye!"

The learned mandarins looked at each other — it was their task to judge the answer and say whether it was right. Slowly, their faces began to light up; then they nodded their heads emphatically.

The chief mandarin rose from his place, and turned to Kalaf. "You have answered the first question wisely and well, my young friend," he said solemnly. "The riddle is solved!"

When he had delivered judgement, the Emperor turned to Turandot.

"Do you acknowledge, daughter, that your suitor has solved this riddle?"

"I acknowledge that he was lucky!" replied Turandot angrily. "The answer is correct. But I wonder how he will deal with the second riddle? Listen, stranger!" she cried.

"What is that thing few value much,
And yet it graces any hand?
Formed to do hurt, its power is such
As, like the sword's, none can withstand.

It makes wounds, though no blood is shed.
Robs none, yet brings prosperity.
Through all the world its rule has spread,
Softening life's severity.

It has built cities tall and strong,
Founded great empires with its power,
Yet brings no war nor other wrong.
Men trust it in a happy hour!"

Complete silence reigned in the hall. Turandot, the Emperor, the learned mandarins, the chamberlains, the counsellors, the bodyguards armed with swords and halberds, the crowd, even the executioner in his red robe — everyone was watching the young man. Would this handsome stranger who chose his words so well be able to solve the second riddle, too? There was concern in the eyes of many of the onlookers. But Prince Kalaf had his answer ready.

"It makes wounds, though no blood is shed?
Your words are clever, I allow!
And yet I think it may be said,
The riddle's answer is: the plough?"

Once again the learned mandarins looked at each other, and once again their faces cleared. They put their heads together and nodded, and the chief mandarin, raising his voice, announced, "The second answer is correct, just like the first!"

Turandot stamped her foot angrily.

"Daughter, daughter!" the Emperor rebuked her. "Do you not care for truth and justice? Or do you really wish to take this young man's life? I do not understand your anger! You should be glad that at last a suitor has managed to answer two of your riddles. If you will take my advice, you will spare this brave man the third question, and give him your hand instead. He has already earned it with his two answers!"

"I would not dream of such a thing!" replied Turandot. "He has three riddles to solve — no more, no less! Perhaps the first two were too easy. The third will be harder."

The Emperor turned to Prince Kalaf. "It seems that my daughter wishes to ruin you at any price! I advise you not to tempt fate any longer. Renounce Turandot's hand, and go your way in peace! Or, if you like, you may stay at my court. Your wisdom, and the proof you have given of it, are quite enough for me; I will take you into my household as an imperial counsellor of state."

"I thank you, your Majesty," replied Kalaf, "but glorious as the position you offer may be, I cannot accept it. I love Princess Turandot. I am ready for the third test, even if it costs me my life."

With a sigh, the Great Khan of China turned to his daughter. "You may speak again, then. Let us hear the third riddle."

Turandot rose, and said:

"This bridge is built of pearls most fair,
High-arching over waters grey.
It rises swiftly in the air,
Up to the heavens it makes its way.

The tallest ships can pass below,
Yet of all burdens it is free.
Broad as this bridge may seem to grow,
When you draw near it still will flee.

The water raised it from the ground,
And with the water it will go.
Now tell me where this bridge is found,
And who was he that built it so?"

For a few seconds Kalaf remained deep in thought. The mandarins glanced at each other anxiously, and the Emperor, too, looked uneasy. But in a minute the prince's face cleared, and he broke the tense silence, uttering this verse in a loud voice:

"A bridge is built of pearls most fair?
By this the rainbow may be known:
You ask who built it in the air —
That can be none but God alone!"

At these words, the mandarins leaped to their feet, waving their scarves and hats. You would never have dreamed those wise and dignified men could show so much enthusiasm! Their cheers echoed through the great hall.

"He has passed all the tests!" they cried, and they, the court and the onlookers all applauded. The bodyguard sheathed their swords. The executioner by the door disappeared. And outside, the horns and trumpets sounded, the drums rolled, and the music was as gay and merry as if it were announcing some great victory to the whole city of Peking.

The Emperor rose from his throne, came down the steps and embraced Kalaf.

"The law is satisfied at last!" he said. "All our misfortunes are over! Come to my arms, young man! I am overjoyed to receive you as my son-in-law. You have conquered Turandot, and now she must yield to you."

"Let me ask him one more question, Father!" Turandot asked, rising from her seat. "Allow me one last riddle!"

"What is this?" cried the Great Khan. "Has not this young man fulfilled all your conditions? Not another word! The wedding will take place at once."

Princess Turandot ran down the steps of the throne and clutched at her father's arm.

"In the name of all the gods, Father!" she begged. "Grant me a little more time!"

"More time?" cried the Emperor angrily. "I will give you no more time! I have kept my word, difficult as that was, and now you must keep yours. Off with you to the temple!"

Sobbing, Turandot fell at her father's feet. And Kalaf, looking sadly at the princess, raised his hand.

"I ask your Majesty to hear me!" said he. "I would willingly grant the princess her fourth riddle, but since you have refused it, I have another proposal to make. Give Turandot the time she asks for, and in turn, allow me to ask her a riddle. If she solves it, I will give up my claim to her hand, and leave the palace, the city and the land of China, to return to the unknown, distant place from which I came, for I see that she does not care for me."

A murmur arose in the hall. The Great Khan Altun, astonished, thought he could hardly have heard correctly.

"You will give it all up, stranger?" he asked. "Everything you earned, and earned justly, at the risk of your life?"

"Happiness that is taken by force is no true happiness, your Majesty," replied the young man. "I swear to renounce my claim to Turandot's hand if she can answer my question correctly. Princess Turandot, for her part, may swear that if she fails, she will become my wife gladly and of her own free will."

"I swear it!" cried Turandot quickly, rising from the ground.

The Emperor, quite at a loss, shook his head back and forth.

"I defy anyone to understand this!" said he. "But if they both wish it, let it be so! Ask her your riddle quickly, my son, and make it as difficult as you possibly can!"

"It is difficult enough!" replied the young man. "My riddle runs: what is the name of the happiest man in the world, he who will become instead the unhappiest man alive if you can answer this question, Turandot? What is he called, and from what tribe does he come?"

The princess would not reply at once. "I will give you your answer to-morrow," she said.

"To-morrow?" cried the Emperor. "You are unjust. This young man did not ask for time! Do as he did, and give him your answer at once!"

"Forgive me, your Majesty!" Kalaf interrupted. "I would willingly grant her the respite she asks for."

Again a murmur passed through the hall, and several of the mandarins said to each other, "Has this young man lost his wits? Is he defying the Fates?"

However, the Emperor shrugged his shoulders. "If that is what you wish," said he, "then let it be so. We will meet here again to-morrow morning."

He saluted Kalaf, and left the throne-room with Turandot. The courtiers and the people dispersed.

143

The prince went back to his room. This evening too he went to bed early. It was not his doubts that kept him awake this time; he was so happy and so sure of his good fortune that he could not sleep. No one could possibly answer his question — a man would have to ride more than half a year's journey westward to find anyone who knew the Prince of Astrakhan . . .

In his mind's eye Kalaf already saw himself mounted on his horse with Turandot before him, riding home to the land of the Berla Tartars, where he would present his young, wise and beautiful bride to his parents — the bride he had won by his courage and wit.

To-morrow these flights of fancy would turn to reality!

Suddenly, by the light of his candle, he saw the door-handle move, and the figure of a heavily veiled woman, dressed in white, came into the room.

Kalaf sat up. "Who are you?" he demanded, ready to jump out of bed.

"Hush!" whispered his visitor. "Stay where you are, and listen to me!"

She made a sign to the prince to keep quiet, and went on, "In this palace, terrible penalties await a woman who ventures into the men's apartments. My name is Adelma; I am a slave girl belonging to Turandot and the Emperor."

"What are you doing here?"

"I came to warn you that you are in great danger."

"I — in danger?" asked Kalaf, perplexed.

"Yes, you are in danger of your life."

"Why, who would wish to take my life?" asked the prince incredulously.

"I will tell you, my lord," replied Adelma. "But what I have to say will seem so monstrous you will scarcely believe it. Princess Turandot has bribed two of the bodyguards to stab you when you go to the throne-room to-morrow."

"But why?"

144

"Because she knows she cannot answer your question, and she is so proud that she would not be your wife for anything in the world, neither of her own free will nor by force. My companions and I have tried to persuade her to give up this plan, but in vain. She refuses to change her mind, and so you will perish!"

Kalaf buried his face in his hands. "O false, cruel Turandot!" he groaned. "So you would rather murder Prince Kalaf than become his wife? Oh, Timurtas, my father! Oh, my dear mother Elmazen! I have only one wish now — may you never learn what fate befell your son in China, and how he was so gullible as to bring it on himself!"

"Do not despair, my lord!" the slave girl urged him. "I did not come only to tell you of the danger that threatens you. I want to rescue you! I have already bribed the doorkeepers and the guards at

145

the gate. The way to freedom lies open before you, and I will come with you. Quick, let us hurry — let us leave this place before Turandot's vengeance can overtake us!"

Kalaf looked at the slave girl in surprise. "In heaven's name, why do you take my fate so much to heart?" he asked. "Why should you wish to save my life? Why do you want to escape with me?"

The girl looked at him, her eyes swimming with tears, and fell on her knees. "My lord," she replied in a choked voice, "you could not win Turandot's heart, but you have, unknowingly, robbed me of mine. I love you for your courage, your wisdom and your generosity. I could not live if you fell victim to the Emperor's cruel daughter!"

"Lovely slave girl," replied Kalaf, "I thank you for your kindness and your love for me. But I cannot run away either by myself or with you. What would the Emperor think of me? And what would Turandot say?"

"Turandot! Turandot!" replied the girl angrily. "Nothing but Turandot! All she wants is your downfall, and you still care what she would say if you escaped her assassins!"

Kalaf closed his eyes. "I love Turandot," he whispered. "Whatever may come of it, I cannot give her up."

The girl rose, anger and disappointment showing in her face. "Stay, then, ungrateful man!" she whispered. "Stay, for all I care, and meet the fate that now awaits you. I can tell you this — Turandot will never be yours!"

And she hurried out of the room.

Riddle Upon Riddle

Kalaf lay down on his bed again, but he could not sleep. His thoughts kept coming back to Turandot.

"How can such a diabolical soul dwell in so beautiful a girl?" he asked himself. "And if her soul is so wicked, how can so much goodness shine out of her eyes? How is it possible?"

He passed the night torn by his conflicting thoughts. At dawn he rose from his bed, quite exhausted. Once again, as on the previous day, the servants led him to the bath, rubbed his body and hair with nard and precious ointments, dressed him in festive robes. This time they brought him a caftan of yellow silk, a green cloak embroidered with silver flowers, red stockings, sandals of punched leather and a red turban.

As soon as he was ready, the chamberlain came to his room, and Kalaf followed him to the throne-room. The way led through great rooms, wide halls, long corridors, and past bodyguards carrying swords and halberds. As he passed them, the young man looked keenly at these motionless, stern-faced men. Which of them was the murderer who, in Turandot's name, was to thrust the dagger into his heart? That man, with the long beard? This one, whose eyes glanced aside?

Following the chamberlain, Kalaf walked on with a firm tread. The traitor must not think him a coward! When would he strike? Now? Or now?

But nothing happened. The door of the throne-room opened. Kalaf had not been afraid, yet he breathed a sign of relief. He knew he was safe here. A moment more, and the proud princess would be conquered. She would have to admit defeat — the hour of his triumph was at hand.

The Emperor's court was already waiting in the throne-room, with all the mandarins, counsellors and ministers of state. Once again a great crowd had poured in. The Emperor of China sat on the high silver throne at the end of the hall, with Princess Turandot at his left hand.

She wore no veil today, and her face was as fair as a morning in spring. Kalaf could scarcely take his eyes off her. So beautiful, he thought, yet so cruel and wicked . . .

Outside in the palace courtyard horns brayed, trumpets sounded, drums rolled.

The Emperor raised his hand, and silence fell. The venerable chief minister of the land stood before Kalaf.

"Young man," he began, in a raised voice. "Answer my question clearly! Do you swear to give up all claim to the hand of Princess Turandot if she solves the riddle you asked her yesterday?"

"I swear it!" replied Kalaf.

He was inwardly amused as he took this oath. How could Turandot ever answer his question? There was not a soul who could do it in all the great land of China, the Middle Kingdom, the Celestial Land!

The chief minister turned to Turandot. Her eyes, resting on the young man, had a strange gleam in them.

"And you, daughter of our noble Emperor Altun," asked the minister, "do you swear that you will take this young man as your husband, gladly and of your own free will, if you cannot solve his riddle?"

"I swear it," replied Turandot.

And as she spoke a strange expression crossed her face, an expression that puzzled Kalaf a great deal.

"The young stranger asked his question yesterday," said the Emperor. "Now it is your turn, my daughter. But if you will take your father's advice, you will abandon any idea of answering this riddle, and give this brave, clever and gallant young man your hand without more ado."

"I would like to answer his question," replied Turandot, with a strange smile. So saying, she rose from the throne and cried in a loud voice,

"Now you shall have the answer that you seek!
O bold young man, you think that you have won?
You are – be still, let no one move or speak!
You are Prince Kalaf, Khan Timurtas' son!"

Kalaf became deathly pale and put his hand to his heart, but Turandot laughed out loud. Looking at the two of them, the courtiers realized that the princess had given the right answer, and a murmur arose.

"Alas, that it should come to this!" the counsellors and ministers whispered to one another. "Why did the young man give her time?"

The Emperor jumped up, quite beside himself. "Are you really Prince Kalaf, son of Khan Timurtas?" he cried.

Kalaf was so agitated that he could only stammer, "This is magic! This is witchcraft!"

Turandot looked down at him. Her face was radiant. "What do you mean by magic and witchcraft? All I did was to send a slave girl to visit you in your room and pry your secret out of you. And my plan succeeded! Adelma played her part very well, and Prince Kalaf fell into her trap."

"This is a trick!" cried the Emperor sharply.

"To be sure!" replied Turandot, not at all abashed. "I do not deny it! But I have answered Prince Kalaf's riddle correctly, and so now I am not pledged to become his wife."

The learned mandarins exchanged questioning glances, then they put their heads together, and finally they nodded. The chief mandarin stood up and pronounced judgement.

"It is quite true that Turandot discovered the name and birth of this young man by a trick. However, she has certainly answered Prince Kalaf's question, and she cannot, therefore, be compelled to marry him."

There were loud shouts among the crowd, and out in the courtyard the musicians began to play as they did after every verdict. The trumpets brayed, the horns sounded, the drums rolled. But Turandot called for silence, and, at a sign from her, the noise and music died away.

"Hear what I still have to say!" cried the beautiful princess. "Now that I am freed from my oath, I declare gladly and of my own free will that my hand is Prince Kalaf's, if he still wishes for it!"

Her face was glowing radiantly, and her eyes rested on the prince, who could hardly believe his ears. He felt quite dizzy with happiness.

Murmurs again rose among the courtiers. "Did we hear right, or are we out of our minds?" the ministers, counsellors and mandarins asked each other.

Turandot raised her hand. "I confess that I love the prince!" she cried. "Nothing but my pride kept me from giving him my hand at

150

once. When I heard him solve my riddles, my heart beat faster and faster for him. Even if he had failed to answer one of them, I would have begged my father to show mercy. Let me now admit it! But my pride could never bear any man to say of himself: I conquered Princess Turandot! And so I resorted to my ruse."

Casting down her eyes, she descended the steps of the throne and went up to Prince Kalaf, adding in a voice that the others could hardly hear, "But, of course, you *did* conquer me, Kalaf!"

Kalaf's face lit up. He had regained his self-control. Taking Turandot's hand, he said, "Yours, Turandot, is the greater victory, for you have overcome your pride!"

At that moment, a slave girl thrust her way through the throng of courtiers and flung herself at the feet of Kalaf and Turandot. It was Adelma, the girl who had tricked Kalaf into telling his secret.

"Punish me!" she cried. "I have betrayed you both. I lied to you, my lord, when I told you that Turandot was planning to have you murdered by the guards, and I tricked you, my lady, when I told you I was going to Kalaf only on your account. The truth is that I love him! I hoped to persuade him to run away with me. But when he rejected me, I told you his secret, as you ordered. However, I hoped secretly that if you answered his riddle and refused to marry him, his heart would turn to me. I have nothing to hope for now. Here I am; I await my punishment!"

"We will spare you your punishment," said the Emperor. "The human heart is full of contradictions, and if we look at it rightly, we have to thank you for this happy ending, Adelma! You will certainly find consolation for your unhappy love for Kalaf. There are many young men in China who would think themselves lucky to be allowed to offer it! Rise! I give you your freedom, Adelma. You may go home to your parents' house this very day, laden with gifts."

The slave girl went away, weeping tears of joy. As for the courtiers, they all crowded around Kalaf and Turandot, wishing them long life and happiness.

However, the smile suddenly vanished from Turandot's lips. Her eyes were sad; something was troubling her.

"What is the matter?" asked Kalaf. "Why are you downcast so suddenly?"

Turandot sighed. "I was thinking of all the young princes who have been led to the place of execution because of me. The memory of them will always be on my conscience. I can never make amends for my great sin!"

"You certainly have a great deal on your conscience," said the Emperor, interrupting them. "You have sent many suitors to the place of execution. Thirty-three, if I am not mistaken! And yet your sin is not as great nor as bad as you believe."

He signalled to the captain of the bodyguard, who hurried out of the room. Soon afterward, both halves of the great golden door swung open, and a troop of young men came into the room. They were Turandot's suitors, those who had not been fortunate enough to solve her riddles; there were thirty-three of them. Leading them was the young man who had gone to meet his fate last of all, the Prince of Samarkhand.

Turandot stared at her rejected suitors, wide-eyed. Now it was her turn to stammer, "Magic!" and "Witchcraft!"

While the onlookers stood on tiptoe to stare over the heads of the crowd, so as not to miss anything, the Emperor said, "It is not magic or witchcraft, Turandot, nor have your thirty-three suitors risen from the dead! They were never put to death at all."

"But how can this be possible?" asked the princess, her face beginning to shine with joy. "Did you not swear to deliver to the executioner any man who could not answer my riddles?"

"Oh, no!" replied the Emperor. "I swore that every suitor who failed to answer you should be put in chains and led to the place of execution. If by that you understood that he would also be beheaded, you were mistaken! I did exactly as I swore to do — the thirty-three suitors were put in chains and led to the place of execution. There, behind those grim walls, their fetters were struck off again, on my orders, and they were taken to pleasant, clean rooms where they lacked for nothing — nothing but freedom. Now they have their freedom back!"

Shouts of joy rang out in the throne-room when the Emperor had finished speaking. The crowd could hardly contain its delight. As for Princess Turandot, she fell on her father's neck, tears streaming down her face.

Before long, there was a wedding at the court of the Great Khan of China. Emperor Altun had sent envoys to the settlement of the Barla Tartars to bring Timurtas and Elmazen to Peking, so that they could share in their son's good fortune. The old chronicles say that no less than ten thousand cartloads of rice were required for the guests at this wedding, five thousand cartloads of poultry, four thousand cartloads of different kinds of fruit, and all manner of other things.

After the marriage ceremony, Prince Kalaf, who had been raised by the Emperor to the rank of Crown Prince of China, asked for a short leave of absence. The Emperor placed a great army at his disposal, and he went with his army to free his native land from the tyrannous Sultan of Chosrem. It was a long way to the country of the Nogai Tartars, but they waged war again in Astrakhan, and this time Kalaf overcame the Sultan, who was killed in the fighting.

The triumphant Kalaf and his Chinese warriors marched on to Chosrem. The people of Chosrem had long since heard of the courage and wisdom of the young prince, and they asked him to become ruler of the land he had conquered. Kalaf accepted their offer, and took up his quarters in the Sultan's magnificent palace.

His young wife, who had been parted from him for a year, came to join him. Kalaf rode to the city gate to meet her. When she stepped out of her litter, surrounded by a host of followers, she was carrying a baby in her arms.

As soon as they had greeted each other, the Emperor of China's daughter said to her husband, "I know a riddle, Kalaf! Quick, tell me the answer! Who is he that today cannot sit upright, yet one day will be able to choose between three thrones; he that cannot speak now, yet three kingdoms will listen to his words one day?"

Kalaf's heart leaped with joy, but he was a skilled dissembler. "No, dear wife," said he, "I cannot solve this riddle."

"Yet it is very easy!" replied Turandot. "Look here! This little child in my arms cannot yet sit up, but one day he will rule three kingdoms, the land of the Nogai Tartars, the land of Chosrem and the land of China. For he is the grandson of Timurtas and of Altun — or to put it more simply, he is your son and mine!"

SEMRUDE THE FAIR AND THE CADI

My tale begins with the fortunes of a prince, as a fairy tale ought to do. This same prince, of course, has a part to play — a very important part — in the life of the beautiful and resourceful Semrude, whose story, strictly speaking, this is. But I will begin at the beginning!

This prince's name was Fadlallah, and he was the son of King Ortok of Mossul — in fact, he was the Crown Prince of Mossul.

One day, his father said to him, "Soon you will be king in my place, and it troubles me that you have never yet paid your respects to our noble lord, Haroun al Raschid, the King of Kings!"

"Shall I go to see him, dear Father?" asked Fadlallah. "I can think of nothing I would rather do! What is more, I have never set eyes on the beautiful city of Baghdad, and who would not want to visit Baghdad?"

"Our wishes coincide exactly!" replied King Ortok. "A caravan sets out for Baghdad tomorrow, taking our yearly tribute to Caliph Haroun al Raschid, Commander of the Faithful. You can join this caravan."

So the next day, when porters had loaded up the camels with the tribute — ten sacks of gold — the caravan set out. A hundred horsemen rode with it to act as guards, and, at its head, on a horse with a silver bridle and a saddle-cloth embroidered with gold, rode Crown Prince Fadlallah in person.

On the third evening of their journey, the caravan pitched its tents on the outskirts of a wood. The soldiers lit a camp fire, lay down and soon fell asleep. But in the middle of the night, the sentries gave the alarm. Robbers were attacking the camp. they swooped down on all sides like a swarm of hornets, and although Prince Fadlallah and his men defended themselves bravely, they were finally overpowered by sheer force of numbers.

When day broke, the hundred soldiers from Mossul lay dead or wounded on the battlefield. Only Fadlallah was unharmed, although he had fought in the thick of the battle all the time. His horse had fallen under him, pierced by a lance, and at last he had to surrender.

"I know you!" said the leader of the robbers. "You are Prince Fadlallah! I am not going to kill you here and now; we will take you to our chief, and he will decide upon your fate!"

They tied the Crown Prince's hands and feet, and bound him on a horse. They marched through the forest for many hours, until they came to a deep, hidden valley, where the robbers lived in tents and caves.

The robber chief, of course, lived in the biggest and finest tent.

"You are brave fellows!" he told his men when they arrived. "And this is good plunder you have brought home — but I am best pleased with your prisoner!"

So saying, he turned to Fadlallah. "Son of a dog!" he shouted. "Have you any idea what your father and his followers have made us suffer? They have been persecuting us for years, hunting us down and murdering us, and it is because of them that we live in hiding here. Now the hour of revenge has come! Ortok's son shall die a slow and painful death!"

"Do as you please!" replied the prince proudly. "I will never beg robbers for mercy!"

It would have been useless to do so. The angry robbers seized him and tied him to a tree trunk so tightly that the ropes bit deep into his flesh.

"Now we will leave you to your fate!" the robber chief mocked him. "We need not soil our hands with your — ha, ha! — princely blood! There are plenty of bloodsucking flies and mosquitoes here."

Crown Prince Fadlallah soon realized that the robber chief had spoken the truth. In less than a quarter of an hour, a cloud of thirsty flies and mosquitoes settled on his helpless, half-naked body, and stung and bit and tormented him unmercifully.

However, the robbers no longer paid any attention to their prisoner. There was no need — he was doomed to die; he was bound so tightly to the tree that he could not make the slightest movement.

Slowly, darkness fell. Myriads of stinging insects circled around the prisoner. Their stings made his skin burn and smart. He was covered with hundreds of bloodstained marks and swellings, his arms and legs were trembling with exhaustion, and he felt sure he was doomed if help did not come soon . . .

Help? What help? Who would come looking for him — who could find him in this great forest, in the farthest corner of a remote valley? There was no point in hoping.

Suddenly the prisoner realized that something was scratching and tugging at his feet. It seemed to be a mouse — and so it was. The nimble little creature was gnawing at his bonds. Perhaps some smell that attracted the mouse clung to the ropes; maybe the robbers had once used them to tie up bundles of meat or cheese . . . .

Fadlailah held his breath, so as not to scare the mouse away. Gradually, he felt the ropes beginning to slacken, and, at last, they fell from one of his feet. Slowly he managed to free one leg and one hand.

As everyone knows, once this is done, it is only a matter of time and caution before a man can free himself completely. When Fadlallah had slipped off all the ropes, he flexed his stiff arms and legs and stretched without making a sound. He crept away quietly on tiptoe, and not until the dying embers of the robbers' camp fire were a long way behind him did he dare to run. Then he ran and ran, deeper and deeper into the forest.

From time to time, he stopped to listen, but no one was following him. His escape had gone unnoticed. He had no idea where he was, but in the first light of day he saw a narrow path ahead. This path could only lead to human dwellings, thought Fadlallah, so he walked along it.

It was almost midday by the time the forest cleared, and the fugitive saw an inhabited valley lying at his feet. A donkey and cart, with an old man sitting in it, was just coming toward him.

The old man looked at the exhausted young man and brought his cart to a standstill.

"If you want to go to Baghdad," said he kindly, "jump up into my cart! I'm on my way there myself, and my donkey will pull us both."

Fadlallah thanked him and climbed up.

The minarets of Baghdad came in sight that afternoon. Fadlallah parted from the old man outside the city gates, and went the rest of the way on foot.

Suddenly, he realized his stomach was complaining. He was

hungry, and no wonder – he had had nothing to eat all day but a few berries he had picked from the bushes.

There is an Eastern proverb that says, "Hunger is a good guide!" It was not long before Fadlallah smelled newly baked bread, and following his nose, he soon found himself standing outside a fine house. The tempting smell came from the open window of this house.

Looking inside, Fadlallah saw a young and very beautiful girl who was busy slicing a warm, crusty, golden-brown loaf of bread. When she chanced to look up, she caught sight of the ragged stranger, and, seeing the hunger in his eyes, quickly cut a thick slice from the loaf. Only then did she veil her face, and she handed the bread through the window to Fadlallah with an inviting gesture.

The prince was ashamed to appear as a beggar before this girl, and dared not take the bread. Moreover, her beauty and kindness made such an impression on him that he could not speak a word.

"Pray take it!" the beautiful girl begged him. "It comes to you with Allah's blessing!"

When, at last, the prince took the bread, she gave him a friendly nod and shut the window. Spellbound, Fadlallah started after the girl, until his rumbling stomach brought him down to earth again.

When he had satisfied his hunger, he felt well enough to observe his surroundings. He was in a small square. Several men, whose looks he did not quite trust, were standing near by.

"Whose house is this?" Fadlallah asked one of them.

"It belongs to Adbanes the Rich," replied the young fellow.

"And who was the beautiful girl at the window?"

"Oh, that was his only daughter, Semrude. But who are you, stranger?"

"I'm a poor traveller," replied Fadlallah, thinking it wiser not to tell these people his real name and rank.

"And what do you intend to do in Baghdad?" the man went on.

"I hope to earn a living here," said the prince.

"Hey, look at this fellow!" cried the young man to his companions, pointing at Fadlallah. "He wants to earn his bread by working!"

The men came closer, laughing.

"I don't understand you," said Fadlallah. "How else can I live?"

"Listen to me!" cried one of the band. "We are just as poor as you are!" He turned his pockets inside out with an eloquent gesture. "Look at that! Not a copper coin! But we're not waiting for kindly folk to give us charity, and we have no intention of wasting our time working! We take what we need!"

"Are you thieves, then?" asked Fadlallah, taking a step back.

"Well, if you like to put it that way, yes, we're thieves! Arsonists and murderers too, for all I care!" laughed the rogue. And he added quietly, "To-day, for instance, as soon as it gets dark, we are going to break into the house of Adbanes, the rich baker, and ransack it from attic to cellar. You can join us, if you like. We could do with a strong young fellow like you."

Putting out both hands to keep the thieves off, the prince looked around, wondering how he could escape from the band, who were closing in on him. But there was no time to escape. Suddenly, the Cadi's armed men appeared in the square. They fell upon the band of thieves, tied them up one by one, and took Fadlallah prisoner along with the rest. He protested in vain that he was innocent. "Caught together, hanged together," says another proverb, and, though it was not quite as bad as that yet, the prince had to go with the others.

So he and the whole gang of thieves were taken before the judge, or Cadi.

The judge, who was an old man, squatted on his cushions and looked his prisoners over.

"Well, you gallow-birds — perhaps you're wondering how I guessed your plans?" he asked. "Aha — the police are no fools, you know! We knew exactly what you were up to!"

One by one they tried to lie their way out of it, and one by one they were sentenced to be bastinadoed, beaten, or thrown into prison.

When Fadlallah's turn came, he told the Cadi he had only been in Baghdad for an hour, and had fallen in with the band by chance. But he still felt it was more prudent not to reveal his identity.

"Then what were you doing, loitering outside the house of Adbanes?" the Cadi barked at him.

"His daughter gave me a piece of bread," replied the prince, "and Semrude's beauty so enchanted me that I have no idea how long I stood outside the window."

The mention of Semrude seemed to surprise the judge. He looked long and keenly into the prince's eyes.

"What was that you said?" he asked cautiously. "It was Semrude's beauty that enchanted you?"

"That was what I said," replied Fadlallah, "and it is no more than the simple truth!"

The Cadi appeared to reflect for a moment; he stroked his beard several times and screwed up his wrinkled face more than ever.

"Do you like Semrude well enough to take her as your wife?" he asked at last.

The prince was startled. What could this question mean? He thought for a moment, and then replied, "Semrude is both beautiful and kind. Why should I not marry her, if such an unlikely piece of good fortune should come my way!"

"Good!" said the Cadi, rubbing his hands. "In that case, get ready to celebrate the wedding to-morrow!"

And without waiting for any reply from the astonished Fadlallah, he made a sign to one of his servants, and handed the prisoner over to him.

"Take this young man to the baths!" he ordered. "When he has bathed, dress him in my finest caftan, with silken trousers and my best cloak. And give him plenty of food and drink too — we want to have him in good spirits, as befits a bridegroom!"

As he was led away, Fadlallah turned back several times to look over his shoulder and ask the Cadi what all this meant. But the Cadi would not reply, and the servant who was in charge of him was as dumb as an ox, and would only shake his head at Fadlallah's questions.

162

So the bewildered prince allowed himself to be taken to the baths, dressed in fine robes, and given food and drink, as the judge ordered. What he did not know was that this Cadi was a grasping, miserly man, who had already asked Adbanes for his daughter's hand in marriage three times. In fact, the old man did not even know Semrude himself, but he had heard tell of her beauty, and, above all, it was the baker's wealth that tempted him. However, since his offer was always refused, the judge had sworn to take revenge on Adbanes. Now he intended to use Fadallah as his tool.

While the young prisoner was being prepared to play his part, the Cadi sent one of his men to Adbanes the baker, with a message that he was to visit the judge at once on important business. So, accompanied by two lantern bearers, the rich baker came to see the Cadi.

"What do you want, so late at night?" he asked.

"My dear Master Adbanes," replied the hypocritical Cadi, pretending to be friendly, "I have good news for you, and it is never too late to hear good news!"

"Peace be with you!" replied Adbanes. "What kind of news is this?"

"I want to ask for Semrude's hand in marriage," replied the Cadi.

The rich baker's face darkened. Even in the flickering light of the lanterns, the veins could be seen standing out on his forehead.

"Haven't I told you three times already that I cannot give you my daughter? You are far too old for her!"

"Let me finish what I was saying!" replied the Cadi. "I am not asking for Semrude's hand for myself this time — I am speaking on behalf of a prince who comes from distant lands. Think of that, Adbanes — a real prince wants to marry your daughter!"

As far as the Cadi knew, he was lying like a trooper; of course, he did not know how close what he was saying came to the truth.

However, Adbanes started at the judge's words. "Are you trying to make fun of me?" he demanded angrily.

163

"No, no!" the Cadi assured him. "This is no laughing matter! I really am speaking to you on behalf of a prince. The only son of Abdul Kasim, Sultan of Basra, has come to visit my humble home. He came to our city in disguise, and happened to catch a glimpse of your daughter, who gave him alms, thinking he was a beggar. Now the prince can think of nothing but her beauty and kindness. His most fervent wish is to have Semrude as his wife, to share the royal throne with him. And you, my friend, still seem to hesitate!"

"You are sure you are not making fun of me?" asked Adbanes incredulously.

"What an idea!" replied the deceitful Cadi. "But if you doubt my words, the prince himself will talk to you."

So saying, he led him to Fadlallah's room.

At the sight of the young man in his magnificent robes, Adbanes touched his forehead, mouth and heart with his hand and bowed low.

"Your Royal Highness," said he, deeply moved, "I am Adbanes, the father of Semrude, and your most devoted servant!"

Fadlallah looked at the baker in astonishment. He had kept his name and rank a secret from everyone – how had this worthy man of Baghdad learned of his royal title?

"Why do you call me prince?" he inquired.

"Should I not do so, noble lord?" replied Adbanes. "Are you not the son of a mighty ruler, and heir to the throne of a great king?"

Fadlallah was amazed. Since he did not know what the Cadi had been saying about him, he thought that, somehow or other, the rich baker must have guessed his secret, so he replied, "Very well, then, I *am* what you take me for – why should I conceal my rank any longer?"

"Thank you for trusting your secret to me, O prince!" replied Adbanes. "The Cadi tells me that you want to marry my daughter."

"I would be happy to do so," replied Fadlallah, "if you would give her to me."

"If?" cried Adbanes. "Blessed be the hour that led you to my humble house!"

All this time, the crafty Cadi was laughing up his sleeve. Of course, he thought the vagabond was simply pretending, and he had to admit that Fadlallah was doing very well.

"I am delighted that you two have agreed so quickly," said the Cadi. "Why put off the wedding any longer than necessary? We had better celebrate it to-morrow! Do you agree?"

"Why not?" replied Adbanes.

As for Fadlallah — well, he was perfectly happy with this arrangement!

So the next morning the rich baker's men ran through the city, spreading the news of the wedding, as was the custom. At midday, when the Imam married the young couple, the fashionable world of Baghdad poured into the baker's house, which was especially decorated for the occasion.

The Cadi was not present among the guests, and in the crowd no one noticed his absence. But while the master of the house was busy receiving his guests, the door opened, and in came the judge's servant with a bundle of dirty, ragged clothes in his hand. Carrying this bundle, he went up to the bridegroom, held it up, and cried, "My master the Cadi sends me to tell you to put on these ragged old clothes of yours again, and send him back the robes he loaned you for you to play your part in the deception!"

All the guests fell silent, in amazement. Semrude leaned for support on Fadlallah, whose face was crimson to the roots of his hair.

"What does this mean?" asked Adbanes hoarsely.

"Only that this fellow, whom your daughter married believing he was a prince, is nothing but a common vagabond!" replied the servant. "He was taken prisoner with the gang of thieves who were arrested outside your house yesterday."

"This cannot be true!" cried Adbanes.

But the servant would say no more. Throwing down the rags, he left the festive room, his head held high. All the guests turned to the young husband, a question in their eyes.

"He was telling the truth," Fadlallah said.

"Do you mean you are not the son of Abdul Kasim, Sultan of Basra?" asked Adbanes in a voice that trembled.

"What made you think that?" replied Fadlallah. "What have I to do with Basra, or Abdul Kasim, or — "

"O vile and wicked man!" cried Adbanes. "Now I see it all — you plotted with the Cadi to make a fool of me before the whole city! Who are you really, you wretch?"

But before Fadlallah could reply, Semrude stepped in front of him.

"Let me speak first!" she cried. "Father, I have no more idea than you do who this young man is, though I have just married him. I know only that I love him, and that I loved him from the moment I first saw him outside my window, dressed as a beggar. What do I care for his name and rank? I promise to be a good wife to him, as long as I live!"

"Oh, my dear daughter!" wailed Adbanes. "The wife of a vagabond, a common criminal . . ."

"I am neither a vagabond nor a criminal!" Fadlallah interrupted his father-in-law. "Now you may learn who I really am, which you would know already if you had not interrupted me! I have nothing to do with the Sultan of Basra, but I am descended from as great a house. My name is Fadlallah, and my father is Ortok, King of Mossul!"

"Can this be true?" cried Adbanes.

"I swear it, by the head of your fair daughter Semrude!" replied Fadlallah.

Adbanes almost threw himself at the prince's feet. He cried, "Forgive me, forgive me!" over and over again, trying to kiss Fadlallah's hand.

Semrude, however, could contain herself no longer. Questions tumbled from her lips, and Fadlallah had to tell the whole story: how he fell into the hands of the robbers, how the mouse saved his life, how he happened to be with the thieves and became the unsuspecting tool of the vengeful Cadi. When Fadlallah had finished, Adbanes completed his son-in-law's tale with a brief account of his own dealings with the Cadi.

"So when he asked for your daughter's hand in marriage in the name of a prince, he was really deceiving himself!" laughed Fadlallah.

"So he was!" replied the baker. "Nevertheless, he should be punished for his villainy."

"That is only right and proper!" cried several of the guests, and they all began to talk at once. Then Semrude raised her voice.

"Pray leave it to me, dear father!" she asked. "After all, I was the one whom the Cadi wanted to harm, by marrying me to a beggar. He does not know me yet, but he soon will! I already have a good idea how we can best fool the old man and punish him!"

Fadlallah consented to his young wife's wishes, and so did her father. She went to her own rooms to prepare for the trick she was planning.

He Who Digs a Pit for Others . . .

Once in her own room, the first thing Semrude did was to take off her rich wedding dress and put on a plain, simple dress, such as poor girls wore. Then she veiled her face and left her father's house, without telling anyone where she was going. She went straight to the old Cadi.

The judge was in the best of tempers. His servant had just described the astonishment his appearance and the revelations he made had produced at the wedding. Of course, he did not know what had happened after that, since he left directly after carrying out his errand. So the Cadi was happy in the belief that his ruse had succeeded. He was still chuckling to himself, when Semrude entered the room.

"Well, and who are you?" he asked, forcing himself to appear suitably grave and serious.

"My name is Zuleika," replied Semrude, "and my father is Omar the cobbler who lives by the city gates — I am sure he has done work for you."

"Yes, I know him," replied the Cadi. "Omar has a good business. But I had no idea he had a daughter."

"Of course — how could you?" said Semrude. "My father always claims that he has no children. Ever since I was born he has kept me hidden in a secret room in the house, where he shuts me up in a cage every day to keep me prisoner. Today, by chance, he left the cage door unlocked, so I have come here to complain of my hard lot and to ask for justice."

"And a very good thing, too!" cried the Cadi. "Why, your father's conduct is infamous! It's against the law! It cries out to heaven! Have none of the folk who live near by noticed the wrong he does you?"

"Yes, they have," replied Semrude. "But whenever anyone sees me in the cage and asks who that girl is, my father always chases him away at once, crying, 'Do you take that for a girl? What in the world makes you think so? It's nothing but an ugly monkey!' And since people are easily duped, they have accepted what he says."

"This is incredible!" said the Cadi. "Your father can't be quite right in the head!"

"I think all he wants is to save the dowry he would have to pay at my wedding," replied Semrude. "Other girls of my age have long been married, and surely, in different circumstances, someone would have married me — don't you think so, my lord Cadi?"

She lifted her veil with a graceful gesture — only for a moment, but that was enough to kindle the old Cadi's desires.

"What a crying shame!" said he. "Imagine pretending you are a monkey and hiding you away!"

"Do you think I might venture to show my face?" asked Semrude. "Would some man really marry me?"

"What a question!" said the judge indignantly. "Why, I myself would be happy to ask for your hand, if you would care to be my wife!"

Semrude modestly cast down her eyes, which showed above the veil.

"Is that really true?" she asked, acting as though she could hardly conceal her joy. "A man like you — ah, I would like to marry a man like you better than anything in the world!"

"Then go home at once, fair Zuleika!" the judge told her. "I will send for your father and talk to him. He will never refuse his

169

daughter to the chief Cadi of Baghdad — especially since he has incurred the penalties of the law!"

"Ah, but you don't know my father!" cried Semrude. "He will pretend I don't exist. Why, I can already hear him saying, 'But I have no daughter!' And if you should ask him, 'Well then, who is it that crouches in the cage in the little back room of your house?' he is so obstinate that he is sure to reply, 'That's an ugly monkey!' "

"Leave it to me!" said the judge. "If he tries to fool *me* — the chief Cadi! — with this tale, I will simply say, 'Very well then, I want to marry that monkey!' "

He laughed heartily, well-pleased with himself.

"You have a ready tongue, my lord!" Semrude flattered the old man, joining in his laughter. "Yes, that would be the way to get the better of him!"

So saying, she bowed, and hurried home. As for the Cadi, he called a servant and told him to go to Omar the cobbler, who lived by the city gates, and summon him to the Cadi's house at once. In less than a half hour the servant came back with the cobbler.

"Omar, listen to me!" said the Cadi. "Do you know me?"

"Everyone knows you, my lord!" replied the cobbler. "You are the chief Cadi of the city of Baghdad."

"Good! And what would a cobbler say if the supreme judge of the city of Baghdad wanted to marry his daughter?"

"Why, he would say he was overwhelmed by so much good fortune, of course!"

"I suppose he would not, by any chance, refuse and say he had no daughter?"

Omar could not understand what the Cadi meant. He shrugged his shoulders. "If he had a daughter, and if he was in his right mind," he replied, "why, he certainly would not refuse!"

"Excellent, cobbler!" said the Cadi. "Then we are agreed upon it!"

·"Agreed?" replied the puzzled Omar. "Agreed upon what, my lord?"

"Why, we have agreed that I am to marry your daughter!"

"But I have no daughter!" cried the cobbler.

"Oh, this is too much!" said the judge angrily. "Are you trying to make fun of me?"

"God forbid!" the cobbler protested. "It is nothing but the truth, my lord. I have no children."

"You are a stupid, obstinate old fellow!" raged the judge. "But I know how to deal with you! Tell me this — who is the girl you keep in a cage in your back room?"

"That is not a girl, my lord! It's nothing but an ugly monkey!" replied Omar. "I bought it years ago from a travelling merchant. When my wife was alive, she liked to play with it."

The cobbler was telling the truth, as Semrude knew very well. Omar had often made her slippers, and when she went to his workshop, she always saw Zuleika, the friendly monkey, and would give her a date, a fig or an orange. She used this knowledge for her trick.

"Oh, so your wife used to play with it?" jeered the Cadi. "And it's an ugly monkey in your cage, eh? Would you mind telling me this monkey's name?"

"Zuleika," replied Omar innocently.

"Ah! Now, you listen to me, cobbler!" shouted the Cadi, bringing his fist down on the table. "I have just been talking to Zuleika!"

"How can that be, my lord?" asked the bewildered cobbler.

"She has just been here, complaining that you keep her a prisoner and will not allow her to marry. Aha — that surprises you, does it?"

"I will not allow her to marry? Pray don't make fun of me, my lord Cadi!"

"Oh, you are surprised to learn how much your judge knows, my good man? In a word, I have settled it all with Zuleika, and she is to be my wife."

"You want to marry a monkey?" asked the cobbler, dumbfounded.

"You are beginning to bore me!" cried the Cadi. "Be careful, or I'll soon change my tune!"

Omar scratched his head. The chief Cadi of Baghdad was a powerful man — no one would want to offend him.

"Then you're not joking, my lord?" he asked. "Zuleika is to be your wife?"

"I have made up my mind!" replied the Cadi sternly.

"Well then, in the name of Allah!" said the cobbler. "Everyone to his own taste! You can have Zuleika."

"Ah, at last!" said the Cadi. "Here is my hand — let us strike the bargin!"

But the cobbler was no fool. Once he realized that the judge was determined to have Zuleika at all costs, he decided to get what he could out of it. "We have not struck any bargin yet, my lord!" said he. "I'm very fond of Zuleika. I will only part with her if you pay me a thousand pieces of gold."

"A thousand pieces of gold?" growled the judge. "That's a fortune! *You* should really be paying the dowry . . . "

"But I don't want to lose her," replied the cobbler. "A thousand pieces of gold — I won't let her go for less."

The Cadi scratched his ear. But Semrude's lovely face, once glimpsed behind her veil, came before his mind's eye. He struggled with his avarice for a few moments.

"Very well, then," said he at last. "I got the better of an old enemy today, and that has put me in a generous mood. Here are your thousand pieces of gold."

And with no more hesitation, he opened a chest, took out a big bag of money and pushed it toward the cobbler. "Now, be off with you!" he cried. "And send Zuleika to me!"

Omar picked up the bag, but he still hesitated.

"What's the matter now?" asked the judge impatiently.

"I have just one more thing to ask, my lord!" replied the cobbler. "I have pointed out to you several times that Zuleika is a monkey and not a girl — a big, hairy monkey! I would like you to acknowledge that in writing."

"What a confounded nuisance you are!" grumbled the Cadi. "However, you shall have it in black and white, if you must!"

Taking pen and ink, he wrote down what the cobbler asked, signed his name and added his seal.

"Many thanks!" said Omar, bowing. "Everything is settled now. I will go home and send you Zuleika."

The judge summoned all his servants. "Deck the gates with flowers!" he ordered. "Lay out my finest carpets, prepare a royal wedding feast, and don't forget to provide good music! What are you gaping for? Off with you — I want to receive my young bride in a suitable manner."

Before the hour was up, two porters stopped outside the Cadi's house, carrying a litter covered with a cloth. Growling, muttering, hissing sounds came from the litter.

"What have you got there?" asked the Cadi, who was waiting at the gate, dressed in his finest robes.

"Zuleika!" replied the porters. "Omar the cobbler told us to tell you she likes to eat carrots, and dates and figs, too, if possible."

With these words they put down their burden. The Cadi took off the cloth — and what should he see but a big, ugly, hairy monkey crouching in the cage, showing its teeth?

Furious, the chief judge of Baghdad tore his hair and ran straight to the cobbler's house by the city gates.

"What have you sent me, you rascal?" he shouted at Omar. "I asked you for your daughter, not that horrible brute!"

"Calm yourself, my lord!" the cobbler tried to soothe him. "Anyway, Zuleika is not a brute! I kept telling you she was a monkey, not a girl. Thanks be to Allah, you admitted it in writing! Do you want to see what you wrote?"

"Devil take what I wrote!" cried the Cadi. "You come with me to the Caliph! He'll soon settle this matter."

"Just as you please, my lord!" replied Omar, and without another word the two of them went to the Caliph.

They were stopped outside Haroun al Raschid's throne-room.

"Halt!" cried the guards. "You cannot go in, at the moment; our gracious lord is busy. Prince Fadlallah, son of the King of Mossul, and his young wife are with him."

Quite beside himself with rage, the chief judge thrust the guards aside and burst into the throne-room.

"My lord Caliph!" he cried, flinging himself before the throne. "Pass judgement in this matter that I am about to lay before you!"

And without waiting for permission to speak, he laid his complaint against Omar, telling the Caliph how a very beautiful girl had visited him, saying that she was Zuleika, the cobbler's daughter, and now he had been given an ugly monkey instead of the lovely Zuleika.

Haroun al Raschid smiled at the young couple beside him. They had already told him the story of their wedding.

"Have this cobbler put in irons, gracious lord!" begged the Cadi. "He has deceived one of your highest officials and forfeited his life! Have him drawn and quartered or broken on the wheel — but make him give back my thousand gold pieces first! Have him . . ."

Haroun al Raschid halted the flow of words with a movement of his hand.

"First," said he, "I would like to know who the beautiful girl was that visited you, saying she was the cobbler's daughter."

"If only I knew!" wailed the Cadi. "It's a mystery to me!"

Now Semrude stood up at Fadlallah's side. "I will tell you!" she cried, unveiling her face. "Look at me, Cadi, and you will know who punished you for your wickedness."

"Zuleika!" whispered the Cadi.

"My name is Semrude," Fadlallah's young wife corrected him. "I am the daughter of Adbanes the baker, and this man on my left is my husband Prince Fadlallah, son of the King of Mossul, whom you took for a vagabond."

The chief judge went pale, and struck his forehead with his fist. So he had fallen into the pit he had dug for others! He groaned aloud.

As for Haroun al Raschid, he laughed so heartily that tears came into his eyes. Then, controlling himself, he told the Cadi, "I hear that you paid a thousand pieces of gold for Zuleika. Not an unreasonable price! Very fair, indeed. And what did the cage cost you?"

"The — the — cage?" stammered the Cadi. "Nothing at all, O Commander of the Faithful."

"Nothing at all?" inquired the Caliph. "But that is impossible! You must pay for the cage. Give Omar a hundred pieces of gold for it. Come, no shilly-shallying, Cadi — or else . . ."

Moaning and groaning, the judge put his hand in his pocket and counted out the money, which he gave to Omar. The cobbler thanked him, and then he and the Cadi were allowed to leave the palace.

Soon afterward, Fadlallah and his young wife also took their leave.

"Tell your royal father," said Haroun al Raschid to the Crown Prince as they parted, "that I will ask no yearly tribute from him in future, for the sake of his brave son and that son's clever and beautiful wife!"

Besides this, the Caliph gave Fadlallah and Semrude magnificent robes and two fine horses, richly harnessed. Now the prince could send back the Cadi's clothes. He helped his wife to mount, swung himself into the saddle, and after saying an affectionate good-bye to Adbanes they rode to the court of King Ortok in Mossul. But on the way, whenever they thought of the Cadi, and tried to picture what he was doing with his ugly monkey, Fadlallah and Semrude reined in their horses and laughed and laughed and laughed.

This story is many, many years old, said Faruknas's nurse, Sutlumene, when she began telling the Tale of the Three Dooms. It belongs to the days when the Pharoahs still ruled Egypt, and we know when that was — two thousand, three thousand or even four thousand years ago. Their power passed away long ago, and their mummified bodies, their treasures and inscriptions are now kept and displayed in places called museums in the lands of the West.

In one of these museums, there is a roll of papyrus that tells the tale of a Pharoah who was childless for a long time. This made him very sad; not a day went by but he prayed to Amon-Ra, king of the gods, for the gift of a son. At last Pharoah's prayer was heard, and his wife gave birth to a baby prince.

At the naming ceremony Hathor, the cow-headed Queen of Heaven, appeared, and foretold the newborn child's fate. "The prince," said she, "is doomed to die young, and his death will be caused either by a snake, a crocodile or a dog."

Pharoah's heart was full of grief when he heard this. He had a strong fortress built for the prince up in the mountains, and sent servants there, and all kinds of beautiful things that are proper for a prince's house. But in order to safeguard the boy's life, the prince was never allowed to leave this palace.

One day, when he had grown to be a fine young man, he climbed up to the flat roof of the palace, and saw a dog following a man along the road. The prince turned to his bodyguard and asked, "What is that, running along the road behind the man?"

"It is a dog, your Highness," replied the servant.

"Bring me a dog like that at once!" the young man ordered.

The guard went to the Pharoah and told him what the prince wanted. The king had not forgotten Hathor's words, but at last he said, "Very well, give him a young hound for hunting. I do not want him to be sad."

So the young man was given a dog, and he was happy. Two or three years later, he sent a message to his father, saying, "Father, I want to go away! Am I to waste away my whole life at home? I know that a sad fate was foretold for me — but I also know that the great Amon-Ra may not be cheated, and he keeps all his promises. What am I to do in my lonely palace?"

Pharoah did not refuse his son's request. He had weapons and a war chariot made ready for the prince; then he took him to the eastern borders of his kingdom and said, "Very well, now go wherever you wish."

Mounting his chariot, the young man took his dog with him and drove away. At last he came to the land of the King of Mesopotamia, who had no heirs except his only daughter. A castle had been built for her; this castle had seventy windows, which were all twenty ells above the ground. The king had summoned all the princes' sons of Mesopotamia, and told them, "Whichever of you can jump up and reach my daughter's window shall have her for his wife."

Day after day, the princes' sons tried their luck, but so far none of them had jumped high enough even to touch the window sill. When Pharoah's son approached in his chariot, they welcomed him, saw that his horse was fed, and asked him where he came from.

"I am the son of a warrior, an Egyptian charioteer," he replied. "My mother is dead. My father married again, and when his second wife had children she began to hate me, so I left my father's house. Now, tell me what you are all doing here!"

They explained what they were attempting to do, and the prince, who had said he was the son of a common soldier, watched them try to jump. One day, as he watched, he saw the king's daughter standing at her window, watching the vain attempts of the princes' sons. Her face was so kind and beautiful that the prince fell in love with her on the spot.

The next day he, too, tried to jump up and reach the window, and, lo and behold, he succeeded, which no one had ever done before. He leaped right up to the window sill, and the king's daughter caught him in her arms and rewarded him with kisses.

This news was told to the king.

"Well," said the king, "and which of the princes' sons was it that reached the window sill?"

"Why, none of them!" replied the messenger. "It was the son of an Egyptian soldier. He drove up in his chariot, escaping from his cruel stepmother, and joined our company."

"What? Am I to give my daughter to a runaway Egyptian?" cried the king, flying into a rage. "He had better go home at once!"

This was told to the prince, who was still celebrating his victory in the arms of the king's daughter.

"You must not leave me!" she cried. And turning to her father's messenger, she said, "By Amon-Ra, if you take him away from me, I will neither eat nor drink, and I will die this very hour."

The messenger told this to the king, but the king would have none of it. He hired men to lie in wait for the supposed Egyptian charioteer's son in his daughter's palace, in order to put him to death. However, the king's daughter intercepted them, and on learning what their task was, she repeated her oath again.

"In the name of Amon-Ra," said she, "if you put him to death, I will not live another hour. Go and tell my father that!"

Now the king realized how much his daughter loved the Egyptian, and he sent for both of them. He took a long and searching look at the prince.

"Are you really the son of an Egyptain charioteer?" he asked at last.

"Yes I am," replied the prince — for he wished to owe his good fortune to his own qualities, not to his royal rank. "My mother is dead. My father married a second wife, and when she had children of her own, she came to hate me, so I left my father's house and ran away."

The king liked the open way in which the Egyptian admitted to his lowly rank in life, and because he spoke sensibly and put on no airs, he changed his mind and gave the young man his daughter's hand in marriage. He presented the Egyptian with a house and slaves, as well as land and livestock, and hundreds of other things, besides. So the young couple lived happily and in great contentment, lacking for nothing that they had in their childhood and youth at their fathers' royal courts.

One day the prince took his young wife aside. "I have something to tell you," said he. "The goddess Hathor foretold that three dooms lay in wait for me, and my death would be caused either by a crocodile, a snake or a dog!"

"Then have the hound who is always at your side killed!" replied his young wife.

"How could I do such a thing?" he replied. "I have reared him ever since he was a puppy. You cannot ask me to do that."

This ended the conversation, and he never mentioned the dreadful prophecy again. But his young wife could not help thinking of his words. She was full of anxiety for her husband, and could hardly bear to see him go out alone.

One day, while they were journeying to the borders of Egypt, they came to a great lake where a crocodile dwelt. The wife never moved from her husband's side, and would not let him go out by himself.

Now there happened to be a giant in the same place, standing guard over the crocodile to make sure it did not leave the water. While the giant slept, the young wife kept watch, and in this way a whole month and two days passed by.

One night, when the prince was asleep, his wife awakened suddenly from a dream. Still drowsy, she got up, filled a bowl with milk, and placed it by her husband's bedside.

Soon a poisonous snake came gliding out of its hole. It was just approaching the prince when it found the milk. The snake lapped up the milk, and since the prince's wife had mixed an intoxicating drink in the bowl, it fell asleep drunk, belly upward. This was what the young wife was waiting for; she took a spear and killed the snake.

The noise awakened her husband. "What are you doing?" he asked, bewildered.

"Amon-Ra has given one of your three dooms to me!" she replied joyfully. "He will deliver the other two to you."

Full of hope, she sacrificed to the king of the gods and praised his goodness.

Some time later, the Egyptian prince happened to be strolling along the banks of the lake. His wife, believing he was now out of danger, was not with him. However, his hound was running behind him. The dog was so full of high spirits that he jumped too far and fell into the water. The prince ran to save his dog, and at that moment the crocodile emerged from the water and seized the prince.

"This is a lucky chance for me!" hissed the crocodile. "I know that your wife is in league with the giant against me! The giant is asleep just now, and if you promise to kill him, I will let you go free."

"How can I kill someone who has done me a service?" replied the prince.

"Well, I will give you the night to think it over," answered the crocodile, "and I will ask you again in the morning."

So saying, the monster bore his prisoner off to his lair. But the next morning the prince still refused to do as the crocodile wanted, so the crocodile gave him a little more time, until sunset.

However, the dog had heard everything, and when the crocodile was not looking, he ran to his mistress. The prince's wife had spent the whole night weeping and wailing. In her terror, she felt sure some harm had come to her husband, and her fears were confirmed when the dog came back alone. She smeared her forehead with dust, wailed and lamented and beat her breast.

The dog, however, paid no attention to her grief, but leaped around her, barking, now snapping at her dress, now bounding toward the door and looking back. He was trying every way he knew to make her understand she was to follow him. At last she realized what he wanted. She dried her eyes, picked up the spear she had used to kill the snake, and followed the dog. On the bank of the lake she lay down among the reeds and waited for the crocodile to appear at sunset.

At last she heard the reptile's voice. "Now, will you kill the giant?" asked the monster. "Otherwise you will die."

The prince's wife ran to the giant and shook him awake.

"Follow me!" she cried. "It is a matter of life and death!"

And she came back to the waterside with him just as the crocodile was crawling up on land with her husband.

"Now, for the last time, will you obey my wish?" snarled the crocodile.

"I cannot and will not do it!" replied the prince. The crocodile opened his jaws wide to swallow him up, but the next moment the prince's wife leaped out of the reeds and thrust her spear into the reptile's open mouth, while the giant fell upon the monster, overpowered it and beat it to death with his club.

The happy wife embraced her husband.

"Amon-Ra has given the second doom to me!" she cried. "The third he will give to you!" Merry, and full of hope, she sacrificed to the king of the gods and praised his goodness.

On the way home the prince's wife said, "We have now averted the fate that threatened you twice. Part with your dog, so that he cannot bring the third doom upon you."

However, her husband made the same reply as before, "I have reared my dog ever since he was a puppy, and now he has saved my life. How could I be so ungrateful?"

Some time passed, and war broke out in the land. The princes' sons who had tried in vain to jump up to the window rebelled against

the King of Mesopotamia. They were angry because none of them had won the king's daughter, and instead she had married the son of a simple Egyptian charioteer. They conquered the Mesopotamian army, invaded the capital city with a host of warriors and chariots, and took the king prisoner. But they searched the palace in vain for the Egyptian and his wife.

"Where are your daughter and her husband?" they asked the captured king.

"They have gone on a journey," he replied. "How should I know where they are?"

The princes' sons held a council together. "We will divide into small groups," they decided, "and go this way and that. One of our groups is sure to find the young couple, and whoever finds them must have the Egyptian killed at once. As for his wife, she is to be treated like any other of the spoils of war."

So some of them went east, others west, north and south. Eventually one group came to the borders of Egypt, where the prince and his wife were. The giant was the first to catch sight of the troop of soldiers. He heard what they were saying and learned what they planned to do.

Since he was grateful to the prince, he hurried straight to him and said, "Save yourself and your wife! I have seen a host of warriors coming this way in search of you. They want to put you to death and treat your wife like any other of the spoils of war. There are too many of them for us to be able to resist them. I will go to my brothers . . ."

So saying, he strode away. The prince took his wife and his dog, and hid in a cave in the mountains near by.

They spent two days and two nights in this cave, and on the third day they saw the princes' sons and their men approaching. But the troop passed the cave and never noticed the couple hiding there. As the last soldier passed the mouth of the cave, the dog suddenly broke loose and dashed out into the open, barking loudly and snapping at the men. The princes' sons, recognizing the animal, turned and made their way into the cave. There they found the man they were looking for and attacked him with swords and spears. As one of their lances seemed about to pierce the prince, the king's daughter covered him with her own body. She took the spear thrust instead of him, and sank to the ground, kissing the dust at his feet.

The prince defended himself more fiercely than ever, striking left and right with his sword. The dog fought at his side, and those he did not throw to the ground were killed by the prince's blade. Then a stone hit the dog. He breathed his last, and as the prince bent over him a spear pierced his breast, and he sank to the ground like a dying man.

The soldiers carried the bodies out into the open, and left them to

be devoured by the wolves. Then they went home to carry news of their victory to their companions, and divide the country between them. When the last man had disappeared, the prince opened his eyes, and seeing the corpses of his wife and dog beside him, he groaned aloud.

"Amon-Ra may not be cheated," he lamented, "and he keeps all his promises. At my naming ceremony, the cow-headed Queen of Heaven prophesied that a snake, a crocodile or a dog would cause my death, and it is so! My faithful dog betrayed me! Now I am ready to die; life means nothing to me without my wife and my dog . . ."

Summoning up the last of his strength, he raised his hands and cried out loud, "O Amon-Ra, I am innocent of all the sins that you abhor! Grant decent burial for myself, my wife and my dog, and speak for me to my judges in the world of the dead!"

As soon as he had uttered his prayer, he sank back and died.

The nine gods had heard his prayer, and they gathered together.

"Fate has run its course for them," said Amon-Ra, pointing to the three corpses outside the cave. "Now, however, we should bring them to life again, for life is still sweet to them, and it is only right to reward such constancy."

So the nine gods came down to earth. One of them touched the hearts of the young couple, and they began to beat. Another touched their feet, and they stood up. The third touched their mouths, and they spoke, the fourth their eyes, and their glances met, the fifth touched their arms, and they embraced one another, the sixth promised them health and happiness, and the seventh brought the dog back to life. He jumped happily around his master and mistress, yelping and leaping up at them.

The prince and his wife went home with the dog, and offered a sacrifice to the gods.

"Let us rejoice!" said the prince. "We have overcome the three dooms and tasted the grace of the gods of Heaven."

As the smoke of their sacrifice arose, and they offered thanks, the prince embraced his wife.

"Now I have something to confess to you," said he. "I am not the son of a simple charioteer, as I told you. I am Pharoah's son. You may ask why I pretended to be a man of a lower rank than I really am. I wished to win renown on my own, and I did not want you to love me for my royal birth — which you did not! Now let us go home to my own country. You will share the throne with me when my father the Pharoah goes to join his ancestors."

No sooner said than done. They went home to Egypt, and the prince's father was so overjoyed at his return that he made him ruler of the country together with himself, and had the King of Mesopotamia's daughter crowned queen. She was given the name, "Revived by Constancy".

Then he equipped a great army and sent it eastward with warriors and chariots. The young king himself was its general. He drove the rebellious princes' sons out of Mesopotamia, set the king free and gave him back his land and his treasures. As for the spoils he had taken, when he came home he gave them to the temple of Amon-Ra in Thebes. The king of the gods rewarded him and his wife with a long life; they lived for a hundred and ten years, and after their deaths, many sons and daughters kept their names alive.

THE PRINCE OF THE FLOWERY MEADOW
(continued)

And so for a thousand and one days the old nurse, Sutlumene, told
tales to Faruknas, the sorrowful princess. The nurse never tired; some
story either new or old was sure to come into her head.

She told tales of good and evil spirits, of dragons and monsters,
mysterious treasures, treasure seekers, journeys and enchantments,
beautiful and clever maidens, enchanted princes, wicked stepsisters —
tales of poor folk made rich and sad folk made happy, and many,
many other things.

At first, Sutlumene seemed to be speaking to a stone wall as she
was telling the princess her stories. Faruknas did not even listen. She
was so lost in her dreams and her longing that she scarcely heard a
word of the tales, and took no interest in them at all. But then an
occasional phrase began to arouse her attention. She listened, and
suddenly she would forget her grief for a minute, two minutes, for
quarter of an hour or even longer. Before that, neither the learned
doctors, nor the court jesters, nor her friends' songs had been able to
lift the weight of her sorrow from her — not even the wise men of
the land, with their long beards, who had been summoned by the
king, although they were paid for just such tasks . . .

It seemed as though the nurse's tales might indeed bring the
princess back to life. And it must be admitted that Sutlumene was a
true mistress of the storyteller's art, so skilfully did she weave her
strands together, happiness and sadness, pleasure and pain. Where
there was a chance to do so, she embroidered her tales, but she was
never boring. She knew just how to capture the princess's interest
and attention, and like the clever Sheherazade in the Tales of the
Thousand and One Nights, she would tell only part of the story at a

time. On reaching the most exciting point, she would break off, and leave the rest for another time.

"That's enough for now!" Sutlumene would say. "To-morrow is another day." And she would rise from her cushions at the princess's feet and wish her audience good night, disregarding all Faruknas's entreaties for her to go on.

Soon, the princess was waiting impatiently for her nurse when she came the next day, urging her to go on with her story.

"I must know what happened next!" Faruknas would say.

So Sutlumene did as she had promised the king; for a thousand and one days she amused and cheered the princess with her stories, and gave her the will to live. Not once in all this time did Faruknas express any wish to set out on her travels in search of the prince of the flowery meadow.

But at the end of a thousand and one days, suddenly the nurse knew no more tales to tell. She racked her brains, but she could not think of a single story. This was a sad state of affairs, since by now Faruknas was living so much in the world of fairy tales that she could not do without them.

"What is the matter with you, Sutlumene?" she cried. "Tell me another story, do!"

At her wits' end, Sutlumene began her stories all over again.

"Would you like me to tell you the tale of Abdallah the Ungrateful, or Abdul Kasim the Rich? Or would you care to hear the tale of Prince Monkey again, or the tale of King Solomon's Ring? Or the story of Harchand the Just, who was as patient as Job?"

"What is the meaning of this?" cried the princess indignantly. "I want to hear new stories!"

What was to be done? Gradually, the little spark of life that the old nurse had kindled with her tales died out of Faruknas's eyes and before long the princess was lying motionless on her couch again. She had been eating her meals in silence as she listened to the stories, but now she could not eat a morsel. It was a desperate state of affairs.

189

Sutlumene went to the king again and threw herself at his feet.

"You know the difficulty we are in, your Majesty!" said she. "My tales have lasted for a thousand and one days, and the princess was recovering her will to live. But now I have no more stories. I am afraid Faruknas will die, or that we will not be able to keep her here much longer, and she will go out into the world."

The king sighed. "I myself have seen that there is a strange power in such stories, able to drive away sadness and despondency," said he. "I think you said much the same yourself, at the time. Can you not think of any more stories?"

"Not one!" replied the nurse sadly.

"Were you hoping that the prince of the flowery meadow might have sent some message by now?"

"I did, indeed, hope for that, great king, but alas, no message has come, and now I do not know what to do."

The king hung his head. Tears came into the eyes of the queen, who had joined them, and they sat, sorrowful and silent, when suddenly the doorkeeper entered the room.

"There is a stranger outside asking to speak to Princess Faruknas," he announced.

"A stranger?" cried the king. "Could it be . . . Show him in at once!"

They all looked expectantly at the man as he came in. However, he was not the prince of the flowery meadow, as they had perhaps secretly hoped, but an elderly, bearded man.

"Who are you?" asked the King of Kashmir.

"My name is Simurg," replied the stranger, kneeling, "and I am the Prince of Egypt's weapon-bearer."

"And what do you want?" asked the king. "Why do you wish to speak to my daughter?"

"That I can disclose only to her," said the stranger.

The king frowned, for this reply vexed him, but being anxious for his daughter's well-being, he overcame his annoyance, and signalled to Simurg to rise.

"Take this man to my daughter's room," he told Sutlumene. "Let her hear what he has to say, if he will not disclose it to me!"

Faruknas was lying on her couch as usual, not saying a word. She was neither asleep, nor awake; she might have been somewhere else altogether, staring straight ahead with wide-open eyes. She was hardly aware of the old nurse when she spoke to her and stroked her forehead, and she took no notice of the stranger.

When Sutlumene left the room, Simurg knelt before her.

"I bring you a message, sorrowful princess!" said he. "It comes

from one who is even more sorrowful than you. It is from my master Prince Farukshad, son of the King of Egypt."

The princess, with a weary gesture, indicated that she did not know Prince Farukshad, and wanted to be left alone.

"Yes, you do know him!" the stranger assured her. "You met him in a broad, flowery meadow, beside a tall thistle. You accepted a bunch of wild flowers that he offered you, and you still wear it on your dress."

Starting up, the princess cried, "I have been waiting for this prince for years! What message does he send me? Quick — tell me where to find him!"

"I will tell you the whole story," replied Simurg, "and then, if you wish, I will take you to him. But it is a difficult and dangerous journey, so listen to my tale before you make your decision."

He bowed low, knelt down beside the couch, and began to tell his tale. The princess hung on his words, as if filled by a new wish to live, letting not a syllable escape her.

The Prince's Adventure

One fine, sunny day, Prince Farukshad, nicknamed 'The Dreamer' by his family, was walking in the rose garden of his father's palace. The palace grounds were surrounded by walls. As Farukshad strolled among the lawns and flowerbeds, a wind suddenly arose. Farukshad closed his eyes for a moment, and when he opened them, the palace and the rose garden had disappeared. The prince found himself in the middle of a broad, flowery meadow.

"What does this mean?" he asked — but no one was there to answer him. Slowly, Farukshad wandered through the tall grass. Beautiful, bright wild flowers grew in the meadow; they took his fancy, and he picked a bunch of them and stuck a buttercup in the jewelled clasp of his turban.

Suddenly he saw a young girl.

"Who are you, beautiful maiden?" Farukshad asked. "And how did you come here?"

He bowed, and offered her the bunch of wild flowers, stretching out his hand over a tall thistle plant.

"Who are you? Tell me your name!" replied the girl.

"I am a prince," replied Farukshad — but before he could go on, a gentle breeze arose again. The prince closed his eyes for a moment, and when he opened them, he found himself back in the walled rose garden of his father's palace. There was no sign of the flowery meadow, the tall thistle or the girl who was as beautiful as the day.

I, as Farukshad's weapon-bearer, was the first to hear of his strange adventure.

"Your mind must be wandering," I said to him. "Or were you asleep and dreaming, in broad daylight?"

"What do you mean, Simurg?" replied the prince. "I was not dreaming, and my mind is not wandering either! Look, I still have the buttercup in the clasp of my turban, and you can see thistles clinging to my silken cloak!"

Since there were no buttercups or thistles growing anywhere in the king's gardens, I had to agree that, as the prince had said, some mysterious power seemed to have spirited him away briefly from the palace grounds, and then brought him back again. But what kind of power was it, and why had he been carried off?"

No one could answer these questions, neither the king nor the queen, nor I myself, the prince's weapon-bearer, least of all the wise men of the land with their long beards, although they were kept at court and paid to solve just such problems.

But Prince Farukshad said, "Whatever power it was, and however this may have happened, one thing is certain! I cannot rest or have a moment's peace until I find that beautiful girl again."

His father shook his head. "What are you saying, my son?" he asked. "Can we be sure that the girl in the flowery meadow was not just a vision? A phantom creature? A lovely apparition that will never return again? However, if you wish to go in search of her, we will not keep you here. It can do no harm for a prince to see the world and gain experience before he succeeds to the throne."

As for me, Simurg the weapon-bearer, I said to Farukshad, "I will follow you wherever you go, my lord. Have you any plans? Do you know where you are bound?"

"We will go straight ahead of us, and trust to luck!" replied the prince.

Farukshad took leave of his parents. We mounted our horses and rode away. As we travelled on, we met many girls, fair of face and form, but Farukshad always said, "This is not the one I am looking for. The maiden I seek is a thousand times more beautiful than any other!"

However, wherever we went we could not find the girl who was as beautiful as the day. I can scarcely number all the cities through which we rode, and who could count the huts and inns, the houses and palaces where we put up for the night? Everywhere we went we inquired about the girl, but no one could tell us where to find her. Many folk did not even believe that she was real; they took her to be a figment of the prince's imagination.

One day, our way led through a forest in a distant land. It was a strange forest; suddenly we saw many deer coming out from the trees and bushes. We were armed, but they did not seem to be afraid of us. They did not run away, but came right up to our horses, and began to nudge us gently with their antlers. Several of the hinds took the ends of our cloaks in their mouths, whimpering softly, and looking at us with pleading, almost human glances. Many of them had tears in their eyes.

"I never saw such creatures before," said Farukshad to me. "There is something the matter with these deer! What is it they want to tell us?"

We went on, deeper and deeper into the forest, although the deer

194

kept barring our way and trying to stop us. Suddenly, we saw a great palace of white marble in the middle of a clearing ahead of us.

"This is strange!" I cried. "Who could have built a palace in such a desolate place?"

"Let us ride over there!" said the prince. "Perhaps the lord of this palace may have news of the beautiful maiden." For he could think of nothing else.

As soon as the deer realized what we intended to do, they acted as if they were completely out of their senses. They uttered loud cries, belled and wailed so lamentably that we could hardly bear to hear them. Several of them flung themselves in our path, and we had to ride over them before at last, and with great difficulty, we reached the palace gates.

The Enchantress Mechmerevza

Looking through the gates, we saw a girl standing on a balcony of red sandalwood. She kept flinging out her hands as if to ward us off. There was no doubt about it, she wanted us to turn back.

"Well, this is not a very friendly reception!" said Farukshad.

The next moment, an old woman came out on the balcony. She seemed to be very strong, in spite of her age, for she seized the girl and roughly pushed her back into the palace. Then she bent down and beckoned to us. As she did so, the gates opened of their own accord.

"Where are you going?" asked the old woman, with a strange smile, as she leaned over the balustrade.

"We are looking for a certain maiden," replied the prince, "a maiden who is a thousand times more beautiful than any other. Do you happen to have seen her?"

"Ah, if you mean the maiden who is as beautiful as the day, you

195

have come to the right place," said the old woman. "I can tell you where to find her."

Prince Farukshad swung himself off his horse, flung the reins around a post, and ran up the steps leading to the palace. I had difficulty in keeping up with him. The old woman came to meet us at the top of the steps, invited us into a room, gave us soft cushions to sit on, and ordered her serving maids to bring us refreshing drinks.

"First tell me where to find the maiden I long for!" cried the prince.

"How impatient you are!" chuckled the old woman. "Well, then, the maiden as beautiful as the day is none other than Princess Faruknas, daughter of the King of Kashmir."

"Kashmir?" cried the prince, leaping up. "Kashmir is far away — we must not delay any longer, Simurg!"

And he went to the door of the room. But the old woman barred his way.

"Why are you in such a hurry?" she rebuked him. "If you have waited so long to find this maiden who is as beautiful as the day, young man, surely an hour more or less will make no difference! It is a long and dangerous journey to Kashmir. Have you never heard that the way there leads through moors and deserts, over mountains and deep chasms, where monsters and robbers lie in wait for travellers?"

The prince thought for a moment. "I am not afraid of such dangers!" said he.

"It is good to have courage, but unwise to be over-confident, my friend," replied the old woman, laughing slyly. "Now, I could give you a charm that would protect you against many dangers. The enchantress Mechmerevza once gave me this remedy. It is a magic powder; I need only sprinkle it over you, and then you can be in any place you desire, instantly. That is the only way you can reach Kashmir in a hurry. But you are so sure of yourself that I suppose you will scorn an old woman's gift, young man?" finished the old woman, with another strange laugh, screwing up her wrinkled face.

196

"Why should I scorn this magic powder, if it will take us to Kashmir so quickly?" cried the prince. "Pray fetch it!"

The old woman nodded, went to a corner of the room and opened a chest. She took out a little bag of silk. It was black, and tied together at the top. She undid it, and put her hand in, saying, "Now close your eyes. When you open them again in a moment, a strange thing will have happened to you."

We did as the old woman said, closed our eyes, and felt a fine strange-smelling powder fall like dust on our cheeks and foreheads.

"There!" laughed the old woman — and now her laugh sounded so cruel and evil that we opened our eyes at once. And, indeed, a strange thing *had* happened, but not what we had hoped for. We had

not been transported to Kashmir; we were still in the room with the old woman, and we had been changed. Prince Farukshad and I, his weapon-bearer, were no longer men, but deer. Thick, grey fur covered our bodies, great antlers grew from our foreheads, and we were standing on four legs, with hoofs on our feet. We could only utter cries of pain, like tormented animals.

As for the old woman, she shook with laughter, and the sound cut us to the heart.

"Now can you guess who I am?" she asked. "I am Mechmerevza, and now you are under my spell until you die, like all the other princes and princesses out there in the forest. You would not listen to them when they barred your way!"

Now we realized that the deer had tried to warn us.

"I know very well who you are, Prince Farukshad and Simurg!" the enchantress went on. "When you were walking in the rose garden of your palace, young man, I carried you away, just as I did Princess Faruknas. I wanted you to see each other and to fall in love, since I have an old quarrel with each of your fathers. They insulted me, and I wished for revenge."

Farukshad lowered his horned head, as if to charge the old woman, but she seized him, and held me fast, as well. No one would ever have believed there could be such strength in the enchantress's old body.

"I knew that you and Princess Faruknas would never be rid of your longing for each other," Merchmervza went on. "One day you would be sure to set out to find each other, and after much travelling you would reach my castle. You and your weapon-bearer are the first to arrive, and it will not be very long before the Princess of Kashmir arrives too, to be turned into a hind."

Farukshad tried in vain to break free from the enchantress.

"I expect you would like to help her," laughed the wicked Mechmerevza. "But even if you could reach Kashmir in your present form, if you could escape all the bears and wolves, hounds and

198

huntsmen you would encounter on the way — who would understand your plaintive whimpering and belling when you got there? Faruknas, perhaps, or her clever old nurse, Sutlumene the storyteller? Why, no one would understand you, little stag! Off you go now, and Simurg the antler-bearer too, to join the other animals in the forest. You'll find plenty of grass and plants out there; you can eat your fill!"

Her tone was one of pure mockery. The next moment we were being pushed down the steps. Servants chased us off the grounds, and there we were in the forest again, stags among the other stags and hinds who had tried to warn us, and now stood gazing at us, sadly.

Gulnas the Good

Who can tell how much time passed? We lived with the other animals, feeding on the grass and plants of the forest, wordlessly lamenting our sad fate.

Then, one day, we met a girl on the path leading from the wicked enchantress's castle into the forest. She was not ugly, but no one could have said she was as beautiful as the day. I recognized her as the girl who had waved to us from the sandalwood balcony as we approached the palace.

When she saw me and the prince in the form of deer, she stopped. Then she seemed to recognize us, too. She stepped behind a tree trunk, telling us to come closer.

"Do not be afraid, either of you!" said she. "My name is Gulnas, and I am Mechmerevza's stepsister. But I hate her and her wicked ways, and I want to help you. See, I have a magic powder with me, not the same sort as the one Mechmerevza sprinkled over you. If I scatter this powder on you you will return to human form. But then you must make haste to get away, for if my wicked stepsister finds

199

out what I have done, she will avenge herself on you as well as on me. I am taking this risk only because no one should ever torment true lovers. For the sake of Princess Faruknas, and for your sake too, Prince Farukshad, I will now break the spell."

Taking a white silk bag out of the pocket of her dress, she opened it, and next minute I felt fine, light powder being sprinkled over me. For, as luck would have it, I was standing closer to Gulnas at that moment than my master. I was my old self again — Simurg the weapon-bearer.

The next moment, however, there was a rushing sound overhead. Mechmerevza descended from the air and seized Gulnas by her long hair.

"Run!" cried the girl. "Save yourself!"

"But what about my prince?" I cried.

"Save yourself!" cried Gulnas. "Save yourself, and then save us!"

There was no time to be lost. I could still see the sad look Farukshad cast at me, I could still hear the piteous cries of Gulnas as the enchantress beat her. "You will pay for this!" I heard the old woman screech, shaking her stepsister and dragging her up and down. I leaped away and ran and ran, over stock and stone, and it was a long time before poor Gulnas's cries of pain and the cursing and raging of Mechmerevza died away behind me. But I saw no more of my dear master. I set out for Kashmir at once, to tell you what had happened, Princess Faruknas. I have fought robbers and monsters, crossed mountains and deep chasms, and now I kneel here, begging for help. I await your commands!"

Faruknas laid her hand on the shoulder of her lover's faithful old weapon-bearer.

"Go to the royal stables, Simurg!" said she. "Have two horses saddled, one for you and one for me! We will start at once!"

"O Princess," stammered Simurg, "do you really mean to . . . ?"

"Why, what did you expect?" the princess interrupted him. "We will ride to Mechmerevza's castle."

She called for her serving maids to get everything ready for her journey, while she went to see her mother and father. They were greatly surprised when she came in, looking so full of high spirits, but when they heared her plan they were alarmed. However, despite objections raised by the king and queen, Faruknas stood firm and stuck to her decision. Finally, when Sutlumene had given her approval and put in a good word for the princess, her parents, too, agreed. They were afraid for their child's safety, but they felt that it would be for the best in the end.

In Mechmerevza's Enchanted Castle

You can picture for yourselves the difficulties of the journey from Kashmir to the wicked enchantress's castle. They went on and on, through moors and deserts, over mountains and chasms. However, in spite of all the hardships Faruknas and Simurg finally reached their destination; the princess because her love and longing sustained her and made her strong, and the weapon-bearer because of his faithful devotion to his master.

When the two of them at last reached the forest surrounding the castle, a great herd of stags and hinds crossed their path, and tried to stop them. The reason for that was now quite plain.

Suddenly, however, Farukshad appeared in his stag's form — the Egyptian prince who was called 'The Dreamer' at home, and who had met the princess in the flowery meadow. It was touching to see the heart-rending eloquence of his glances when he caught sight of Faruknas. Faruknas herself seemed to feel it; she understood exactly what he was trying to say when he shook his horned head, or turned it left or right, for the language of the heart needs no words.

So she and Simurg followed her lover in his enchanted form when he fell out of the herd and chased away the other deer that followed

him. He did not lead Faruknas and Simurg to the great gate of the castle, through which he and his weapon-bearer had once entered the courtyard. Instead, they entered the palace through a secret, back way, unknown to Mechmerevza. Here the stag stopped at the door barred by a grating, and Simurg realized that he was supposed to open it. He succeeded in breaking it open softly. Behind it, in a musty room, poor Gulnas lay bound on the floor, a prisoner. She was only half conscious, and did not come to her senses until the princess moistened her dry lips with fresh water.

Then she whispered, "Flee!" She sat up and pointed away from the castle. "For God's sake, have nothing to do with my wicked stepsister!"

Gradually, however, she became calmer, realizing that something must be done if Farukshad and all the other enchanted princes and princesses were to be released from the spell.

"When Mechmerevza caught me," Gulnas told them, "she took the white silk bag away from me. She may have hidden it in the chest where she keeps the black one. If only we could lay our hands on that white bag," the prisoner sighed, "then all would be well, and we could break the spell on the enchanted princes and princesses. But who could go to look for the magic powder? I must not appear in Mechmerevza's sight . . ."

"I will go to look for it," said Simurg.

"That will never do," Faruknas objected. "The enchantress knows you; if she sees you, you will perish -- and so will the rest of us. I will go myself."

She put her arm around the neck of the enchanted Farukshad, and although the stag's eyes filled with tears as they looked into hers, he made no move to prevent her, for he realized that this was the only solution.

"Yes, it is the only way," said the princess. "Let us delay no longer!"

They left the castle again by the back way, and returned to the forest. At a certain spot, the enchanted stag stopped, with Simurg and Gulnas. Faruknas mounted her horse, and exchanged one more tender glance with her beloved. Then she spurred on her steed, and galloped briskly to the great gate of the castle. She did not want to arouse the witch's suspicions.

Sure enough, the enchantress soon caught sight of Faruknas. As before, Mechmerevza stood on the red sandalwood balcony.

"Where are you going, fair maiden?" she asked.

"I am looking for a prince who wears a faded buttercup in his turban," replied the princess. "Have you seen him?"

"Ah, so you are the princess who is as beautiful as the day!" replied the enchantress. "Be happy, for you have come to the right place! I, and I alone, can tell you where to find your prince."

The castle gate again opened by itself, and Faruknas rode through. Dismounting from her horse, she threw the reins over a post, and began to climb the great flight of steps. Mechmerevza came to meet her at the top. She showed her into a room, invited her to sit down, and offered her a refreshing drink.

But the princess refused it. "I want to speak to the young man I am looking for," said she.

"How impatient you are!" replied the witch, just as she had done when Farukshad and Simurg came to her. "The young man you are looking for is Prince Farukshad, the Dreamer, one of the King of Egypt's sons. He is in Cairo at his father's court."

"In Cairo?" cried Faruknas, jumping up. "That is far away! I will waste no more time here!" And she went to the door of the room at once. The old woman, who had no idea that the princess was only pretending, barred her way.

"Why are you in such a hurry?" the enchantress rebuked her. "If you have waited for your prince so long, an hour more or less will make no difference, either way. You may have come from Kashmir, but that was nothing compared to the journey to Cairo."

"I am not afraid of danger," replied Faruknas, just as her lover had said before her.

And again Mechmerevza replied, "It is good to have courage, but foolish to be over-confident, my dear. I could give you a charm that would save you a great deal of trouble. The enchantress Mechmerevza once gave it to me. It is a magic powder. I need only to sprinkle it over you, and then you can be in any place you desire, instantly. That is the only way you can reach Cairo in a hurry. But you are so sure of yourself that I suppose you will scorn an old woman's gift!"

"Oh, no, indeed!" replied Faruknas, who was only waiting for these words. "Why should I scorn this powder? Pray fetch it quickly!"

So the old woman went to the corner of the room, where Faruknas had already seen the chest standing. The enchantress lifted the lid, put her hand in the chest and brought out a little black silk bag.

"Now, close your eyes!" she said. "When you open them again, you will find that something very strange has happened."

Faruknas appeared to be doing as she was told, but in fact she only half-closed her eyes. She kept them open just enough to watch what Mechmerevza was doing, and so she saw the enchantress undoing the string that tied the bag . . .

The next moment the princess sprang at the old woman and tore the bag from her grasp.

"I know you! You are Mechmerevza!" cried Faruknas, as soon as she had the magic powder in her hand. "It was you who turned the prince of the flowery meadow into a stag, and bewitched all the other princes and princesses out in the forest. You were waiting for me — well, here I am, and now your power is at an end."

Mechmerevza let out a scream of rage. She fell upon the princess, and even managed to get hold of the bag again — but she tugged at it so violently that it fell open, and some of the magic powder flew into her own face.

In a twinkling she turned into a hind — and what a hind! She looked quite different from the deer in the forest. She had a bright-red coat like a fox, with spots like a big hyena. Her eyes glared. She stamped her hoofs, and who knows what she might have done next if the door had not been flung open by Simurg and Gulnas. They had secretly followed Faruknas to help her if necessary.

When she saw them, the bewitched enchantress cried out loud. She leaped down the steps with great bounds. Outside the gate, many deer, both stags and hinds, had gathered. They all fell back as the frantic animal flew past, and disappeared into the darkness of the forest. No one tried to stop it.

Simurg and Gulnas watched from the balcony as Mechmerevza escaped into the forest. "She will not get far," said the weapon-bearer. "Huntsmen are quick to track such creatures down."

Meanwhile, Faruknas went to the chest, and was searching inside it. Suddenly she uttered a cry of joy, and triumphantly lifted out a white silk bag. She had found the power that could break the spell! Faruknas ran down the steps into the open air, so fast that Simurg and Gulnas could hardly keep up with her. Down by the gate, she sprinkled the white powder over the deer standing there, and in a moment they were changed back into human form, the stags to princes, the hinds to princesses. But the handsomest and most splendid figure among them all was that of Farukshad, son of the King of Egypt, the prince of the flowery meadow. Smiling radiantly, he took the faded buttercup from the clasp on his turban and offered it to Faruknas. Before he took her in his arms, Faruknas removed the withered bunch of wild flowers from her breast, and put it in the prince's turban.

Then a wonderful thing happened. The faded buttercup rose up; suddenly, it looked as fresh as if it had just been picked in the meadow and put in water. The same thing happened to the bunch of wild flowers; it bloomed and smelled as sweet as if it had been freshly gathered, and not many, many more than a thousand days earlier.

What more is there to tell? Arm in arm, Farukshad and Faruknas turned to the princes and princesses who were freed from their enchantment. Many of them had come together to form loving

couples, ready to go through life together in human form, as perhaps they had already done as stags and hinds.

Simurg, the good old weapon-bearer, was also among the wooers on this occasion. He announced that he and Gulnas were to be married, and his bearded old face shone with such pride that it looked almost young.

Gulnas herself was so radiant with happiness that she could almost be called beautiful. The two of them took their leave at once. They were going to Cairo to tell the king and queen the happy outcome of the adventure, bearing greetings from their son 'The Dreamer'.

Then the other princes and princesses set off for their own countries. None of them spared a thought for the magic castle — it could crumble into ruins in the forest, for all they cared. They only wanted to go home!

As for Farukshad and Faruknas, they rode to Kashmir, and there was great rejoicing when they arrived. The king and queen were beside themselves with joy, and the good old nurse Sutlumene embraced both the prince of the flowery meadow and the princess. No one thought it strange of the old women to forget herself so far as to treat royal personages as if they were her own family. Soon the wedding was held, and it lasted a whole month, as the old tales tell. Even Sutlumene danced at the wedding, and she did not dance so badly either — though not, of course, as well as she told stories.

Her story-telling was over now, since no one wanted to hear her old tales again. Farukshad had never heard them, to be sure, but for the time being he had other things to do.

Not long after the wedding, he and his wife and their royal retinue visited his family in Cairo. After the couple had returned to Kashmir, and the old king and queen had died, Farukshad and Faruknas succeeded to the throne. The new king reigned so wisely and well that he was never called 'The Dreamer' again.

And then — what? Why, then Farukshad and Faruknas had many children, little princes and princesses who all grew up to delight their parents' hearts. And Sutlumene came into her own again. Day after day, evening after evening, she had to tell the royal children stories, which she was able to do very well. She twined so many threads together, merry tales and sad ones, and did it so skilfully that one moment her listeners could not stop laughing, and the next they were quite sad. Occasionally, King Farukshad came to listen when he wanted a rest from the cares of state. The stories were all new to him, and they sounded as fresh and blooming as the bunch of wild flowers and the buttercup looked after their magical transformation ... after all, there were enough of them to last a long, long time; to be exact, a thousand and one days.

About three hundred years ago, a Frenchman visited Isfahan, which at that time was the capital of Persia, the country we know today as Iran. It was in the seventeenth century; the exact date is not known. The Frenchman's name was Pétis de la Croix. Since he spoke Persian, in a short time he made friends in Isfahan, and came to know the land and its people.

Pétis de la Croix expressed his delight in the beauties of Isfahan in many letters and other writings. He was full of admiration for the numerous palaces, mosques and minarets, the palm groves and rose gardens, baths and fountains. At that time, there were over forty thousand houses and palaces in the Persian capital, two thousand inns and caravanserais, a hundred and fifty mosques and fifty schools.

Isfahan owed its magnificence to Abbas the Great, a member of the Safavid dynasty, who ruled at the time when the East was entering on a period of great unrest, marked by religious differences and a thirty years' war.

"The city is like a fairy tale," de la Croix wrote of Isfahan, "one of those oriental fairy tales generally acknowledged to surpass all others in the wealth of their invention . . ." The Frenchman knew a great deal about folk tales himself, and so was well qualified to make this comparison.

One day, as he was walking in the streets of Isfahan, he heard a festive procession in the distance. There were men on foot and on horseback, preceded by a band playing drums, trumpets and cymbals. The by-standers made way as the procession approached. They cleared away from the streets and pressed close against the walls of the houses, waiting with great deference for the glittering cavalcade to pass. It was led by Soliman, a Safavid, the current occupant of the Peacock Throne.

Suddenly the Frenchman, who was in the middle of the crowd of spectators, noticed a dervish — a Muslim monk — in a simple brown robe, riding on a donkey toward the Shah and his retinue. Several students and followers, five or six of them, accompanied him. To the Frenchman's surprise, they, like their master, showed no signs of giving way to the royal procession.

Curious, Pétis de la Croix watched to see what would happen next. Would the dervish and his companions be swept out of the way? Would the Shah's armed men seize them? Nothing of the kind happened. When the Shar recognized the old dervish, he gave a brief word of command to his retinue. The band stopped playing. Soliman dismounted from his horse and hurried on foot to meet the dervish, who remained seated on his donkey. The ruler of Persia bowed before the monk, and even kissed the hem of his cloak. Then he signalled to his servants. Those who had not already done so stepped aside, following the example of the horsemen, and gave way to the wise old man and his followers. Not until he had disappeared around the street corner did the royal procession set off and the music begin to play again.

"Who was that dervish?" Pétis de la Croix asked one of the Persians standing near him.

"Pir Mochles," replied the man. "He is head of the learned monks who have enjoyed many privileges in the land of the Silver Lion, since the time of Abbas. Have you never heard of Pir Mochles?"

The Frenchman shook his head.

"He has no equal in wisdom and enlightenment!" added the Persian fervently. "As you see, even the Shahinshah pays homage to him. Pir Mochles, versed in a hundred branches of knowledge, knows

211

the holy scriptures as well as he knows the poetry of Firdausi and Hafiz. It is said that he also has all the folk tales of the East stored in his memory, or written down for his library."

Folk tales? The Frenchman pricked up his ears. He himself was a collector and a scholar in this field, which had just been opened up in his native land by Charles Perrault. Moreover, it was at this time that Antoine Galland had brought to Paris the first news of a famous collection of Arabian tales, *The Thousand and One Nights*. The full manuscript of this collection was to reach Europe through the agency of the Austrian diplomat and orientalist, Joseph, Baron von Hammer-Purgstall, a hundred and fifty years later.

Deeply impressed by what he had seen and heard in the streets of Isfahan, Pétis de la Croix tried to make the acquaintance of the learned *pir*, or prior. The Persian scholar consented to receive the French traveller, and the two men talked for many hours. Pir Mochles was so impressed by the Frenchman's knowledge that he gave him access to his documents and his treasures. It is said that it was through him that Pétis de la Croix learned of the existence in the East of the companion piece to the famous *Thousand and One Nights*, called *Hesariek Rus – The Thousand and One Days*. Pir Mochles is reputed to have assembled most of them, and translated them from Indian dialects, and since the Frenchman had won his confidence he allowed him to study this extensive collection, write down some of the stories and translate them into French.

So the story runs – and with the help of the proficient linguist Pétis de la Croix, the first stories from the *Hesariek Rus* came to the West toward the end of the seventeenth century. But it was not until a hundred years later, in 1785, that they were first printed, by an Amsterdam publisher. This small selection is partly based on that work.

As in *The Thousand and One Nights*, these tales are set in a

212

framework story. In *The Thousand and One Nights,* as we all know, the beautiful Sheherazade tells tale after tale; here the narrator is the old nurse Sutlumene. Whether this framework goes back to the *Thousand and One Days* of Pier Mochles and Pétis de la Croix, or dates from a later version, cannot be ascertained.

The editor of this book shares the opinion of the skilled storytellers that may still be heard today in the *suks* of markets of Isfahan or Tetuan, or other places where the Eastern way of life still prevails. These dignified old men like to close their tales with the words, "Allah kerim" — "Allah is kindly", or, more freely, but conveying the sense of the phrase, "Allah will set all things right".

Made and printed in Great Britain by
Thomas Nelson (Printers) Ltd, London and Edinburgh

DC-DC Switching
Regulator
Analysis

DC-DC Switching Regulator Analysis

Daniel M. Mitchell

Advanced Technology and Engineering Department
Collins Defense Communications
Rockwell International Corporation
Cedar Rapids

Adjunct Instructor
Department of Electrical and Computer Engineering
University of Iowa
Iowa City

McGraw-Hill Book Company

New York St. Louis San Francisco Auckland
Bogotá Hamburg London Madrid Mexico
Milan Montreal New Delhi Panama
Paris São Paulo Singapore
Sydney Tokyo Toronto

Library of Congress Cataloging-in-Publication Data

Mitchell, Daniel M.
  DC-DC switching regulator analysis.

  1. Electronic apparatus and appliances—Power
supply—Direct current. I. Title.
TK7868.P6M58 1988   621.381′044   87-16976
ISBN 0-07-042597-3

  234567890 DOC/DOC   9210

ISBN 0-07-042597-3

*The editors for this book were Daniel A. Gonneau and Lucy Mullins,
the designer was Naomi Auerbach, and the production supervisor
was Dianne Walber. It was set in Century Schoolbook
by Techna Type, Inc.*

Printed and bound by R. R. Donnelley & Sons Company.

To Ginny

Contents

Preface   ix
Acknowledgments   xii

Chapter 1. Introduction to Switching Regulation   1

Chapter 2. Basic Switching Regulator Topologies   5

2.1. Second-Order Voltage Converters   6
2.2. Critical Inductance Criterion   10
2.3. Discontinuous Conduction Mode   12
2.4. Second-Order Current Converters   14
2.5. Critical Capacitance Criterion   18
2.6. Fourth-Order Voltage Converters   19
2.7. Some Practical Considerations   22
2.8. Voltage Converters with Transformer Isolation   23
2.9. Illustrative Problems   28

Chapter 3. Pulse-Width Modulation (PWM)   35

3.1. Hysteretic Controllers   37
3.2. Fixed-Frequency Controllers   37
3.3. PWM Waveform Spectral Analysis   41
3.4. Illustrative Problems   45

Chapter 4. State-Space Averaging and Linearization   51

4.1. Review of Modern Linear Systems Analysis   52
4.2. State-Space-Averaging Approximation for Continuity   56
4.3. Discontinuous Conduction Mode   61
4.4. Small-Signal Approximation for Linearity   64
4.5. Application of Approximation Techniques   65
4.6. General Second-Order Linear Equivalent Circuit   69
4.7. The DC Transformer   71
4.8. Illustrative Problems   73

Chapter 5. Voltage-Mode Switching Regulator Transfer Functions   83

5.1. General Control-Law Considerations   83
5.2. Source-to-State Transfer Functions   84

5.3. Source-to-Output Transfer Functions   86
5.4. Classic Stability Considerations   90
5.5. Voltage-Mode Loop-Compensation Techniques   93
5.6. DC Characteristics   97
5.7. Illustrative Problems   100

Chapter 6. Current-Injected Control   **109**

6.1. Limit-Cycle Controllers   109
6.2. Fixed-Frequency Control-Law Derivation   111
6.3. Current-Mode Switching Stability Criterion   114
6.4. Open-Loop Gain Calculation   118
6.5. Performance Comparisons with Voltage-Mode Control   123
6.6. Illustrative Problems   130

Chapter 7. Effects of Input EMI Filtering   **137**

7.1. Stability Considerations   138
7.2. Performance Considerations   140
7.3. Derivation of Feed-Forward State Control Laws   144
7.4. Improvements with Feed-Forward State Control   149
7.5. Illustrative Problems   152

Index   160

Preface

A consequence of the microelectronics revolution is that the power supply has become an increasingly larger portion of the overall electronic system from the viewpoint of size versus functionality. The reasons for this include: (1) the use of microelectronics, in conjunction with advanced packaging techniques, permits higher load power densities; (2) as microelectronic process dimensions become smaller, correspondingly lower power supply voltages are required in order to prevent voltage breakdown, thereby reducing power supply efficiency and increasing the required thermal mass of the power supply; and (3) an increasingly larger portion of the power delivered to these new, more sophisticated, more sensitive electronic loads must be well regulated. The trend away from high-voltage low-current vacuum tube power amplifiers toward high-current low-voltage solid-state power amplifiers has created similar burdens on the power supply.

These pressures have spawned a parallel revolution in power supply design based on much of the same semiconductor physics used in these new loads themselves. Power supplies that use large low-frequency power-line transformers and inefficient linear regulators are being replaced with power supplies that use highly efficient switching regulation techniques together with much smaller higher-frequency transformers operating from high-power semiconductor switches. Because of the higher frequency, filter components are similarly smaller.

This new breed of switching regulated power supplies is not without its own set of problems. Switching supplies generally have many more components than their predecessors, they are less forgiving of source and load disturbances, and their switching behavior contributes to electromagnetic interference. As a result, reduced size has, all too often, resulted in reduced reliability at both the power supply module and system levels. Furthermore, these more complex switching power supplies are more difficult to design. This is manifested by the fact that the field reliability of switching power supplies is worse than what would be predicted by parts count alone (see NAVMAT P4855-1, "Navy Power Supply Reliability—Design and Manufacturing Guidelines,"

Section 1). Thus, additional attention to the design problem itelf is required in all respects—electrical, mechanical, and thermal. This implies improved models, improved design disciplines, and improved technical understanding of the principles involved. What is needed are more power supply designers who are familiar with state-of-the-art switching techniques and who have a broad enough understanding to apply these techniques in a system context.

This brings up a second consequence of the microelectronics revolution. The tremendous demand for digital and computer engineers has overshadowed the demand for additional power supply design engineers. This problem has been aggravated by two factors. First, power supplies have generally had a negative image compared to computers and other microelectronic applications. At least in part, this is because the power supply's simplicity of functional concept belies the technical challenge of its design. Furthermore, any problems encountered during product development tend to have more dramatic consequences for the power supply engineer than for the computer engineer; there may be noise and smoke instead of an unobtrusive bit error. Second, largely in response to industry requirements, engineering curricula have become more digitally oriented, often at the expense of courses needed for understanding power supply design fundamentals and overall system concepts. As a result, the power supply may be designed by someone who lacks good qualifications, whose difficulties may be compounded by an attitude problem, and who may not be getting the support that is deserved.

The prognosis for improvement in this situation is positive. First, several schools, such as the California Institute of Technology, Duke, the Massachusetts Institute of Technology, and Virginia Polytechnic Institute and State University, have instituted formal programs in power electronics and, in the process, have performed much valuable missionary work to promote the idea that power supply design can be interesting, challenging, and rewarding. Second, corporate management, partly in response to customer pressure, is more in tune with the fact that the power supply is an undeniable, integral part of any delivered system and that resources must be applied accordingly, including continued education.

Finally, there seems to be a grass-roots movement among the students themselves to seek out non-computer-oriented courses. After all, the student of today has literally grown up with the computer. If the student chooses to major in computer engineering, it is more likely to be because of genuine interest rather than because of superficial fascination.

This book is an outgrowth of a one-semester course in power electronics taught at the University of Iowa as part of its effort to meet the needs of industry, including those of the Collins Defense Communications organization of Rockwell International. The course is a senior- or graduate-level elective for which core courses in linear systems analysis and control systems are prerequisites. The book concentrates on the mathematical principles of switching regulator behavior and, as such, is intended to complement books that focus on power supply applications and circuit design techniques. As such, the goal of this book is to allow the reader to develop a better understanding of switching regulator technology in order to facilitate performance analyses and to minimize design risk. It is hoped that the book will serve both as a basis for extending the student's knowledge into the field of power electronics and as a means for solidifying the skills of power supply designers in industry.

Daniel M. Mitchell

Acknowledgments

The author wishes to express sincere appreciation to Collins Defense Communications of Rockwell International, whose support and facilities helped make this work possible. The author would also like to acknowledge Mr. Charles Lagerstrom and Dr. Sudhakar Reddy for their assistance and encouragement, Mr. Steve Hageman, Mr. Gordon (Ed) Bloom, Mr. Jerry Tucker, and the Power Electronics students at the University of Iowa for their review of the manuscript and helpful suggestions, and Mrs. JoAnn Wilson for her conscientious preparation of the manuscript.

Introduction to Switching Regulation

Switching regulation is the technique by which unregulated source power is efficiently converted to regulated load power through the use of controlled power switching devices. The devices themselves have evolved over the years from the mercury-arc tubes of the 1920s and 1930s, through the magnetic amplifiers of the 1940s and 1950s, to the power semiconductor devices of the 1960s and beyond. The emphasis upon switching techniques, as opposed to linear techniques, relates to efficiency. An ideal switch has no losses. There is either voltage or current, but not both simultaneously. As the switching characteristics of these semiconductor devices improve—lower saturation voltages, higher blocking voltages, and faster transition times—power switching techniques will assume increasing importance. Faster transition times permit higher switching frequencies resulting in smaller transformers, smaller filter components, and increased signal bandwidths. Although, in principle, switching techniques can be applied to any possible combination of current or voltage sources and current or voltage outputs, this book, as a practical matter, will concentrate on voltage-to-voltage conversion.

Switching regulation can take the form of alternating-current–direct-current (ac-dc), ac-ac, dc-ac, or dc-dc. The ac-ac switching regulator may involve frequency conversion, or it may not. The familiar silicon-controlled rectifier (SCR) light dimmer circuit, shown in Fig. 1.1, is an example of an ac-ac switching circuit that regulates the output voltage, by varying the phase-back angle α. The cycloconverter[1] is an example of a device which directly converts ac of one frequency to ac of another frequency (which must be lower). However, most ac-ac converters involve the formation of an intermediary dc link. That is, they are really cascaded stages of ac-dc conversion (rectification) and dc-ac conversion (inversion).

Rectifier stages that use only two-terminal diodes are, by definition, not switching regulators since no control means is available. An SCR phase-controlled full-wave bridge rectifier is shown in Fig. 1.2. In this case, dc regulation is achieved by the same principle that is used for the light dimmer circuit of Fig. 1.1. SCR phase control can be thought of as a form of switching regulation in which the switching frequency is equal to the ac input frequency times the effective number of phases. This form of switching regulation is already thoroughly covered in the literature.[2,3] The rectification process in general can be degrading to power sources and common-bus equipments because of the harmonic content of the input current waveform. For this reason, higher-frequency switching techniques that require less passive filtering and that actively shape the input current waveform for improved power factor are becoming increasingly popular, particularly at higher power levels.[4]

Inverters may operate at the desired output frequency, or they may operate at much higher frequencies than the output frequency as a means of achieving active filtering in order to help produce sinusoidal

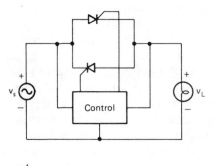

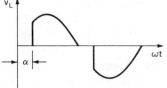

Figure 1.1 SCR light dimmer circuit.

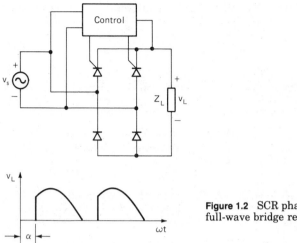

Figure 1.2 SCR phase-controlled full-wave bridge rectifier.

waveshapes with less passive filtering. SCR inverters for motor control, in which the inertia of the motor itself provides output filtering, are prime examples of inverters of the first type and, like SCR rectifiers, are well covered in the literature.[5] For inverters of the second type, the switching frequency is analogous to the carrier frequency of a radio communications system.[6]

Dc-dc switching regulators may be direct-coupled, or they may be isolated by means of a transformer that is sized in accordance with the power level and the switching frequency. This brings out another advantage of switching versus linear techniques, namely, that a switching-frequency ac link is established which can be used in conjunction with inductors and transformers for voltage scaling and isolation. In almost all other respects, signals at the switching frequency are undesirable and must be adequately filtered.

The mathematical concepts and analytical techniques associated with higher-frequency switching regulation are largely independent of the specific application, whether it be waveshaping an ac input current, waveshaping an ac output voltage, or simply providing efficient dc-dc power conversion, with or without isolation. What is considered important here is to meet the need for a compact, orderly, analytically based book that will serve both as a text for a one-semester power electronics course (augmented as appropriate by the available literature on practical switching regulator circuits and design techniques[7–9]) and as a reference book for practicing engineers. Thus, the book will unapologetically concentrate on direct-coupled dc-dc switching regulators. In this context, switching regulation refers to the use of switches such as bipolar and field-effect transistors operating at frequencies from 20 to several hundred kilohertz and above, versus SCRs operating at power-line frequencies.

References

1. B. R. Pelly, *Thyristor Phase-Controlled Converters and Cycloconverters,* Wiley, New York, 1971.
2. S. B. Dewan and A. Straughen, *Power Semiconductor Circuits,* Wiley, New York, 1975.
3. A. Kloss, *A Basic Guide to Power Electronics,* Wiley, Chichester, 1984.
4. D. M. Mitchell, Rockwell International, AC-DC Converter Having an Improved Power Factor, U.S. Patent 4,412,277, Oct. 25, 1983.
5. B. D. Bedford and R. G. Hoft, *Principles of Inverter Circuits,* Reprint ed., Krieger, Malabar, FL, 1985.
6. D. M. Mitchell, Rockwell International, DC to Low Frequency Inverter with Pulse Width Modulated High Frequency Link, U.S. Patent 4,339,791, July 13, 1982.
7. A. I. Pressman, *Switching and Linear Power Supply, Power Converter Design,* Hayden, Rochelle Park, NJ, 1977.
8. R. P. Severns and G. E. Bloom, *Modern DC-to-DC Switchmode Power Converter Circuits,* Van Nostrand, New York, 1985.
9. K. K. Sum, *Switch Mode Power Conversion,* Dekker, New York, 1984.

Chapter 2

Basic Switching
Regulator Topologies

A linear regulator can be thought of as an active voltage divider that maintains a regulated output voltage v_2 over variations in input voltage v_1 and load Z_L (Fig. 2.1). The efficiency η of a linear regulator is determined by

$$\eta = \frac{P_{\text{out}}}{P_{\text{in}}} \times 100\% = \frac{v_2 i_2}{v_1 i_1} \times 100\% \qquad (2.1a)$$

where P represents power and i represents current. The maximum theoretical efficiency, corresponding to $i_3 = 0$, is

$$\eta = \frac{v_2}{v_1} \times 100\% \qquad i_2 = i_1 \qquad (2.1b)$$

where v_2 must be less than v_1.

For practical linear regulators, $i_3 > 0$ and the constraint on v_2 is

$$v_2 < v_1 - V_T \qquad (2.2)$$

where V_T represents the minimum voltage [typically 2 to 3 volts (V)] necessary to keep the linear regulator in its active region. Switching techniques can be used to overcome both the efficiency limitation of the linear regulator and the constraint that v_2 must be less than v_1. In

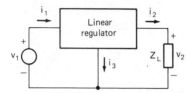

Figure 2.1 Linear regulator block diagram.

this chapter, a structured approach is used to derive the set of basic switching regulator topologies which are then logically extended to more complex configurations.

2.1 Second-Order Voltage Converters*

Suppose we have a load R that requires an average voltage V_2 and a dc voltage source $V_1 > V_2$. Conceivably, we could simply close the switch connecting the load to the source (Fig. 2.2) and then open it again in such a way that $v_{2(avg)} = V_2$. If S1 is switched at a fixed frequency f_s, then its required ON time duty factor D is V_2/V_1. That is,

$$D = t_{ON}f_s = \frac{V_2}{V_1} \tag{2.3}$$

If f_s is high enough, then a voltmeter across the load will read V_2, even though v_2 actually is either zero or V_1 at any given time. This may be satisfactory for heating, lighting, and mechanical loads but not for electronic loads. In general, the effects of switching are undesirable and are regarded as noise. That is the penalty for achieving a higher efficiency (theoretically 100 percent) than linear regulation would allow. If the load does not inherently provide adequate filtering of the

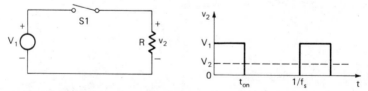

Figure 2.2 Simplest switching voltage converter.

---

* The term "converter" is used instead of the term "regulator" when the power circuit is being considered alone, in the absence of the control circuit. Alternatively, we can say that a switching regulator is a power converter circuit that is connected to an appropriate means of control.

switching frequency and its harmonics, then the switching regulator itself must include the necessary filtering.

The first obvious step in filtering a voltage converter is to place a capacitor in parallel with the load. However, we cannot switch a voltage source into a capacitor without infinite current. Thus, we use an inductor as a nondissipative means of limiting the value of source current. In doing so we impose the additional constraint that we cannot instantaneously interrupt the inductor current, since that would result in infinite voltage. Therefore, if we open one switch supplying inductor current, we must simultaneously close a second switch in order to provide a continuous inductor current path. Consequently, the simplest practical voltage converter consists of a parallel combination of the load resistor and a filter capacitor connected to the voltage source by means of two switches and an inductor. The next question is, how many ways are there of making these connections? Figure 2.3 represents the set of simplest practical voltage converter topologies. From here on in this chapter, we assume that the filtering is effective enough to permit the switching component of the output voltage, or "ripple," to be neglected.

We begin with the finite current constraint that disallows a closed switch between node 1 and ground, node 2 and ground, or node 1 and node 2. However, there is nothing wrong with connecting the inductor between any of the above three node pairs. Furthermore, these three are the only node pair combinations. Thus, there are but three switch conditions corresponding to Fig. 2.3, which are shown in Fig. 2.4.

These three switch conditions permit the formation of three converter topologies, each of which has two switch conditions. In Fig. 2.5, for example, converter a has conditions I and III, converter b has conditions I and II, and converter c has conditions II and III. Note that, for each configuration, L is in a different leg of a T network consisting of S1, S2, and L. By the finite current constraint, S1 and S2 cannot both be on. S1 and S2 can theoretically both be off (corresponding to $i_L = 0$), resulting in a degenerate third switch condition for each converter. In this condition the load is literally out of control of the switches. The

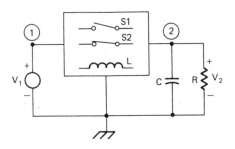

Figure 2.3 Representation of simplest practical voltage converter topologies.

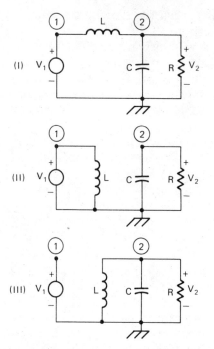

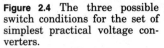

Figure 2.4 The three possible switch conditions for the set of simplest practical voltage converters.

practical consequences of this depend upon whether the switch control scheme is dedicated to that particular load and will be discussed in the next section. For the remainder of this section, we consider only the first two switch conditions.

To determine V_2, we use the finite current constraint that $v_{L(\text{avg})}$ per cycle must be zero for steady-state operation. For only two switch conditions, we have

$$V_{L1}D + V_{L2}(1 - D) = 0 \qquad (2.4)$$

where

$$V_L = \begin{cases} V_{L1} & \text{S1 ON/S2 OFF} \\ V_{L2} & \text{S1 OFF/S2 ON} \end{cases} \qquad (2.5)$$

From Fig. 2.5, for converter a we have

$$(V_1 - V_2)D - V_2(1 - D) = 0 \qquad (2.6a)$$

or $\qquad\qquad\qquad\qquad V_2 = DV_1 \qquad\qquad\qquad\qquad (2.6b)$

For converter b, we have

$$V_1 D + (V_1 - V_2)(1 - D) = 0 \qquad (2.7a)$$

or
$$V_2 = \frac{V_1}{1 - D} \tag{2.7b}$$

For converter c, we have

$$V_1 D + V_2(1 - D) = 0 \tag{2.8a}$$

or
$$V_2 = -\frac{DV_1}{1 - D} \tag{2.8b}$$

Note the polarity reversal in Eq. (2.8b). Given that $0 \le D < 1$, the ranges of output voltage magnitudes in terms of input voltage are

Converter a. $V_2 < V_1$

Converter b. $V_2 > V_1$

Converter c. $|V_2| > V_1$ if $D > 0.5$
                     $|V_2| < V_1$ if $D < 0.5$

In accordance with these ranges, the three voltage converters are named, respectively, (a) buck, (b) boost, and (c) buck-boost.

For $i_L > 0$, only one unidirectional controlled switch, such as a transistor, is necessary for the practical implementation of these converters. The second switch can be a diode which is naturally commutated by

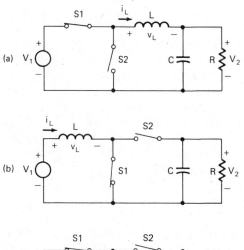

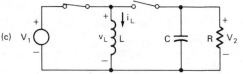

Figure 2.5 The three simplest practical voltage converter topologies. (a) Buck, (b) boost, and (c) buck-boost.

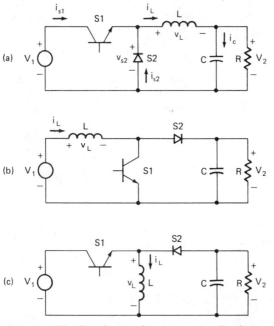

Figure 2.6 The three basic voltage converter circuits using NPN transistors. (*a*) Buck, (*b*) boost, and (*c*) buck-boost.

the transistor. That is, when the transistor is on, the diode is back-biased off; when the transistor is off, the diode is forced on by the fact that $i_L > 0$. These considerations imply unique converter circuits as shown in Fig. 2.6, where NPN transistors are arbitrarily shown. By convention, D is the ON time duty factor of the controlled switch, which has been arranged to correspond to S1.

These basic voltage converter circuits are second-order since they each include an inductor and a capacitor. That is, for any given switch condition, two independent first-order differential equations are required to describe the total behavior. Control is achieved by varying the duty factor as will be discussed further in Chap. 3.

2.2 Critical Inductance Criterion

For $i_L > 0$, the inductor voltage waveforms are rectangular, being either of amplitude V_{L1} or V_{L2} in accordance with Eq. (2.5). Therefore, the ac inductor current waveforms are triangular, assuming component linearity [see Fig. 2.7(*a*) for buck converter waveforms]. For very large L, the ac component of the inductor current may be considered negligible with respect to the dc component for the purposes of designing the inductor and selecting the power semiconductors. As L becomes smaller, for a given value of load resistance, the ratio of peak inductor current I_p to average inductor current I_L becomes larger. Eventually the peak-to-peak sawtooth amplitude becomes large enough that i_L would dip below zero if S2 were not a diode; instead, there is a time interval during which both v_L and i_L are zero [see Fig. 2.7(b) for buck converter waveforms]. Alternatively, one can think of forcing a time interval where v_L and i_L are equal to zero by increasing R (that is, reducing the load) for a given value of inductance.

The value of L for which $i_L = 0$ at one and only one point per cycle is defined as critical inductance L_c. At critical inductance, the peak

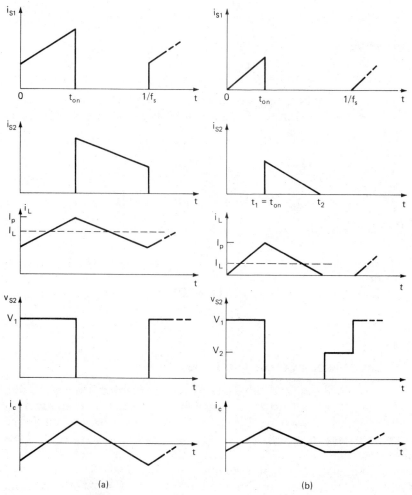

(a)   (b)

Figure 2.7 Buck converter waveforms for (a) $L > L_c$ and (b) $L < L_c$.

inductor current is twice the average according to the equation

$$I_p = 2I_L = \frac{V_{L1}t_{ON}}{L_c} = \frac{V_{L1}D}{f_s L_c} \tag{2.9}$$

To help solve explicitly for L_c, we use the fact that for an ideal switching regulator, input power is equal to output power.

Buck.

$$V_1 I_L D = \frac{V_2{}^2}{R} \tag{2.10a}$$

Boost.

$$V_1 I_L = \frac{V_2{}^2}{R} \tag{2.10b}$$

Buck-boost.

$$V_1 I_L D = \frac{V_2{}^2}{R} \tag{2.10c}$$

In Eqs. (2.10a) and (2.10c), we make use of the fact that the average inductor current during the ON time of S1 is also I_L. Combining Eqs. (2.4) through (2.10) results in

Buck.

$$L_c = \frac{R(1 - D)}{2f_s} \tag{2.11a}$$

Boost.

$$L_c = \frac{R(1 - D)^2 D}{2f_s} \tag{2.11b}$$

Buck-boost.

$$L_c = \frac{R(1 - D)}{2f_s} \tag{2.11c}$$

2.3   Discontinuous Conduction Mode

For $L < L_c$, V_2 does not behave simply in accordance with Eqs. (2.6b), (2.7b), and (2.8b), but rather is also dependent upon R in an algebraically complicated way.[1] In Fig. 2.7(b), we define t_1 as t_{ON} and define t_2, which is less than $1/f_s$, as the time at which i_L goes to zero. Since there is a time interval during which the inductor is not conducting current, namely $1/f_s - t_2$, it is common practice to refer to the situation of $L < L_c$ as the discontinuous conduction mode (DCM) of operation. For the DCM buck regulator, the average inductor voltage per cycle is still zero in accordance with the equation

$$(V_1 - V_2)t_1 f_s - V_2(t_2 - t_1)f_s = 0 \qquad (2.12)$$

where V_{L1} and V_{L2} are as defined in Eq. (2.5). Also, the average capacitor current per cycle is still zero, so

$$\frac{I_p t_2 f_s}{2} = \frac{V_2}{R} \qquad (2.13)$$

Equation (2.13) merely expresses the unknown t_2 in terms of another unknown I_p. Thus, yet another equation is needed. By using $v_L = L \, di_L/dt$, we can say that

$$(V_1 - V_2)t_2 = LI_p \qquad (2.14)$$

Combining Eqs. (2.11a), (2.12), (2.13), and (2.14) and substituting $D = t_1 f_s$ results in

$$V_2 = \frac{V_1 D(\sqrt{4L(1 - D)/L_c + D^2} - D)}{2L(1 - D)/L_c} \qquad L < L_c \qquad (2.15a)$$

$$t_2 = \frac{2L(1 - D)/L_c f_s}{\sqrt{4L(1 - D)/L_c + D^2} - D} \qquad L < L_c \qquad (2.15b)$$

$$I_p = \frac{2V_1 D}{R}\left[\frac{\sqrt{4L(1 - D)/L_c + D^2} - D}{2L(1 - D)/L_c}\right]^2 \qquad L < L_c \qquad (2.15c)$$

Note that for $L = L_c$, Eq. (2.15) yields $V_2 = V_1 D$, $t_2 = 1/f_s$, and $I_p = 2V_1 D/R$. Furthermore, for $L \to 0$, applying L'Hospital's rule to Eq. (2.15a) yields $V_2 \to V_1$. These are the expected results. Corresponding equations can be similarly derived for the boost and buck-boost topologies.

In a single-output feedback-controlled switching regulator, output voltage regulation can be achieved regardless of L. For multiple-output switching regulators, where only one output is directly controlled, additional so-called postregulators may be required. Helping out is the fact that many, if not most, switching voltage converters use several times critical inductance at full load in order to achieve minimum filter size for a given maximum ripple voltage requirement. Because of the increased computational complexity associated with $L < L_c$ and because the switching regulator dynamics of most interest are typically in the vicinity of full load, $L > L_c$ will be assumed, unless otherwise indicated, throughout the remainder of this book. However, the analytical principles are the same, and the reader should be able to infer results for $L < L_c$ from the material presented.

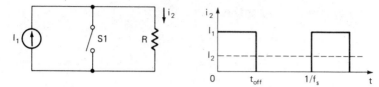

Figure 2.8 Simplest switching current converter.

2.4   Second-Order Current Converters

Although nature may be partial to voltage sources, mathematics is not, and we can derive a set of basic current converter circuits in a manner similar to that of Sec. 2.1. We will find these current converter circuits to be useful as building blocks for more complex voltage converter circuits. The simplest switching current converter consists of a shunt switch that alternately diverts the current source from the load, as shown in Fig. 2.8.

Assuming that, as before, a pulsed output waveform is unacceptable, we add a filter inductor in series with the load. However, we cannot switch a current source into an inductor without infinite voltage. Thus, we use a shunt capacitance as a nondissipative means of absorbing the difference between source current and load current. However, we cannot close a switch across a capacitor without infinite current. Thus, when we close the first switch, we must simultaneously open a second switch in order to provide capacitor voltage continuity. Consequently, the simplest practical current converter consists of a series combination of the load resistor and a filter inductor connected to the current source by means of two switches and a capacitor. The question now becomes, how many ways are there of making the connections implied by Fig. 2.9? In this case, we assume that, for present purposes, the filtering is effective enough to permit the switching component of the output current to be neglected.

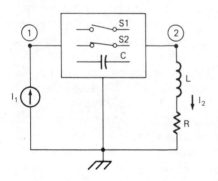

Figure 2.9 Representation of simplest practical current converter topologies.

The finite voltage constraint disallows an open circuit between node 1 and ground or node 2 and ground. Thus, there must either be the capacitor or a closed switch across these pairs at all times. Furthermore, since, in general, $I_1 \neq I_2$, the source and load cannot be simply connected in series with either the capacitor or a closed switch. Thus, there are but three switch conditions corresponding to Fig. 2.9, which are shown in Fig. 2.10.

The three converter topologies formed by combining pairs of the three possible combinations of Fig. 2.10, corresponding to S1 ON/S2 OFF and S1 OFF/S2 ON, are shown in Fig. 2.11. Note that, this time, C is in a different leg of a pi network consisting of S1, S2, and C, for each topology. For v_c greater than zero, S1 and S2 cannot both be on; otherwise the capacitor current would be infinite. A degenerate third condition of S1 ON/S2 ON is theoretically possible for the case where

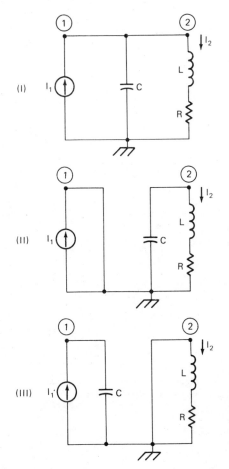

Figure 2.10 The three possible switch conditions for the set of simplest practical current converters.

the capacitor is allowed to discharge to $v_c = 0$, and we can define a corresponding critical capacitance. Just as S1 and S2 could not both be on for voltage converters because of the finite current constraint, S1 and S2 cannot both be off for current converters because of the finite voltage constraint. In fact, it should be clear by now that the three current converters of Fig. 2.11 are duals of the three voltage converters of Fig. 2.5.

To determine I_2 as a function of I_1 and D, we use the constraint that for steady-state dc operation, $i_{c(avg)}$ per cycle is zero. For only two switch

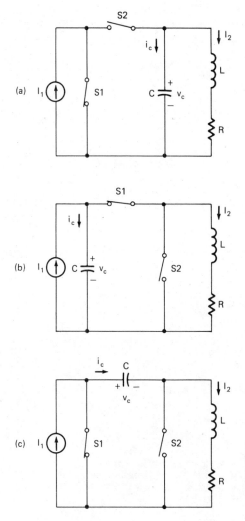

Figure 2.11 The three simplest practical current converter topologies. (a) Buck, (b) boost, and (c) buck-boost.

conditions, we have

$$I_{c1}D + I_{c2}(1 - D) = 0 \qquad (2.16)$$

where

$$i_c = \begin{cases} I_{c1} & \text{S1 ON/S2 OFF} \\ I_{c2} & \text{S1 OFF/S2 ON} \end{cases} \qquad (2.17)$$

From Fig. 2.11, for converter a, we have

$$-I_2 D + (I_1 - I_2)(1 - D) = 0 \qquad (2.18a)$$

or

$$I_2 = (1 - D)I_1 \qquad (2.18b)$$

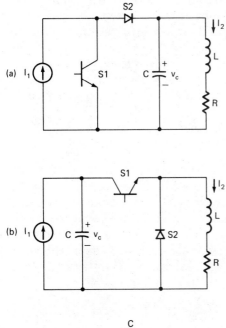

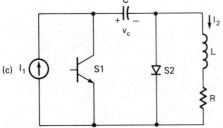

Figure 2.12 The three basic current converter circuits using NPN transistors. (a) Buck, (b) boost, and (c) buck-boost.

For converter b, we have

$$(I_1 - I_2)D + I_1(1 - D) = 0 \tag{2.19a}$$

or

$$I_2 = \frac{I_1}{D} \tag{2.19b}$$

For converter c, we have

$$I_2D + I_1(1 - D) = 0 \tag{2.20a}$$

or

$$I_2 = -\frac{(1 - D)I_1}{D} \tag{2.20b}$$

Note the correspondence of Eqs. (2.18), (2.19), and (2.20) to Eqs. (2.6), (2.7), and (2.8). Using physical reasoning, we use a transistor for S1 and a diode for S2, to arrive at the basic current converter circuits of Fig. 2.12. The terms buck, boost, and buck-boost relate to the magnitude of I_2 with respect to I_1. (If operation with less than critical capacitance is to be allowed, S1 must be bidirectional.) Again, these converters are second-order because, for any given switch condition, two independent first-order differential equations are required to describe the total behavior.

2.5   Critical Capacitance Criterion

For current converters with $v_c > 0$, the capacitor current waveforms are rectangular and the ac capacitor voltage waveforms are triangular. For either small enough C or large enough R, there can be a time interval during which both v_c and i_c are zero. The value of C for which $v_c = 0$ at one and only one point per cycle is defined as critical capacitance C_c. At critical capacitance, the peak capacitor voltage v_p is twice the average voltage V_c according to the equation

$$V_p = 2V_c = \frac{-I_{c1}t_{ON}}{C_c} = \frac{-I_{c1}D}{f_sC_c} \tag{2.21}$$

To help solve explicitly for C_c, we again use the fact that for an ideal switching regulator, input power is equal to output power.

Buck.

$$V_cI_1(1 - D) = I_2^2R \tag{2.22a}$$

Boost.

$$V_cI_1 = I_2^2R \tag{2.22b}$$

Buck-boost.

$$V_c I_1 (1 - D) = I_2^2 R \qquad (2.22c)$$

Combining Eqs. (2.16) through (2.22) results in

Buck.

$$C_c = \frac{D}{2 f_s R} \qquad (2.23a)$$

Boost.

$$C_c = \frac{(1 - D)D^2}{2 f_s R} \qquad (2.23b)$$

Buck-boost.

$$C_c = \frac{D^2}{2 f_s R} \qquad (2.23c)$$

2.6   Fourth-Order Voltage Converters

The converters of Fig. 2.12 are of little practical interest as they are, because of the current source, although there are applications where a current output rather than a voltage output is desired. Nevertheless, it is of interest to use these topologies as a basis for forming voltage converters that represent the next higher level of complexity compared to the circuits of Fig. 2.6. We begin by adding a capacitor in parallel with the load resistor to form a voltage output. We cannot directly replace the current source with a voltage source without violating the finite current constraint. The simplest nondissipative practical transformation of the current source is a voltage source in series with an inductor. When these two topological changes are made to the three basic current converter circuits, we arrive at three extended voltage converter circuits, as shown in Fig. 2.13.

The first of these circuits is the basic boost converter with an additional output filter stage. The second is the basic buck converter with an additional input filter stage. The input/output dc voltage relationships for these two circuits are the same as for the corresponding basic circuits of Fig. 2.6. The third extended converter circuit is the Ćuk converter,[2] named for Dr. Slobodan Ćuk of the California Institute of Technology. One of its main advantages is that the input and output inductors can be coupled in such a way that the switching component of either the input current or the output current can be nulled to zero.

To find V_c and V_2 in terms of D and V_1 for the Ćuk converter with two switch conditions (i.e., $L_2 > L_c$ and $C_1 > C_c$), we use the average voltage constraint for both L_1 and L_2. Since, for each inductor, the average inductor current for either of the two switch conditions is the same as the corresponding steady-state dc value, it is no longer necessary to assume that the switching current component is negligible. Applying the average voltage constraint to L_1 gives

$$V_1 D + (V_1 - V_c)(1 - D) = 0 \qquad (2.24a)$$

or

$$V_c = \frac{V_1}{1 - D} \qquad (2.24b)$$

and, for L_2,

$$-(V_2 + V_c)D - V_2(1 - D) = 0 \qquad (2.25a)$$

or

$$V_2 = -DV_c \qquad (2.25b)$$

Combining Eqs. (2.24b) and (2.25b) results in

$$V_2 = -\frac{DV_1}{1 - D} \qquad (2.26)$$

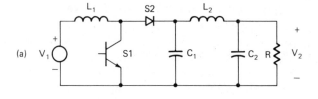

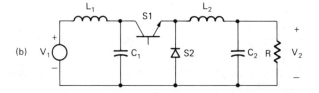

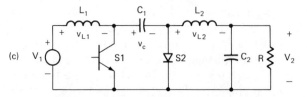

Figure 2.13 The three extended voltage converter circuits based on the basic current converters. (a) Boost with additional output filter, (b) buck with additional input filter, and (c) Ćuk.

Thus, V_c is greater than V_1 and the output is buck-boost with a polarity reversal.

We now generalize the situation to find all possible physically realizable topologies, with an input consisting of a voltage source in series with an inductor and an output consisting of a capacitor in parallel with the load resistor, that are connected by means of two switches, a second inductor, and a second capacitor. Disallowed topologies include topologies that have a shunt input inductor, since this would provide a shorted dc input path, and topologies that have a series output capacitor, since this would block the desired dc output path. The set of three possible configurations using the second inductor in the output path is shown in Fig. 2.13. What remain, then, are the three configurations using a switch in the output path. These circuits are shown in Fig. 2.14.

The first two circuits represent the buck-boost and boost converters with additional input filtering. The third converter circuit is called the "single-ended primary inductor converter," or SEPIC.[3] In its original

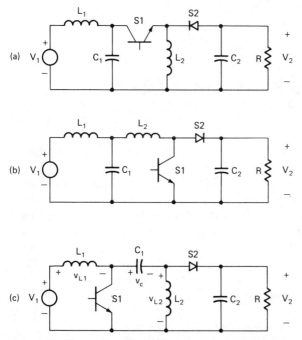

Figure 2.14 Three allowable additional extended voltage converter circuits. (*a*) Buck-boost with additional input filter, (*b*) boost with additional input filter, and (*c*) SEPIC.

application at Bell Labs, a transformer was used on the load side of L_2 to achieve isolation with a single-ended topology. Its advantage compared to using the buck-boost converter with a similarly placed transformer is that the possibility of transformer saturation due to dc offset is precluded by the series capacitor. Applying the average voltage constraint to L_1 and L_2 under the conditions of $L_2 > L_c$ and $C_1 > C_c$, we have, for L_1,

$$V_1 D + (V_1 - V_c - V_2)(1 - D) = 0 \qquad (2.27a)$$

or
$$V_c + V_2 = \frac{V_1}{1 - D} \qquad (2.27b)$$

and, for L_2,
$$-V_c D + V_2(1 - D) = 0 \qquad (2.28a)$$

or
$$V_2 = \frac{DV_c}{1 - D} \qquad (2.28b)$$

Combining Eqs. (2.27b) and (2.28b) results in

$$V_c = V_1 \qquad (2.29a)$$

and
$$V_2 = \frac{DV_1}{1 - D} \qquad (2.29b)$$

Note that, compared to the Ćuk converter, output voltage polarity is preserved and V_c is smaller. On the other hand, mutual coupling of L_1 and L_2 can be used to cancel only the input switching current component.

These extended topologies represent fourth-order voltage converters, corresponding to the four independent energy storage elements. For any given switch condition, four independent first-order differential equations are required to describe the total behavior. For the sake of completeness, it should be noted that two additional physically realizable fourth-order topologies can be created by simply adding an LC output filter stage to the basic buck and buck-boost topologies. However, the input/output relationships are obviously unchanged. Furthermore, there would be few, if any, applications where it would be more desirable to add a second output filter stage than to add a first input stage.

2.7 Some Practical Considerations

In the simplified dc analyses we have performed, lossless components have been assumed and the switching component of the output voltage, or ripple, has been neglected. In practice, an inductor has series power losses in the wire and shunt power losses in the magnetic core. Also, care must be taken during the design of the inductor to ensure that it remains basically linear over the expected range of current. A capacitor has an ac equivalent series resistance (ESR) and a dc leakage resistance. In the case of an output capacitor, which is usually electrolytic for small size, the ESR not only degrades efficiency but has a major effect on the output ripple and can influence the overall loop dynamics of the switching regulator. It is not uncommon for the ESR to dominate over the capacitive impedance at modern-day switching frequencies (20 kHz to 1 MHz), and, particularly at the higher end of this frequency range, equivalent series inductance (ESL) must be taken into consideration as well.

The major sources of inefficiency are the power switches themselves. The controlled switch S1 has saturation losses during its ON time, leakage losses during its OFF time (usually negligible), and switching losses. In almost all cases, the peak instantaneous power dissipation in S1 occurs either at turn-on, when the current is increasing and the voltage is decreasing, or at turnoff, when the current is decreasing and the voltage is increasing. The diode has saturation losses comparable to those of the transistor and a reverse recovery time* that can result in large transistor turn-on current spikes. These current spikes, in turn, can lead to damaging voltage spikes which, in practice, are limited by so-called snubber circuits that have their own associated losses.

Whether switching losses or saturation losses predominate depends upon the frequency of operation, the magnitude of the output voltage, the power semiconductors used, the converter topology, and any special turn-on or turnoff drive circuit techniques that may be used to advantage. As a generalization for silicon devices, it is probably fair to say that switching losses begin predominating at a few tens of kilohertz with bipolar switches and at a few hundreds of kilohertz with field-effect switches.

2.8   Voltage Converters with Transformer Isolation

The converter circuits examined in this chapter so far provide a baseline for the design, analysis, and evaluation of more complex circuits. Many other circuits can be derived from these baseline topologies using transformers, coupled inductors, and additional switches. Although it is not one of the stated goals of this book to dwell on these various circuits, we would be remiss in not presenting some simple trans-

---

* The time it takes for the depletion region to be reformed after forward conduction.

former-isolated versions of the basic second-order circuits, since so many practical applications require input-to-output isolation and/or voltage scaling. Of course, the associated control circuitry for these converters must also be isolated, using either transformers or optical couplers.

Figure 2.15 shows four of the most common buck-derived transformer-isolated voltage converters. The term "buck-derived" means, after Severns and Bloom,[4] that, with appropriate transformations, these converters can be modeled as the basic buck converter of Fig. 2.6.

The forward converter of Fig. 2.15(a) is a single-ended topology using only one controlled switch. S3 conducts during the S1 ON time. For $L > L_c$, S2 conducts during the S1 OFF time, as before. S4 begins conducting the transformer magnetizing current as S1 is turned off, and it remains on until the transformer is reset (i.e., until the magnetizing current returns to zero). V_z represents the transformer reset voltage under the constraint that $|V_z t_{OFF}| > |V_1 t_{ON}|$. S4 withstands V_1 during the ON time and S3 withstands nV_z during the OFF time. S1 must withstand V_1 plus V_z during its OFF time. The transformer is used only in the first quadrant of its B-H characteristic. The use of the forward converter is generally confined to relatively low voltage, low power applications of, say, below 100 watts (W).

The push-pull converter of Fig. 2.15(b) permits first- and third-quadrant operation of the transformer (which can, therefore, be smaller) at the expense of two controlled switches that operate 180° apart. Assuming S1 and S2 have equal ON times and saturation voltages, the transformer operation is inherently balanced. Of course, in practice, the switches are not perfectly equal, and therein lies the design challenge for this circuit. S3 turns on with S2, and S4 turns on with S1. When S1 and S2 are both off, inductor current conducts through both S3 and S4. For a well-designed tightly coupled transformer, there is no need for an additional so-called free-wheeling diode for the inductor; S3 and S4 suffice. The effective frequency of operation of this converter is twice the switching frequency of either S1 or S2 individually. Similarly, the effective duty factor D_{eff} is twice that of either S1 or S2. Unlike the forward converter, full conduction ($D_{eff} = 1$) is allowed. The output voltage V_2 is equal to $nV_1 D_{eff}$. Because of transformer action, S1 and S2 must be able to withstand at least $2V_1$ in their OFF conditions; S3 and S4 must be able to withstand at least $2nV_1$. Because of improved transformer utilization, push-pull converters are used at much higher power levels than forward converters. However, they are still confined to relatively low input voltage applications.

Figure 2.15(c) and (d) shows the bridge (sometimes called "full-bridge") and half-bridge converters, respectively. In the bridge con-

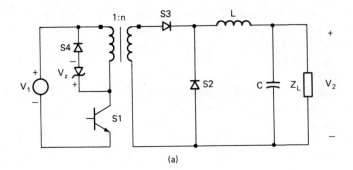

(a)

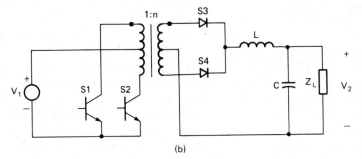

(b)

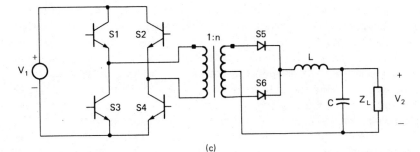

(c)

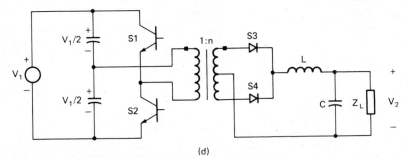

(d)

Figure 2.15 Buck-derived converters with transformer isolation. (*a*) Forward converter, (*b*) push-pull converter, (*c*) bridge converter, and (*d*) half-bridge converter.

verter, S1 and S4 are synchronized, as are S2 and S3. The two sets of switches operate 180° out of phase. Since the controlled switches need to withstand only V_1, not $2V_1$, the bridge converter is often used for higher input voltage applications. However, because of the complexity of four controlled switches and their associated drive circuits, its cost-effective use is generally confined to higher power applications of, say, above 1 kW. The half-bridge converter is very popular for single-phase ac input applications where the input power is first rectified and filtered to form a dc link, as represented by V_1. (This is called "off-line rectification.") A large input filter capacitor is needed anyway for single-phase inputs, so there is little penalty associated with arranging the input capacitors as shown. Again, S1 and S2 need to withstand only V_1; however, only $V_1/2$ is applied to the transformer primary. Thus, compared to the bridge converter, the primary switches must conduct twice the current for the same output power. In any of the converters b through d, the output diodes may be arranged in a bridge configuration for higher output voltage applications.

Figure 2.16 shows a push-pull arrangement of the boost converter, commonly called the "current-fed converter." This converter and its relatives are particularly useful in high output voltage applications where the inductor prevents what otherwise might be damaging switching current spikes due to the primary-reflected transformer winding capacitance. Current-fed converters may also be of the bridge configuration. With buck-derived converters, overlapping conduction of transistors that are intended to operate 180° apart is the classic failure mode. With boost-derived converters, overlapping conduction is essential to their mode of operation. The simultaneous conduction of S1 and S2 in Fig. 2.16 corresponds to the ON time of the basic boost converter of Fig. 2.6. The minimum transistor duty factor in Fig. 2.16 is 0.5, in order to assure a continuous conduction path for the inductor current. The output voltage V_2 is equal to $nV_1/(1 - D_{eff})$, where D_{eff} is the duty factor of simultaneous conduction.

The final example we will show is, perhaps, the most common of all

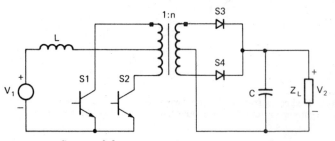

Figure 2.16 Current-fed converter.

switching regulators. Figure 2.17 shows the transformer-isolated buck-boost converter, or "flyback" converter. A version of this circuit appears in nearly every commercial television set and is used to generate the CRT voltages using a control signal from the horizontal oscillator. Energy is stored in the magnetic core of the flyback transformer while S1 is on and "flies back" to the output through S2 while S1 is off. Normally, a transformer is designed so that magnetizing current is minimized. However, the flyback transformer is designed with an appropriate air gap so that it serves the dual role of inductor and transformer. As such, isolation and polarity reversal can be achieved in a practical flyback converter with no more power components than are in the basic buck-boost converter. The output voltage V_2 is equal to $nV_1D/(1 - D)$. This concept of "integrated magnetics" can also be applied to the Ćuk converter, and its more widespread application in switching regulators is a topic of current investigation.[5]

Not all of the practical switching regulator topologies are directly derivable from the basic converters presented in this chapter. Two classes of circuits whose ON time durations are determined not by the control circuitry but rather by the power circuitry are saturable reactor circuits[6] and resonant converters. As the name implies, the ON time of a saturable reactor circuit is determined by the length of time it takes to saturate a magnetic core. Advanced power semiconductors and low-cost integrated control circuits have contributed to the decrease of activity in this area.

Resonant converters use additional inductor(s) and capacitor(s) that cause the switching currents to be sinusoidal. The ON time of a resonant converter is the duration between a turn-on signal from the control circuit and the time that the resulting sinusoidal current naturally goes to zero. Resonant techniques are often used in SCR converters,[7] where gate control is lost after turn-on anyway, and in higher-frequency transistor converters,[8–10] where "square-wave" switching losses are unacceptable and the influence of parasitic inductance and capacitance is not negligible. Some resonant topologies allow these parasitics to help rather than hinder. Although the treatment of resonant converters is beyond the scope of this book, it should be observed

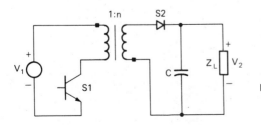

Figure 2.17 The flyback converter.

that they are becoming increasingly popular as the maximum practical switching frequency of advanced power semiconductors increases.

2.9 Illustrative Problems

2.1 You are asked to design a flyback converter as shown in Fig. P2.1 such that $V_2 = 100$ V for 10 V $< V_1 <$ 14 V. You are told to assume that the voltage drops $V_{(sat)}$ and V_f across S1 and S2 during their respective ON times are 0.8 V each, and that for best transformer utilization (i.e., size vs. power) the duty factor should be 0.5 under the nominal condition of $V_1 = 12$ V.   (a) Find n. (b) For $R = 100$ ohms (Ω) and $f_s = 24$ kilohertz (kHz), what is the primary reflected critical inductance L_c?   (c) For $L = L_c$, determine the minimum value of C that is required to assure that the peak-to-peak output voltage ripple is less than 1 percent of the dc value.   (d) Examine the possible benefits of increasing L to $10L_c$.

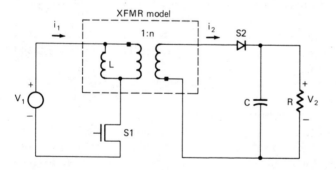

Figure P2.1

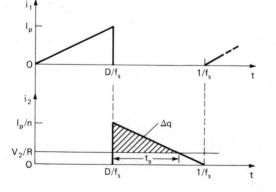

SOLUTION: (a) For volt-second transformer balance, in accordance with Eq. (2.4), we have

$$(V_1 - V_{(sat)})D = \frac{V_2 + V_f}{n}(1 - D)$$

or

$$(12 - 0.8)(0.5) = \frac{100 + 0.8}{n}(1 - 0.5)$$

$$n = 9$$

(b) From Eq. (2.9), we have

$$I_p = \frac{(V_1 - V_{(sat)})D}{f_s L_c}$$

Since we are not neglecting the ON voltage drops of the switches, input power does not equal output power and Eq. (2.10c) does not apply. However, we still have

$$i_{2(avg)} = \frac{I_p(1 - D)}{2n} = \frac{V_2}{R}$$

Using the results of Part (a) of this problem, the equation for critical inductance is

$$L_c = \frac{(V_2 + V_f)R(1 - D)^2}{2n^2 V_2 f_s}$$

Notice that for $V_f = 0$ and $n = 1$, this agrees with Eq. (2.11c). To assure that there are only two switching conditions over the entire input voltage range, the minimum value of D must be substituted above. From Part (a), we arrive at

$$D_{min} = \frac{V_2 + V_f}{V_2 + V_f + n(V_{1(max)} - V_{(sat)})}$$

$$= \frac{100 + 0.8}{100 + 0.8 + 9(14 - 0.8)} = 0.459$$

$$L_c = \frac{(100 + 0.8)100(1 - 0.459)^2}{2(9)^2 100(24 \times 10^3)}$$

$$= 7.59 \text{ microhenrys (}\mu\text{H)}$$

(c) During the ON time of S1, $i_2 = 0$. During the OFF time of S1, i_2 ramps down from I_p/n as shown in Fig. P2.1.

$$C\Delta V_2 = \Delta q$$

$$\Delta q = \left(\frac{I_p}{n} - \frac{V_2}{R}\right)\frac{t_a}{2}$$

$$\frac{I_p}{n} - \frac{(V_2 + V_f)t_a}{n^2 L_c} = \frac{V_2}{R}$$

$$C\Delta V_2 = \frac{n^2 L_c}{2(V_2 + V_f)}\left(\frac{I_p}{n} - \frac{V_2}{R}\right)^2$$

From Part (b), we have

$$I_p = \frac{2nV_2}{R(1 - D)}$$

$$C\Delta V_2 = \frac{n^2 L_c}{2(V_2 + V_f)}\left(\frac{1 + D}{1 - D}\right)^2 \left(\frac{V_2}{R}\right)^2$$

For a given value of C, ΔV_2 is maximum at maximum duty factor D_{max}. From Part (a), we have

$$D_{max} = \frac{V_2 + V_f}{V_2 + V_f + n(V_{1(min)} - V_{(sat)})}$$

$$= \frac{100 + 0.8}{100 + 0.8 + 9(10 - 0.8)} = 0.549$$

$$\Delta V_2 = (0.01)(100) = 1$$

$$C = \frac{(9)^2(7.59 \times 10^{-6})}{2(100 + 0.8)}\left(\frac{1 + 0.549}{1 - 0.549}\right)^2 \left(\frac{100}{100}\right)^2 > 36 \text{ microfarads } (\mu F)$$

In practice, ESR and ESL contribute to the total impedance of the physical capacitor, so the actual value of C may have to be significantly higher or an additional higher-frequency output filter may be required. Note that 1 percent ripple is clearly small enough to justify neglecting the effect of the ac component of capacitor voltage on the current waveforms.

(d) The first obvious benefit is that I_p is reduced from $2i_{1(avg)}$ at $D = D_{min}$, to $1.1I_p$, thus reducing turnoff losses in S1. Secondly, if we assume that i_1 and i_2 are rectangular pulses for $L = 10L_c$, then the rms currents in the transformer windings are reduced by $\sqrt{2/3}$, so either copper losses are reduced by $2/3$ or the wire can be made smaller for the same losses as with $L = L_c$. The value of Δq, for an assumed rectangular pulse (i.e., $L \to \infty$), is determined by the equation

$$\Delta q = \left[\frac{V_2}{R(1 - D)} - \frac{V_2}{R}\right]\frac{(1 - D)}{f_s} = \frac{V_2 D}{Rf_s}$$

For $D = D_{max} = 0.549$ and $\Delta V_2 = 1$, as before, the result is

$$C > 23 \ \mu F$$

It should be clear from this example that in the boost and buck-boost converters, a minimum value of C is required regardless of the value of L. This is in contrast to the buck converter where, for a given ripple requirement, $C \to 0$ as $L \to \infty$.

2.2 The following questions relate to the current converter of Fig. P2.2, where it is assumed that the ac component of inductor current is negligible. (a) Prove Eq. (2.22c). (b) Determine V_c as a general function of V_2 and D, where it is assumed that V_2 is held constant by the control circuitry (not shown). (c) Plot i_c and v_c for $I_1 = 4$ amperes (A), $R = 2 \ \Omega$, $D = 0.25$, and $C = C_c$. (d) What is C_c for $f_s = 24$ kHz?

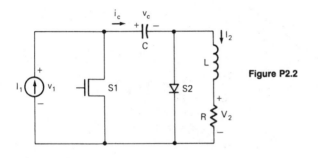

Figure P2.2

SOLUTION:

(a)
$$P_{in} = P_{out}$$

$$I_1 v_{1(avg)} = I_2^2 R$$

$$v_{1(avg)} = 0 \times D + V_c \times (1 - D)$$

$$\therefore V_c I_1(1 - D) = I_2^2 R \qquad C \geq C_c$$

Incidentally, this also shows that, physically, V_c must be in the polarity as shown. That is, the switching regulator cannot generate power to the source.

(b) Combining Eqs. (2.20b) and (2.22c) with the equation $I_2 = V_2/R$ results in

$$V_c = -\frac{V_2}{D}$$

Alternatively, one may view Fig. P2.2 and observe that V_2 is the average inductor voltage (which must be zero) plus the average voltage across S2. Defining v_{S2} as positive from anode to cathode, we have

$$V_2 = v_{S2(avg)} = -V_c D + 0 \times (1 - D)$$

where we take advantage of the fact that V_c is the average value of v_2 for any given switch condition as well as for the entire switching cycle. Viewed in this way, it is clear that this result also applies to the Ćuk converter of Fig. 2.13c.

(c) The values for the plots shown in Fig. S2.2 are determined below.

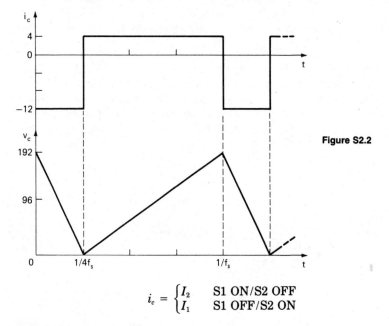

Figure S2.2

$$i_c = \begin{cases} I_2 & \text{S1 ON/S2 OFF} \\ I_1 & \text{S1 OFF/S2 ON} \end{cases}$$

From Eq. (2.20b), we have

$$I_2 = -12 \text{ A}$$

$$V_2 = -24 \text{ V}$$

From Part (b), we have

$$V_c = 96 \text{ V}$$

(d) From Eq. (2.23c), we have directly that

$$C_c = 0.651 \text{ }\mu\text{F}$$

The peak voltage rating must be greater than 192 V, and the ac rms current rating must be greater than

$$i_{c\text{(rms)}} = \sqrt{(12)^2(\frac{1}{4}) + (4)^2(\frac{3}{4})} = 6.93 \text{ A}$$

2.3   The task is to design the output filter of a 5-V/100-A 24-kHz push-pull converter so that the output ripple is less than 100 mV peak-to-peak (p-p) for $D = 0.5$. You are advised to use at least 10 times critical inductance in order to contain peak current stresses, and to use a family of 10-V dc aluminum electrolytic capacitors whose ESR predominates over the capacitive reactance at frequencies above 1 kHz and whose product of ESR in ohms and capacitance C in microfarads is approximately 750.

SOLUTION: Since the converter is push-pull, the effective switching frequency to the output filter is 48 kHz. From Eq. (2.11a), we have

$$L = 10L_c = \frac{10R(1 - D)}{2f_s}$$

$$= \frac{10(5/100)(1 - 0.5)}{2(48 \times 10^3)} = 2.6 \; \mu H$$

At critical inductance, the peak-to-peak inductor current $i_{L(p\text{-}p)}$ is twice $i_{L(dc)}$; at 10 times, it is one-fifth as much. The peak-to-peak ripple voltage $v_{r(p\text{-}p)}$ is as follows:

$$v_{r(p\text{-}p)} \approx ESR \times i_{L(p\text{-}p)}$$

$$0.1 \approx ESR \times \frac{100}{5}$$

$$ESR = 5 \; m\Omega$$

$$C = \frac{750}{(5 \times 10^{-3})} \; \mu F = 150,000 \; \mu F$$

2.4   In relation to Prob. 2.3, the magnetics vendor tells you that the estimated volume for a 2.6-μH 100-A inductor is approximately 6 cubic inches (in^3). Looking in the capacitor catalog, you determine that you will need to parallel at least two capacitors to achieve the 150,000 μF, totaling approximately 60 in^3. Since this is one of your first design assignments, you are surprised to discover that you cannot fit the filter into the prescribed volume. Assuming that the inductor volume is roughly proportional to L and that the capacitor volume is roughly proportional to C, investigate the possibility of reducing overall filter volume by increasing L and reducing C (i.e., increasing ESR).

SOLUTION:

$$v_{r(p\text{-}p)} = 0.1 \; V = 0.1 \frac{2.6 \times 10^{-6}}{L} \frac{ESR}{5 \times 10^{-3}}$$

$$C = (0.15)(5 \times 10^{-3}ESR)$$

$$LC = 3.9 \times 10^{-7}$$

$$Vol_C \approx \frac{C}{0.15} \; 60 \; in^3$$

$$Vol_L \approx \frac{L}{2.6 \times 10^{-6}} \; 6 \; in^3$$

$$\mathrm{Vol}_{LC} = \mathrm{Vol}_L + \mathrm{Vol}_C$$

$$= \frac{C}{0.15}\, 60 + \frac{L}{2.6 \times 10^{-6}}\, 6 \ \mathrm{in}^3$$

$$= \frac{C}{0.15}\, 60 + \frac{3.9 \times 10^{-7}}{2.6C \times 10^{-6}}\, 6 \ \mathrm{in}^3$$

To find a minimum, we set $d\mathrm{Vol}_{LC}/dC = 0$.

$$0 = \frac{60}{0.15} - \frac{3.9 \times 10^{-7}}{2.6C^2 \times 10^{-6}}\, 6$$

Multiplying through by C, we have

$$\frac{C}{0.15}\, 60 = \frac{3.9 \times 10^{-7}}{2.6C \times 10^{-6}}\, 6$$

$$C = 47{,}000 \ \mu\mathrm{F}$$

$$\mathrm{ESR} = 0.016$$

$$L = 8.3 \ \mu\mathrm{H} = 32L_c$$

$$\mathrm{Vol}_L = \mathrm{Vol}_C = 18.8 \ \mathrm{in}^3$$

$$\mathrm{Vol}_{LC} = 37.6 \ \mathrm{in}^3$$

$$\mathrm{Savings} = 28.4 \ \mathrm{in}^3$$

References

1. S. Ćuk and R. D. Middlebrook, "A General Unified Approach to Modelling Switching DC-to-DC Converters in Discontinuous Conduction Mode," *IEEE Power Electronics Specialists Conference Record,* June 1977, pp. 36–57.
2. S. Ćuk and R. D. Middlebrook, "A New Optimum Topology Switching DC-to-DC Converter," *IEEE Power Electronics Specialists Conference Record,* June 1977, pp. 160–169.
3. R. P. Massey and E. C. Snyder, "High Voltage Single-Ended DC-DC Converter," *IEEE Power Electronics Specialists Conference Record,* June 1977, pp. 156–159.
4. R. P. Severns and G. E. Bloom, *Modern DC-to-DC Switchmode Power Converter Circuits,* Van Nostrand, New York, 1985, chaps. 5, 6.
5. Ibid., chap. 12.
6. W. A. Geyger, *Nonlinear-Magnetic Control Devices,* McGraw-Hill, New York, 1964.
7. S. B. Dewan and A. Straughen, *Power Semiconductor Circuits,* Wiley, New York, 1975, sec. 7.7.
8. V. Vopérian and S. Ćuk, "A Complete DC Analysis of the Series Resonant Converter," *IEEE Power Electronics Specialists Conference Record,* June 1982, pp. 85–100.
9. R. L. Steigerwald, "High-Frequency Resonant Transistor DC-DC Converters," *IEEE Transactions on Industrial Electronics,* vol. IE-31, no. 2, May 1984, pp. 181–191.
10. K. H. Liu, R. Oruganti, and F. C. Lee, "Resonant Switches—Topologies and Characteristics," *IEEE Power Electronics Specialists Conference Record,* June 1985, pp. 106–116.

Chapter 3

Pulse-Width Modulation (PWM)

Electronic control of the basic power converter circuits discussed in Chap. 2 is achieved by modulating the duty factor d of the controlled switch S1, where the duty factor now consists of a variable term $\hat{d}$ in addition to the steady-state term D, which we have been using for steady-state analyses. For topologies with multiple-controlled switches that can be derived from the basic power converter circuits, d represents the total effective duty factor. Typically, the intent is to keep the output voltage constant, as determined by a dc reference signal, in the presence of time-varying sources and loads. However, there are applications where the reference signal may also be time-varying. As we shall see in Chap. 4, the amplitudes of these variations, relative to their respective steady-state values, help determine the analytical approach that may be taken to describe the total switching regulator behavior. In particular, for small enough amplitudes and low enough frequencies, relative to the switching frequency, it is possible to approximate the switching regulator as a linear system when, in fact, it is not even continuous.

Since the duty factor of S1 is defined as the ratio of its ON time to the switching period $1/f_s$ according to the equation

$$d = t_{ON}f_s = \frac{t_{ON}}{t_{ON} + t_{OFF}} \tag{3.1}$$

we see that d can be modulated by modulating either t_{ON} or t_{OFF}, or both. The technique of modulating the duration (or width) of the ON and/or OFF pulses that are applied from the control circuit to the control input of S1 is called "pulse-width modulation" (PWM).

Switching regulators can be classified as either variable-frequency or fixed-frequency. This is a useful distinction when considering electromagnetic interference (EMI) and compatibility (EMC). In principle, variable-frequency regulators can have (1) fixed t_{ON} and variable t_{OFF}, (2) fixed t_{OFF} and variable t_{ON}, or (3) variable t_{ON} and variable t_{OFF}. Naturally, PWM-controlled fixed-frequency regulators must have both variable t_{ON} and variable t_{OFF}.

Fixed ON time controllers are occasionally used in low-power boost and buck-boost regulators, where L is designed to be less than L_c, to provide a simple means of limiting peak switching current. Fixed OFF time control is sometimes used to ensure proper resetting of the transformer in single-ended configurations. Variable-frequency controllers with variable ON and OFF times are discussed in Sec. 3.1. Fixed-frequency controllers are discussed in Sec. 3.2.

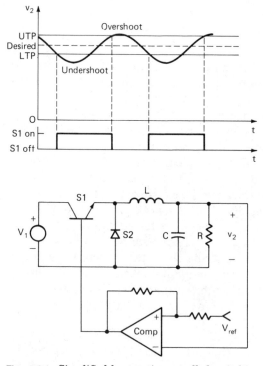

Figure 3.1 Simplified hysteretic-controlled switching regulator.

3.1   Hysteretic Controllers

Prior to the introduction of fixed-frequency integrated-circuit PWM controllers, perhaps the most common PWM control technique consisted simply of comparing the actual output, or an analog thereof, to a reference signal corresponding to the desired output (Fig. 3.1). With this technique, when the actual output becomes too low, S1 is turned on; when the output becomes too high, S1 is turned off. Neither t_{ON} nor t_{OFF} is fixed, and the variable frequency of operation is a function of R, L, C, and the hysteresis h, where h is the difference between the upper and lower trip points of the Schmitt-trigger comparator.* These regulators are variously described as hysteretic, free-running, asynchronous, or simply as bang-bang regulators. Hysteretic-controlled regulators are simple to implement and respond rapidly to sudden load changes, but they have an unpredictable noise spectrum, making EMI control more difficult.

3.2   Fixed-Frequency Controllers

Fixed-frequency PWM control is, by far, the switching regulator control technique that is most widely used today. Two reasons for this are (1) the ready availability of low-cost highly sophisticated fixed-frequency PWM integrated-circuit (IC) controllers and (2) the growing need to minimize the spurious emissions of switching regulators in increasingly sensitive computational and communicative environments. As we shall see in the next section, the switching regulator is a prolific noise generator. The task of containing this noise is made easier by fixed-frequency operation. With proper filtering, grounding, bonding, and shielding, switching regulators can be successfully used in EMI-sensitive applications.

There are many ways that fixed-frequency PWM control can be implemented, including the use of microprocessors and digital signal processing circuits with appropriate analog-to-digital converters. Nevertheless, the basic ingredients of almost all existing PWM IC controllers that are used for simple voltage control are (1) an adjustable clock for setting the switching frequency, (2) an output voltage error amplifier, (3) a sawtooth generator for providing a sawtooth signal that is synchronized to the clock, and (4) a comparator that compares the output error signal with the sawtooth signal. The output of the comparator is the signal from which the drive to the controlled switches is derived.

---

* In practice, the value of capacitor ESR may dominate over the value of C.

Figure 3.2 shows a simple PWM controller with a fixed-frequency fixed-amplitude sawtooth signal applied to the basic buck converter. The width of the PWM ON pulse is the time between the reset of the sawtooth generator and the intersection of the error voltage with the positive-going sawtooth signal, or ramp. If v_e is the error voltage amplitude, which is assumed to change slowly with respect to the switching frequency, and V_p is the sawtooth voltage amplitude, then the duty factor can be approximated by the continuous expression

$$d = \frac{v_e}{V_p} \tag{3.2}$$

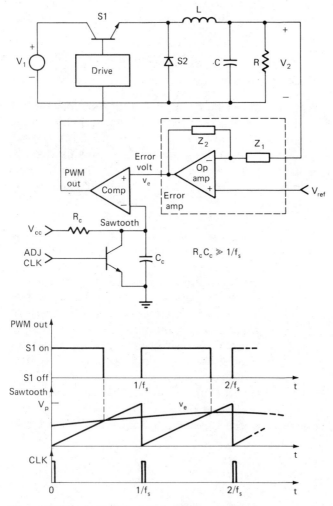

Figure 3.2 Simple fixed-frequency PWM controller.

A lower than desired output voltage produces a high error voltage and, thus, a longer ON pulse which, in turn, results in an increased output voltage. The operational amplifier's feedback network, consisting of Z_1 and Z_2, helps determine the stability and response of the switching regulator. If K is the dc gain of the error amplifier and V_2' is the open-loop input voltage to the error amplifier, then the dc open-loop gain $G_0 H_0$ is

$$G_0 H_0 = \frac{V_2}{V_2'} = \frac{V_1 D}{V_2'} = \frac{V_1 V_e}{V_2' V_p} = \frac{V_1 K V_2'}{V_2' V_p} = \frac{V_1 K}{V_p} \qquad (3.3)$$

If the output voltage is divided down to the reference voltage prior to being fed to the error amplifier, then $G_0 H_0$ is correspondingly reduced. Note that the value of dc gain in Eq. (3.3) depends directly upon the value of input voltage V_1. For applications with wide input voltage ranges, there may be a problem in maintaining enough gain at $V_{1(min)}$ to meet performance requirements without risking instability at $V_{1(max)}$.

This problem can be overcome by using so-called feed-forward control in which the sawtooth supply voltage V_{cc} is derived from the input supply voltage V_1. In this case, the peak sawtooth voltage V_p is directly proportional to V_1. As can be seen from Eq. (3.3), the dc open-loop gain $G_0 H_0$ is then constant over the full range of values of V_1. Furthermore, for a fixed value of v_e, V_2 is constant over variations in V_1. This means that, ideally, line regulation can be maintained using only feed-forward control, allowing the feedback control loop to be optimized for load regulation. This feed-forward PWM control technique as described is limited to buck-derived regulators. Unfortunately, the sawtooth generators of most present-day IC controllers operate from an internally derived V_{cc}, so feed-forward control is not possible. On the other hand, these IC controllers have many built-in protection and monitoring features that designers did not always include in their older discrete-component PWM control circuit designs.

PWM controllers that are modeled after Fig. 3.2, whether they use a fixed sawtooth amplitude or not, are often called "voltage-mode" controllers since only voltage information is used. It will be shown in Chap. 6 that current information, in addition to voltage information, can be used to significant advantage, particularly for boost- and buck-boost-derived switching regulators. One way of adding current information is to use an analog of the switching current waveform in place of the sawtooth generator; after all, the ac component of the inductor current waveform is a sawtooth also. A voltage analog of the switching current waveform can be provided with a small current-sense resistor that is otherwise negligible. In practice, a resettable current transformer for isolation and scaling might also be used. Since only the positive-going portion of the sawtooth waveform is required, the current-sense means can be placed in series with the controlled switches. This control technique is variously called "current-mode" control, to distinguish it from voltage-mode control, or "current-injected" control. The author's preference is current-injected control, since this term more accurately conveys the notion that voltage information is being augmented by, not replaced by, current information. Figure 3.3 shows, in simplified form, the basic boost converter implemented with current-injected control.

For a given cycle of operation, turn-on is coincident with the clock pulse and turnoff is coincident with the time that the analog voltage of the controlled switch current intercepts the error voltage v_e. In ad-

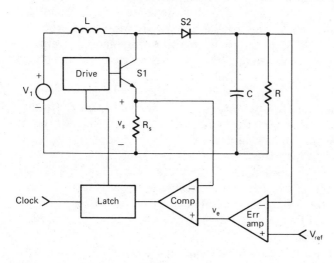

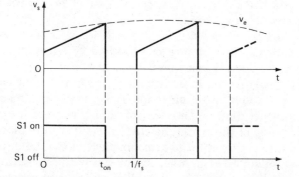

Figure 3.3 Basic boost converter with simplified current-injected control.

dition to any performance advantages, current-injected control provides inherent peak current limiting, thus enhancing the reliability of the controlled switches. Peak current limiting is a desirable feature that must be separately provided in the basic voltage-mode controller. However, as we shall see, there are applications where voltage-mode control may still be preferred. Also, as practical matters, current-injected control is somewhat more difficult to implement and there are fewer available PWM IC current-injected controllers today.

3.3 PWM Waveform Spectral Analysis

Regardless of which of the above control techniques is used, the PWM output waveform can be represented by the normalized pulse train $m(t)$ shown in Fig. 3.4. The pulse width of the nth cycle d_n/f_s is the duty factor of the nth cycle divided by the switching frequency. It consists of (1) a fixed component D/f_s that is determined by the steady-state values of source, load, and reference, and (2) a modulating component $\hat{d}_n/f_s$ that is determined by the time variations in source, load, and reference. As shown, turn-on always occurs at the beginning of the cycle, whereas the relative turnoff times are variable. Consequently, this particular method of PWM control is sometimes described as "trailing-edge" modulation. Conceptually, one could just as well have "leading-edge" modulation or a combination of both trailing-edge and leading-edge modulation. However, the practical differences are small[1] and only trailing-edge modulation will be considered further, particularly since nearly all PWM IC controllers use this method.

The pulse train of Fig. 3.4 is representative of the input switching current in buck-derived converters, the output switching current in boost-derived converters, and both input and output switching currents in buck-boost-derived converters. It also represents the voltage waveform applied to the output filter of buck-derived converters. Furthermore, for any of the PWM switching regulators, it is representative of

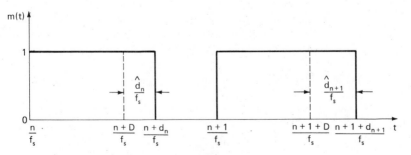

Figure 3.4 Normalized PWM output waveform.

the source of radiated electric and magnetic fields. Thus, an analysis of the frequency spectrum of the PWM output waveform would provide useful information for predicting system noise and for designing associated filters.

In performing this analysis, we consider the situation where the error voltage v_e consists of a dc component V_e and a time-varying component $V_{e1} \sin 2\pi f_m t$, where f_m is the modulation frequency of a variation in source, load, or reference signal. The modulation in error voltage gives rise to a corresponding modulation in duty factor. The duty factor for any given cycle is determined by the exact time at which the positive-going sawtooth intercepts the modulating error signal in accordance with the transcendental equation

$$d_n = D + D_1 \sin \frac{2\pi f_m(n + d_n)}{f_s} \tag{3.4}$$

where D_1 is the peak variation in duty factor. Such a system is sometimes referred to as a "real-time" sampling system, since the pulse widths are not determined prior to the completion of the pulses. In an explicit sample-and-hold PWM system, the pulse widths are predetermined at the beginnings of the pulses, coincident with the clock pulses, according to the equation

$$d_n = D + D_1 \sin \frac{2\pi f_m n}{f_s} \tag{3.5}$$

For the sample-and-hold case, there is an associated transport lag of $2\pi f_m D/f_s$ radians (rad). For high enough modulation frequencies with respect to the switching frequency, the transport lag can be significant and must be included in any loop stability analysis. Real-time sampling systems exhibit no transport lag.[2,3]

The PWM output waveform $m(t)$, as shown in Fig. 3.4, can be expressed as a Fourier series according to the equation

$$m(t) = \sum_{k=1}^{\infty} a_k \sin 2\pi k f_m t + \sum_{k=1}^{\infty} b_k \cos 2\pi k f_m t + D \tag{3.6}$$

where

$$a_k = 2f_m \int_0^{1/f_m} m(t) \sin 2\pi k f_m t \, dt = 2f_m \sum_{n=1}^{r} \int_{n/f_s}^{(n+d_n)/f_s} \sin 2\pi k f_m t \, dt$$

$$\tag{3.7a}$$

and

$$b_k = 2f_m \int_0^{1/f_m} m(t) \cos 2\pi k f_m t \, dt = 2f_m \sum_{n=1}^{r} \int_{n/f_s}^{(n+d_n)/f_s} \cos 2\pi k f_m t \, dt \tag{3.7b}$$

where r is the ratio of switching frequency to modulation frequency f_s/f_m. Solving Eqs. (3.7a) and (3.7b) results in

$$a_k = \frac{1}{\pi k} \sum_{n=1}^{r} \left[\cos \frac{2\pi k n}{r} - \cos \frac{2\pi k(n + d_n)}{r} \right] \tag{3.8a}$$

and

$$b_k = \frac{1}{\pi k} \sum_{n=1}^{r} \left[\sin \frac{2\pi k(n + d_n)}{r} - \sin \frac{2\pi k n}{r} \right] \tag{3.8b}$$

or

$$a_k = \frac{1}{\pi k} \sum_{n=1}^{r} \left(\cos \frac{2\pi k n}{r} - \cos \frac{2\pi k n}{r} \cos \frac{2\pi k d_n}{r} \right.$$
$$\left. + \sin \frac{2\pi k n}{r} \sin \frac{2\pi k d_n}{r} \right) \tag{3.9a}$$

and

$$b_k = \frac{1}{\pi k} \sum_{n=1}^{r} \left(\sin \frac{2\pi k n}{r} \cos \frac{2\pi k d_n}{r} + \sin \frac{2\pi k d_n}{r} \cos \frac{2\pi k n}{r} - \sin \frac{2\pi k n}{r} \right) \tag{3.9b}$$

Since Eq. (3.4) is transcendental, there is no sense in using it for d_n in Eq. (3.9) at this point; we would only get d_n back again. Therefore, some sort of reasonable approximation must be made in order to carry this analysis forward in closed form. We recognize from Eq. (3.4) that

$$\hat{d}_n = D_1 \sin \frac{2\pi(n + d_n)}{r} \tag{3.10}$$

Trigonometrically expanding Eq. (3.10), substituting $d_n = D + \hat{d}_n$, and expanding again results in

$$\hat{d}_n = D_1 \sin \frac{2\pi n}{r} \left(\cos \frac{2\pi D}{r} \cos \frac{2\pi \hat{d}_n}{r} - \sin \frac{2\pi D}{r} \sin \frac{2\pi \hat{d}_n}{r} \right)$$
$$+ D_1 \cos \frac{2\pi n}{r} \left(\sin \frac{2\pi D}{r} \cos \frac{2\pi \hat{d}_n}{r} + \sin \frac{2\pi \hat{d}_n}{r} \cos \frac{2\pi D}{r} \right) \tag{3.11}$$

It will now be assumed that the peak duty factor variation D_1 is small enough and the ratio of switching frequency to modulation frequency r is large enough so that the following approximations are valid:

$$\cos \frac{2\pi \hat{d}_n}{r} \approx 1 \qquad (3.12a)$$

and

$$\sin \frac{2\pi \hat{d}_n}{r} \approx \frac{2\pi \hat{d}_n}{r} \qquad (3.12b)$$

Combining Eqs. (3.11) and (3.12) results in

$$\hat{d}_n = \frac{D_1 \sin [2\pi(n + D)/r]}{1 - (2\pi D_1/r) \cos [2\pi(n + D)/r]} \qquad (3.13)$$

or

$$d_n = D + \frac{D_1 \sin [2\pi(n + D)/r]}{1 - (2\pi D_1/r) \cos [2\pi(n + D)/r]} \qquad (3.14)$$

Equation (3.14) can now be substituted into Eq. (3.9) to solve explicitly for a_k and b_k, given r, D_1, and D.

Computer design aids can be used to good advantage in predicting the spectrum of a PWM waveform. For example, a personal computer

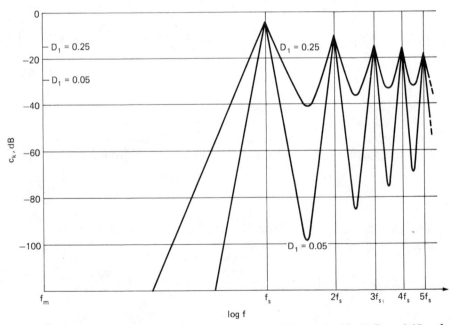

Figure 3.5 Normalized PWM spectrum for $f_s = 10f_m$ and $D = 0.5$ with (1) $D_1 = 0.05$ and (2) $D_1 = 0.25$.

program[4] has been written that, for user-entered values of r, D, and D_1, calculates $c_k = \sqrt{a_k^2 + b_k^2}$ for $k = 1$ (i.e., the modulation frequency), for $k = r$, $r \pm 1$, $r \pm 2$, $r \pm 3$, $r \pm 4$ and $r \pm 5$ (i.e., the switching frequency and the first five modulation frequency increments about either side), and for the corresponding points about the first four harmonics of the switching frequency. Figure 3.5 shows these spectral points for $r = 10$, $D = 0.5$, and $D_1 = 0.05$, and also for $D_1 = 0.25$. A factor of 5 corresponds to 14 decibels (dB); however, several points were increased by more than 14 dB in going from $D_1 = 0.05$ to $D_1 = 0.25$, showing the nonlinear operation of a pulse-width modulator.

In addition to providing a quantitative means for predicting noise external to the switching regulator, programs such as this can be used to predict the behavior of the switching regulator itself in the presence of its own noise. In particular, it is possible for harmonics of the modulation frequency to mix with the switching frequency in such a way that the harmonics are reinforced, according to the equation

$$f_s - kf_m = kf_m \qquad (3.15a)$$

or

$$f_m = \frac{f_s}{2k} \qquad (3.15b)$$

Switching regulators have been observed that sustain so-called subharmonic oscillations at one-half and sometimes even one-fourth of the switching frequency. Particularly susceptible are push-pull and bridge converters, where a significant $f_s/2$ component may inherently exist because of power circuit imbalances. In general, the higher the unity-gain cross-over frequency of the open-loop gain, the greater the susceptibility to subharmonic oscillations. With computer design aids, this risk can be quantitatively assessed.

3.4 Illustrative Problems

3.1 A 100 kHz half-bridge converter [Fig. 2.15(d)] operates from a three-phase full-wave-rectified 400-Hz aircraft bus and produces 50 V dc at 20 A dc for a solid-state power amplifier with a nominal effective duty factor of 0.5. The wideband feedback control circuitry is designed to maintain good dynamic output voltage regulation for load modulation frequencies up to 20 kHz, where the ac duty factor variation can be as much as ±10 percent. To save the development effort of a second power supply, a low-power 24-V dc output was included whose regulation depends upon the 50-V dc control loop. The 24-V dc output has an LC filter with $L > L_c$ and 40-dB rejection at 200 kHz.

It now turns out that although the 24-V dc load is nearly constant and is tolerant to absolute voltage variations, it is extremely sensitive to any 160-kHz signals greater than 1 mV rms. The original power supply designer says that there is no problem since there can only be the 200-kHz effective frequency component and harmonics thereof. What do you say?

SOLUTION: Consider the situation at $f_m = 20$ kHz.

$$r = \frac{f_s}{f_m} = \frac{200 \text{ kHz}}{20 \text{ kHz}} = 10$$

$$k = \frac{160 \text{ kHz}}{20 \text{ kHz}} = 8 = r - 2$$

$$D_1 = 0.1(D) = 0.01$$

From Fig. 3.5, the spectral content of the normalized PWM waveform at 160 kHz is -50 dB. For $D = 0.5$, the pulse amplitude must be 48 V dc for a 24-V dc output. Thus, the peak 160-kHz component into the output filter is

$$-50 \text{ dB} + 20 \log 48 = -16.4 \text{ dB}$$

The filter rejection at 160 kHz is

$$-40 \text{ dB} + 20 \log \left(\frac{200}{160}\right)^2 = -36.1 \text{ dB}$$

Thus, the peak 160-kHz component out of the filter is

$$-16.4 \text{ dB} - 36.1 \text{ dB} = -52.5 \text{ dB}$$

$$-52.5 \text{ dB} \rightarrow 2.5 \text{ mV pk} = 1.78 \text{ mV root mean square (rms)}$$

$$1.78 \text{ mV rms} > 1 \text{ mV rms}$$

Therefore, trouble is possible, even without considering the imbalancing effects of the half-bridge converter, which can produce a 100-kHz output that is subject to modulation as well, and without considering possible source modulations.

3.2   In Sec. 3.3, it was stated that real-time sampling systems exhibit no transport lag. What is the effect of a time delay t_d between the "real time" that the sawtooth intercepts the error signal and the time that S1 actually turns off?

SOLUTION: The duty factor of the nth cycle d_n, instead of being $D + \hat{d}_n$, is now determined by the equation

$$d_n = D + \hat{d}_n + t_d f_s$$

The control loop still maintains nearly constant dc output voltage, so the new value of D is smaller by the amount $t_d f_s$, corresponding to a lower value of dc error voltage v_e. From Eq. (3.6), it is clear that any phase shift at the modulation frequency between the PWM output signal $m(t)$ and the time-varying error voltage component $v_{e1} \sin 2\pi f_m t$ can be expressed as

$$\phi_1 = \tan^{-1} \frac{b_1}{a_1}$$

Substituting the new expression for d_n into Eq. (3.8a) for $k = 1$ results in

$$a_1 = \frac{1}{\pi} \sum_{n=1}^{r} -\cos \frac{2\pi}{r}(n + D + \hat{d}_n + t_{df_s})$$

where it is recognized that

$$\sum_{n=1}^{r} \cos \frac{2\pi n}{r} = 0 \qquad r > 1$$

Trigonometrically expanding, we have

$$a_1 = \frac{1}{\pi} \sum_{n=1}^{r} \left[\sin \frac{2\pi}{r}(n + D) \sin \frac{2\pi}{r}(\hat{d}_n + t_{df_s}) \right.$$

$$\left. - \cos \frac{2\pi}{r}(n + D) \cos \frac{2\pi}{r}(\hat{d}_n + t_{df_s}) \right] \qquad r > 1$$

Using Eq. (3.12) and expanding again gives us

$$a_1 = \frac{1}{\pi} \sum_{n=1}^{r} \left[\sin \frac{2\pi}{r}(n + D) \sin \frac{2\pi t_{df_s}}{r} \right.$$

$$+ \frac{2\pi \hat{d}_n}{r} \cos \frac{2\pi t_{df_s}}{r} \sin \frac{2\pi}{r}(n + D)$$

$$- \cos \frac{2\pi}{r}(n + D) \cos \frac{2\pi t_{df_s}}{r}$$

$$\left. + \frac{2\pi \hat{d}_n}{r} \sin \frac{2\pi t_{df_s}}{r} \cos \frac{2\pi}{r}(n + D) \right] \qquad r > 1$$

Substituting Eq. (3.13), where it is assumed that $2\pi D_1/r \ll 1$, for $\hat{d}_n$ above and recognizing that

$$\sum_{n=1}^{r} \sin \frac{2\pi}{r}(n + D) = \sum_{n=1}^{r} \cos \frac{2\pi}{r}(n + D) = 0 \qquad r > 1$$

results in

$$a_1 = \frac{1}{\pi} \sum_{n=1}^{r} \left[\frac{2\pi D_1}{r} \cos \frac{2\pi t_{df_s}}{r} \sin^2 \frac{2\pi}{r}(n + D) \right.$$

$$\left. + \frac{2\pi D_1}{r} \sin \frac{2\pi t_{df_s}}{r} \sin \frac{2\pi}{r}(n + D) \cos \frac{2\pi}{r}(n + D) \right] \qquad r > 1$$

Substituting the trigonometric identities

$$\sin^2\alpha = \tfrac{1}{2}(1 - \cos 2\alpha)$$

and

$$\sin\alpha \cos\alpha = \tfrac{1}{2}\sin 2\alpha$$

into the equation above yields

$$a_1 = \frac{D_1}{r}\sum_{n=1}^{r}\left\{\cos\frac{2\pi t_d f_s}{r}\left[1 - \cos\frac{4\pi}{r}(n+D)\right]\right.$$

$$\left. + \sin\frac{2\pi t_d f_s}{r}\sin\frac{4\pi}{r}(n+D)\right\}\qquad r > 1$$

Since

$$\sum_{n=1}^{r}\cos\frac{4\pi}{r}(n+D) = \sum_{n=1}^{r}\sin\frac{4\pi}{r}(n+D) = 0\qquad r > 2$$

and

$$\sum_{n=1}^{r}1 = r$$

we arrive at

$$a_1 = D_1\cos\frac{2\pi t_d f_s}{r}$$

Similarly,

$$b_1 = -D_1\sin\frac{2\pi t_d f_s}{r}$$

Thus,

$$\phi_1 = -\tan^{-1}\left(\tan\frac{2\pi t_d f_s}{r}\right) = -\frac{2\pi t_d f_s}{r} = -2\pi t_d f_m$$

This is, for example, the phase shift due to a switching transistor with a storage time t_d, even in a so-called real-time sampling system. If the storage times of the transistors in a push-pull converter operating at 300 kHz are 1 microsecond (μs), then the modulator phase shift at one-tenth the effective switching frequency is

$$\phi_1 = -2\pi \times 10^{-6} \times 60 \times 10^3 = -0.377\text{ rad} = -21.6°$$

This may not be a trivial consideration in a wideband lead-compensated*

---

* This is discussed further in Chap. 5.

system. The result of $\phi_1 = -2\pi t_d f_m$ is also sufficient to prove the statement that transport lag of a sample-and-hold pulse-width modulator is $\phi_1 = -2\pi f_m D/f_s$, where D/f_s is interpreted here as the total delay for the case where the pulse width is determined at the beginning of the switching period.

References

1. W. R. Kolk, "A Study of Pulse Width Modulation in Feedback Control Systems," Ph.D. dissertation, Univ. of Conn., 1972.
2. D. M. Mitchell, "Pulsewidth Modulator Phase Shift," *IEEE Transactions on Aerospace and Electronic Systems,* vol. AES-16, no. 3, May 1980, pp. 272–278.
3. R. D. Middlebrook, "Predicting Modulator Phase Lag in PWM Converter Feedback Loops," *Proceedings of Powercon 8,* Power Concepts, Inc., Ventura, CA, April 1981.
4. D. M. Mitchell, "Spectral Analysis of Pulse-Width Modulated (PWM) Waveforms," Rockwell International Working Paper WP84-2023, July 1984.

Chapter 4

State-Space Averaging
and Linearization

State-space averaging and linearization are analytical approximation techniques that allow switching regulators to be represented as linear systems. More specifically, (1) state-space averaging allows the switched (i.e., discontinuous) system to be approximated as a continuous but, as we shall see, nonlinear system, and (2) linearization allows the resulting nonlinear system to be approximated as a linear system. The criterion for the continuity approximation is that the circuit natural frequencies and all modulation, or signal, frequencies of interest must be sufficiently low with respect to the switching frequency. The criterion for the linearity approximation is that the time variations, or ac excursions, of the pertinent variables about their respective dc operating points must be sufficiently small.

One might well question the motivation for approximating the switching regulator as a linear system in the first place. After all, computer-aided analyses[1,2] could be performed that would be highly accurate without the need for these approximations. In fact, for cases where the frequencies are not low enough or the amplitudes are not small enough, one has no choice. However, aside from the obvious situations where a computer is not readily available or where the time and cost of any necessary programming cannot be easily accommodated, an approximated linear analysis may prove useful as a basis for corroborating the computer solutions. Furthermore, it can be argued that understanding the techniques of linearized switching regulator analysis facilitates the understanding of switching regulator behavior in general. Needless to say, the computer can often be used to good advantage even for linear analyses. Before explaining exactly what we mean by "low enough" and "small enough," and how these two approximation techniques are applied, a brief review of modern linear systems analyses will be presented, along with the rationale for choosing this approach over the classical approach.

4.1   Review of Modern Linear Systems Analysis

Any nth-order linear or nonlinear differential equation in one time-dependent variable y can be written as n first-order differential equations in n time-dependent variables x_1 through x_n. Consider, for example, the third-order equation

$$\dddot{y} + a_2\ddot{y} + a_1\dot{y} + a_0y = 0 \tag{4.1}$$

Let y be x_1. Then Eq. (4.1) can be represented by the three equations

$$\dot{x}_1 = x_2 \tag{4.2a}$$

$$\dot{x}_2 = x_3 \tag{4.2b}$$

$$\dot{x}_3 = -a_0x_1 - a_1x_2 - a_2x_3 \tag{4.2c}$$

In either case, n initial conditions must be known before an exact solution can be found. For any nth-order system, a set of n independent variables is necessary and sufficient to describe that system completely. These variables are called the "state variables." x_1, x_2, and x_3 are the state variables for the third-order system represented by Eq. (4.2). If we know the n independent initial conditions for a linear system at time $t = t_0$, then, for a given set of sources, we know everything about that system (i.e., its state) for all time $t > t_0$. For nonlinear systems, the initial conditions must be updated on a moment-to-moment basis, making computer-aided analysis virtually essential. Any linear system output variable can be uniquely expressed in terms of the state variables and the source variables.

Any output variable and its $n - 1$ derivatives can serve as a set of state variables. In fact, that is how Eq. (4.2) was obtained from Eq. (4.1). State variables chosen in this way are referred to as "phase variables." However, any choice of variables that results in n independent first-order differential equations is mathematically acceptable. Thus, the state variables are not unique.* Nevertheless, for systems involving switching regulators, the n initial conditions can be related to capacitor voltages and inductor currents. Therefore, we might as well use capacitor voltages and inductor currents for state variables in the first place. Although the effects of component nonlinearity are beyond the scope of this book, a side benefit of this choice of state variables is that systems for which inductance is a function of inductor current and capacitance is a function of capacitor voltage can be more easily described. Furthermore, even in a so-called linear system, any inductor with a magnetic core will eventually saturate with high enough current and any capacitor will eventually break down with high enough voltage; this choice of state variables allows the associated linearity and breakdown constraints to be more easily observed. It should be pointed out that all inductor currents and all capacitor voltages are not necessarily independent. Two obvious degenerate cases are capacitors in parallel and inductors in series. However, as we shall see, there is a simple test for independence. None of the basic switching regulator topologies discussed in Chap. 2 has any degenerate case.

As an illustrative example of modern linear systems analysis, consider the simple second-order network in Fig. 4.1. To be consistent with the literature on modern network analysis,[3] all state variables are subscripted x's and all source variables are subscripted u's.

We can apply Kirchoff's voltage law to arrive at a first-order equation in $\dot{x}_1$, namely,

$$u_1 = L\dot{x}_1 + x_2 \tag{4.3}$$

and apply Kirchoff's current law to arrive at a first-order equation in $\dot{x}_2$, namely,

$$x_1 = C\dot{x}_2 + \frac{1}{R}x_2 \tag{4.4}$$

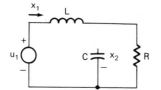

Figure 4.1 Simple second-order network.

---

* For example, any point on this two-dimensional page can be expressed in terms of one of an infinite number of unit vector pairs, as long as the two vectors comprising such a pair are not parallel.

Suppose we want to find the transfer function $X_2(s)/U_1(s)$. In the classical approach, Eqs. (4.3) and (4.4) are combined to form the equation

$$\ddot{x}_2 + \frac{1}{RC}\dot{x}_2 + \frac{1}{LC}x_2 = \frac{1}{LC}u_1 \tag{4.5}$$

resulting in the transfer function

$$\frac{X_2(s)}{U_1(s)} = \frac{\dfrac{1}{LC}}{s^2 + \dfrac{1}{RC}s + \dfrac{1}{LC}} \tag{4.6}$$

Visibility of x_1 is lost. However, we still need to know the initial value $x_1(t_0)$ to solve for x_2 where $t > t_0$. [We might also have arrived at Eq. (4.6) by using circuit impedances.]

In the modern approach, we rearrange Eqs. (4.3) and (4.4):

$$\dot{x}_1 = \frac{-1}{L}x_2 + \frac{1}{L}u_1 \tag{4.7a}$$

$$\dot{x}_2 = \frac{1}{C}x_1 - \frac{1}{RC}x_2 \tag{4.7b}$$

These equations then fit the universal format

$$\dot{\mathbf{x}} = \mathbf{Ax} + \mathbf{Bu} \tag{4.8}$$

where $\mathbf{x}$ = state vector
  $\mathbf{A}$ = state coefficient matrix
  $\mathbf{u}$ = source vector
  $\mathbf{B}$ = source coefficient matrix

For our example, we have the following:

(a)
$$\mathbf{x} = \begin{bmatrix} x_1 \\ x_2 \end{bmatrix}$$

(b)
$$\mathbf{A} = \begin{bmatrix} 0 & -\dfrac{1}{L} \\ \dfrac{1}{C} & -\dfrac{1}{RC} \end{bmatrix}$$

(c)
$$\mathbf{u} = u_1$$

(d)
$$\mathbf{B} = \begin{bmatrix} \dfrac{1}{L} \\ 0 \end{bmatrix}$$

$$\tag{4.9}$$

In the most general case, $\mathbf{A}$ and $\mathbf{B}$ may be functions of $\mathbf{x}$ and/or $\mathbf{u}$, in which case Eq. (4.8) is nonlinear.

If we assume that Eq. (4.8) is linear, then the dc solution, obtained by setting $\dot{\mathbf{x}} = \mathbf{0}$, is $\mathbf{x} = -\mathbf{A}^{-1}\mathbf{Bu}$. The inverse of a matrix is the adjoint divided by the determinant. Since division by zero is not allowed, the criterion for a valid dc solution, corresponding to a linearly independent set of state variables, is that the determinant of $\mathbf{A}$ be nonzero. That is, a necessary and sufficient condition for linearly independent state variables is that det $\mathbf{A} \neq 0$. If Eq. (4.8) is linear, we can take the Laplace transform, resulting in the equation

$$s\mathbf{X}(s) = \mathbf{A}\mathbf{x}(s) + \mathbf{B}\mathbf{U}(s) \tag{4.10a}$$

or

$$\mathbf{X}(s) = (s\mathbf{I} - \mathbf{A})^{-1}\mathbf{B}\mathbf{U}(s) \tag{4.10b}$$

where $\mathbf{I}$ is the identity matrix. The general transfer function between state and source variables is $(s\mathbf{I} - \mathbf{A})^{-1}\mathbf{B}$. For our example, we have the equation

$$\begin{bmatrix} X_1(s) \\ X_2(s) \end{bmatrix} = \frac{\begin{bmatrix} s + \dfrac{1}{RC} & -\dfrac{1}{L} \\ \dfrac{1}{C} & s \end{bmatrix} \begin{bmatrix} \dfrac{1}{L} \\ 0 \end{bmatrix} U_1(s)}{s^2 + \dfrac{1}{RC}s + \dfrac{1}{LC}} \tag{4.11}$$

or

$$\frac{X_1(s)}{U_1(s)} = \frac{\dfrac{1}{L}\left(s + \dfrac{1}{RC}\right)}{s^2 + \dfrac{1}{RC}s + \dfrac{1}{LC}} \tag{4.12a}$$

and

$$\frac{X_2(s)}{U_1(s)} = \frac{\dfrac{1}{LC}}{s^2 + \dfrac{1}{RC}s + \dfrac{1}{LC}} \tag{4.12b}$$

With the modern approach, visibility of all state variables is maintained, at the expense of finding the inverse of an $n \times n$ matrix. This brings up yet another advantage of the modern approach, namely, its adaptability to feedback control systems. In an nth-order system, n independent variables must, in general, be fed back for optimal control. The feedback variables do not necessarily have to be the state variables; however, the state variables must be known in order for the feedback variables to be known. As a matter of fact, it was the pursuit of solutions to optimal control problems that provided much of the motivation for the development of the modern approach. Finally, the uniform notation of the modern approach facilitates generalized computer analysis programs and conceptually emphasizes system similarities instead of system differences. Having established the basic analytical approach and associated notation, we shall carry on our discussion of the two subject approximation techniques.

4.2   State-Space-Averaging Approximation for Continuity

The first point to be made is that we are all already familiar with the concept of state-space averaging, whether we realize it or not. In our everyday lives we are constantly averaging out discrete phenomena, either in space or time, to achieve continuity. When we watch television, we are not usually aware of the raster nor of the color dots, unless there is a convergence problem; at the cinema, we are not conscious of the fact that we are watching 24 discrete frames per second, until the wagon wheel spokes start going backward; we do not see Monet's brush strokes from across the room; ever since utilities went from 25 to 60 Hz, we are not bothered by flicker in incandescent lamps; a spinning top that is half yellow and half red appears orange if it spins fast enough; and you can think of your own even better examples.

The key ingredient for space continuity is, of course, that the size of interest must be large with respect to the size of the discrete parts. The key ingredients for time continuity are that (1) the rate of change of the desired information must be slow with respect to the rate of change of the discrete events (otherwise, as in the case of rotating wagon wheels in a cinema, the information received can be false) and (2) there must be some means of storing information from one discrete event to the next.

In the case of switching regulators, the inductors and capacitors serve to store information, or energy, as dictated by the control signals. If we color the switch condition S1 ON/S2 OFF red and the switch condition S1 OFF/S2 ON yellow, we can get orange if the switching frequency is high enough, and, through pulse-width modulation, we can vary the shade of that orange. With these introductory remarks we are now prepared for the mathematical treatment of state-space averaging for switching regulators.

As can be inferred from Eq. (4.8), all of the state variables and their derivatives must be continuous in order for the system to be continuous. Switching regulators fail this test since the voltage across the main filter inductor, hence, the derivative of inductor current, is discontinuous (assuming ideal switching). As a result, we cannot describe any of the basic switching regulator topologies by Eq. (4.8) for any time interval that is long enough to include a discontinuity. However, for any given switch condition, Eq. (4.8) does apply, and, in fact, the coefficient matrices are constant. This indicates that the discontinuous system consists of two alternating linear systems. We define $\mathbf{A}_1$ and $\mathbf{B}_1$ as the coefficient matrices for the switch condition S1 ON/S2 OFF and define $\mathbf{A}_2$ and $\mathbf{B}_2$ as the coefficient matrices for the switch condition S1 OFF/S2 ON. S1 ON refers to the ON time of a single controlled switch or, in the case of multiple dependently controlled switches as in Sec. 2.7, to the effective ON time as viewed from either the source or the load.

Thus, the system under discussion can be represented by

$$\dot{\mathbf{x}}(t) = \mathbf{A}_1\mathbf{x}(t) + \mathbf{B}_1\mathbf{u}(t) \qquad \frac{n}{f_s} \le t < \frac{n + d_n}{f_s} \qquad (4.13a)$$

and

$$\dot{\mathbf{x}}(t) = \mathbf{A}_2\mathbf{x}(t) + \mathbf{B}_2\mathbf{u}(t) \qquad \frac{n + d_n}{f_s} \le t < \frac{n + 1}{f_s} \qquad (4.13b)$$

where the switching times correspond to the PWM waveform of Fig. 3.4, and where, for present purposes, the time dependency of $\mathbf{x}$ and $\mathbf{u}$ is explicitly noted. The time intervals have been chosen so that $\dot{\mathbf{x}}(t)$ in either Eq. (4.13a) or (4.13b) is single-valued. However, Eq. (4.13b) cannot continuously follow Eq. (4.13a) since $\dot{\mathbf{x}}[(n + d_n)/f_s - \epsilon]$ as described by Eq. (4.13a) cannot equal $\dot{\mathbf{x}}[(n + d_n)/f_s]$ as described by Eq. (4.13b) no matter how closely ϵ approaches zero. Therefore, the only hope of achieving a continuous description of the discontinuous system is to exclude the switching components of the $\mathbf{x}(t)$ waveforms.

Obviously, this does not mean that switching information is unimportant. Even though this information may be strictly noise to the outside world, it is very important for the switching regulator designer to know such things as peak inductor current and the output ripple voltage. What this does mean is that the switching information must be determined by separate time-domain analyses. In practice, these analyses are very straightforward, since only fixed worst-case duty factors are typically assumed. In the case of the basic buck converter, for example, the output-related switching model is as shown in Fig. 4.2, where v_1 is a rectangular-wave source at the switching frequency.

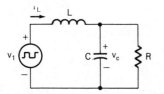

Figure 4.2 Output-related switching frequency model of the basic buck converter.

In order to avoid the notational complexities of differentiating between state variables that include switching information and those that do not, it will henceforth be understood that switching components are to be analyzed separately so that $\mathbf{x}$ can be regarded as continuous. With this understanding, the time interval of Eq. (4.13a) can include $(n + d_n)/f_s$ and the time interval of Eq. (4.13b) can include $(n + 1)/f_s$. If the switching frequency is high enough relative to the circuit natural frequencies and the signal frequencies, then the switching period is short enough to approximate the derivatives of $\mathbf{x}$ at $t = n/f_s$ and at $t = (n + d_n)/f_s$, as follows:

$$\dot{\mathbf{x}}\left(\frac{n}{f_s}\right) = \frac{\mathbf{x}[(n + d_n)/f_s] - \mathbf{x}(n/f_s)}{d_n/f_s} \tag{4.14a}$$

and
$$\dot{\mathbf{x}}\left(\frac{n + d_n}{f_s}\right) = \frac{\mathbf{x}[(n + 1)/f_s] - \mathbf{x}[(n + d_n)/f_s]}{(1 - d_n)/f_s} \tag{4.14b}$$

Combining Eqs. (4.13) (where closed time intervals are now permitted) and (4.14) to eliminate $\dot{\mathbf{x}}(n/f_s)$ and $\dot{\mathbf{x}}[(n + d_n)/f_s]$ results in

$$\mathbf{x}\left(\frac{n + d_n}{f_s}\right) = \mathbf{x}\left(\frac{n}{f_s}\right) + \frac{d_n}{f_s} \cdot \left[\mathbf{A}_1\mathbf{x}\left(\frac{n}{f_s}\right) + \mathbf{B}_1\mathbf{u}\left(\frac{n}{f_s}\right)\right] \tag{4.15a}$$

and
$$\mathbf{x}\left(\frac{n + 1}{f_s}\right) = \mathbf{x}\left(\frac{n + d_n}{f_s}\right) + \frac{1 - d_n}{f_s}$$
$$\cdot \left[\mathbf{A}_2\mathbf{x}\left(\frac{n + d_n}{f_s}\right) + \mathbf{B}_2\mathbf{u}\left(\frac{n + d_n}{f_s}\right)\right] \tag{4.15b}$$

Combining Eqs. (4.15a) and (4.15b) to eliminate $\mathbf{x}[(n + d_n)/f_s]$ results in

$$\mathbf{x}\left(\frac{n + 1}{f_s}\right) = \mathbf{x}\left(\frac{n}{f_s}\right) + \frac{d_n}{f_s} \cdot \left[\mathbf{A}_1\mathbf{x}\left(\frac{n}{f_s}\right) + \mathbf{B}_1\mathbf{u}\left(\frac{n}{f_s}\right)\right]$$
$$+ \frac{1 - d_n}{f_s} \mathbf{A}_2 \cdot \left\{\mathbf{x}\left(\frac{n}{f_s}\right) + \frac{d_n}{f_s} \cdot \left[\mathbf{A}_1\mathbf{x}\left(\frac{n}{f_s}\right) + \mathbf{B}_1\mathbf{u}\left(\frac{n}{f_s}\right)\right]\right\}$$
$$+ \frac{1 - d_n}{f_s} \mathbf{B}_2\mathbf{u}\left(\frac{n + d_n}{f_s}\right) \tag{4.16}$$

The term $\mathbf{u}[(n + d_n)/f_s]$ can be eliminated using the approximation

$$\dot{\mathbf{u}}\left(\frac{n}{f_s}\right) = \frac{\mathbf{u}[(n + d_n)/f_s] - \mathbf{u}(n/f_s)}{d_n/f_s} \tag{4.17}$$

Substituting Eq. (4.17) into Eq. (4.16), and rearranging, results in

$$\frac{\mathbf{x}[(n+1)/f_s] - \mathbf{x}(n/f_s)}{1/f_s} = [d_n\mathbf{A}_1 + (1-d_n)\mathbf{A}_2]\mathbf{x}\left(\frac{n}{f_s}\right)$$

$$+ [d_n\mathbf{B}_1 + (1-d_n)\mathbf{B}_2]\mathbf{u}\left(\frac{n}{f_s}\right)$$

$$+ \frac{1}{f_s}[d_n(1-d_n)]\left\{\mathbf{A}_2 \cdot \left[\mathbf{A}_1\mathbf{x}\left(\frac{n}{f_s}\right)\right.\right.$$

$$\left.\left. + \mathbf{B}_1\mathbf{u}\left(\frac{n}{f_s}\right)\right] + \mathbf{B}_2\dot{\mathbf{u}}\left(\frac{n}{f_s}\right)\right\} \qquad (4.18)$$

For large enough f_s, the left-hand side (LHS) of Eq. (4.18) approximates $\dot{\mathbf{x}}(n/f_s)$, and the $1/f_s$ terms of the RHS are negligible; hence we have

$$\dot{\mathbf{x}}\left(\frac{n}{f_s}\right) = [d_n\mathbf{A}_1 + (1-d_n)\mathbf{A}_2]\mathbf{x}\left(\frac{n}{f_s}\right)$$

$$+ [d_n\mathbf{B}_1 + (1-d_n)\mathbf{B}_2]\mathbf{u}\left(\frac{n}{f_s}\right) \qquad (4.19)$$

for which the continuous-time state-space-averaged representation

$$\dot{\mathbf{x}} = [\mathbf{A}_1 d + \mathbf{A}_2(1-d)]\mathbf{x} + [\mathbf{B}_1 d + \mathbf{B}_2(1-d)]\mathbf{u} \qquad (4.20)$$

applies, where once again it is understood that $\mathbf{x} = \mathbf{x}(t)$ and $\mathbf{u} = \mathbf{u}(t)$. In feedback control systems, d is a function of $\mathbf{x}$ and may, in principle, be a function of $\mathbf{u}$ as well. Thus, the continuous approximation of two switched linear systems is a nonlinear system. Using the notation of Eq. (4.8), we have

$$\mathbf{A} = \mathbf{A}_1 d + \mathbf{A}_2(1-d) \qquad (4.21a)$$

and

$$\mathbf{B} = \mathbf{B}_1 d + \mathbf{B}_2(1-d) \qquad (4.21b)$$

Note that this is the same result that would have been achieved by initially assuming that, on the average, $\mathbf{A}_1$ and $\mathbf{B}_1$ apply dth of the time and $\mathbf{A}_2$ and $\mathbf{B}_2$ apply $(1-d)$th of the time. Equation (4.18) establishes the exact criteria for which the assumption is valid.

In sum, state-space averaging can be thought of as an approximation technique that, for high enough switching frequencies, allows a continuous-time signal frequency analysis to be carried out separately from the switching frequency analysis. The total solution, then, is the sum of the terms from each analysis. The penalty, however, is that even if the original system is linear for any given switch condition, the resulting system will generally be nonlinear, and small-signal approximations have to be employed before familiar techniques such as Laplace transforms and Bode plots are applicable.

As a simple illustrative example of state-space averaging, consider the basic second-order buck converter of Fig. 2.6(a), which is redrawn in Fig. 4.3, where the dc source V_1 is replaced with the more general source u_1. The following analysis applies:

S1 ON/S2 OFF.

$$u_1 = L\dot{x}_1 + x_2 \implies \dot{x}_1 = -\frac{1}{L}x_2 + \frac{1}{L}u_1$$

$$C\dot{x}_2 = x_1 - \frac{1}{R}x_2 \implies \dot{x}_2 = \frac{1}{C}x_1 - \frac{1}{RC}x_2$$

$$\therefore \ \mathbf{A}_1 = \begin{bmatrix} 0 & -\dfrac{1}{L} \\ \dfrac{1}{C} & -\dfrac{1}{RC} \end{bmatrix} \qquad \mathbf{B}_1 = \begin{bmatrix} \dfrac{1}{L} \\ 0 \end{bmatrix}$$

S1 OFF/S2 ON.

$$0 = L\dot{x}_1 + x_2 \implies \dot{x}_1 = -\frac{1}{L}x_2$$

$$C\dot{x}_2 = x_1 - \frac{1}{R}x_2 \implies \dot{x}_2 = \frac{1}{C}x_1 - \frac{1}{RC}x_2$$

$$\therefore \ \mathbf{A}_2 = \begin{bmatrix} 0 & -\dfrac{1}{L} \\ \dfrac{1}{C} & -\dfrac{1}{RC} \end{bmatrix} \qquad \mathbf{B}_2 = \begin{bmatrix} 0 \\ 0 \end{bmatrix}$$

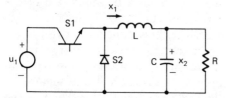

Figure 4.3 Updated basic buck converter.

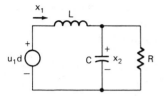

Figure 4.4 A continuous equivalent circuit of the basic buck converter.

Applying Eq. (4.21) results in

$$\mathbf{A} = \begin{bmatrix} 0 & -\dfrac{1}{L} \\ \dfrac{1}{C} & -\dfrac{1}{RC} \end{bmatrix} \tag{4.22a}$$

$$\mathbf{B} = \begin{bmatrix} \dfrac{d}{L} \\ 0 \end{bmatrix} \tag{4.22b}$$

which, in turn, leads to

$$\dot{x}_1 = -\frac{1}{L}x_2 + \frac{d}{L}u_1 \tag{4.23a}$$

and

$$\dot{x}_2 = \frac{1}{C}x_1 - \frac{1}{RC}x_2 \tag{4.23b}$$

A continuous but nonlinear circuit that is described by Eq. (4.23) is shown in Fig. 4.4. It is nonlinear because, in the general case, d can be a function of any combination of x_1, x_2, and u_1.

4.3 Discontinuous Conduction Mode

For DCM operation (Chap. 2, Sec. 2.3) there is a third switch condition of S1 OFF/S2 OFF for which corresponding matrices $\mathbf{A}_3$ and $\mathbf{B}_3$ can be derived. In this case, $\mathbf{A}_1$ and $\mathbf{B}_1$ apply dth of the time as before, but the duty factor of $\mathbf{A}_2$ and $\mathbf{B}_2$ is $(t_2 f_s - d)$ and the duty factor of $\mathbf{A}_3$ and $\mathbf{B}_3$ is $(1 - t_2 f_s)$, where t_2 is as shown in Fig. 2.7(b). That is,

$$\mathbf{A} = \mathbf{A}_1 d + \mathbf{A}_2(t_2 f_s - d) + \mathbf{A}_3(1 - t_2 f_s) \tag{4.24a}$$

and

$$\mathbf{B} = \mathbf{B}_1 d + \mathbf{B}_2(t_2 f_s - d) + \mathbf{B}_3(1 - t_2 f_s) \tag{4.24b}$$

For the DCM buck regulator, the equivalent circuit corresponding to the switch condition S1 OFF/S2 OFF is simply the output capacitor in parallel with the load resistor, so the following analysis applies:

S1 OFF/S2 OFF.

$$x_1 = 0 \implies \dot{x}_1 = 0$$

$$C\dot{x}_2 = 0 \cdot x_1 - \frac{1}{R} x_2 \implies \dot{x}_2 = -\frac{1}{RC} x_2$$

$$\therefore \quad \mathbf{A}_3 = \begin{bmatrix} 0 & 0 \\ 0 & -\dfrac{1}{RC} \end{bmatrix} \qquad \mathbf{B}_3 = \begin{bmatrix} 0 \\ 0 \end{bmatrix}$$

Applying Eq. (4.24) results in

$$\mathbf{A} = \begin{bmatrix} 0 & -\dfrac{t_2 f_2}{L} \\ \dfrac{t_2 f_s}{C} & -\dfrac{1}{RC} \end{bmatrix} \tag{4.25a}$$

and, as before,

$$\mathbf{B} = \begin{bmatrix} \dfrac{d}{L} \\ 0 \end{bmatrix} \tag{4.25b}$$

which, in turn, leads to

$$\dot{x}_1 = \frac{t_2 f_s}{L} x_2 + \frac{d}{L} u_1 \tag{4.26a}$$

and

$$\dot{x}_2 = \frac{t_2 f_s}{C} x_1 - \frac{1}{RC} x_2 \tag{4.26b}$$

where t_2 is defined in Eq. (2.15b).

Updating the voltage balance equation [Eq. (2.12)] to the new terminology, rearranging, and simplifying, results in

$$u_1 d = x_2 t_2 f_s \tag{4.27}$$

Substituting Eq. (4.27) into Eq. (4.26a) gives us the result that, for the state-space-averaged DCM buck regulator, $\dot{x}_1 = 0$. This is a restatement of the fact that, for any given cycle of DCM operation, the inductor switching current always starts at zero and always resets to zero, so there can be no net increase. This does not mean that x_1 cannot be variable in time, but it does mean that x_1 no longer qualifies as a state variable. Thus, the state-space-averaged DCM buck regulator is a first-order system.

If x_1 is not a state variable, then it must be expressible in terms of u_1 and x_2. To determine this relationship, we first update Eq. (2.14) to arrive at

$$\frac{(u_1 - x_2)d}{f_s} = LI_p \qquad (4.28)$$

The next step is to find x_1 in terms of I_p. From Fig. 2.7(b), it may be tempting to equate x_1 to $i_{L(avg)}$. However, in order for the state equations for switch conditions S1 ON/S2 OFF and S1 OFF/S2 ON [upon which Eq. (4.26) is based] to be true, x_1 must be $I_p/2$, not $I_p t_2 f_s/2$. For the switch condition S1 OFF/S2 OFF, we can think of the x_1 coefficient being zero rather than x_1 itself. We can verify that

$$x_1 = \frac{I_p}{2} \qquad (4.29)$$

by considering Eq. (4.26b) under steady-state conditions. In particular,

$$x_1 = \frac{x_2}{Rt_2f_s} \qquad \dot{x}_2 = 0 \qquad (4.30)$$

Furthermore, we know that

$$i_{L(avg)} = \frac{I_p t_2 f_s}{2} = \frac{x_2}{R} \qquad \dot{x}_2 = 0 \qquad (4.31)$$

Combining Eqs. (4.30) and (4.31) results in Eq. (4.29). Combining Eq. (4.29) with Eq. (4.28) to eliminate I_p and substituting the resultant value of x_1 into Eq. (4.26b) gives us

$$\dot{x}_2 = \frac{(u_1 - x_2)t_2 d}{2LC} - \frac{1}{RC}x_2 \qquad (4.32)$$

Finally, using Eq. (4.27) to eliminate t_2, we have the first-order DCM buck regulator equation

$$\dot{x}_2 = \frac{(u_1 - x_2)u_1 d}{2LCx_2 f_s} - \frac{1}{RC}x_2 \qquad (4.33)$$

Similar results can be derived for the boost and buck-boost topologies.

Certainly one of the conclusions that is reinforced in this section, upon inspection of Eq. (4.33), is that the state-space-averaging process approximates a switched system as a continuous but *nonlinear* system. This helps provide motivation for the small-signal approximation for linearity, as will be discussed in the next section.

4.4 Small-Signal Approximation for Linearity

Any continuous nonlinear system can be approximated as a linear system within a small enough neighborhood about its dc operating point. We begin the linearization of Eq. (4.20) by separating the dc terms of $\mathbf{x}$, $\mathbf{u}$, and d from the signal frequency ac terms. (Remember that the switching frequency terms were already effectively separated in the state-space-averaging process.) In particular, we say that

$$\mathbf{x} = \mathbf{x}_0 + \hat{\mathbf{x}} \qquad (4.34a)$$

$$\mathbf{u} = \mathbf{u}_0 + \hat{\mathbf{u}} \qquad (4.34b)$$

and
$$d = D + \hat{d} \qquad (4.34c)$$

The signal frequency ac terms are identified by the hat ($\char94$) notation. We next assume that the ac amplitudes are small enough so that the product of any two ac terms is negligible. This assumption is not always valid, but it is necessary for a linear system approximation. If the assumption is not valid, then computer-aided analysis will probably be required.

Substituting Eq. (4.34) into Eq. (4.20) results in a dc equation

$$0 = [\mathbf{A}_1 D + \mathbf{A}_2(1 - D)]\mathbf{x}_0 + [\mathbf{B}_1 D + \mathbf{B}_2(1 - D)]\mathbf{u}_0 \qquad (4.35)$$

and an ac equation

$$\dot{\hat{\mathbf{x}}} = [\mathbf{A}_1 D + \mathbf{A}_2(1 - D)]\hat{\mathbf{x}} + [\mathbf{B}_1 D + \mathbf{B}_2(1 - D)]\hat{\mathbf{u}}$$
$$+ [(\mathbf{A}_1 - \mathbf{A}_2)\mathbf{x}_0 + (\mathbf{B}_1 - \mathbf{B}_2)\mathbf{u}_0]\hat{d} \qquad (4.36)$$

Defining

$$\mathbf{A}_0 = [\mathbf{A}_1 D + \mathbf{A}_2(1 - D)] \qquad (4.37a)$$

$$\mathbf{B}_0 = [\mathbf{B}_1 D + \mathbf{B}_2(1 - D)] \qquad (4.37b)$$

and
$$\mathbf{E} = (\mathbf{A}_1 - \mathbf{A}_2)\mathbf{x}_0 + (\mathbf{B}_1 - \mathbf{B}_2)\mathbf{u}_0 \qquad (4.37c)$$

we can write

$$0 = \mathbf{A}_0\mathbf{x}_0 + \mathbf{B}_0\mathbf{u}_0 \qquad (4.38)$$

and

$$\dot{\mathbf{x}} = \mathbf{A}_0\hat{\mathbf{x}} + \mathbf{B}_0\hat{\mathbf{u}} + \mathbf{E}\hat{d} \qquad (4.39)$$

Adding Eqs. (4.38) and (4.39) results in the linear equation

$$\dot{\mathbf{x}} = \mathbf{A}_0\mathbf{x} + \mathbf{B}_0\mathbf{u} + \mathbf{E}\hat{d} \qquad (4.40)$$

where it is recognized that $\dot{\mathbf{x}}$ is equal to $\dot{\hat{\mathbf{x}}}$.

4.5 Application of Approximation Techniques

We now have at our disposal an overall strategy for approximating a switching regulator as a linear system. This strategy is depicted in the flow graph shown in Fig. 4.5. In addition, we have identified the criteria for the validity of these approximations.

As an illustrative example, we shall apply these techniques to the basic second-order boost converter of Fig. 2.6(b), which is redrawn in Fig. 4.6 using the designation u_1 for the voltage source. In addition, an ac current source u_2 is placed in parallel with the load to simulate load modulation. The first step is to write the linear differential equations for each of the two switch conditions in order to determine the matrices $\mathbf{A}_1$, $\mathbf{A}_2$, $\mathbf{B}_1$, and $\mathbf{B}_2$. Figure 4.7 shows the basic boost converter

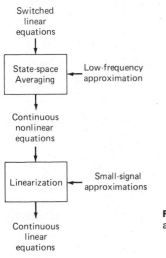

Figure 4.5 Flow graph for linear analysis of switching regulators.

for (a) the switch condition S1 ON/S2 OFF and (b) the switch condition S1 OFF/S2 ON. The corresponding analysis follows below:

S1 ON/S2 OFF.

$$u_1 = L\dot{x}_1 \implies \dot{x}_1 = \frac{1}{L} u_1$$

$$u_2 = C\dot{x}_2 + \frac{1}{R} x_2 \implies \dot{x}_2 = -\frac{1}{RC} x_2 + \frac{1}{C} u_2$$

$$\therefore \quad \mathbf{A}_1 = \begin{bmatrix} 0 & 0 \\ 0 & -\dfrac{1}{RC} \end{bmatrix} \quad \mathbf{B}_1 = \begin{bmatrix} \dfrac{1}{L} & 0 \\ 0 & \dfrac{1}{C} \end{bmatrix}$$

S1 OFF/S2 ON.

$$u_1 = L\dot{x}_1 + x_2 \implies \dot{x}_1 = -\frac{1}{L} x_2 + \frac{1}{L} u_1$$

$$u_2 + x_1 = C\dot{x}_2 + \frac{1}{R} x_2 \implies \dot{x}_2 = \frac{1}{C} x_1 - \frac{1}{RC} x_2 + \frac{1}{C} u_2$$

$$\therefore \quad \mathbf{A}_2 = \begin{bmatrix} 0 & -\dfrac{1}{L} \\ \dfrac{1}{C} & -\dfrac{1}{RC} \end{bmatrix} \quad \mathbf{B}_2 = \begin{bmatrix} \dfrac{1}{L} & 0 \\ 0 & \dfrac{1}{C} \end{bmatrix}$$

Applying Eq. (4.21) results in

$$\mathbf{A} = \begin{bmatrix} 0 & \dfrac{-(1-d)}{L} \\ \dfrac{1-d}{C} & -\dfrac{1}{RC} \end{bmatrix} \tag{4.41a}$$

and

$$\mathbf{B} = \begin{bmatrix} \dfrac{1}{L} & 0 \\ 0 & \dfrac{1}{C} \end{bmatrix} \tag{4.41b}$$

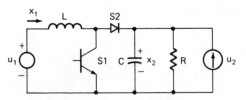

Figure 4.6 Updated basic boost converter.

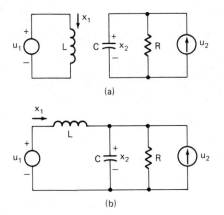

Figure 4.7 The basic boost converter for switch conditions (a) S1 ON/S2 OFF and (b) S1 OFF/ S2 ON.

This, in turn, leads to

$$\dot{x}_1 = \frac{-(1 - d)}{L} x_2 + \frac{1}{L} u_1 \tag{4.42a}$$

and

$$\dot{x}_2 = \frac{1 - d}{C} x_1 - \frac{1}{RC} x_2 + \frac{1}{C} u_2 \tag{4.42b}$$

A continuous but nonlinear equivalent circuit that is described by Eq. (4.42) is shown in Fig. 4.8.

The next step is to apply the small-signal approximations shown in Eq. (4.34) to Eq. (4.42). Neglecting products of ac terms, we have

$$\dot{x}_1 = -\frac{1 - D}{L} x_2 + \frac{x_{20}}{L} \hat{d} + \frac{1}{L} u_1 \tag{4.43a}$$

and

$$\dot{x}_2 = \frac{1 - D}{C} x_1 - \frac{x_{10}}{C} \hat{d} - \frac{1}{RC} x_2 + \frac{1}{C} u_2 \tag{4.43b}$$

Therefore,

$$\mathbf{A}_0 = \begin{bmatrix} 0 & \dfrac{-(1 - D)}{L} \\ \dfrac{1 - D}{C} & -\dfrac{1}{RC} \end{bmatrix} \tag{4.44a}$$

$$\mathbf{B}_0 = \begin{bmatrix} \dfrac{1}{L} & 0 \\ 0 & \dfrac{1}{C} \end{bmatrix} \tag{4.44b}$$

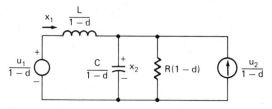

Figure 4.8 A continuous equivalent circuit of the basic boost converter.

and

$$\mathbf{E} = \begin{bmatrix} \dfrac{x_{20}}{L} \\[2mm] -\dfrac{x_{10}}{C} \end{bmatrix}$$

(4.44c)

From our dc analyses in Chap. 2, we know that

$$x_{20} = \frac{u_{10}}{1 - D}$$

(4.45a)

and

$$x_{10} = \frac{u_{10}}{R(1 - D)^2}$$

(4.45b)

These values can also be directly inferred from the equivalent circuit of Fig. 4.8.

We can now draw a linearized equivalent circuit that is described by Eq. (4.43), as shown in Fig. 4.9. The effective values of the circuit elements and the independent sources are a function of the dc operating point, as represented by the dc duty factor D. In addition, there are dependent voltage and current sources, also functions of D, that are due to signal frequency ac variations in the duty factor, as represented by $\hat{d}$. In the next chapter we will "close the loop" by relating the duty factor to the state and source variables in accordance with the control law.

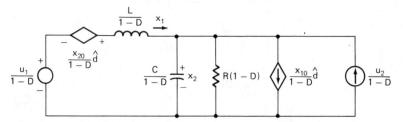

Figure 4.9 Linearized equivalent circuit of the basic boost converter.

4.6 General Second-Order Equivalent Circuit

Just as we developed a general linearized equation for analyzing switching regulator behavior, namely Eq. (4.40), it is possible to develop general linearized equivalent circuits. Since the synthesis problem is unbounded, equivalent circuits are not unique and other approaches are possible besides the one taken here. Because of the risk of misapplying equivalent circuits, they are perhaps most useful as aids in understanding basic concepts. In any event, a general equivalent circuit for a basic second-order voltage converter with an ac current source in parallel with the load will be developed below. For this case, $\mathbf{A}_0$ is 2×2, $\mathbf{B}_0$ is 2×2, and $\mathbf{E}$ is 2×1. In particular,

$$\mathbf{A}_0 = \begin{bmatrix} a_{11} & a_{12} \\ a_{21} & a_{22} \end{bmatrix} \tag{4.46a}$$

$$\mathbf{B}_0 = \begin{bmatrix} b_{11} & b_{12} \\ b_{21} & b_{22} \end{bmatrix} \tag{4.46b}$$

$$\mathbf{E} = \begin{bmatrix} e_1 \\ e_2 \end{bmatrix} \tag{4.46c}$$

For a second-order system, substituting Eq. (4.46) into (4.40) results in the linear differential equations

$$\dot{x}_1 = a_{11}x_1 + a_{12}x_2 + b_{11}u_1 + b_{12}u_2 + e_1\hat{d} \tag{4.47a}$$

$$\dot{x}_2 = a_{21}x_1 + a_{22}x_2 + b_{21}u_1 + b_{22}u_2 + e_2\hat{d} \tag{4.47b}$$

By choosing x_1 to represent inductor current and x_2 to represent capacitor voltage, we can synthesize a second-order equivalent circuit which is described by one first-order loop equation, namely Eq. (4.47a), and one first-order nodal equation, namely Eq. (4.47b).

In order to isolate the original state variables, we multiply Eq. (4.47a) by a_{12}^{-1} and Eq. (4.47b) by a_{21}^{-1} resulting in

$$a_{12}^{-1}\dot{x}_1 = a_{12}^{-1}a_{11}x_1 + x_2 + a_{12}^{-1}b_{11}u_1 + a_{12}^{-1}b_{12}u_2$$
$$+ a_{12}^{-1}e_1\hat{d} \tag{4.48a}$$

$$a_{21}^{-1}\dot{x}_2 = x_1 + a_{21}^{-1}a_{22}x_2 + a_{21}^{-1}b_{21}u_1 + a_{21}^{-1}b_{22}u_2$$
$$+ a_{21}^{-1}e_2\hat{d} \tag{4.48b}$$

We can see that the equivalent circuit will consist of voltage sources, an inductor with losses, current sources, and a capacitor with losses.

Thus, we hypothesize the circuit of Fig. 4.10, where the polarity of x_1 is chosen so that positive x_1 contributes to positive x_2. For greater generality, both series and shunt losses are inserted for the energy storage elements. In the case of the capacitor, the practical configuration of equivalent series resistance (ESR) and load resistance is preserved. Any nonnegligible capacitor shunt leakage resistance would thus be included in the ESR and the equivalent load resistance.

Writing the equations for Fig. 4.10, we have

$$k_1 u_1 + k_2 \hat{d} = L_e \dot{x}_1 + R_{1e}\left(x_1 + \frac{L_e \dot{x}_1}{R_{4e}}\right) + R_{2e}C_e \dot{x}_2 + x_2 \quad (4.49a)$$

and $\quad x_1 + \dfrac{L_e \dot{x}_1}{R_{4e}} + k_4 u_2 + k_3 \hat{d} = C_e \dot{x}_2 + \dfrac{1}{R_{3e}}(x_2 + R_{2e}C_e \dot{x}_2) \quad (4.49b)$

Rearranging and combining to correlate with Eq. (4.48) results in

$$L_e \dot{x}_1 = -(R_{1e} + R_{2e})x_1 - x_2 + k_1 u_1 - R_{2e}k_4 u_2$$
$$+ (k_2 - R_{2e}k_3)\hat{d} \quad (4.50a)$$

and $\quad C_e \dot{x}_2 = x_1 - \dfrac{1}{R_{3e}}x_2 + \dfrac{k_1}{R_{4e}}u_1 + k_4 u_2 + k_3 \hat{d} \quad (4.50b)$

where it is assumed that $R_{1e} \ll R_{4e}$, $R_{2e} \ll R_{3e}$, and $R_{2e} \ll R_{4e}$.

Multiplying Eq. (4.50a) by -1, for a positive x_2 term, and correlating Eqs. (4.48) and (4.50) term by term results in

$$(a) \;\; L_e = -\frac{1}{a_{12}} \qquad\qquad (b) \;\; R_{1e} + R_{2e} = \frac{a_{11}}{a_{12}}$$

$$(c) \;\; k_1 = -\frac{b_{11}}{a_{12}} \qquad\qquad (d) \;\; R_{2e}k_4 = \frac{b_{12}}{a_{12}}$$

$$(e) \;\; k_2 - R_{2e}k_3 = -\frac{e_1}{a_{12}} \qquad (f) \;\; C_e = \frac{1}{a_{21}} \qquad (4.51)$$

$$(g) \;\; R_{3e} = -\frac{a_{21}}{a_{22}} \qquad\qquad (h) \;\; \frac{k_1}{R_{4e}} = \frac{b_{21}}{a_{21}}$$

$$(i) \;\; k_4 = \frac{b_{22}}{a_{21}} \qquad\qquad (j) \;\; k_3 = \frac{e_2}{a_{21}}$$

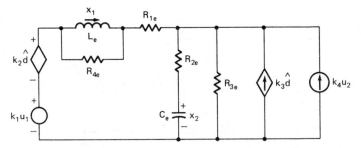

Figure 4.10 General linearized second-order switching regulator equivalent circuit.

From Eqs. (4.51c) and (4.51h), we have

$$R_{4e} = -\frac{a_{21}b_{11}}{a_{12}b_{21}} \qquad (4.52a)$$

From Eqs. (4.51d) and (4.51i),

$$R_{2e} = \frac{a_{21}b_{12}}{a_{12}b_{22}} \qquad (4.52b)$$

From Eqs. (4.51b) and (4.52b),

$$R_{1e} = \frac{a_{11}b_{22} - a_{21}b_{12}}{a_{12}b_{22}} \qquad (4.52c)$$

From Eqs. (4.51e), (4.51j), and (4.52b),

$$k_2 = \frac{b_{12}e_2 - b_{22}e_1}{a_{12}b_{22}} \qquad (4.52d)$$

To help validate these expressions, we reconsider the lossless basic boost converter of Fig. 4.6, whose matrix elements appear in Eq. (4.44). Inserting the values of these elements into Eqs. (4.51) and (4.52), and applying these equations to Fig. 4.10, results in the equivalent circuit of Fig. 4.9, as would be expected.

4.7 The DC Transformer

Although the equivalent circuits derived in the previous two sections are valid for the purpose of graphically depicting the corresponding state equations and are representative of the influence of duty factor modulation, they do not accurately represent the switching regulator

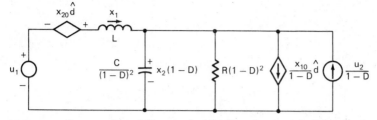

Figure 4.11   Source-reflected linearized equivalent circuit of the basic boost converter.

as presented either to the source or to the load. For example, in comparing Fig. 4.6 to Fig. 4.9, we see that the voltage source u_1 has become $u_1/(1 - D)$, for the same input current x_1, and the load resistor R has become $R(1 - D)$, for the same output voltage x_2. However, again, the equivalent circuits are not unique, and it is possible to manipulate Eq. (4.43) to help form suitable source- and load-reflected equivalent circuits, as will now be shown.

A suitable source-reflected equivalent circuit for the basic boost converter should preserve $u_1, x_1,$ and L. Equation (4.43a) can be rearranged as

$$L\dot{x}_1 = -x_2(1 - D) + u_1 + x_{20}\hat{d} \tag{4.53}$$

in which case u_1, x_1, and L can be preserved by defining the capacitor voltage as $x_2(1 - D)$ instead of x_2. Separating $x_2(1 - D)$ as an explicit variable, Eq. (4.43b) can be rearranged as

$$\frac{C}{(1 - D)^2} \dot{x}_2(1 - D) = x_1 - \frac{x_2(1 - D)}{R(1 - D)^2}$$

$$+ \frac{u_2}{1 - D} - \frac{x_{10}}{1 - D}\hat{d} \tag{4.54}$$

for which the equivalent circuit of Fig. 4.11 applies.

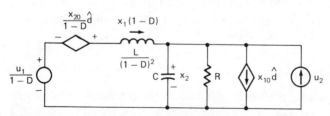

Figure 4.12   Load-reflected linearized equivalent circuit of the basic boost converter.

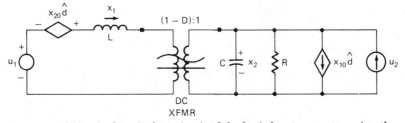

Figure 4.13 Linearized equivalent circuit of the basic boost converter using the dc transformer.

Similarly, a suitable load-reflected equivalent circuit for the basic boost converter should preserve u_2, x_2, C, and R. Equation (4.43b) can be rearranged as

$$C\dot{x}_2 = x_1(1 - D) - \frac{1}{R}x_2 + u_2 - x_{10}\hat{d} \qquad (4.55)$$

in which case u_2, x_2, C, and R can be preserved by defining the inductor current as $x_1(1 - D)$ instead of x_1. Separating $x_1(1 - D)$ as an explicit variable, Eq. (4.43a) can be rearranged as

$$\frac{L}{(1 - D)^2}\dot{x}_1(1 - D) = -x_2 + \frac{u_1}{1 - D} + \frac{x_{20}}{1 - D}\hat{d} \qquad (4.56)$$

for which the equivalent circuit of Fig. 4.12 applies.

By using a pseudo element called a "dc transformer," which has the same transformation properties as an ac transformer, it is possible to combine the equivalent circuits of Figs. 4.11 and 4.12 into a single equivalent circuit, as shown in Fig. 4.13. Since both the input and the output interfaces are preserved, this equivalent circuit, after Middlebrook and Ćuk,[4] is particularly useful in power systems analysis where the basic switching regulator is but a component part.

4.8 Illustrative Problems

4.1 As a review of matrix algebra, do the following problems.

(a)

$$[1 \quad 2 \quad 3]\begin{bmatrix} 1 \\ 2 \\ 3 \end{bmatrix}$$

(b)

$$\begin{bmatrix} 1 & 2 \\ 3 & 0 \end{bmatrix}\begin{bmatrix} 4 \\ -1 \end{bmatrix}$$

(c)

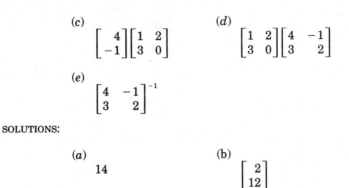

(d)

(e)

$$\begin{bmatrix} 4 & -1 \\ 3 & 2 \end{bmatrix}^{-1}$$

SOLUTIONS:

(a)

14

(b)

$$\begin{bmatrix} 2 \\ 12 \end{bmatrix}$$

(c)

Undefined

(d)

$$\begin{bmatrix} 10 & 3 \\ 12 & -3 \end{bmatrix}$$

(e)

$$\begin{bmatrix} \frac{2}{11} & \frac{1}{11} \\ -\frac{3}{11} & \frac{4}{11} \end{bmatrix}$$

4.2   For the circuit in Fig. P4.2, determine the transfer functions $Y_1(s)/U_1(s)$, $Y_2(s)/U_1(s)$, $Y_1(s)/U_2(s)$, and $Y_2(s)/U_2(s)$ using the modern approach. Confirm the output impedance $Z_2(s) = Y_2(s)/U_2(s)$ using the impedance technique.

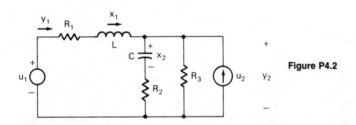

Figure P4.2

SOLUTION: The strategy will be to determine the transfer functions $X_1(s)/U_1(s)$, etc., using Eq. (4.10b) and then to relate the so-called output vector **y** to the state vector **x**. Summing voltages, we have

$$u_1 = R_1 x_1 + L\dot{x}_1 + x_2 + R_2 C\dot{x}_2$$

Rearranging yields the result

$$\dot{x}_1 = -\frac{R_1}{L}x_1 - \frac{1}{L}x_2 + \frac{1}{L}u_1 - \frac{R_2 C}{L}\dot{x}_2$$

As it stands, this equation does not conform to the format of Eq. (4.8), so it will have to be combined with the current summation equation, which is

$$x_1 + u_2 = C\dot{x}_2 + \frac{x_2 + R_2 C\dot{x}_2}{R_3}$$

Rearranging produces

$$\dot{x}_2 = \frac{R_3}{(R_2 + R_3)C} x_1 - \frac{1}{(R_2 + R_3)C} x_2 + \frac{R_3}{(R_2 + R_3)C} u_2$$

Substituting the rearranged current equation into the rearranged voltage equation gives us

$$\dot{x}_1 = \frac{-(R_1R_2 + R_1R_3 + R_2R_3)}{(R_2 + R_3)L} x_1 - \frac{R_3}{(R_2 + R_3)L} x_2$$
$$+ \frac{1}{L} u_1 - \frac{R_2R_3}{(R_2 + R_3)L} u_2$$

If the matrix **A** contains the elements a_{jk}, and the matrix **B** contains the elements b_{jk}, then we have

$$a_{11} = -\frac{R_1R_2 + R_1R_3 + R_2R_3}{(R_2 + R_3)L}$$

$$a_{12} = -\frac{R_3}{(R_2 + R_3)L}$$

$$a_{21} = \frac{R_3}{(R_2 + R_3)C}$$

$$a_{22} = -\frac{1}{(R_2 + R_3)C}$$

$$b_{11} = \frac{1}{L}$$

$$b_{12} = -\frac{R_2R_3}{(R_2 + R_3)L}$$

$$b_{21} = 0$$

$$b_{22} = \frac{R_3}{(R_2 + R_3)C}$$

$$s\mathbf{I} - \mathbf{A} = \begin{bmatrix} s - a_{11} & -a_{12} \\ -a_{21} & s - a_{22} \end{bmatrix}$$

$$(s\mathbf{I} - \mathbf{A})^{-1}\mathbf{B} = \frac{\begin{bmatrix} s - a_{22} & a_{12} \\ a_{21} & s - a_{11} \end{bmatrix}\begin{bmatrix} b_{11} & b_{12} \\ b_{21} & b_{22} \end{bmatrix}}{s^2 - (a_{11} + a_{22})s + a_{11}a_{22} - a_{12}a_{21}}$$

$$\Delta \triangleq s^2 - (a_{11} + a_{22})s + a_{11}a_{22} - a_{12}a_{21}$$

Thus, the state-to-source transfer functions are

$$\frac{X_1(s)}{U_1(s)} = \frac{(s - a_{22})b_{11} + a_{12}b_{21}}{\Delta}$$

$$\frac{X_2(s)}{U_1(s)} = \frac{a_{21}b_{11} + (s - a_{11})b_{21}}{\Delta}$$

$$\frac{X_1(s)}{U_2(s)} = \frac{(s - a_{22})b_{12} + a_{12}b_{22}}{\Delta}$$

$$\frac{X_2(s)}{U_2(s)} = \frac{a_{21}b_{12} + (s - a_{11})b_{22}}{\Delta}$$

Expressing the outputs in terms of the states gives us

$$y_1 = x_1$$

$$Y_1(s) = X_1(s)$$

$$y_2 = x_2 + R_2 C \dot{x}_2$$

$$Y_2(s) = (1 + R_2 Cs)X_2(s)$$

Thus, the output-to-source transfer functions are

$$\frac{Y_1(s)}{U_1(s)} = \frac{1}{L}\left[s + \frac{1}{(R_2 + R_2)C} \right] \div \Delta$$

$$\frac{Y_2(s)}{U_1(s)} = \frac{R_2 R_3(s + 1/R_2 C)}{(R_2 + R_3)L} \div \Delta$$

$$\frac{Y_1(s)}{U_2(s)} = -\frac{R_2 R_3}{(R_2 + R_3)L}\left[s + \frac{1 + R_3/R_2}{(R_2 + R_3)C} \right] \div \Delta$$

$$\frac{Y_2(s)}{U_2(s)} = \frac{R_2 R_3}{R_2 + R_3}\left(s + \frac{1}{R_2 C} \right)\left(s + \frac{R_1}{L} \right) \div \Delta$$

$$\Delta = s^2 \left[\frac{R_1 R_2 + R_1 R_3 + R_2 R_3}{(R_2 + R_3)L} + \frac{1}{(R_2 + R_3)C} \right] s$$

$$+ \frac{R_1 R_2 + R_1 R_3 + R_2 R_3 + R_3^2}{(R_2 + R_3)^2 LC}$$

4.3 The initial conditions of x_1 and x_2 at $t = 0$ for the circuit in Fig. P4.3 are $x_{10} = x_{20}/R$ and x_{20}, respectively. Assuming an ideal diode, draw the trajectory of the state vector $\mathbf{x} = [x_1 \ x_2]^T$ in the two-dimensional state space formed by x_1 and x_2 for $0 \le t < \infty$. Assume that the damping factor $\zeta = \sqrt{L/C}/2R$ is less than unity.

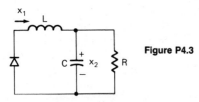

Figure P4.3

SOLUTION: The voltage equation is

$$0 = L\dot{x}_1 + x_2$$

or

$$\dot{x}_1 = -\frac{1}{L}x_2$$

The current equation is

$$x_1 = C\dot{x}_2 + \frac{1}{R}x_2$$

or

$$\dot{x}_2 = \frac{1}{C}x_1 - \frac{1}{RC}x_2$$

Dividing $\dot{x}_2$ by $\dot{x}_1$, we have

$$\frac{dx_2}{dx_1} = \frac{L}{C}\left(\frac{1}{R} - \frac{x_1}{x_2}\right)$$

As shown in Fig. S4.3, $dx_2/dx_1 = \infty$ along the x_1 axis, where $x_2 = 0$; $dx_2/dx_1 = 0$ along the line $x_1 = x_2/R$; and $dx_2/dx_1 = L/RC$ along the x_2 axis,

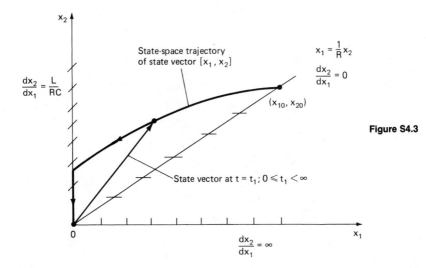

Figure S4.3

where $x_1 = 0$. Since the circuit is stable and since there are no sources, the state vector will move from its initial position $[x_{10} \quad x_{20}]$ to a final position of $[0 \quad 0]$. If it were not for the diode, the state-space trajectory of the state vector would encircle the origin with an ever decreasing radius, corresponding to damped sinusoids for x_1 and x_2 in the time domain. As it is, as soon as x_1 reaches zero, the inductor and diode are out of the picture and the circuit is first-order, or one-dimensional.

4.4 Determine the $\mathbf{A}_0$, $\mathbf{B}_0$, and $\mathbf{E}$ matrices for the Ćuk converter of Fig. P4.4, and develop a linearized equivalent circuit that preserves the input and output circuits, i.e., u_1, x_1, L_1, x_3, L_2, x_4, C_2, R, and u_2.

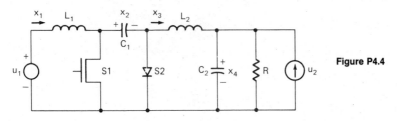

Figure P4.4

SOLUTION: The first step is to write the four equations corresponding to the four state variables for each of the two switch conditions.

S1 ON/S2 OFF.

$$u_1 = L_1\dot{x}_1 \Longrightarrow \dot{x}_1 = \frac{1}{L_1} u_1$$

$$C_1\dot{x}_2 = x_3 \Longrightarrow \dot{x}_2 = \frac{1}{C_1} x_3$$

$$x_2 + L_2\dot{x}_3 + x_4 = 0 \Longrightarrow \dot{x}_3 = -\frac{1}{L_2} x_2 - \frac{1}{L_2} x_4$$

$$x_3 + u_2 = C_2\dot{x}_4 + \frac{1}{R} x_4 \Longrightarrow \dot{x}_4 = \frac{1}{C_2} x_3 - \frac{1}{RC_2} x_4 + \frac{1}{C_2} u_2$$

S1 OFF/S2 ON.

$$u_1 = L_1\dot{x}_1 + x_2 \Longrightarrow \dot{x}_1 = -\frac{1}{L_1} x_2 + \frac{1}{L_1} u_1$$

$$C_1\dot{x}_2 = x_1 \Longrightarrow \dot{x}_2 = \frac{1}{C_1} x_1$$

$$L_2\dot{x}_3 + x_4 = 0 \Longrightarrow \dot{x}_3 = -\frac{1}{L_2} x_4$$

$$x_3 + u_2 = C_2\dot{x}_4 + \frac{1}{R} x_4 \Longrightarrow \dot{x}_4 = \frac{1}{C_2} x_3 - \frac{1}{RC_2} x_4 + \frac{1}{C_2} u_2$$

The second step is to use the state-space-averaging approximation to achieve a continuous set of equations.

$$\dot{x}_1 = -\frac{1-d}{L_1} x_2 + \frac{1}{L_1} u_1$$

$$\dot{x}_2 = \frac{1-d}{C_1} x_1 + \frac{d}{C_1} x_3$$

$$\dot{x}_3 = -\frac{d}{L_2} x_2 - \frac{1}{L_2} x_4$$

$$\dot{x}_4 = \frac{1}{C_2} x_3 - \frac{1}{RC_2} x_4 + \frac{1}{C_2} u_2$$

The third step is to use the small-signal approximation to achieve a linear set of equations.

AC equations.

$$\dot{\hat{x}}_1 = -\frac{1-D}{L_1} \hat{x}_2 + \frac{1}{L_1} \hat{u}_1 + \frac{x_{20}}{L_1} \hat{d}$$

$$\dot{\hat{x}}_2 = \frac{1-D}{C_1} \hat{x}_1 + \frac{D}{C_1} \hat{x}_3 + \frac{x_{30} - x_{10}}{C_1} \hat{d}$$

$$\dot{\hat{x}}_3 = -\frac{D}{L_2} \hat{x}_2 - \frac{1}{L_2} \hat{x}_4 - \frac{x_{20}}{L_2} \hat{d}$$

$$\dot{\hat{x}}_4 = \frac{1}{C_2} \hat{x}_3 - \frac{1}{RC_2} \hat{x}_4 + \frac{1}{C_2} \hat{u}_2$$

DC equations (assume $u_{20} = 0$).

$$0 = -\frac{1-D}{L_1} x_{20} + \frac{1}{L_1} u_{10}$$

$$0 = \frac{1-D}{C_1} x_{10} + \frac{D}{C_1} x_{30}$$

$$0 = -\frac{D}{L_2} x_{20} - \frac{1}{L_2} x_{40}$$

$$0 = \frac{1}{C_2} x_{30} - \frac{1}{RC_2} x_{40}$$

Solving the dc equations results in

$$x_{20} = \frac{u_{10}}{1 - D}$$

$$x_{40} = -Dx_{20} = -\frac{Du_{10}}{1 - D}$$

$$x_{30} = \frac{x_{40}}{R} = -\frac{Du_{10}}{(1 - D)R}$$

$$x_{10} = -\frac{Dx_{30}}{1 - D} = \frac{D^2 u_{10}}{(1 - D)^2 R}$$

We next substitute the dc solutions into the $\hat{d}$ coefficients and then add the ac and dc equations to arrive at a total equation set of the form

$$\dot{\mathbf{x}} = \mathbf{A}_0 \mathbf{x} + \mathbf{B}_0 \mathbf{u} + \mathbf{E}\hat{d}$$

in which case

$$\mathbf{A}_0 = \begin{bmatrix} 0 & \dfrac{-(1 - D)}{L_1} & 0 & 0 \\ \dfrac{1 - D}{C_1} & 0 & \dfrac{D}{C_1} & 0 \\ 0 & -\dfrac{D}{L_2} & 0 & -\dfrac{1}{L_2} \\ 0 & 0 & \dfrac{1}{C_2} & -\dfrac{1}{RC_2} \end{bmatrix}$$

$$\mathbf{B}_0 = \begin{bmatrix} \dfrac{1}{L_1} & 0 \\ 0 & 0 \\ 0 & 0 \\ 0 & \dfrac{1}{C_2} \end{bmatrix} \qquad \mathbf{E} = \begin{bmatrix} \dfrac{u_{10}}{(1 - D)L_1} \\ \dfrac{-Du_{10}}{(1 - D)^2 RC_1} \\ \dfrac{-u_{10}}{(1 - D)L_2} \\ 0 \end{bmatrix}$$

The $\dot{x}_1$, $\dot{x}_3$, and $\dot{x}_4$ equations can be rearranged such that all desired variables and parameters are preserved as shown below.

$$u_1 + x_{20}\hat{d} = L_1\dot{x}_1 + (1 - D)x_2$$

$$-Dx_2 = x_{20}\hat{d} + L_2\dot{x}_3 + x_4$$

$$u_2 + x_3 = C_2\dot{x}_4 + \frac{1}{R}x_4$$

These three equations describe the partial equivalent circuit shown in Fig. S4.4(a). The $\dot{x}_2$ equation cannot be rearranged so that both x_1 and x_3 are preserved. However, with the aid of the dc transformer concept, we can write

$$C_1\dot{x}_2 = (1 - D)x_1 + Dx_3 + (x_{30} - x_{10})\hat{d}$$

for which the partial equivalent circuit in Fig. S4.4(b) applies. The total equivalent circuit is then obtained by combining the two figures. Note the dependency upon the dc operating point, as would be expected as a result of the linear approximation.

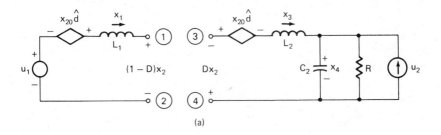

(a)

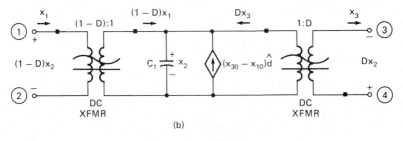

(b)

Figure S4.4

References

1. R. C. Wong, H. A. Owen, Jr., and T. G. Wilson, "A Fast Algorithm for the Time-Domain Simulation of Switched-Mode Piecewise-Linear Systems," *IEEE Power Electronics Specialists Conference Record,* June 1984, pp. 281–296.
2. G. F. Pierce and P. R. Troyk, "Switchmode Power Supply Transfer Determination Using SPICE-2," *IEEE Power Electronics Specialists Conference Record,* June 1984, pp. 297–303.
3. W. L. Brogan, *Modern Control Theory,* Quantum, New York, 1974.
4. R. D. Middlebrook and S. Ćuk, "A General Unified Approach to Modelling Switching-Converter Power Stages," *IEEE Power Electronics Specialists Conference Record,* June 1976, pp. 18–34.

Voltage-Mode
Switching Regulator
Transfer Functions

In order to allow the switching regulator to be viewed in a proper systems context, it is necessary to know such things as (1) its input and output impedances, (2) the extent to which a modulating input voltage is transmitted to the output, and (3) the extent to which a modulating load current is reflected to the input. Also, we need to know whether or not the switching regulator is stable. In short, what is necessary is to use the analytical approach that was presented in the previous chapter to find the switching regulator closed-loop transfer functions and the open-loop gain function. Because the ac solutions are dependent upon the dc operating point, the strategy will be first to find the ac solutions in terms of a general dc operating point, represented by $\mathbf{u}_0$ and D, and then to find the particular dc solution, from which the particular ac solutions follow directly.

5.1 General Control-Law Considerations

Since Eq. (4.39) is linear, we can apply Laplace transforms to arrive at the equation

$$\hat{\mathbf{X}}(s) = (s\mathbf{I} - \mathbf{A}_0)^{-1}\mathbf{B}_0\hat{\mathbf{U}}(s) + (s\mathbf{I} - \mathbf{A}_0)^{-1}\mathbf{E}\,\hat{d}(s) \qquad (5.1)$$

If $\hat{d}(s)$ is independent of $\hat{\mathbf{X}}(s)$ and $\hat{\mathbf{U}}(s)$, then the two transfer function matrices $(s\mathbf{I} - \mathbf{A}_0)^{-1}\mathbf{B}_0$ and $(s\mathbf{I} - \mathbf{A}_0)^{-1}\mathbf{E}$ are useful as is. However, in the most general case, d is a function of $\mathbf{x}$ (feedback control) and $\mathbf{u}$ (feed-forward control). The dependency of $\mathbf{u}$ may be either intentional or a consequence of the feedback control implementation. The equation that describes the dependency of $\hat{d}(s)$ on $\hat{\mathbf{X}}(s)$ and $\hat{\mathbf{U}}(s)$ is called the "control law."

The control law is not necessarily linear. For example, in the feed-forward control of the buck-derived regulator discussed in Chap. 3, Sec. 3.2, the duty factor is, by design, inversely proportional to the input voltage. When the control law is nonlinear, it must be linearized using small-signal approximations. To demonstrate, the nonlinear term $1/u_1$ is linearized as follows:

$$\frac{1}{u_1} = \frac{1}{u_{10} + \hat{u}_1} = \frac{1}{u_{10}(1 + \hat{u}_1/u_{10})} \approx \frac{1}{u_{10}}\left(1 - \frac{\hat{u}_1}{u_{10}}\right) \qquad (5.2)$$

After linearization, as appropriate, the generalized control law can be expressed as

$$\hat{d}(s) = \mathbf{F}^T(s)\hat{\mathbf{X}}(s) + \mathbf{Q}^T(s)\hat{\mathbf{U}}(s) \qquad (5.3)$$

The coefficient matrices are functions of s since the control circuit may include integration and differentiation, as required, for loop compensation.

5.2   Source-to-State Transfer Functions

Combining Eq. (5.3) with the Laplace transform of Eq. (4.39) results in

$$\hat{\mathbf{X}}(s) = [s\mathbf{I} - \mathbf{A}_0 - \mathbf{E}\mathbf{F}^T(s)]^{-1}[\mathbf{B}_0 + \mathbf{E}\mathbf{Q}^T(s)]\hat{\mathbf{U}}(s) \qquad (5.4)$$

The expression $[s\mathbf{I} - \mathbf{A}_0 - \mathbf{E}\mathbf{F}^T(s)]^{-1}[\mathbf{B}_0 + \mathbf{E}\mathbf{Q}^T(s)]$ is the general ac transfer function matrix relating state variables to source variables, which we shall designate by $\mathbf{T}_{xu}(s)$.

As an illustrative example, we again consider the basic boost converter, this time implemented with the simple voltage-mode PWM controller of Fig. 3.2. Since $d = v_e/V_p$, we have

$$d(s) = \frac{V_e(s)}{V_p} = \frac{[1 + K(s)]V_R(s) - K(s)X_2(s)}{V_p} \qquad (5.5)$$

where $K(s)$ is the error amplifier gain and $V_R(s)$ is the transform of the reference voltage. Assuming that the reference is dc only and, therefore, not modulated, the ac duty factor can be expressed by the equation

$$\hat{d}(s) = -\frac{K(s)}{V_p}\hat{X}_2(s) \qquad (5.6)$$

in which case

$$\mathbf{F}^T(s) = \begin{bmatrix} 0 & -\dfrac{K(s)}{V_p} \end{bmatrix} \qquad (5.7a)$$

and

$$\mathbf{Q}^T(s) = \mathbf{0} \qquad (5.7b)$$

Combining Eqs. (4.44) and (5.7) results in the transfer function matrix

$$\mathbf{T}_{xu}(s) = \begin{bmatrix} s & \dfrac{1-D}{L} + \dfrac{x_{20}K(s)}{V_pL} \\ -\dfrac{(1-D)}{C} & s + \dfrac{1}{RC} - \dfrac{x_{10}K(s)}{V_pC} \end{bmatrix}^{-1} \begin{bmatrix} \dfrac{1}{L} & 0 \\ 0 & \dfrac{1}{C} \end{bmatrix}$$

$$(5.8a)$$

or

$$\mathbf{T}_{xu}(s) = \frac{\begin{bmatrix} s + \dfrac{1}{RC} - \dfrac{x_{10}K(s)}{V_pC} & -\dfrac{(1-D)}{L} - \dfrac{x_{20}K(s)}{V_pL} \\ \dfrac{1-D}{C} & s \end{bmatrix} \begin{bmatrix} \dfrac{1}{L} & 0 \\ 0 & \dfrac{1}{C} \end{bmatrix}}{s^2 + s\left[\dfrac{1}{RC} - \dfrac{x_{10}K(s)}{V_pC}\right] + \dfrac{(1-D)^2}{LC} + \dfrac{x_{20}(1-D)K(s)}{V_pLC}}$$

$$(5.8b)$$

The final form of the above transfer function matrix is obtained by substituting the dc values of Eq. (4.45) into Eq. (5.8b) and carrying out the matrix multiplication. Each element of $\mathbf{T}_{xu}(s)$ corresponds to a specific source-to-state transfer function as follows:

$$[\mathbf{T}_{xu}(s)]_{11} = \frac{\hat{X}_1(s)}{\hat{U}_1(s)} =$$

$$\frac{\dfrac{1}{L}\left\{s + \dfrac{1}{RC}\left[1 - \dfrac{u_{10}K(s)}{V_p(1-D)^2}\right]\right\}}{s^2 + \dfrac{s}{RC}\left[1 - \dfrac{u_{10}K(s)}{V_p(1-D)^2}\right] + \dfrac{(1-D)^2}{LC}\left[1 + \dfrac{u_{10}K(s)}{V_p(1-D)^2}\right]}$$

$$(5.9a)$$

$$[\mathbf{T}_{xu}(s)]_{12} = \frac{\hat{X}_1(s)}{\hat{U}_2(s)} =$$

$$\frac{\dfrac{-(1-D)}{LC}\left[1 + \dfrac{u_{10}K(s)}{V_p(1-D)^2}\right]}{s^2 + \dfrac{s}{RC}\left[1 - \dfrac{u_{10}K(s)}{V_p(1-D)^2}\right] + \dfrac{(1-D)^2}{LC}\left[1 + \dfrac{u_{10}K(s)}{V_p(1-D)^2}\right]}$$

$$(5.9b)$$

$$[\mathbf{T}_{xu}(s)]_{21} = \frac{\hat{X}_2(s)}{\hat{U}_1(s)} =$$

$$\frac{\dfrac{1-D}{LC}}{s^2 + \dfrac{s}{RC}\left[1 - \dfrac{u_{10}K(s)}{V_p(1-D)^2}\right] + \dfrac{(1-D)^2}{LC}\left[1 + \dfrac{u_{10}K(s)}{V_p(1-D)^2}\right]}$$

$$(5.9c)$$

and

$$[\mathbf{T}_{xu}(s)]_{22} = \frac{\hat{X}_2(s)}{\hat{U}_2(s)} =$$

$$\frac{\dfrac{s}{C}}{s^2 + \dfrac{s}{RC}\left[1 - \dfrac{u_{10}K(s)}{V_p(1-D)^2}\right] + \dfrac{(1-D)^2}{LC}\left[1 + \dfrac{u_{10}K(s)}{V_p(1-D)^2}\right]}$$

$$(5.9d)$$

These transfer functions are important in their own right, but the state variables do not necessarily correspond to the output variables of interest.

5.3   Source-to-Output Transfer Functions

Of particular interest are the input current y_1 and the output voltage y_2 as shown in Fig. 5.1. For a linear system, any output vector $\mathbf{y}$ can be expressed as a linear combination of the state vector $\mathbf{x}$ and the source vector $\mathbf{u}$. In the linearized switching regulator, the output vector may also be a function of $\hat{d}$. In our basic boost regulator example, y_1 is simply equal to x_1, and y_2 is equal to x_2. However, in the basic buck regulator, y_1 is equal to x_1 for the condition S1 ON/S2 OFF and is equal to zero for the condition S1 OFF/S2 ON. After state-space averaging, y_1 becomes $x_1 d$, and after linearization, y_1 becomes $x_1 D + x_{10} \hat{d}$. In general, the linearized output vector can be expressed as

$$\mathbf{y} = \mathbf{C}_0 \mathbf{x} + \mathbf{D}_0 \mathbf{u} + \mathbf{P} \hat{d} \tag{5.10}$$

where, as before, the coefficient matrices generally depend on the dc operating point. Since $\hat{d}$ is expressible in terms of $\dot{\mathbf{x}}$, $\mathbf{x}$, and $\mathbf{u}$, in accordance with Eq. (4.40), it follows that $\mathbf{y}$ can also be expressed in terms of $\dot{\mathbf{x}}$, $\mathbf{x}$, and $\mathbf{u}$, in which case we can say that

$$\hat{\mathbf{Y}}(s) = \mathbf{M}(s)\hat{\mathbf{X}}(s) + \mathbf{N}_0 \hat{\mathbf{U}}(s) \tag{5.11}$$

Using Eq. (5.11), instead of the Laplace transform of the ac output vector derived from Eq. (5.10), provides an economy of algebra and is more appropriate in instances where the output variable can be expressed directly in terms of the state variables, their derivatives, and the source variables. Such is the case, for example, for the output voltage y_2 in any of the topologies where ESR is not negligible. In these instances, $Y_2(s)$ is simply $(1 + R_{ESR}Cs)X_2(s)$, independent of the control law.

Combining Eqs. (5.4) and (5.11) results in the general ac source-to-output transfer function matrix

$$\mathbf{T}_{yu}(s) = \mathbf{M}(s)[s\mathbf{I} - \mathbf{A}_0 - \mathbf{E}\mathbf{F}^T(s)]^{-1}[\mathbf{B}_0 + \mathbf{E}\mathbf{Q}^T(s)] + \mathbf{N}_0 \tag{5.12}$$

which, for the variables shown in Fig. 5.1, consists of the following elements:

$$\frac{\hat{Y}_1(s)}{\hat{U}_1(s)} = \text{input admittance} \overset{\Delta}{=} Z_1^{-1}(s) \tag{5.13a}$$

$$\frac{\hat{Y}_1(s)}{\hat{U}_2(s)} = \text{output current susceptibility} \tag{5.13b}$$

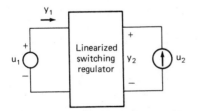

Figure 5.1 General two-port model of linearized switching regulator.

$$\frac{\hat{Y}_2(s)}{\hat{U}_1(s)} = \text{input voltage susceptibility} \qquad (5.13c)$$

$$\frac{\hat{Y}_2(s)}{\hat{U}_2(s)} = \text{output impedance} \overset{\Delta}{=} Z_2(s) \qquad (5.13d)$$

As an illustrative example, we consider the output impedance of our voltage-mode-controlled boost regulator, updated further to include ESR. For notational clarity, we use R_1 for the load resistance and R_2 for the ESR (Fig. 5.2). For algebraic simplicity, R_2 has been neglected so far. However, since R_2 affects phase shift at much lower frequencies than it affects amplitude, it is always well to include it. Certainly, at some high enough frequency, R_2 is not negligible, even for amplitude considerations. Similarly, at some low enough frequency, the series resistance of the inductor is not negligible, and it should also be included in any detailed analysis. However, its practical influence on switching regulator behavior is less significant, and it will continue to be neglected here. Since

$$y_1 = x_1 \qquad (5.14a)$$

and
$$y_2 = x_2 + R_2 C \dot{x}_2 \qquad (5.14b)$$

we have

$$\mathbf{M}(s) = \begin{bmatrix} 1 & 0 \\ 0 & 1 + R_2 C s \end{bmatrix} \qquad (5.15a)$$

and
$$\mathbf{N}_0 = \mathbf{0} \qquad (5.15b)$$

The updated $\mathbf{A}_0$ and $\mathbf{B}_0$ matrices are

$$\mathbf{A}_0 = \begin{bmatrix} -\dfrac{R_2(1-D)}{L} & -\dfrac{(1-D)}{L} \\ \dfrac{1-D}{C} & -\dfrac{1}{R_1 C} \end{bmatrix} \qquad (5.16a)$$

and
$$\mathbf{B}_0 = \begin{bmatrix} \dfrac{1}{L} & -\dfrac{R_2(1-D)}{L} \\ 0 & \dfrac{1}{C} \end{bmatrix} \qquad (5.16b)$$

The $\mathbf{E}$ matrix is unaffected by ESR. Combining Eqs. (4.44c) and (4.45) results in the equation

$$\mathbf{E} = \begin{bmatrix} \dfrac{u_{10}}{L(1 - D)} \\[3mm] -\dfrac{u_{10}}{R_1 C(1 - D)^2} \end{bmatrix} \tag{5.16c}$$

The updated $\mathbf{F}^T(s)$ matrix in the control law becomes

$$\mathbf{F}^T(s) = \begin{bmatrix} 0 & -\dfrac{(1 + R_2 Cs)K(s)}{V_p} \end{bmatrix} \tag{5.16d}$$

Thus, $\mathbf{T}_{yu}(s)$ becomes

$$\mathbf{T}_{yu}(s) = \begin{bmatrix} 1 & 0 \\ 0 & 1 + R_2 Cs \end{bmatrix}$$

$$\cdot \left[\begin{array}{c|c} s + \dfrac{R_2(1 - D)}{L} & \dfrac{(1 - D)}{L}\left[1 + \dfrac{u_{10}(1 + R_2 Cs)K(s)}{V_p(1 - D)^2}\right] \\ \hline -\dfrac{(1 - D)}{C} & s + \dfrac{1}{R_1 C}\left[1 - \dfrac{u_{10}(1 + R_2 Cs)K(s)}{V_p(1 - D)^2}\right] \end{array} \right]^{-1}$$

$$\cdot \begin{bmatrix} \dfrac{1}{L} & -\dfrac{R_2(1 - D)}{L} \\[3mm] 0 & \dfrac{1}{C} \end{bmatrix} \tag{5.17}$$

from which it can be determined that

$$Z_2(s) = R_2 s \left(s + \dfrac{1}{R_2 C}\right) \Big/ \left(s^2 + s\left\{\dfrac{1}{R_1 C}\left[1 - \dfrac{u_{10}(1 + R_2 Cs)K(s)}{V_p(1 - D)^2}\right]\right.\right.$$

$$\left.\left. + \dfrac{R_2(1 - D)}{L}\right\} + \dfrac{(1 - D)^2}{LC}\left[1 + \dfrac{u_{10}(1 + R_2 Cs)K(s)}{V_p(1 - D)^2}\right]\right) \tag{5.18}$$

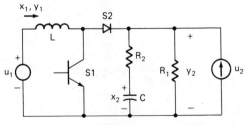

Figure 5.2 Basic boost converter with ESR.

where some terms are neglected on the assumption that $R_2/R_1 \ll 1$. Note that for $s \to \infty$, we get the expected result that $Z_2 \to R_2$. For $s \to 0$, we get $Z_2 \to 0$ as a result of the assumption that the series resistance of the inductor is neglected.

It is clear from Eq. (5.12) that the actual closed-loop static and dynamic performance characteristics of a switching regulator are determined by a combination of the power circuitry and the control circuitry. Static performance requirements include output voltage regulation over variations in load and input voltage; dynamic performance requirements include input ripple voltage susceptibility and output impedance over the ranges of source and load modulation frequencies, respectively. In addition, there are switching-related performance requirements, such as output ripple and EMI, that must be dealt with using switching models rather than the state-space-averaged linearized model, as discussed in the previous chapter. As with any feedback control system, the object is to achieve the specified performance requirements without violating the stability criteria.

5.4 Classic Stability Considerations

The stability of a linearized switching regulator can be evaluated using any of the classical stability criteria. For example, the Routh–Hurwitz criterion can be applied directly to the closed-loop characteristic polynomial, $\det [s\mathbf{I} - \mathbf{A}_0 - \mathbf{E}\mathbf{F}^T(s)]$. Alternatively, Nyquist plots or Bode plots of the open-loop gain function can be drawn and examined for adequate gain and phase margins.

The feedback control loops can be mathematically opened by replacing the transformed ac state vector $\hat{\mathbf{X}}(s)$ with an independent test vector $\hat{\mathbf{V}}(s)$ in the control law [Eq. (5.3)]. The general ac open-loop transfer function matrix $\mathbf{T}_{xv}(s)$ that relates the state vector to the test vector is then determined by combining the equation

$$\hat{d}(s) = \mathbf{F}^T(s)\hat{\mathbf{V}}(s) + \mathbf{Q}^T(s)\hat{\mathbf{U}}(s) \tag{5.19}$$

with the transform of Eq. (4.39), or

$$s\hat{\mathbf{X}}(s) = \mathbf{A}_0\hat{\mathbf{X}}(s) + \mathbf{B}_0\hat{\mathbf{U}}(s) + \mathbf{E}\hat{d}(s) \tag{5.20}$$

to arrive at the equation

$$\mathbf{T}_{xv}(s) = (s\mathbf{I} - \mathbf{A}_0)^{-1}\mathbf{E}\mathbf{F}^T(s) \tag{5.21}$$

For negative-feedback systems with touching feedback loops, the total open-loop gain function $G(s)H(s)$ is simply the sum of the individual open-loop gain functions $-\hat{X}_k(s)/\hat{V}_k(s)$.[1] That is, for an nth-order system, where there may be as many as n loops,

$$G(s)H(s) = -\sum_{k=1}^{n} \frac{\hat{X}_k(s)}{\hat{V}_k(s)} \tag{5.22}$$

This equation is valid for switching regulators that use a single comparator, since all loops touch at the comparator. Switching regulators with two or more *independently* controlled switches may fall out of this category, and their associated stability analyses are necessarily more complex. All of the switching regulator topologies presented in this book have only one independently controlled switch, even though there may be multiple switches. The transfer functions $\hat{X}_k(s)/\hat{V}_k(s)$ are the diagonal elements of the open-loop transfer function matrix, so Eq. (5.22) can be rewritten as

$$G(s)H(s) = -\sum_{k=1}^{n} \text{diag}\,[(s\mathbf{I} - \mathbf{A}_0)^{-1}\mathbf{E}\mathbf{F}^T(s)] \tag{5.23}$$

We shall now apply Eq. (5.23) to the basic boost converter with ESR, shown in Fig. 5.2, with voltage-mode control. Equation (5.6) becomes

$$\hat{d}(s) = -\frac{K(s)}{V_p} Y_2(s) \tag{5.24}$$

After applying Eq. (5.14b), the control-law feedback coefficient matrix becomes

$$\mathbf{F}^T(s) = \left[0 \quad -\frac{K(s)}{V_p}(1 + R_2Cs) \right] \tag{5.25}$$

Combining Eqs. (5.16) and (5.25) results in

$$\mathbf{T}_{xv}(s) = \left[\begin{array}{c|c} s + \dfrac{R_2(1 - D)}{L} & \dfrac{1 - D}{L} \\ \hline -\dfrac{(1 - D)}{C} & s + \dfrac{1}{R_1C} \end{array} \right]^{-1}$$

$$\cdot \left[\begin{array}{c|c} 0 & -\dfrac{u_{10}K(s)}{V_pL(1 - D)}(1 + R_2Cs) \\ \hline 0 & \dfrac{u_{10}K(s)}{V_pR_1C(1 - D)^2}(1 + R_2Cs) \end{array} \right] \tag{5.26}$$

or, neglecting the R_2/R_1 term in the determinant,

$$
\mathbf{T}_{xv}(s) = \frac{
\begin{bmatrix}
s + \dfrac{1}{R_1C} & \bigg| & -\dfrac{(1-D)}{L} \\[2mm]
\hline
\dfrac{1-D}{C} & \bigg| & s + \dfrac{R_2(1-D)}{L}
\end{bmatrix}
\begin{bmatrix}
0 & \bigg| & -\dfrac{u_{10}K(s)}{V_pL(1-D)}(1+R_2Cs) \\[2mm]
\hline
0 & \bigg| & \dfrac{u_{10}K(s)}{V_pR_1C(1-D)^2}(1+R_2Cs)
\end{bmatrix}
}{
s^2 + s\left[\dfrac{1}{R_1C} + \dfrac{R_2(1-D)}{L}\right] + \dfrac{(1-D)^2}{LC}
}
$$

(5.27)

We see that the current-loop gain $[\mathbf{T}_{xv}(s)]_{11}$ is zero,* so

$$G(s)H(s) = -[\mathbf{T}_{xv}(s)]_{22} \tag{5.28}$$

or

Boost.

$$
G(s)H(s) = \frac{\dfrac{u_{10}K(s)R_2}{V_pR_1(1-D)^2}\left(s + \dfrac{1}{R_2C}\right)\left[\dfrac{R_1(1-D)^2}{L} - s\right]}{s^2 + s\left[\dfrac{1}{R_1C} + \dfrac{R_2(1-D)}{L}\right] + \dfrac{(1-D)^2}{LC}} \tag{5.29}
$$

where, again, the numerator is simplified by assuming that $R_2 \ll R_1$.

Similar analyses for the corresponding buck-boost and buck regulators yield, respectively, the following:

Buck-boost.

$$
G(s)H(s) = \frac{\dfrac{u_{10}K(s)R_2D}{V_pR_1(1-D)^2}\left(s + \dfrac{1}{R_2C}\right)\left[\dfrac{R_1(1-D)^2}{LD} - s\right]}{s^2 + s\left[\dfrac{1}{R_1C} + \dfrac{R_2(1-D)}{L}\right] + \dfrac{(1-D)^2}{LC}} \tag{5.30}
$$

Buck.

$$
G(s)H(s) = \frac{\dfrac{u_{10}K(s)R_2}{V_pL}\left(s + \dfrac{1}{R_2C}\right)}{s^2 + s\left(\dfrac{1}{R_1C} + \dfrac{R_2}{L}\right) + \dfrac{1}{LC}} \tag{5.31}
$$

Note that for the boost and buck-boost regulators, the open-loop gain amplitude and the complex pole angular frequency $(1-D)/\sqrt{LC}$ are

---

* As would be expected with voltage-mode control.

dependent upon the steady-state duty factor D. Furthermore, the open-loop gain function for each of these two regulators includes a right-half-plane (RHP) zero that contributes to phase lag. These characteristics place additional constraints on the loop compensation of these regulators compared to the buck regulator. For all three regulators, the gain amplitude is directly dependent upon the dc input voltage for fixed V_p. This confirms one of the advantages of feed-forward control for buck-derived regulators as described in Chap. 3, Sec. 3.2; namely, by designing the sawtooth generator so that V_p is proportional to u_1, the open-loop gain can be made independent of u_{10} so that open-loop gain bandwidth is not compromised at minimum input voltage for the sake of stability at maximum input voltage.

5.5   Voltage-Mode Loop-Compensation Techniques

A Bode plot of the uncompensated open-loop gain function for the voltage-controlled buck regulator is shown in Fig. 5.3(a), where $s = j\omega$. By "uncompensated," we mean that $K(s)$ in Eq. (5.31) is simply equal to a constant value K. That is, there are no poles or zeros in the error amplifier gain function. For simplicity, we have made the worst-case assumption that R_2 is small enough so that the zero at $1/R_2C$ is beyond the frequency range of interest for classical stability considerations. Theoretically, no minimum-phase* second-order system can be unstable. However, as shown, the open-loop phase lag can be arbitrarily close to 180°, so any additional phase lag, such as the transport lag due to switching time delays, can render the system unstable. The dc value of Eq. (5.31) is $u_{10}K/V_p$, ω_n is the resonant frequency $1/\sqrt{LC}$, and ω_c is the unity-gain cross-over angular frequency. The -2 slope implies an amplitude roll-off of -2 times 20 dB per decade.

The two basic voltage-mode loop-compensation techniques are phase lag and phase lead. As applied to a second-order system of resonant angular frequency ω_n, the pole angular frequency of the lag-compensation network ω_p must be low enough so that the gain amplitude, including resonant peaks, is below unity gain when the open-loop phase lag is 180°.† The margin below unity gain is defined as the gain margin and is typically chosen to be 6 dB in order to assure stability under all conditions, including component tolerance and temperature variations. A Bode plot for the lag-compensated version of the buck reg-

---

* A minimum-phase system has no RHP poles or zeros.

† Since any series resistance R_3 associated with the inductor contributes to damping, neglecting R_3 is a worst-case assumption for stability considerations.

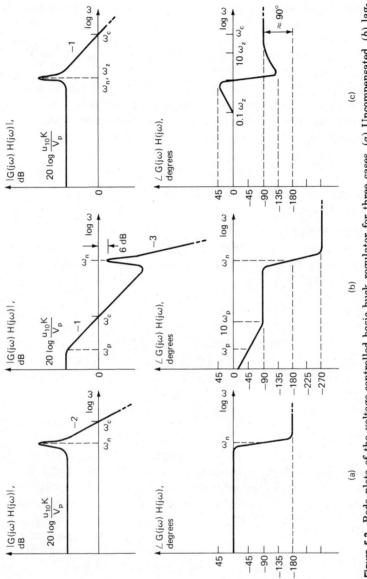

Figure 5.3 Bode plots of the voltage-controlled basic buck regulator for three cases. (*a*) Uncompensated, (*b*) lag-compensated, and (*c*) lead-compensated.

ulator is shown in Fig. 5.3(b), for which

$$K(s) = \frac{\omega_p K}{s + \omega_p} \tag{5.32}$$

For lead compensation, the zero angular frequency ω_z must be low enough so that the open-loop phase lag is less than 180° when the gain is unity. The margin between 180° and the actual phase lag at unity gain is called the "phase margin." A common design practice, which provides nearly 90° of phase margin and which results in essentially a first-order closed-loop system over much of the frequency range, is to choose ω_z equal to ω_n. Since $\omega_z = \omega_n$, this compensation technique is sometimes referred to as "pole cancellation," although the resonant peak associated with the complex pole remains unaffected. A Bode plot for the lead-compensated version of the buck regulator is shown in Fig. 5.3(c), for which $\omega_z = \omega_n$ and

$$K(s) = \frac{K}{\omega_n} (s + \omega_n) \tag{5.33}$$

A pure lead network is not physically realizable, and there must always be an associated lag. However, it is implicitly assumed that lead compensation can be implemented so that the corresponding pole frequency is beyond the frequency range of concern.

It is readily apparent from the Bode plots of Fig. 5.3 that lead compensation results in a much wider open-loop bandwidth than lag compensation. This means that a lead-compensated buck regulator can dynamically respond to load and/or source modulations over a much wider frequency range than its lag-compensated counterpart. However, as we shall see in Chap. 7, the input impedance of a switching regulator is negative for frequencies within its bandwidth of regulation, so extending the frequency range for which this impedance is negative may complicate the design of the input EMI filter, which is used to reduce power-line-conducted interference to acceptable levels.

A second potential disadvantage of lead compensation for switching regulators is that, compared to lag compensation, the open-loop gain at the switching frequency and subharmonics thereof is much, much higher. Especially for push-pull or bridge topologies, where a nontrivial $f_s/2$ component due to inherent circuit imbalances may exist, there is a much greater risk of excessive or even damaging $f_s/2$ or $f_s/4$ output voltage ripple, due to reinforcement by the control circuit. This subharmonic switching instability is popularly known as "tail chasing." A more detailed analysis of this phenomenon, using describing function techniques, is beyond the scope of this book. Although a well-established design criterion for preventing tail chasing does not seem to exist, a suggested rule of thumb is that the open-loop gain should be 40 dB below unity at twice the switching angular frequency $\omega_s = 2\pi f_s$. Tail chasing can be aggravated by ESR, since the slope of the open-loop gain function increases 20 dB per decade at the zero angular frequency $1/R_2C$. In practice, additional filtering must be wedged in between the unity-gain cross-over frequency and the switching frequency to prevent subharmonic switching instability without degrading classical stability. Thus, avoidance of tail chasing places a practical upper limit on the bandwidth of voltage-controlled lead-compensated buck-derived switching regulators that may be well below the allowable bandwidth that would be inferred from the state-space-averaged linearized switching regulator model alone. Of course, the bandwidth can always be increased by increasing the switching frequency, at the expense of lower efficiency.

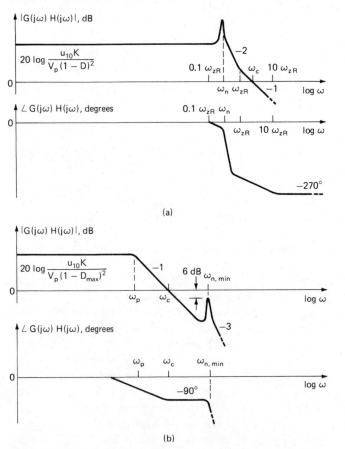

Figure 5.4 Bode plots of the voltage-controlled basic boost regulator for two cases. (a) Uncompensated and (b) lag-compensated.

A Bode plot of the uncompensated open-loop gain function for the voltage-controlled boost regulator is shown in Fig. 5.4(a). In Eq. (5.29), the RHP zero $\omega_{zR} = R_1(1 - D)^2/L$ is shown to be greater than the resonant frequency $\omega_n = (1 - D)/\sqrt{LC}$. From Fig. 4.9, it can be determined that the condition $\omega_{zR} = \omega_n$ corresponds to a load-related damping factor $\zeta_{\text{load}} = \sqrt{L/C}/2R_1(1 - D)$ of 0.5 and that typical values of ζ_{load} are below 0.1. Thus, the supposition that $\omega_{zR} > \omega_n$ is justified. Again, ESR is neglected as a worst-case assumption for classical stability considerations. Because of the duty-factor dependent resonant frequency and the additional 90° phase lag due to the RHP zero, lead compensation is not generally applicable to boost and buck-boost regulators. Figure 5.4(b) shows a Bode plot for the lag-compensated version of the boost regulator, where Eq. (5.32) applies for $K(s)$. The pole frequency ω_p must be low enough so that the worst-case condition of $D = D_{\text{max}}$ can be accommodated. That is, for $D = D_{\text{max}}$, the gain amplitude is highest, the resonant frequency is lowest, and the RHP zero frequency is lowest. As can be seen from Eq. (5.30), the same is true for the buck-boost regulator. Thus, in general, voltage-controlled boost and buck-boost regulators have inherently narrow bandwidths and, therefore, relatively poor frequency response. Again, bandwidth can always be increased by increasing the switching frequency.

In Sec. 5.3, we determined the output impedance of the voltage-mode-controlled boost regulator, as an illustrative example, in terms of the general error-amplifier gain function $K(s)$. To determine the output impedance for the lag compensation described by Eq. (5.32), we simply substitute Eq. (5.32) into Eq. (5.18) to arrive at

$$Z_2(s) =$$

$$R_2s \left(s + \frac{1}{R_2C}\right) \bigg/ \left(s^2 + s \left\{\frac{1}{R_1C}\left[1 - \frac{u_{10}\omega_p K(1 + R_2Cs)}{V_p(1 - D)^2(s + \omega_p)}\right]\right.\right.$$

$$\left.\left. + \frac{R_2(1 - D)}{L}\right\} + \frac{(1 - D)^2}{LC}\left[1 + \frac{u_{10}\omega_p K(1 + R_2Cs)}{V_p(1 - D)^2(s + \omega_p)}\right]\right) \quad (5.34)$$

Further discussion of Eq. (5.34) is deferred until Chap. 6, Sec. 6.5, where performance comparisons are made between voltage-mode control and current-injected control.

5.6 DC Characteristics

There are many applications where good frequency response may not be necessary. However, almost all applications require good dc output voltage regulation over variations in load and input voltage (load regulation and line regulation, respectively). Therefore, it is desirable to make the dc open-loop gain $G_0 H_0$ as large as possible. For the lag-compensated cases, Z_2 and Z_1 of Fig. 3.2 can be configured as a pure integrator, in which case the dc gain in Figs. 5.3(b) and 5.4(b) can be as much as the operational amplifier will allow. For the lead-compensated case, a low-frequency zero at $\omega < 0.1\omega_n$ is needed in addition to the integrator in order to achieve higher dc gain without adding phase lag at ω_n. The low-frequency gain of Fig. 5.3(c) then becomes the so-called gain plateau $G_p H_p$ as shown in Fig. 5.5.

The state-variable dc solutions for the basic switching regulators were determined in Chap. 2 using the constraints that the average inductor voltage and average capacitor current must be zero. Alternatively, we can use Eq. (4.38) to arrive at

$$\mathbf{x}_0 = -\mathbf{A}_0^{-1}\mathbf{B}_0\mathbf{u}_0 \tag{5.35}$$

and, based on Eq. (5.11), we have the equation

$$\mathbf{y}_0 = \mathbf{M}_0\mathbf{x}_0 + \mathbf{N}_0\mathbf{u}_0 \tag{5.36}$$

where $\mathbf{M}_0 \triangleq \mathbf{M}(0)$. Combining Eqs. (5.35) and (5.36) results in the equation

$$\mathbf{y}_0 = (-\mathbf{M}_0\mathbf{A}_0^{-1}\mathbf{B}_0 + \mathbf{N}_0)\mathbf{u}_0 \tag{5.37}$$

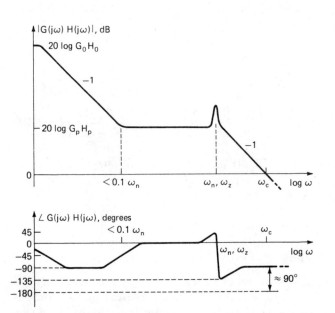

Figure 5.5 Bode plot of the lead-compensated voltage-controlled basic buck regulator with high dc gain.

Continuing with our boost regulator example and applying Eq. (5.15) for $s = 0$, we get

$$\begin{bmatrix} y_{10} \\ y_{20} \end{bmatrix} = \begin{bmatrix} 1 & 0 \\ 0 & 1 \end{bmatrix} \begin{bmatrix} x_{10} \\ x_{20} \end{bmatrix} \tag{5.38a}$$

or

$$y_{10} = x_{10} \tag{5.38b}$$

and

$$y_{20} = x_{20} \tag{5.38c}$$

Now, using Eq. (5.16), we get

$$\begin{bmatrix} x_{10} \\ x_{20} \end{bmatrix} = - \begin{bmatrix} -\dfrac{R_2(1-D)}{L} & -\dfrac{(1-D)}{L} \\ \dfrac{1-D}{C} & -\dfrac{1}{R_1 C} \end{bmatrix}^{-1} \begin{bmatrix} \dfrac{1}{L} & -\dfrac{R_2(1-D)}{L} \\ 0 & \dfrac{1}{C} \end{bmatrix} \begin{bmatrix} u_{10} \\ 0 \end{bmatrix} \tag{5.39a}$$

where it is understood that $u_{20} = 0$. Solving Eq. (5.39a) results in

$$\begin{bmatrix} x_{10} \\ x_{20} \end{bmatrix} = \dfrac{\begin{bmatrix} \dfrac{1}{R_1 C} & -\dfrac{(1-D)}{L} \\ \dfrac{1-D}{C} & \dfrac{R_2(1-D)}{L} \end{bmatrix} \begin{bmatrix} \dfrac{1}{L} & -\dfrac{R_2(1-D)}{L} \\ 0 & \dfrac{1}{C} \end{bmatrix} \begin{bmatrix} u_{10} \\ 0 \end{bmatrix}}{-\dfrac{(1-D)}{LC}\left(1 + \dfrac{R_2}{R_1}\right)} \tag{5.39b}$$

or

$$\begin{bmatrix} x_{10} \\ x_{20} \end{bmatrix} = \dfrac{\begin{bmatrix} \dfrac{1}{R_1 LC} & -\dfrac{(1-D)}{LC}\left(1 + \dfrac{R_2}{R_1}\right) \\ \dfrac{1-D}{LC} & \dfrac{R_2 D(1-D)}{LC} \end{bmatrix} \begin{bmatrix} u_{10} \\ 0 \end{bmatrix}}{\dfrac{(1-D)^2}{LC}\left[1 + \dfrac{R_2}{R_1(1-D)}\right]} \tag{5.39c}$$

Neglecting R_2/R_1 with respect to unity, we can write

$$x_{10} = \dfrac{u_{10}}{R_1(1-D)^2} \tag{5.40a}$$

and

$$x_{20} = \dfrac{u_{10}}{1-D} \tag{5.40b}$$

which coincide with Eq. (4.45). Based on Eq. (5.5), the steady-state duty factor D is determined by the expression

$$D = \frac{V_e(0)}{V_p} = \frac{V_R + K_0(V_R - x_{20})}{V_p} \tag{5.41}$$

where $K_0 \triangleq K(0)$. When the error amplifier feedback network includes a pure integrator, K_0 is simply the dc gain of the operational amplifier. Combining Eqs. (5.40) and (5.41) leads to the obvious result of

$$x_{20} \approx V_R \tag{5.42a}$$

and

$$x_{10} \approx \frac{V_R}{R_1} \tag{5.42b}$$

in which case

$$D \approx 1 - \frac{u_{10}}{V_R} \tag{5.43}$$

In practice, particularly for the boost regulator, an output voltage divider would be used. For a divider attenuation factor a, Eq. (5.42c) becomes

$$D \approx 1 - \frac{au_{10}}{V_R} \tag{5.44}$$

The dc solutions for other switching regulator topologies can be similarly determined.

5.7 Illustrative Problems

5.1   Determine the general source-to-output transfer function matrix for the buck regulator of Fig. P5.1 where $K(s)$ is the error-amplifier gain, V_R is the fixed reference voltage, and V_P is the fixed sawtooth peak voltage.

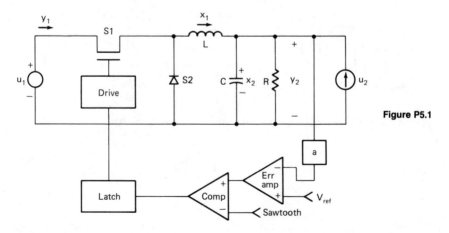

Figure P5.1

SOLUTION:

S1 ON/S2 OFF:

$$u_1 = L\dot{x}_1 + x_2 \Longrightarrow \dot{x}_1 = -\frac{1}{L}x_2 + \frac{1}{L}u_1$$

$$x_1 + u_2 = C\dot{x}_2 + \frac{1}{R}x_2 \Longrightarrow \dot{x}_2 = \frac{1}{C}x_1 - \frac{1}{RC}x_2 + \frac{1}{C}u_2$$

$$y_1 = x_1$$

$$y_2 = x_2$$

S1 OFF/S2 ON:

$$\dot{x}_1 = -\frac{1}{L}x_2$$

$$\dot{x}_2 = \frac{1}{C}x_1 - \frac{1}{RC}x_2 + \frac{1}{C}u_2$$

$$y_1 = 0$$

$$y_2 = x_2$$

State-space averaging gives us

$$\dot{x}_1 = -\frac{1}{L}x_2 + \frac{1}{L}u_1 d$$

$$\dot{x}_2 = \frac{1}{C}x_1 - \frac{1}{RC}x_2 + \frac{1}{C}u_2$$

$$y_1 = x_1 d$$

$$y_2 = x_2$$

Linearizing gives us

$$\dot{x}_1 = -\frac{1}{L}x_2 + \frac{D}{L}u_1 + \frac{u_{10}}{L}\hat{d}$$

$$\dot{x}_2 = \frac{1}{C}x_1 - \frac{1}{RC}x_2 + \frac{1}{C}u_2$$

$$y_1 = Dx_1 + x_{10}\hat{d}$$

$$y_2 = x_2$$

$$\mathbf{A}_0 = \begin{bmatrix} 0 & -\dfrac{1}{L} \\ \dfrac{1}{C} & -\dfrac{1}{RC} \end{bmatrix} \qquad \mathbf{B}_0 = \begin{bmatrix} \dfrac{D}{L} & 0 \\ 0 & \dfrac{1}{C} \end{bmatrix} \qquad \mathbf{E} = \begin{bmatrix} \dfrac{u_{10}}{L} \\ 0 \end{bmatrix}$$

Using Eq. (5.5) with the attenuation factor a, we have

$$\mathbf{F}^T(s) = \begin{bmatrix} 0 & -\dfrac{aK(s)}{V_p} \end{bmatrix} \qquad \mathbf{Q}^T(s) = \mathbf{0}$$

Taking the Laplace transform of the output equations and using Eq. (5.6) with the attenuation factor a results in

$$\hat{Y}_1(s) = D\hat{X}_1(s) - \frac{ax_{10}K(s)}{V_p}\hat{X}_2(s)$$

$$\hat{Y}_2(s) = \hat{X}_2(s)$$

$$\therefore \quad \mathbf{M}(s) = \begin{bmatrix} D & -\dfrac{ax_{10}K(s)}{V_p} \\ 0 & 1 \end{bmatrix} \qquad \mathbf{N}_0 = \mathbf{0}$$

From dc considerations, we can determine that

$$D = \frac{V_R}{au_{10}}$$

$$x_{10} = \frac{V_R}{aR}$$

We now combine the above matrices in accordance with Eq. (5.12) to arrive at the equation

$$\mathbf{EF}^T(s) = \begin{bmatrix} 0 & -\dfrac{au_{10}K(s)}{V_pL} \\ 0 & 0 \end{bmatrix}$$

$$s\mathbf{I} - \mathbf{A}_0 - \mathbf{EF}^T(s) = \begin{bmatrix} s & \dfrac{1}{L}\left[1 + \dfrac{au_{10}K(s)}{V_p}\right] \\ -\dfrac{1}{C} & s + \dfrac{1}{RC} \end{bmatrix}$$

$$[s\mathbf{I} - \mathbf{A}_0 - \mathbf{EF}^T(s)]^{-1} = \frac{\begin{bmatrix} s + \dfrac{1}{RC} & -\dfrac{1}{L}\left[1 + \dfrac{au_{10}K(s)}{V_p}\right] \\ \hline \dfrac{1}{C} & s \end{bmatrix}}{s^2 + \dfrac{s}{RC} + \dfrac{1}{LC}\left[1 + \dfrac{au_{10}K(s)}{V_p}\right]}$$

$$[s\mathbf{I} - \mathbf{A}_0 - \mathbf{EF}^T(s)]^{-1}\mathbf{B}_0 = \cfrac{\begin{bmatrix} \dfrac{D}{L}\left(s + \dfrac{1}{RC}\right) & \Bigg| & -\dfrac{1}{LC}\left[1 + \dfrac{au_{10}K(s)}{V_p}\right] \\[2ex] \hline \dfrac{D}{LC} & \Bigg| & \dfrac{s}{C} \end{bmatrix}}{s^2 + \dfrac{s}{RC} + \dfrac{1}{LC}\left[1 + \dfrac{au_{10}K(s)}{V_p}\right]}$$

Since $\mathbf{Q}^T(s) = \mathbf{N}_0 = \mathbf{0}$, we have

$$\mathbf{T}_{yu}(s) = \mathbf{M}(s)[s\mathbf{I} - \mathbf{A}_0 - \mathbf{EF}^T(s)]^{-1}\mathbf{B}_0$$

$$[\mathbf{T}_{yu}(s)]_{11} = \left[\frac{D^2}{L}\left(s + \frac{1}{RC}\right) - \frac{aDx_{10}K(s)}{V_pLC}\right] \div \Delta = \frac{\hat{Y}_1(s)}{\hat{U}_1(s)}$$

$$[\mathbf{T}_{yu}(s)]_{12} = \left\{-\frac{D}{LC}\left[1 + \frac{au_{10}K(s)}{V_p}\right] - \frac{sax_{10}K(s)}{V_pC}\right\} \div \Delta = \frac{\hat{Y}_1(s)}{\hat{U}_2(s)}$$

$$[\mathbf{T}_{yu}(s)]_{21} = \frac{D}{LC} \div \Delta = \frac{\hat{Y}_2(s)}{\hat{U}_1(s)}$$

$$[\mathbf{T}_{yu}(s)]_{22} = \frac{s}{C} \div \Delta = \frac{\hat{Y}_2(s)}{\hat{U}_2(s)}$$

$$\Delta = s^2 + \frac{s}{RC} + \frac{1}{LC}\left[1 + \frac{au_{10}K(s)}{V_p}\right]$$

Observe that the input admittance $[\mathbf{T}_{yu}(s)]_{11}$ can be negative at low frequencies where $K(s) \gg 1$. This may have adverse system repercussions, as will be discussed in Chap. 7. For $au_{10}K(s)/V_p \gg 1$, we have

$$[\mathbf{T}_{yu}(s)]_{11} \approx \frac{D^2}{L}\left[s - \frac{au_{10}K(s)}{V_pRC}\right] \div \Delta$$

$$[\mathbf{T}_{yu}(s)]_{12} \approx -\frac{au_{10}DK(s)}{V_pRC}\left(s + \frac{R}{L}\right) \div \Delta$$

where $u_{10}D/R$ has been substituted for x_{10} and where

$$\Delta \approx s^2 + \frac{s}{RC} + \frac{au_{10}K(s)}{V_pLC}$$

5.2 Figure P5.1 is given to you as the equivalent circuit of a 40-kHz 20-V/20-A push-pull converter for which $L = 100$ µH and $C = 10,000$ µF. Feedforward compensation (where V_p is proportional to u_{10}) is used so that the dc open-loop gain $au_{10}K(0)/V_p$ is 40 dB regardless of the value of u_{10}. Compare the peak values of output impedance $Z_2(s) = \hat{Y}_2(s)/\hat{U}_2(s)$ for lag compensation and pole-cancelling lead compensation.

SOLUTION: For lag compensation, the unity-gain cross-over frequency ω_c must be much less than $\omega_n = 1/\sqrt{LC}$, since

$$\zeta = \frac{1}{2R} \sqrt{\frac{L}{C}} = \frac{1}{2} \sqrt{\frac{100}{10,000}} = 0.05$$

Therefore, $au_{10}K(s)/V_P \ll 1$ at $\omega = \omega_n$ and, using the results of Prob. 5.1, we have

$$Z_{2(max)} \approx \frac{j\omega_n/C}{-\omega_n^2 + j\omega_n/RC + \omega_n^2} = R = 1\ \Omega \qquad \text{lag comp.}$$

For pole-cancelling lead compensation with feed-forward and a dc gain of 40 dB, we have

$$\frac{au_{10}K(s)}{V_p} = 100\left(1 + \frac{s}{\omega_n}\right)$$

Since $100 \gg 1$ and $100/\omega_n \gg 1/RC$, the determinant Δ can be approximated as

$$\Delta \approx s^2 + \frac{100s}{\omega_n} + 100\omega_n^2 \approx (s + \omega_n)(s + 100\omega_n)$$

$$Z_2(s) \approx \frac{s/C}{(s + \omega_n)(s + 100\omega_n)}$$

For $s < j\omega_n$, $Z_2(s)$ is approximated by the expression

$$Z_2(s) = \frac{s/C}{100\omega_n^2} = \frac{Ls}{100}$$

For $s > j100\omega_n$, $Z_2(s)$ is approximated by the expression

$$Z_2(s) = \frac{s/C}{s^2} = \frac{1}{Cs}$$

For $j\omega_n < s < j100\omega_n$, $Z_2(s)$ is approximated by the expression

$$Z_2(s) = \frac{s/C}{s(100\omega_n)} = \frac{1}{100}\sqrt{\frac{L}{C}}$$

so

$$Z_{2(max)} = \frac{1}{100}\sqrt{\frac{100}{10,000}} = 0.001\ \Omega \qquad \text{lead comp.}$$

Thus, $Z_{2(max)}$ is three orders of magnitude lower with pole-cancelling lead compensation than with lag compensation. This problem illustrates the large potential performance improvements possible with a so-called wide-bandwidth feedback control scheme.

5.3 In an effort to verify the low output impedance of the lead-compensated switching regulator of Prob. 5.2, you measure over 0.003 Ω (i.e., 10 dB higher than predicted) at the critical modulation frequency of 2 kHz. Although you determine that this value may still be satisfactory, your supervisor suggests that you investigate the possible effects of ESR. You discover that, for the chosen capacitor, ESR is 0.025 Ω.

SOLUTION: The damping effect of ESR is determined by the equation

$$\zeta_{ESR} = \frac{ESR}{2}\sqrt{\frac{C}{L}} = \frac{0.025}{2}\sqrt{\frac{10,000}{100}} = 0.125$$

This is significant with respect to the load-related damping factor of 0.05 calculated in Prob. 5.2, and, as a result, it will cause the lag-compensated value of $Z_{2(max)}$ to be somewhat reduced. However, the ESR-related damping term in the new characteristic polynomial is still much less than the term $100s/\omega_n$ for the lead-compensated case. Thus, the lead-compensated determinant is basically unchanged, and the major effect is the addition of a zero at $1/R_2C$ to the expression for $Z_2(s)$, where R_2 is ESR. That is, for lead compensation, $Z_2(s)$ is determined by the expression

$$Z_2(s) \approx \frac{(1 + R_2Cs)s/C}{(s + \omega_n)(s + 100\omega_n)} = \frac{R_2s(s + 1/R_2C)}{(s + \omega_n)(s + 100\omega_n)}$$

Figure S5.3 is a plot of $Z_2(s)$, with appropriate numerical values, showing the influence of ESR for lead compensation. Figure S5.3 also reflects the fact that the dc resistance (DCR) of the inductor and the ON resistances of the switches

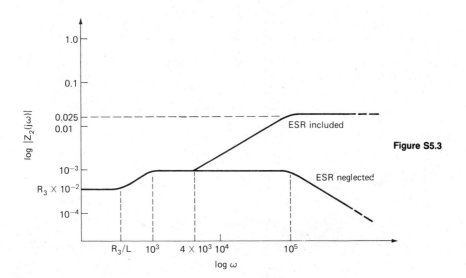

Figure S5.3

provide a lower bound on $Z_2(s)$ for low frequencies. If the total effective series resistance is R_3, then the lead-compensated output impedance becomes

$$Z_2(s) = \frac{R_2(s + R_3/L)(s + 1/R_2C)}{(s + \omega_n)(s + 100\omega_n)}$$

such that $Z_2(0) = R_3/100$ for a dc gain of 40 dB.

5.4 You are asked to design a programmable version of the power supply of Prob. 5.2, in which the output tracks a time-varying reference signal. Derive the small-signal transfer function between the output voltage and the reference voltage for the lead-compensated buck-derived switching regulator modeled in Fig. P5.1. Assume that $a = 0.25$ so that a 20-V output corresponds to a 5-V reference.

SOLUTION: We define the reference voltage as a third independent source u_3. Equation (5.5) then becomes

$$d(s) = \frac{1 + K(s)}{V_p} U_3(s) - \frac{aK(s)}{V_p} X_2(s)$$

so

$$\mathbf{Q}^T(s) = \begin{bmatrix} 0 & 0 & \dfrac{1 + K(s)}{V_p} \end{bmatrix}$$

From Prob. 5.1, we can write

$$\mathbf{EQ}^T(s) = \begin{bmatrix} 0 & 0 & \dfrac{u_{10}[1 + K(s)]}{V_pL} \\ 0 & 0 & 0 \end{bmatrix}$$

Updating $\mathbf{B}_0$ yields

$$\mathbf{B}_0 = \begin{bmatrix} \dfrac{D}{L} & 0 & 0 \\ 0 & \dfrac{1}{C} & 0 \end{bmatrix}$$

in which case

$$\mathbf{B}_0 + \mathbf{EQ}^T(s) = \begin{bmatrix} \dfrac{D}{L} & 0 & \dfrac{u_{10}[1 + K(s)]}{V_pL} \\ 0 & \dfrac{1}{C} & 0 \end{bmatrix}$$

Again using the results of Prob. 5.1, we have

$$[s\mathbf{I} - \mathbf{A}_0 - \mathbf{E}\mathbf{F}^T(s)]^{-1}[\mathbf{B}_0 + \mathbf{E}\mathbf{Q}^T(s)] =$$

$$
\frac{\begin{bmatrix}
\dfrac{D}{L}\left(s + \dfrac{1}{RC}\right) & -\dfrac{1}{LC}\left[1 + \dfrac{au_{10}K(s)}{V_p}\right] & \dfrac{u_{10}[1 + K(s)](s + 1/RC)}{V_pL} \\[3mm]
\hline
\dfrac{D}{LC} & \dfrac{s}{C} & \dfrac{u_{10}[1 + K(s)]}{V_pLC}
\end{bmatrix}}{\Delta}
$$

where Δ is the same as before. It follows that

$$\frac{\hat{Y}_2(s)}{\hat{U}_3(s)} = [\mathbf{T}_{yu}(s)]_{23}$$

$$= \frac{M_{21}(s)u_{10}[1 + K(s)](s + 1/RC)}{V_pL\Delta}$$

$$+ \frac{M_{22}(s)u_{10}[1 + K(s)]}{V_pLC\Delta}$$

$$= \frac{u_{10}[1 + K(s)]}{V_pLC\Delta}$$

where $M_{21}(s)$ and $M_{22}(s)$ are appropriately designated elements of the matrix $\mathbf{M}(s)$. Using the control law of Prob. 5.2, we have

$$\frac{au_{10}K(s)}{V_p} = 100\left(1 + \frac{s}{\omega_n}\right)$$

Because of the lead-compensation feature, we can say that $K(s) \gg 1$ over the frequency range of interest. That is, the associated pole that must be present in any physically realizable system is assumed to be beyond the frequency range of concern. Thus,

$$\frac{\hat{Y}_2(s)}{\hat{U}_3(s)} \approx \frac{u_{10}K(s)}{V_pLC\Delta}$$

Since $a = 0.25$, we have

$$\frac{\hat{Y}_2(s)}{\hat{U}_3(s)} = \frac{400(1 + s/\omega_n)/LC}{(s + \omega_n)(s + 100\omega_n)} = \frac{400\omega_n}{(s + 100\omega_n)}$$

This gives us the result that for a wideband pole-cancelling lead-compensated regulator, the output tracks the reference, at least in a small-signal sense, in accordance with the attenuation constant of 0.25 up to a frequency of $100\omega_n$, corresponding to nearly 16 kHz. It is left as an exercise to show that when

ESR is included, good tracking is possible at even higher frequencies. Circuit imbalances may ultimately limit the bandwidth, and hence the tracking that is achievable in practice, because of tail chasing.

It should be noted that the accuracy of this analysis may suffer as the signal frequency approaches 16 kHz for a switching frequency of 50 kHz. In addition, for larger signals, besides the possibility that ac products may no longer be negligible, one frequently encounters the constraints that $0 < D < 1$ and that, in practice, there would be a current limit circuit associated with S1. Nevertheless, there is a broad range of applications for which these linearized analytical techniques give surprisingly good results, or at least very useful results, even for relatively large signals and relatively high signal frequencies.

References

1. S. J. Mason and H. J. Zimmermann, *Electronic Circuits, Signals, and Systems,* Wiley, New York, 1960, Chap. 4.

Chapter 6

Current-Injected Control

Since optimal control of an nth-order system generally requires n independent feedback variables, it follows that the performance of a basic second-order switching regulator could be improved by including the inductor current state variable along with the capacitor voltage state variable in the PWM control law. As introduced in Chap. 3, Sec. 3.1, one such technique is current-injected control. In this chapter we present a general analysis of these controllers followed by a performance comparison between current-injected control and voltage-mode control for the boost converter as a specific example. The principles presented here can be used as a basis for similar evaluations of other switching regulator topologies.

6.1 Limit-Cycle Controllers

Current-injected control (CIC) was introduced in the U.S. literature as early as 1978 by the European Space Agency Technology Center.[1] As first implemented, CIC switching regulators were free-running, rather than fixed-frequency, and were called "limit-cycle controllers" in apparent reference to the state-space trajectory of the state vector formed by the capacitor voltage and the inductor current. In limit-cycle controllers, an analog of the inductor current ai_L is fed to the negative input of a Schmitt-trigger comparator whose positive input is the output of the output voltage error amplifier. This control technique is

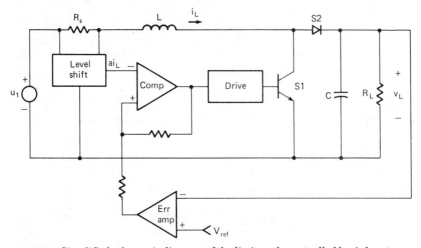

Figure 6.1 Simplified schematic diagram of the limit-cycle-controlled basic boost converter.

shown in Fig. 6.1 for our boost converter example. Turn-on occurs at the lower trip point (LTP), $v_e - h/2$, and turnoff occurs at the UTP, $v_e + h/2$, where h is the hysteresis of the Schmitt trigger. The relevant control waveforms are shown in Fig. 6.2. As can be seen, the average inductor current analog ax_1 is equal to the error voltage which, in turn, depends upon the average output voltage. This means that x_1 is dependent upon x_2 for signal frequencies which are much less than the switching frequency, so there is only one true state variable. Thus, the state-space-averaged limit-cycle-controlled switching regulator is a first-order system.

Since the inductor current signal leads the capacitor voltage signal, wideband frequency response can be achieved with limit-cycle control at the expense of variable frequency operation and, hence, more difficult EMI control, whether the topology is buck, boost, or buck-boost. We shall now investigate the extent to which the desirable features of

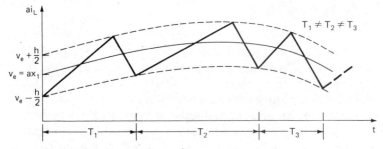

Figure 6.2 Limit-cycle control waveforms.

wideband first-order response can be incorporated into fixed-frequency switching regulators using current-injected control.

6.2 Fixed-Frequency Control-Law Derivation

The usual method of implementing fixed-frequency current-injected control[2,3] is shown in Fig. 6.3. When the frequency is fixed, the control waveforms of Fig. 6.2 no longer apply. In particular, it is not possible to have a fixed period ($T_1 = T_2 = T_3$) with both a constrained UTP and a constrained LTP; one of the trip points must be a free variable. The fixed-frequency control waveforms that correspond to Fig. 6.3 are shown in Fig. 6.4, where turn-on is coincident with a fixed-frequency clock pulse train, and turnoff occurs when the current analog is equal to the error voltage. Since only the positive-going portion of the inductor current waveform is used, an analog of the controlled switch current i_{S1} is adequate. Notice that the locus of lower trip points $R_s i_1$ no longer bears a fixed relationship to the error voltage. As a result, x_1 is not absolutely dependent upon x_2, and the fixed-frequency CIC switching regulator is not categorically first-order.

Nevertheless, as will be shown, it is possible to develop fixed-frequency CIC design criteria for significantly improved performance relative to voltage-mode control, particularly for the boost and buck-boost converters. (From here on, CIC will imply fixed-frequency current-injected control.) The design considerations for the buck-boost converter are virtually identical to those for the boost converter, since their respective analyses differ only by an occasional factor of D. For

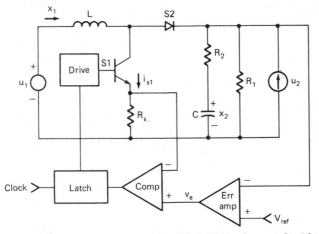

Figure 6.3 Basic boost converter with ESR implemented with fixed-frequency current-injected control.

example, compare Eqs. (5.29) and (5.30). In the case of buck regulators, CIC, as implemented here, does not categorically result in improved performance when compared to lead-compensated voltage control.[4] This is because differentiation of the capacitor voltage state variable in the buck regulator, which is what lead compensation* corresponds to, already provides direct information about the inductor current state variable. Thus, CIC is mainly used in buck converters for instantaneous current limiting, e.g., for minimizing transformer imbalance problems in push-pull topologies, and for current sharing in parallel power supplies. In parallel voltage-mode-controlled supplies, whichever supply has a tendency to produce a higher output voltage tends to produce most of the output current. In parallel CIC supplies, the average output currents track the near-equivalent error voltages. This feature is inherent in any CIC regulator topology. We now derive the CIC control law for the boost converter.

For large enough f_s, the discrete-time equation that relates the nth-cycle error voltage to the nth-cycle current analog of Fig. 6.4, for the power circuit parameters of Fig. 6.3, can be expressed as

$$v_e \left(\frac{n + d_n}{f_s} \right) = R_s \left[i_1 \left(\frac{n}{f_s} \right) + \frac{u_1 d_n}{L f_s} \right] \tag{6.1}$$

where the time dependency of v_e and i_1 is explicitly shown. The continuous-time approximation of Eq. 6.1 is then

$$v_e = R_s \left(i_1 + \frac{u_1 d}{L f_s} \right) \tag{6.2}$$

From Fig. 6.3, we can express i_1 in terms of x_1 and v_e, according to the

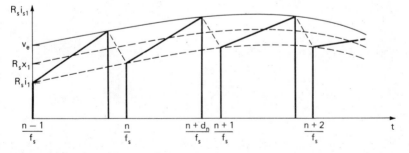

Figure 6.4 Fixed-frequency CIC control waveforms.

---

* Sometimes called "rate feedback."

equation

$$\tfrac{1}{2}(i_1 R_s + v_e) = R_s x_1 \tag{6.3}$$

Combining Eqs. (6.2) and (6.3) results in the continuous control law

$$u_1 d = \frac{2 v_e L f_s}{R_s} - 2 x_1 L f_s \tag{6.4}$$

As we saw in Chap. 4, the penalty for the continuity approximation is nonlinearity, as evidenced by the term $u_1 d$. However, just as before, we can linearize Eq. (6.5) using small-signal approximations. Substituting $u_1 = u_{10} + \hat{u}_1$ and $d = D + \hat{d}$ into Eq. (6.5) and neglecting $\hat{u}_1 \hat{d}$ results in the linear equation

$$\hat{d} = \frac{2 \hat{v}_e L f_s}{u_{10} R_s} - \frac{2 \hat{x}_1 L f_s}{u_{10}} - \frac{\hat{u}_1 D}{u_{10}} \tag{6.5}$$

to which Laplace transforms can now be applied to give

$$\hat{d}(s) = \frac{2 L f_s}{u_{10} R_s} \hat{V}_e(s) - \frac{2 L f_s}{u_{10}} \hat{X}_1(s) - \frac{D}{u_{10}} \hat{U}_1(s) \tag{6.6}$$

Substituting the equation

$$\hat{V}_e(s) = -K(s)(1 + R_2 Cs)\hat{X}_2(s) \tag{6.7}$$

into Eq. (6.6), where $K(s)$ is again the general error-amplifier gain function, we arrive at

$$\hat{d}(s) = -\frac{2 L f_s}{u_{10}} \hat{X}_1(s) - \frac{2 L f_s (1 + R_2 Cs)K(s)}{u_{10} R_s} \hat{X}_2(s) - \frac{D}{u_{10}} \hat{U}_1(s) \tag{6.8}$$

in which case

$$\mathbf{F}^T(s) = -\frac{2 L f_s}{u_{10}} \left[1 \quad \frac{(1 + R_2 Cs)K(s)}{R_s} \right] \tag{6.9a}$$

and

$$\mathbf{Q}^T(s) = -\frac{D}{u_{10}} [1 \quad 0] \tag{6.9b}$$

At first glance, it may seem implausible that the CIC control law should be dependent upon switching frequency, particularly after the continuity approximation has been made. However, by inspection of Fig. 6.4, we see that if f_s is treated as an independent parameter of variation, then the higher f_s is, the more closely x_1 follows the demands of the error signal which, in turn, is dependent upon x_2; that is, the higher f_s is, the more closely the CIC switching regulator approximates a first-order system.

6.3   Current-Mode Switching Stability Criterion

In the previous chapter, two different kinds of instability were discussed: the classic instability of the linearized switching regulator and the subharmonic switching instability, or tail chasing, due to excessive loop gain at subharmonics of the switching frequency in voltage-mode lead-compensated buck-derived regulators. A third type of instability is a switching instability associated with control schemes in which turn-on is coincident with a clock pulse and turnoff occurs when the inductor current analog reaches an upper limit. As we have just seen, this is the normal mode of operation for current-injected control. This mode of operation can also occur in voltage-mode-controlled switching regulators that have a peak current-limiting circuit that overrides the output voltage controller at start-up or in case of overload.

Figure 6.5(a) shows the normal inductor current waveform for a switching regulator with such a control scheme. The current at turn-on is i_1, and the current at turnoff is i_2. Now, suppose that there is some perturbation in the system that causes the initial current of the nth cycle to deviate by an amount δ_n as shown in Fig. 6.5(b). As will now be shown, if the duty factor is less than 0.5, then the subsequent deviations become smaller, converging to zero, and the system is stable; if the duty factor is greater than 0.5, then the subsequent deviations grow indefinitely and the system is unstable.[5]

Assume, for the sake of analysis, that the positive-going slope m_1 and the negative-going slope $-m_2$ of the inductor current waveform are constant. Then,

$$i_2 = i_1 + \delta_n + m_1 \frac{d_n}{f_s} \tag{6.10}$$

and the deviation δ_{n+1} for the next cycle can be determined from the equation

$$i_1 + \delta_{n+1} = i_2 - m_2 \left(\frac{1 - d_n}{f_s} \right) \tag{6.11}$$

Combining Eqs. (6.10) and (6.11) results in the equation

$$\delta_{n+1} = (i_2 - i_1)\left(1 + \frac{m_2}{m_1}\right) - \frac{m_2}{f_s} - \frac{m_2}{m_1}\delta_n \tag{6.12}$$

Similarly, we can say that

$$\delta_{n+2} = (i_2 - i_1)\left(1 + \frac{m_2}{m_1}\right) - \frac{m_2}{f_s} - \frac{m_2}{m_1}\delta_{n+1} \tag{6.13}$$

which, when combined with Eq. (6.12), results in the equation

$$\delta_{n+2} = \left(1 - \frac{m_2}{m_1}\right)\left[(i_2 - i_1)\left(1 + \frac{m_2}{m_1}\right) - \frac{m_2}{f_s}\right] + \left(\frac{m_2}{m_1}\right)^2\delta_n \tag{6.14}$$

By induction,

$$\delta_{n+k} = \left[1 - \frac{m_2}{m_1} + \left(\frac{m_2}{m_1}\right)^2 + \cdots + \left(-\frac{m_2}{m_1}\right)^k\right]$$
$$\cdot\left[(i_2 - i_1)\left(1 + \frac{m_2}{m_1}\right) - \frac{m_2}{f_s}\right] + \left(-\frac{m_2}{m_1}\right)^k\delta_n \tag{6.15}$$

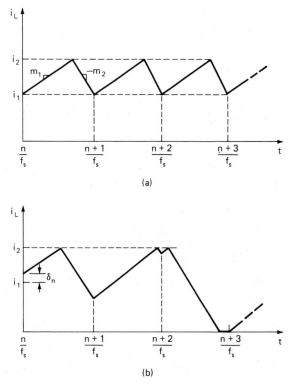

(a)

(b)

Figure 6.5 Inductor current waveforms with fixed-frequency peak-current control for (a) stable operation and (b) unstable operation.

Using the infinite series equivalency

$$1 + \sum_{j=1}^{\infty} (-a)^j = \frac{1}{1 + a} \tag{6.16}$$

we can write

$$\delta_{n+k} = i_2 - i_1 - \frac{m_2/f_s}{1 + m_2/m_1} + \left(-\frac{m_2}{m_1}\right)^k \delta_n \qquad k \longrightarrow \infty \tag{6.17}$$

By combining the stable steady-state equations

$$i_2 = i_1 + \frac{m_1 d_n}{f_s} \tag{6.18}$$

and

$$i_1 = i_2 - \frac{m_2(1 - d_n)}{f_s} \tag{6.19}$$

we have the expression

$$i_2 - i_1 = \frac{m_2/f_s}{1 + m_2/m_1} \tag{6.20}$$

Substituting Eq. (6.20) into Eq. (6.17) yields

$$\delta_{n+k} = \left(-\frac{m_2}{m_1}\right)^k \delta_n \qquad k \longrightarrow \infty \tag{6.21}$$

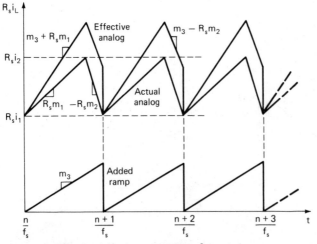

Figure 6.6   Effective inductor current analog.

for which

$$|\delta_{n+k}| \longrightarrow 0 \qquad m_2 < m_1 \qquad (6.22a)$$

and

$$|\delta_{n+k}| \longrightarrow \infty \qquad m_2 > m_1 \qquad (6.22b)$$

By inspection of Fig. 6.5, the current-mode switching stability criterion $m_2 < m_1$ is equivalent to the criterion that the duty factor be less than 0.5.

This is obviously an unsatisfactory operational constraint. However, the situation can be remedied by adding either a negative ramp to the peak current reference or a positive ramp to the inductor current analog $R_s i_L$. The latter technique is shown in Fig. 6.6. Since the step change at the end of the cycle is constant for fixed m_3 and fixed f_s, the current-mode switching stability criterion becomes

$$R_s m_1 + m_3 > -(m_3 - R_s m_2) \qquad (6.23)$$

or

$$m_3 > \frac{R_s}{2}(m_2 - m_1) \qquad (6.24)$$

We apply the results of Chap. 2 for m_1 and m_2 to arrive at the following table:

TABLE 6.1 Switching Stability Criteria for Peak Current Control of Basic Second-Order Converters.

Slope	Buck	Boost	Buck-Boost
m_1	$\dfrac{u_{10}(1 - D)}{L}$	$\dfrac{u_{10}}{L}$	$\dfrac{u_{10}}{L}$
m_2	$\dfrac{u_{10}D}{L}$	$\dfrac{u_{10}D}{L(1 - D)}$	$\dfrac{u_{10}D}{L(1 - D)}$
$m_{3(min)}$	$\dfrac{u_{10}R_s}{2L}(2D - 1)$	$\dfrac{u_{10}R_s}{2L}\dfrac{2D - 1}{1 - D}$	$\dfrac{u_{10}R_s}{2L}\dfrac{2D - 1}{1 - D}$

In each instance, the criterion for m_3 implies that the added slope is unnecessary for $D < 0.5$. It is easily seen that, for all three regulators, worst-case m_3 corresponds to maximum duty factor, as would be expected.

The effective slope of the current analog for the circuit of Fig. 6.3, appropriately augmented with added ramp circuitry, is $u_1 R_s / L + m_3$, as a consequence of the current-mode switching stability criterion, and

Eq. (6.2) must be modified accordingly. On the other hand, m_3 obviously does not affect the actual average current x_1. When Eqs. (6.2), (6.3), and (6.4) are suitably modified, the term u_{10} in Eq. (6.5) becomes $u_{10} + 2m_3L/R_s$. For notational simplicity, we define γ as

$$\gamma = \frac{u_{10}}{u_{10} + 2m_3L/R_s} \le 1 \qquad (6.25)$$

Thus, when the current-mode switching stability criterion is taken into account, the control-law matrices of Eq. (6.9) become

$$\mathbf{F}^T(s) = \frac{-2Lf_s\gamma}{u_{10}} \left[1 \quad \frac{(1 + R_2Cs)K(s)}{R_s} \right] \qquad (6.26a)$$

and
$$\mathbf{Q}^T(s) = \frac{-D\gamma}{u_{10}} [1 \quad 0] \qquad (6.26b)$$

The control-law matrices for the CIC buck and buck-boost converters can be similarly derived.

6.4   Open-Loop Gain Calculation

The CIC open-loop gain calculation is determined by substituting Eq. (6.26) into Eq. (5.23) for the particular converter of interest. Continuing with our example of the basic boost converter with ESR, we apply the corresponding coefficient matrices shown in Eq. (5.16), with the assumption that R_s is negligible except for control considerations, to arrive at a current-loop gain of

$$G_1(s)H_1(s) = \frac{\dfrac{2f_s\gamma}{1 - D}\left(s + \dfrac{2}{R_1C}\right)}{s^2 + s\left[\dfrac{1}{R_1C} + \dfrac{R_2(1 - D)^2}{L}\right] + \dfrac{(1 - D)^2}{LC}} \qquad (6.27)$$

and a voltage-loop gain of

$$G_2(s)H_2(s) = \frac{\dfrac{2Lf_s\gamma(1 + R_2Cs)K(s)}{R_sR_1C(1 - D)^2}\left[\dfrac{R_1(1 - D)^2}{L} - s\right]}{s^2 + s\left[\dfrac{1}{R_1C} + \dfrac{R_2(1 - D)^2}{L}\right] + \dfrac{(1 - D)^2}{LC}} \qquad (6.28)$$

where it is assumed that $R_2/R_1 \ll 1$. As would be expected from the voltage-mode analysis, the voltage loop has an RHP zero and a complex pole that are dependent upon the steady-state duty factor. Summing Eqs. (6.27) and (6.28) in accordance with Eq. (5.23) to arrive at the total open-loop gain function, where once again it is assumed that R_2 is small enough so that any associated corner frequency is beyond the frequency range of interest for stability considerations, we have the equation

$$G(s)H(s) =$$

$$\frac{\dfrac{2f_s\gamma}{1 - D}\left\{s\left[1 - \dfrac{LK(s)}{R_sR_1C(1 - D)}\right] + \dfrac{2}{R_1C}\left[1 + \dfrac{R_1(1 - D)K(s)}{2R_s}\right]\right\}}{s^2 + s\left[\dfrac{1}{R_1C} + \dfrac{R_2(1 - D)^2}{L}\right] + \dfrac{(1 - D)^2}{LC}}$$

$$(6.29)$$

Note that the influence of the additional ramp, as represented by γ, is limited to the gain amplitude; the corner frequencies are not affected. From Eq. (6.29), it can be seen that if it were possible to design the regulator such that

$$\frac{LK(s)}{R_sR_1C(1 - D)} \ll 1 \qquad (6.30)$$

then the RHP zero could be eliminated. Furthermore, if the regulator could be designed such that the inequality

$$\frac{R_1(1 - D)K(s)}{2R_s} \gg 1 \qquad (6.31)$$

is valid as well, then the total open-loop gain function could be accurately expressed as

$$G(s)H(s) = \frac{\dfrac{2f_s\gamma}{(1 - D)}\left[s + \dfrac{(1 - D)K(s)}{R_sC}\right]}{s^2 + s\left[\dfrac{1}{R_1C} + \dfrac{R_2(1 - D)^2}{L}\right] + \dfrac{(1 - D)^2}{LC}} \qquad (6.32)$$

Such a design would permit the possibility of not only eliminating the RHP zero but also of generating an LHP zero that would compensate the complex pole, independent of steady-state duty factor.

For the sake of discussion, suppose that Eqs. (6.30), (6.31), and (6.32) are valid and that $K(s)$ is a constant K over the frequency range of interest from a stability standpoint, that is, from well below the second-order pole frequency $(1 - D)/\sqrt{LC}$ to well past the unity-gain cross-over angular frequency ω_c. Specifically, we say that

$$K(s) = K \qquad \frac{1 - D}{10\sqrt{LC}} < \omega < 10\omega_c \qquad (6.33)$$

Then, it would be conceivable to set the zero frequency $(1 - D)K/R_sC$ equal to the pole frequency $(1 - D)/\sqrt{LC}$, in order to achieve a wideband open-loop gain function with a nearly 90° phase margin independent of steady-state duty factor, in exactly the same way that a lead network was used for pole cancellation in the voltage-mode-controlled buck regulator. This results in a value of K determined by the equation

$$K = R_s \sqrt{\frac{C}{L}} \qquad (6.34)$$

To see whether this is reasonable, we substitute Eq. (6.34) into the assumptions represented by Eqs. (6.30) and (6.31), for $K(s) = K$, to arrive at

$$\frac{1}{R_1(1 - D)\sqrt{C/L}} \ll 1 \qquad (6.35)$$

and

$$\tfrac{1}{2}R_1(1 - D)\sqrt{\frac{C}{L}} \gg 1 \qquad (6.36)$$

respectively. From this it can be seen that compliance with Eq. (6.36) implies compliance with Eq. (6.35) and that, furthermore, there is only a factor of 2 difference between the two assumptions. To get a better feel for the validity of Eq. (6.36), we apply the load-related damping factor for the basic boost converter $\zeta_{load} = \sqrt{L/C}/2R_1(1 - D)$* to Eq. (6.36) to arrive at the expression

$$\zeta_{load} \ll 0.25 \qquad (6.37)$$

Because of the pulsed nature of the current that must be absorbed by the output filter capacitor in boost-derived switching regulators, a large ratio of C to L is generally required in order to meet output ripple

---

* See Fig. 4.6.

specifications. Thus, Eq. (6.37) does not represent a significant design compromise, if any. Substituting Eq. (6.34) into Eq. (6.32) yields the result

$$G(s)H(s) = \frac{\dfrac{2f_s\gamma}{1-D}\left(s + \dfrac{1-D}{\sqrt{LC}}\right)}{s^2 + s\left[\dfrac{1}{R_1C} + \dfrac{R_2(1-D)^2}{L}\right] + \dfrac{(1-D)^2}{LC}} \qquad (6.38)$$

The open-loop gain Bode plot of Fig. 5.3(c) for the lead-compensated voltage-mode-controlled buck regulator applies directly here except that the dc gain is $2f_s\gamma/\omega_n(1 - D)$ where $\omega_n = (1 - D)/\sqrt{LC}$.

Just as before, the dc gain can be enhanced by the addition of an integrator and a zero at $\omega_z \leq 0.1\omega_{n(\min)}$, in which case we have a gain plateau of

$$G_pH_p = \frac{2f_s\gamma}{\omega_n(1 - D)} \qquad (6.39)$$

and the dc gain G_0H_0 is whatever the operational amplifier in the error amplifier will allow (Fig. 5.5). For an ideal operational amplifier, the numerator of Eq. (6.38) then becomes multiplied by $(s + \omega_z)/s$. Equating the updated numerator of Eq. (6.38) to the numerator of Eq. (6.32), with the simplifying assumption that $\omega_z \ll \omega_n$, results in an error-amplifier gain function determined by the equation

$$K(s) = R_s\sqrt{\frac{C}{L}}\left(\frac{s + \omega_z}{s}\right) \qquad (6.40)$$

Because of the pulsed nature of the waveform from which inductor current information is derived, the practical means of measuring the CIC open-loop gain is not necessarily as straightforward as it is for measuring voltage-mode open-loop gains, and digital-to-analog conversion techniques may be required.[6] This is particularly true for the open-loop gain $G_1(s)H_1(s) + G_2(s)H_2(s)$ as defined here, where, in order to determine the total effect of both loops, measurement must take place in a common branch, which does not occur until after the comparator. This definition of open-loop gain has the advantages of good visibility of the individual contributions of the current and voltage loops, and of easy comparison with single-loop control. However, it is not unique. The characteristic equation

$$1 + G_1(s)H_1(s) + G_2(s)H_2(s) = 0 \qquad (6.41)$$

could just as well have been written as

$$1 + \frac{G_1(s)H_1(s)}{1 + G_2(s)H_2(s)} = 0 \qquad (6.42)$$

or
$$1 + \frac{G_2(s)H_2(s)}{1 + G_1(s)H_1(s)} = 0 \qquad (6.43)$$

All three equations must necessarily have exactly the same stability information, although not necessarily in the same form (see Prob. 6.3). In particular, Eq. (6.43) corresponds to the conventional open-loop gain measurement in the voltage loop, with the current loop closed. Thus, digital-to-analog conversion is not required just to determine the stability of a CIC switching regulator.[7]

By design, the CIC boost converter open-loop gain function has been made identical to that of the lead-compensated voltage-mode-controlled buck regulator in an effort to achieve wider-band frequency response than what otherwise might be achievable using lag-compensated voltage control. CIC buck and buck-boost converters can also be designed for this same wideband open-loop gain function. The question arises whether these CIC converters are susceptible to the same potential subharmonic instability, or tail-chasing problem, that lead-compensated voltage-mode-controlled buck regulators are, as discussed previously.

The answer would seem to depend upon the extent to which the total open-loop gain in the neighborhood of the switching frequency is due to the voltage loop. With voltage-mode control, all of the open-loop gain is obviously in the voltage loop. With CIC, some is due to the voltage loop and some is due to the current loop. Looking at Eq. (6.38), it can be determined from the previous equations and assumptions that the s term in the numerator is due to the current loop and the $(1 - D)/\sqrt{LC}$, or ω_n, term is due to the voltage loop. This means that for $\omega > \omega_n$, the current-loop gain is larger than the voltage-loop gain, and, particularly for frequencies in the neighborhood of the switching frequency, the current-loop gain would be expected to predominate (see Prob. 6.2). It is an experimental fact that push-pull CIC buck regulators are not as susceptible to tail chasing as their voltage-mode-controlled counterparts. A more detailed study of this phenomenon and the development of quantitative design criteria to assure subharmonic switching stability are the subjects of current study efforts.

6.5 Performance Comparisons with Voltage-Mode Control

Once the control law has been determined in accordance with both the classical and switching stability criteria, the closed-loop source-to-output transfer function matrix can be found for a particular switching regulator topology from Eq. (5.12). Using the control-law matrices of Eq. (6.26), the transfer function matrix $\mathbf{T}_{yu}(s)$ for the CIC basic boost converter with ESR is

$$\mathbf{T}_{yu}(s) = \begin{bmatrix} 1 & 0 \\ 0 & 1 + R_2Cs \end{bmatrix}$$

$$\cdot \left[\begin{array}{c|c} s + \dfrac{R_2(1 - D)^2}{L} + \dfrac{2f_s\gamma}{1 - D} & \dfrac{1 - D}{L}\left[1 + \dfrac{2Lf_s\gamma(1 + R_2Cs)K(s)}{R_s(1 - D)^2}\right] \\ \hline \dfrac{1 - D}{C}\left[1 + \dfrac{2Lf_s\gamma}{R_1(1 - D)^3}\right] & s + \dfrac{1}{R_1C}\left[1 - \dfrac{2Lf_s\gamma(1 + R_2Cs)K(s)}{R_s(1 - D)^2}\right] \end{array} \right]^{-1}$$

$$\cdot \begin{bmatrix} \dfrac{1}{L}\left(1 - \dfrac{D\gamma}{1 - D}\right) & \dfrac{-R_2(1 - D)}{L} \\ \dfrac{D\gamma}{R_1C(1 - D)^2} & \dfrac{1}{C} \end{bmatrix} \tag{6.44}$$

from which any of the specific transfer functions of Eq. (5.13) can be determined. Two transfer functions of particular practical interest are the output impedance $Z_2(s)$ and the input voltage susceptibility $\hat{Y}_2(s)/\hat{U}_1(s)$. These transfer functions will serve as a basis for comparing CIC and voltage-mode control for our boost regulator example.

In the case of CIC, we substitute Eq. (6.40) into (6.44) to arrive at

$$Z_2(s) = \frac{R_2\left(s + \dfrac{1}{R_2C}\right)\left(s + \dfrac{2f_s\gamma}{1 - D}\right)}{\Delta} \tag{6.45}$$

and

$$\frac{\hat{Y}_2(s)}{\hat{U}_1(s)} = \frac{\dfrac{R_2\gamma D}{R_1(1 - D)^2}\left(s + \dfrac{2f_s}{D}\right)\left(s + \dfrac{1}{R_2C}\right)}{\Delta} \tag{6.46}$$

where Δ is the determinant of $[s\mathbf{I} - \mathbf{A}_0 - \mathbf{EF}^T(s)]$, and is given by the equation

$$\Delta = \frac{1}{s}\left(s + \frac{2f_s\gamma}{1 - D}\right)(s + \omega_n)(s + \omega_z) \tag{6.47}$$

The above equations are subject to the straightforward assumptions of $R_2/R_1 \ll 1$, $L \gg L_c$,* $\omega_z \ll \omega_n$, $\zeta_{\text{load}} = \sqrt{L/C}/R_1(1 - D) \ll 1$, $\zeta_{\text{ESR}} = R_2(1 - D)\sqrt{C/L} \ll 1$, and the not so straightforward assumption

$$R_2 \ll \frac{R_1}{G_p H_p} \tag{6.48}$$

This assumption comes about because the actual s^2 coefficient in Eq. (6.47) of Δ is $1 - R_2 G_p H_p/R_1$. Thus, Eq. (6.48) represents a quantification of the assumption that was made in Sec. 6.4 in the derivation of Eq. (6.29), namely, that R_2 is small enough so that any associated corner frequency is beyond the frequency range of interest for stability considerations. Typically, R_2 is at least two orders of magnitude lower than R_1, and a typical value of $G_p H_p$ is 20 dB. The primary motivation for the assumption of Eq. (6.48) is algebraic simplicity, and it may not be valid in all practical applications. On the other hand, R_2 must certainly be smaller than $R_1/G_p H_p$ from straightforward stability considerations.† Combining Eq. (6.47) with Eqs. (6.45) and (6.46), respectively, results in the expressions

$$Z_2(s) = \frac{sR_2\left(s + \dfrac{1}{R_2 C}\right)}{(s + \omega_z)(s + \omega_n)} \tag{6.49}$$

and

$$\frac{\hat{Y}_2(s)}{\hat{U}_1(s)} = \frac{sR_2\gamma D\left(s + \dfrac{1}{R_2 C}\right)\left(s + \dfrac{2f_s}{D}\right)}{R_1(1 - D)^2(s + \omega_z)(s + \omega_n)\left(s + \dfrac{2f_s\gamma}{1 - D}\right)} \tag{6.50}$$

It is tempting to assert that the signal frequency range of interest is much less than the switching frequency, in which case Eq. (6.50) becomes simply

$$\frac{\hat{Y}_2(s)}{\hat{U}_1(s)} = \frac{sR_2\left(s + \dfrac{1}{R_2 C}\right)}{R_1(1 - D)(s + \omega_z)(s + \omega_n)} \qquad \omega \ll 2\pi f_s \tag{6.51}$$

However, we are clearly interested in signal frequencies up to the unity-gain cross-over frequency ω_c. From Fig. 5.5 and Eq. (6.39), we

---

* See Eq. (2.11b).

† A necessary condition for stability is that all coefficients of the characteristic polynomial be positive.

see that

$$\omega_c = \frac{2f_s\gamma}{1-D} \tag{6.52}$$

From Table 6.1 and Eq. (6.25), we have

$$\gamma_{(max)} = \frac{1-D}{D} \qquad D > 0.5 \tag{6.53}$$

in which case

$$\omega_{c(max)} = \frac{2f_s}{D} \qquad D > 0.5 \tag{6.54}$$

Thus, ω_c can be as high as $4f_s$, which hardly qualifies as much less than $2\pi f_s$. We are faced with the fact that the key assumption of $\omega \ll 2\pi f_s$, upon which state-space averaging is based, is violated as ω_c is approached. This means that the linearized model may not be sufficiently accurate near ω_c. On the other hand, stability is the major concern at $\omega = \omega_c$ and the linearized model predicts a phase margin of approximately 90° (Fig. 5.5), so there is a large tolerance for error. Helping out also is the fact that, in practice, the terms $s + 2f_s/D$ and $s + 2f_s\gamma/(1-D)$ come close to canceling anyway. In fact, for a value of γ in accordance with Eq. (6.53), the terms cancel exactly.

In the case of voltage-mode-controlled boost regulators, we recall that only lag compensation is appropriate because of the duty-factor-dependent complex pole and RHP zero in the open-loop gain function. As pointed out in Chap. 5, Sec. 5.6, dc performance can be maximized by configuring Z_1 and Z_2 in the error amplifier as a perfect integrator. The unity-gain cross-over frequency ω_c must be low enough to assure adequate gain margin as indicated in Fig. 5.4(b). If Z_2 is purely capacitive and Z_1 is purely resistive, then ω_p and K are determined by the operational amplifier itself. Assuming an ideal operational amplifier, as we did for Eq. (6.40), it can be determined from Eq. (5.29) that unity gain at $\omega = \omega_c$ corresponds to an error-amplifier gain function of

$$K(s) = \frac{\omega_c V_p (1-D)^2}{u_{10}s} \tag{6.55}$$

for $\omega_c \ll \omega_n$. As we did in Chap. 5, Sec. 5.3, if we assume a total damping factor of 0.1 (a reasonable practical value) in Eq. (5.29), then the resonant peak is 14 dB. When the 6-dB gain margin is taken into account, this results in a maximum value of ω_c equal to $0.1\omega_{n(min)}$ in order to assure stability, so the assumption $\omega_c \ll \omega_n$ is valid.

The output impedance of the lag-compensated voltage-mode-controlled boost regulator is obtained by substituting Eq. (6.55) directly into Eq. (5.18) to arrive at

$$Z_2(s) = \frac{R_2 s^2 \left(s + \dfrac{1}{R_2 C} \right)}{(s + \omega_c) \left\{ s^2 + s \left[\dfrac{1}{R_1 C} + \dfrac{R_2(1 - D)^2}{L} \right] + \omega_n^2 \right\}} \tag{6.56}$$

where, again, ω_n is $(1 - D)/\sqrt{LC}$, Eq. (6.48) is assumed valid, and the ESR- and load-related damping factors ζ_{ESR} and ζ_{load} are assumed small, as they were for the general CIC analysis. To obtain the input voltage susceptibility transfer function $\hat{Y}_2(s)/\hat{U}_1(s)$, we solve Eq. (5.17) for the $[\mathbf{T}_{yu}(s)]_{21}$ element and substitute Eq. (6.55) into that result to get

$$\frac{\hat{Y}_2(s)}{\hat{U}_1(s)} = \frac{\dfrac{sR_2(1 - D)}{L} \left(s + \dfrac{1}{R_2 C} \right)}{(s + \omega_c) \left\{ s^2 + s \left[\dfrac{1}{R_1 C} + \dfrac{R_2(1 - D)^2}{L} \right] + \omega_n^2 \right\}} \tag{6.57}$$

for the same small damping factor assumptions.

The comparisons of $Z_2(s)$ and $\hat{Y}_2(s)/\hat{U}_1(s)$ for the CIC and voltage-mode-controlled boost converters, with identical power elements, are shown in Figs. 6.7 and 6.8, respectively, where both ω_z for CIC and ω_c

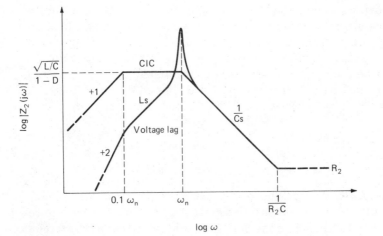

Figure 6.7 Boost converter output impedance comparison.

for voltage-mode control are assumed equal to $0.1\omega_n$ for simplicity. For $\omega < \omega_n$, the output impedance of the voltage-mode-controlled boost regulator is lower than that of the CIC boost regulator, and, for $\omega > \omega_n$, they are the same, as determined by the output capacitor and its ESR. The advantage of CIC for output impedance shows up in the neighborhood of ω_n, where the wider bandwidth provides active damping such that there is no resonant peaking. The input voltage susceptibility for CIC is lower than that for voltage-mode control by a factor of $\sqrt{L/C}/R_1(1 - D)$, or $2\zeta_{\text{load}}$, over a large portion of the frequency range of interest. Since, in practice, $\zeta_{\text{load}} \ll 1$, this is a significant improvement. In addition, there is the advantage of no resonant peaking.

The fact that CIC is more advantageous for input voltage susceptibility than for output impedance makes intuitive sense. Ideally, CIC replaces the inductor with a dependent current source that would have a very high dynamic impedance. This prevents the inductor from helping to reduce the output impedance for $\omega < \omega_n$ but provides additional help in decoupling the output from the input voltage source. Since there is a large frequency range over which the boost converter output impedance is lower with voltage-mode control than with CIC, it certainly cannot be said that CIC, as implemented here, is categorically better than voltage-mode control even though an additional state variable is being fed back. The limitations of CIC, in this regard, are even more evident when this technique is compared with lead-compensated voltage-mode control in buck regulators.[4]

In the foregoing quantitative analyses and trade-offs, a phase margin of 90° was used as the stability criterion for current-injected control. Although this criterion may represent common design practice, it does

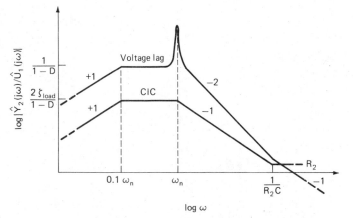

Figure 6.8 Boost converter input voltage susceptibility comparison.

not represent a fundamental requirement. Consider the general lead-compensated second-order open-loop gain function in the equation below.

$$G(s)H(s) = \frac{(G_0 H_0 \omega_n^2 / s_0)(s + s_0)}{s^2 + 2\zeta\omega_n s + \omega_n^2} \tag{6.58}$$

A phase margin of 90° corresponds to the zero frequency s_0 being equal to the resonant frequency ω_n. For $G_0 H_0 \gg 1$, the resulting closed-loop characteristic polynomial can be accurately approximated by the expression $(s + G_0 H_0 \omega_n)(s + \omega_n)$. The pole frequency $G_0 H_0 \omega_n$ is the unity-gain cross-over frequency ω_c, so within the regulating bandwidth of interest, the closed-loop transfer functions are essentially first-order with pole frequency ω_n. Thus, a phase margin of 90° represents a very conservative stability criterion. A less conservative but still very reasonable stability criterion is that the characteristic polynomial be critically damped. For $G_0 H_0 \gg 1$ and $G_0 H_0 \gg 2\zeta s_0 / \omega_n$, the closed-loop characteristic equation for Eq. (6.58) can be expressed as

$$s^2 + \frac{G_0 H_0 \omega_n^2}{s_0} s + G_0 H_0 \omega_n^2 = 0 \tag{6.59}$$

For critical damping,

$$s_0 = \tfrac{1}{2}\sqrt{G_0 H_0}\, \omega_n \tag{6.60}$$

This results in an open-loop gain equal to 15 dB at $s = js_0$, and an ω_c of $4s_0$, independent of $G_0 H_0$. A locus of open-loop gain plots for various values of $G_0 H_0$ is shown in Fig. 6.9. It can be shown that for critical

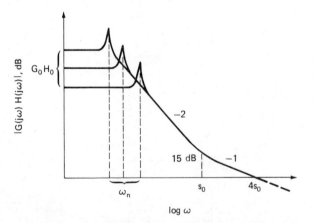

Figure 6.9 Lead-compensated open-loop gain plots for closed-loop critical damping.

damping of the closed-loop characteristic equation, the phase margin is a constant 76°.

Turning our attention back to the output impedance of the CIC boost regulator, we see that for a value of s_0 that is not necessarily equal to ω_n, the $s + \omega_n$ term in the denominator of Eq. (6.49) is replaced with the term $s + s_0$. For $s_0 > \omega_n$, as shown in Fig. 6.10, the CIC output impedance plateau in Fig. 6.7 is correspondingly reduced. The lower limit, based on critical damping, depends upon the maximum allowable value of open-loop gain. As is evident from Eq. (6.60) and Fig. 6.9, the higher the open-loop gain is, the larger s_0 can be with respect to ω_n. Recalling that $G(s)H(s)$ is dependent upon the error-amplifier gain $K(s)$, as shown in Eq. (6.32), we see that for some large enough value of open-loop gain, the inequality of Eq. (6.30) will be violated and the analytical results, which are not presented here, will become more complicated.

Nevertheless, it is clear that by using a less conservative stability criterion than a 90° phase margin, the CIC boost converter output impedance is lower than that of the voltage-mode boost converter over a larger portion of the frequency range. Furthermore, it can be shown that this loop-compensation approach also permits the output impedance of CIC buck converters to compare more favorably with the output impedance of lead-compensated voltage-mode-controlled buck converters, particularly when tail-chasing constraints are taken into account. Potential output impedance reductions in CIC switching regulators using criteria other than a 90° phase margin and using other implementations, such as sensing capacitor current instead of inductor current, are subjects of present study efforts.

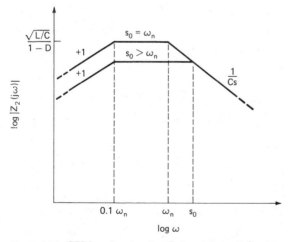

Figure 6.10   CIC boost converter Z_2 improvement for $s_0 > \omega_n$.

6.6 Illustrative Problems

6.1 The following questions relate to the CIC boost regulator of Fig. 6.3. (a) Determine the value of the error-amplifier gain K which would provide pole cancellation in the open-loop gain function $G_1(s)H_1(s) + G_2(s)H_2(s)$ for $L = 200\ \mu\text{H}$, $C = 2000\ \mu\text{F}$, $R_1 = 10\ \Omega$, $R_s = 0.1\ \Omega$, $0 < D < 0.5$, and R_2 negligible. (b) What is the corresponding value of total dc loop gain for $f_s = 40$ kHz and $\gamma = 1$ (since $D < 0.5$)?   (c) How much of the dc gain is provided by the current loop?

SOLUTION: Assume that the inequalities of Eqs. (6.30) and (6.31) are valid. From Eq. (6.34), we have

$$K = R_s \sqrt{\frac{C}{L}} = 0.1 \sqrt{\frac{2000}{200}} = 0.316$$

We now check the two assumptions:

$$\frac{LK}{R_s R_1 C(1 - D)} \ll 1?$$

$$\frac{200(0.316)}{0.1(10)(2000)(0.5)} \ll 1?$$

$$0.0632 \ll 1?\ \text{Yes.}$$

$$\frac{R_1(1 - D)K}{2R_s} \gg 1?$$

$$\frac{10(1 - 0.5)(0.316)}{2(0.1)} \gg 1?$$

$$7.9 \gg 1?\ \text{Yes.}$$

Note that no output voltage divider is included in the model of Fig. 6.3. If the divider attenuation constant is a, then the dc gain of the error amplifier is K/a.

(b) From Eq. (6.38) for $s = 0$, we have

$$G_0 H_0 = \frac{2f_s\sqrt{LC}}{(1 - D)^2} = \frac{2(40 \times 10^3)\sqrt{(200 \times 10^{-6})(2000 \times 10^{-6})}}{(1 - D)^2}$$

$$50.6 < G_0 H_0 < 202.4 \qquad 0 < D < 0.5$$

(c) From Eq. (6.27), we have

$$G_1(0)H_1(0) = \frac{4f_s L}{R_1(1 - D)^3} = \frac{4(40 \times 10^3)(200 \times 10^{-6})}{10(1 - D)^3}$$

$$3.2 < G_1(0)H_1(0) < 25.6 \qquad 0 < D < 0.5$$

It is apparent that almost all of the dc gain is provided by the voltage loop.

6.2 Since the voltage-loop gain of Eq. (6.28) includes a negative s term corresponding to an RHP zero, it is obvious that at some value of ω the current-loop gain becomes larger than the voltage-loop gain. What is that value?

SOLUTION: From Eqs. (6.27) and (6.28), we have

$$\frac{2f_s}{1 - D}\left|j\omega + \frac{2}{R_1 C}\right| = \frac{2Lf_s K}{R_s R_1 C(1 - D)^2}\left|\frac{R_1(1 - D)^2}{L} - j\omega\right|$$

Substituting Eq. (6.34) for K gives us

$$\left|j\omega + \frac{2}{R_1 C}\right| = \frac{\sqrt{L/C}}{R_1(1 - D)}\left|\frac{R_1(1 - D)^2}{L} - j\omega\right|$$

$$\omega^2 + \left(\frac{2}{R_1 C}\right)^2 = \left[\frac{\sqrt{L/C}}{R_1(1 - D)}\right]^2\left\{\left[\frac{R_1(1 - D)^2}{L}\right]^2 + \omega^2\right\}$$

$$\omega^2 = \frac{\dfrac{(1 - D)^2}{LC}\left\{1 - \left[\dfrac{2\sqrt{L/C}}{R_1(1 - D)}\right]^2\right\}}{1 - \left[\dfrac{\sqrt{L/C}}{R_1(1 - D)}\right]^2} = \omega_n^{\,2}\frac{1 - 4\zeta_{load}^2}{1 - 2\zeta_{load}^2}$$

If the value of $\zeta_{load} = \sqrt{L/C}/2R_1(1 - D)$ is low enough, then $|G_1(s)H_1(s)| \geq |G_2(s)H_2(s)|$ for $\omega \geq \omega_n$. For the values of Prob. 6.1, we have

$$\zeta_{load} \leq \frac{\sqrt{200/2000}}{2(10)(1 - 0.5)} = 0.0316$$

Thus $\omega = \omega_n$ is a very good approximation for that problem in particular and, in practice, is a very good general approximation.

6.3 A Bode plot of $G_1(s)H_1(s) + G_2(s)H_2(s)$ in Prob. 6.1 would be similar to Fig. 5.3(c), indicating a phase margin of 90°. What is the corresponding gain margin for the open-loop gain expression below for $D = 0.5$?

$$G(s)H(s) = \frac{G_2(s)H_2(s)}{1 + G_1(s)H_1(s)}$$

SOLUTION: Updating Eqs. (6.27) and (6.28) for $R_2 = 0$ and $\gamma = 1$, we have

$$G_1(s)H_1(s) = \frac{\dfrac{2f_s}{1 - D}\left(s + \dfrac{2}{R_1 C}\right)}{s^2 + \dfrac{s}{R_1 C} + \dfrac{(1 - D)^2}{LC}}$$

and
$$G_2(s)H_2(s) = \frac{\dfrac{2Lf_s K}{R_s R_1 C(1 - D)^2}\left[\dfrac{R_1(1 - D)^2}{L} - s\right]}{s^2 + \dfrac{s}{R_1 C} + \dfrac{(1 - D)^2}{LC}}$$

Hence, we have

$$G(s)H(s) = \cfrac{\cfrac{2Lf_sK}{R_sR_1C(1-D)^2}\left[\cfrac{R_1(1-D)^2}{L} - s\right]}{s^2 + s\left(\cfrac{2f_s}{1-D} + \cfrac{1}{R_1C}\right) + \cfrac{4f_s}{R_1C(1-D)} + \cfrac{(1-D)^2}{LC}}$$

Note that the RHP zero that was eliminated for $G(s)H(s)$ defined as $G_1(s)H_1(s) + G_2(s)H_2(s)$ reappears for $G(s)H(s)$ defined as $G_2(s)H_2(s)/[1 + G_1(s)H_1(s)]$. Assuming that $L \gg L_c$ and $2f_s/(1-D) \gg 1/R_1C$, and substituting in $K = R_s\sqrt{C/L}$, yields

$$G(s)H(s) = \cfrac{\cfrac{2f_s\sqrt{L/C}}{R_1(1-D)^2}\left[\cfrac{R_1(1-D)^2}{L} - s\right]}{s^2 + \cfrac{2f_s}{1-D}s + \cfrac{4f_s}{R_1C(1-D)}}$$

Checking assumptions, we have

$$\frac{2f_s}{1-D} \gg \frac{1}{R_1C}?$$

$$2(40 \times 10^3) \gg \frac{1}{10(2000 \times 10^{-6})}?$$

$$80 \times 10^3 \gg 50? \text{ Yes.}$$

$$L \gg L_c?$$

From Eq. (2.11*b*).

$$L_c = \frac{R(1-D)^2D}{2f_s}$$

For what value of D is L_c maximum?

$$\frac{dL_c}{dD} = \frac{R}{2f_s}[(1-D)^2 - 2D(1-D)] = 0$$

$$(3D - 1)(D - 1) = 0$$

$$D = \tfrac{1}{3}, 1$$

$$L_{c,\text{max}} = \frac{10(1 - 1/3)^2(1/3)}{2(40 \times 10^3)} = 27.8 \ \mu\text{H}$$

$$200 \gg 27.8? \text{ Yes.}$$

Since

$$\frac{2f_s}{1 - D} \gg \frac{2}{R_1 C}$$

we have

$$G(s)H(s) \approx \frac{\dfrac{2f_s\sqrt{L/C}}{R_1(1 - D)^2}\left[\dfrac{R_1(1 - D)^2}{L} - s\right]}{\left(s + \dfrac{2f_s}{1 - D}\right)\left(s + \dfrac{2}{R_1 C}\right)}$$

where, assuming sufficient separation of corner frequencies, we have

$$G(s)H(s) = \begin{cases} \dfrac{R_1(1 - D)}{2}\sqrt{\dfrac{C}{L}} & 0 \le s < \dfrac{j2}{R_1 C} \\[3mm] \dfrac{1 - D}{s\sqrt{LC}} & \dfrac{j2}{R_1 C} < s < \dfrac{jR_1(1 - D)^2}{L} \\[3mm] \dfrac{-\sqrt{L/C}}{R_1(1 - D)} & \dfrac{jR_1(1 - D)^2}{L} < s < \dfrac{j2f_s}{1 - D} \\[3mm] \dfrac{-2f_s\sqrt{L/C}}{sR_1(1 - D)^2} & s > \dfrac{j2f_s}{1 - D} \end{cases}$$

The corresponding Bode plot is shown in Fig. S6.3 for the given numerical values. Note that the RHP zero produces a 90° phase *lag*. Also note that the unity-gain cross-over frequency is ω_n. From Fig. S6.3, we see that the corresponding gain margin is 24 dB.

6.4 There are an increasing number of sensitive communications applications in which it is desirable to minimize the amount of power supply load modulation that appears on the input power lines in order to prevent detection of an important or secret message by an unauthorized party. Investigate the theoretical possibility of using load current information in the control law of the pole-canceled CIC boost converter to minimize the transfer function $\hat{Y}_1(s)/\hat{U}_2(s)$. For algebraic simplicity, assume $R_2 = 0$ and $\gamma = 1$.

SOLUTION: The source-dependent control-law matrix $\mathbf{Q}^T(s)$ in Eq. (6.9b) is first updated to include the possibility of dependency on u_2.

$$\mathbf{Q}^T(s) = \left[\frac{-D}{u_{10}} \quad Q_2(s)\right]$$

The updated matrix $\mathbf{EQ}^T(s)$ then becomes

$$\mathbf{EQ}^T(s) = \begin{bmatrix} \dfrac{-D}{L(1 - D)} & \dfrac{u_{10}Q_2(s)}{L(1 - D)} \\[3mm] \dfrac{D}{R_1 C(1 - D)^2} & \dfrac{-u_{10}Q_2(s)}{R_1 C(1 - D)^2} \end{bmatrix}$$

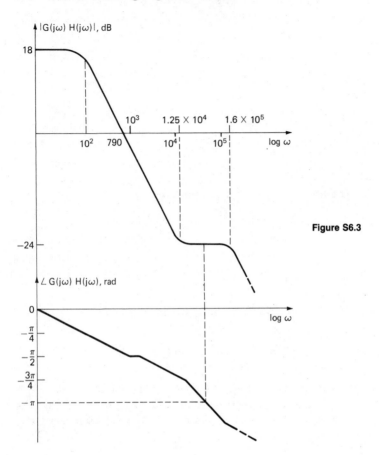

Figure S6.3

Updating Eq. (6.44) in accordance with the above result and for the given assumptions results in

$$
\mathbf{T}_{yu}(s) = \begin{bmatrix} 1 & 0 \\ 0 & 1 \end{bmatrix}
$$

$$
\cdot \left[\begin{array}{c|c} s + \dfrac{2f_s}{1-D} & \dfrac{1-D}{L}\left[1 + \dfrac{2Lf_sK}{R_s(1-D)^2}\right] \\ \hline \dfrac{-(1-D)}{C}\left[1 + \dfrac{2Lf_s}{R_1(1-D)^3}\right] & s + \dfrac{1}{R_1C}\left[1 + \dfrac{2Lf_sK}{R_s(1-D)^2}\right] \end{array} \right]^{-1}
$$

$$
\cdot \begin{bmatrix} \dfrac{1}{L}\left(1 - \dfrac{D}{1-D}\right) & \dfrac{u_{10}Q_2(s)}{L(1-D)} \\ \dfrac{D}{R_1C(1-D)^2} & \dfrac{1}{C}\left[1 - \dfrac{u_{10}Q_2(s)}{R_1(1-D)^2}\right] \end{bmatrix}
$$

Solving for $\hat{Y}_1(s)/\hat{U}_2(s)$ results in

$$\frac{\hat{Y}_1(s)}{\hat{U}_2(s)} = \left(\left\{ s + \frac{1}{R_1C} \left[1 - \frac{2Lf_sK}{R_s(1-D)^2} \right] \right\} \frac{u_{10}Q_2(s)}{L(1-D)} \right.$$
$$\left. - \frac{(1-D)}{LC} \left[1 + \frac{2Lf_sK}{R_s(1-D)^2} \right] \left[1 - \frac{u_{10}Q_2(s)}{R_1(1-D)^2} \right] \right) \div \Delta$$
$$= \left\{ \frac{su_{10}Q_2(s)}{L(1-D)} - \frac{1-D}{LC} \left[1 + \frac{2Lf_sK}{R_s(1-D)^2} \right] \right\} \div \Delta \qquad s \gg \frac{j2}{R_1C}$$

where, again, Δ is the determinant of $[s\mathbf{I} - \mathbf{A}_0 - \mathbf{EF}^T(s)]$. Substituting in $K = R_s\sqrt{C/L}$ and assuming that $f_s \gg \omega_n$, we have

$$\frac{\hat{Y}_1(s)}{\hat{U}_2(s)} = \left[\frac{su_{10}Q_2(s)}{L(1-D)} - \frac{2f_s}{(1-D)\sqrt{LC}} \right] \div \Delta$$

Evidently, the transfer function $\hat{Y}_1(s)/\hat{U}_2(s)$ can be nulled out if $Q_2(s)$ is chosen such that

$$Q_2(s) = \frac{2f_s}{su_{10}} \sqrt{\frac{L}{C}}$$

The author confesses to not having determined the practicality of such a control law. However, this shows the type of question that can be investigated using the mathematical discipline described herein. Using similar analyses as a basis, a control law using u_2 information has been successfully implemented that reduces the output impedance of CIC buck regulators.[8]

References

1. A. Capel, G. Ferrante, D. O'Sullivan, and A. Weinberg, "Application of the Injected Current Model for the Dynamic Analysis of Switching Regulators with the New Concept of LC^3 Modulator," *IEEE Power Electronics Specialists Conference Record,* June 1978, pp. 135–147.
2. F. C. Lee and R. A. Carter, "Investigations of Stability and Dynamic Performances of Switching Regulators Employing Current-Injected Control," *IEEE Power Electronics Specialists Conference Record,* June 1981, pp. 3–16.
3. D. M. Mitchell, "An Analytical Investigation of Current-Injected Control for Constant-Frequency Switching Regulators," *IEEE Power Electronics Specialists Conference— ESA Proceedings,* June 1985, pp. 225–233.
4. G. K. Schoneman and D. M. Mitchell, "Closed-Loop Performance Comparisons of Switching Regulators with Current-Injected Control," *IEEE Power Electronics Specialists Conference Record,* June 1986, pp. 3–12.
5. S. P. Hsu, A. Brown, L. Rensink, and R. D. Middlebrook, "Modelling and Analysis of Switching DC-to-DC Converters in the Constant-Frequency Current-Control Mode," *IEEE Power Electronics Specialists Conference Record,* June 1979, pp. 284–301.
6. B. H. Cho and F. C. Lee, "Measurement of Loop Gain with the Digital Modulator," *IEEE Power Electronics Specialists Conference Record,* June 1984, pp. 363–373.
7. R. D. Middlebrook, "Topics in Multiple-Loop Regulators and Current-Mode Programming," *IEEE Power Electronics Specialists Conference Record,* June 1985, pp. 716–732.

8. G. K. Schoneman and D. M. Mitchell, "Output Impedance Considerations for Switching Regulators with Current-Injected Control," *IEEE Power Electronics Specialists Conference Record*, June 1987, pp. 324–335.

Chapter 7

Effects of
Input EMI Filtering

In previous chapters, our discussion of switching regulator behavior has emphasized the interface between the switching regulator and the load. In particular, we have addressed (1) the need for output filtering to prevent excessive deviations between instantaneous and average output voltages, (2) the switching regulator input voltage susceptibility, or the extent to which input voltage variations at the source are passed on to the load, and (3) the switching regulator output impedance, which represents the source impedance to switching regulator loads.

In this chapter, we turn our attention to the interface between the switching regulator and the source. If the source were ideal, then there would be no concern; an ideal source would have no source impedance and would remain unperturbed regardless of the input current waveform of the switching regulator. However, in addition to the reality of nonideal sources, the effective source impedance presented to the switching regulator includes the transmission and distribution impedances of the input power system. In order to prevent the switching regulator's input current waveform from interfering with the source and to preserve the integrity of the source for other equipment that may be operating from a common input power bus, the switching regulator must include appropriate input electromagnetic interference (EMI) filtering. (Although EMI is a general switching regulator problem that may take many forms, this chapter focuses on differential-mode conducted emissions on the input power line.)

7.1 Stability Considerations

For EMI purposes, we can model the switching regulator as an interfering current source i_s for which the most straightforward EMI filter consists of a shunt capacitance C_1 and a series inductance L_1 as shown in Fig. 7.1. For simplicity, the total effective impedance of the source u_1 is modeled as a single resistance R_d. It can safely be assumed that L_1 and C_1 are large enough to dominate the reactive impedances of the source. By choosing L_1 and C_1 sufficiently large, the switching regulator's interfering signals at the switching frequency and harmonics thereof can be adequately attenuated. However, there may be an associated low-frequency stability problem[1,2] due to interaction between the EMI filter and the basic switching regulator, as will now be discussed.

The efficiency of a practical switching regulator is not very dependent upon input voltage, even over a rather wide range of values. Ideally, of course, it is 100 percent regardless of input voltage. Therefore, for a fixed switching regulator load, the average power demand through the input EMI filter is virtually constant. Assuming that the switching frequency is much higher than the resonant frequency of the EMI filter and that the resonant frequency of the EMI filter is well within the regulating bandwidth of the switching regulator, one can approximate the switching regulator as a continuous constant-power element for lower-frequency stability considerations, in accordance with the concept of state-space averaging. If one considers the EMI filter of Fig. 7.1, followed by a constant-power load P as shown in Fig. 7.2, the nonlinear second-order differential equation shown in Eq. (7.1) applies.

$$\ddot{x}_2 + \left(\frac{R_d}{L_1} - \frac{P}{C_1 x_2{}^2}\right)\dot{x}_2 + \frac{1}{L_1 C_1}\,x_2 = \frac{1}{L_1 C_1}\,u_1 \qquad (7.1)$$

The term $-P/C_1 x_2{}^2$ is due to the negative dynamic input impedance of the constant power load. That is, as the input voltage to the switching

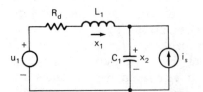

Figure 7.1 Switching regulator EMI model.

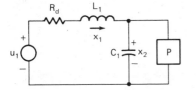

Figure 7.2 Stability model of switching regulator with EMI filter.

regulator incrementally increases, the current drawn by the switching regulator incrementally decreases. It follows naturally that the stability criterion for Eq. (7.1) is

$$\frac{R_d}{L_1} > \frac{P}{C_1 x_{2(\text{min})}^2} \tag{7.2}$$

which suggests that a high ratio of capacitance to inductance is desirable. Actually, both the inductor and the capacitor have small series resistances which contribute to stability and which, to a first-order approximation, can be lumped with the source resistance R_d to arrive at a total effective damping resistance. Nevertheless, in applications where the resonant frequency of the EMI filter is within the regulating bandwidth of the switching regulator and where the inherent source and component resistances are small enough, the possibility of instability exists.

It should be emphasized that what we are considering here is local system stability between the EMI filter and the switching regulator, not the stability of the switching regulator itself. Therefore, the only ways to improve this local system stability are (1) to increase the damping factor of the EMI filter, (2) to modify the switching regulator control so that the regulating bandwidth is reduced to a range that is below the EMI filter resonant frequency, or (3) to modify the switching regulator control law to include EMI filter information.

From an efficiency standpoint, it is undesirable to increase the EMI filter damping factor by inserting additional resistance in series with L_1 or in parallel with C_1. From an EMI attenuation standpoint, it is

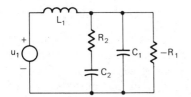

Figure 7.3 RC configuration of damped EMI filter.

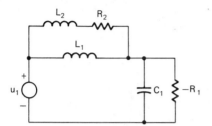

Figure 7.4 *RL* configuration of damped EMI filter.

undesirable to insert additional resistance in series with C_1 or in parallel with L_1. The next apparent level of complexity would be to couple a damping resistor to the LC filter through another inductor or capacitor. Figures 7.3 and 7.4 show two such configurations (1) where the nonlinear resistance $-x_2{}^2/P$ in Eq. (7.1) is replaced with the linear resistor $-R_1$, which is valid in the neighborhood of the corresponding dc operating point x_{20}, and (2) where, for worst case, the effect of the source resistance R_d is assumed negligible compared to the effect of the inserted damping resistance R_2. The respective Routh-Hurwitz stability criteria for Figs. 7.3 and 7.4 are

$$C_2 \left(1 - \frac{R_2}{R_1} \right) \left(R_2 C_2 - \frac{L_1}{R_1} \right) > \frac{L_1 C_1}{R_1} \tag{7.3}$$

and
$$\left(\frac{R_2}{L_2} - \frac{1}{R_1 C_1} \right) \left(\frac{L_1 + L_2}{L_1} - \frac{R_2}{R_1} \right) > \frac{R_2}{L_1} \tag{7.4}$$

The designs of the filters of Figs. 7.3 and 7.4 are amenable to a personal computer design aid in which the user supplies a value of C_1 based on the worst-case assumption that it must accommodate all the switching ripple current i_s, and the program then calculates the remaining three component values based on the three criteria of stability, minimum volume, and the user-supplied value of allowable power-line-conducted interference.[3]

7.2 Performance Considerations

The constant-power model of the switching regulator is useful for the purposes of demonstrating that the low-frequency input impedance of a switching regulator is negative and that there may be associated stability problems when the regulator is coupled with an LC-input EMI filter. However, in order to assess the modified performance of the updated switching regulators, which consist of the switching reg-

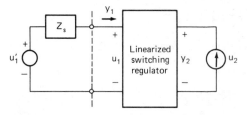

Figure 7.5 Linearized switching regulator model with Thevenin equivalent circuit of EMI filter.

ulators discussed in previous chapters plus their respective EMI filters, and in order to determine more precise stability criteria, a more detailed analysis using the approaches and techniques we have already learned must be performed.

As a first step toward accomplishing this goal, we form a Thevenin equivalent circuit of the EMI filter, with source u_1' and source impedance $Z_s(s)$, as shown in Fig. 7.5. The linearized switching regulator model is the same model that has been discussed in the previous chapters. The effective source for the linearized switching regulator is u_1, as before, and the true source u_1'' is related to the Thevenin equivalent source u_1' in accordance with the specific EMI filter topology. It is of interest now to derive a new set of transfer functions that relate the output vector $\mathbf{y}$ to the new source vector $\mathbf{u}'$ consisting of u_1' and u_2. Once y_1 has been determined, the equivalent circuit of Fig. 7.6 can then be used to determine individual EMI filter currents and voltages. Another, more elegant approach, which will be pursued in the next section, is to treat the EMI filter as an integral part of the updated multiorder switching regulator system and solve for all variables of interest directly. However, this first-step approach will allow us to identify more readily the specific influence of the EMI filter on overall performance.

From Fig. 7.5, we see that

$$\hat{U}_1(s) = \hat{U}_1'(s) - Z_s(s)\hat{Y}_1(s) \tag{7.5}$$

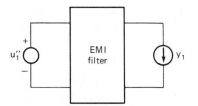

Figure 7.6 Input EMI filter analytical model.

or, using matrix notation for use with our previously derived equations

$$\hat{\mathbf{U}}(s) = \hat{\mathbf{U}}'(s) - \mathbf{Z}(s)\hat{\mathbf{Y}}(s) \qquad (7.6)$$

where

$$\mathbf{Z}(s) = \begin{bmatrix} Z_s(s) & 0 \\ 0 & 0 \end{bmatrix} \qquad (7.7a)$$

and $$\hat{\mathbf{U}}'(s) = [\hat{U}_1'(s) \quad \hat{U}_2(s)]^T \qquad (7.7b)$$

Remembering that the general transfer function $\mathbf{T}_{yu}(s)$ is defined such that $\hat{\mathbf{Y}}(s) = \mathbf{T}_{yu}(s)\hat{\mathbf{U}}(s)$, we now define $\mathbf{T}_{yu}'(s)$ such that $\hat{\mathbf{Y}}(s) = \mathbf{T}_{yr}'(s)\hat{\mathbf{U}}'(s)$, in which case

$$\mathbf{T}_{yu}'(s), = [\mathbf{I} + \mathbf{T}_{yu}(s)\mathbf{Z}(s)]^{-1}\mathbf{T}_{yu}(s) \qquad (7.8)$$

From Eq. (7.8), the individual updated source-to-output transfer functions can be determined in terms of the original transfer functions that were defined in Chap. 5. To simplify notation somewhat, we shall assume that all transfer functions of interest are source-to-output transfer functions (we can always define a state variable as an output variable as well). In particular, we let $\mathbf{T}_{yu}(s) = \mathbf{T}(s)$, and $\mathbf{T}_{yu}'(s) = \mathbf{T}'(s)$. Also, we let the matrix elements $T_{jk}(s)$ and $T_{jk}'(s)$ represent the individual transfer functions of interest for the original and updated switching regulators, respectively. Solving for the elements of Eq. (7.8), we have

$$T_{jk}'(s) = \frac{T_{jk}(s)}{1 + Z_s(s)/Z_1(s)} \qquad (7.9)$$

where it is recognized that $T_{11}(s)T_{22}(s) = T_{12}(s)T_{21}(s)$ and where, as before, $Z_1(s)$ is defined as $T_{11}^{-1}(s)$.

By inspection of Eq. (7.9), it is clear that a necessary and sufficient condition for negligible closed-loop performance modification due to source impedance is that $Z_s(s) \ll Z_1(s)$, as one would surmise from Fig. 7.5. In applications where dynamic performance is not particularly important, so only stability is of major concern, the criterion of $Z_s(s) \ll Z_1(s)$ may represent a gross overdesign. To examine the stability of the updated switching regulator, we combine Eqs. (5.12) and (7.8), using our simplified notation, to arrive at

$$\mathbf{T}'(s) = [\mathbf{I} + \mathbf{T}(s)\mathbf{Z}(s)]^{-1}$$

$$\cdot \{\mathbf{M}(s)[s\mathbf{I} - \mathbf{A}_0 - \mathbf{EF}^T(s)]^{-1}[\mathbf{B}_0 + \mathbf{EQ}^T(s)] + \mathbf{N}_0\} \qquad (7.10)$$

It follows directly that a necessary and sufficient condition for stability of the updated switching regulator is that the updated closed-loop characteristic equation, shown in Eq. (7.11), have no RHP roots.

$$\left[1 + \frac{Z_s(s)}{Z_1(s)}\right] \det\left[sI - A_0 - EF^T(s)\right] = 0 \qquad (7.11)$$

Because of the factorability of Eq. (7.11), we can say that if the original switching regulator is stable, then a necessary and sufficient condition for stability of the updated switching regulator is that the expression $1 + Z_s(s)/Z_1(s)$ have no RHP roots.

As a specific example, we once again consider the basic boost regulator, this time updated with the simplified EMI filter shown in Fig. 7.2. Since the ESR of the output capacitor would not be expected to be as significant for input impedance as it was for output impedance, it will be neglected here for algebraic simplicity. The Thevenin equivalent source impedance Z_s is determined by calculating the impedance $1/C_1 s$ in parallel with the impedance $R_d + L_1 s$ to arrive at

$$Z_s(s) = \frac{(1/C_1)(s + R_d/L_1)}{s^2 + sR_d/L_1 + 1/L_1 C_1} \qquad (7.12)$$

The input impedance $Z_1(s)$ of the basic boost regulator is the inverse of Eq. (5.9a). Applying lag compensation in accordance with Eq. (5.32), we have

$$Z_1(s) = \left\{s^2 + \frac{s}{RC_2}\left[1 - \frac{u_{10}\omega_p K}{V_p(1 - D)^2(s + \omega_p)}\right]\right.$$
$$\left. + \frac{(1 - D)^2}{L_2 C_2}\left[1 + \frac{u_{10}\omega_D K}{V_p(1 - D)^2(s + \omega_p)}\right]\right\} \div \Delta \qquad (7.13a)$$

where

$$\Delta = \frac{1}{L_2}\left\{s + \frac{1}{RC_2}\left[1 - \frac{u_{10}\omega_p K}{V_p(1 - D)^2(s + \omega_p)}\right]\right\} \qquad (7.13b)$$

and where the output filter components are now designated by the subscript 2. Although it may be algebraically cumbersome, it is conceptually straightforward to use Eqs. (7.12) and (7.13) to form the equation $1 + Z_s(s)/Z_1(s) = 0$, multiply through by the denominator of $Z_s(s)/Z_1(s)$, and apply the Routh-Hurwitz stability criterion to determine stability. Alternatively, one can form a Bode plot of the pseudo-gain expression $Z_s(s)/Z_1(s)$.

From Eq. (7.13), it can be determined that, for $u_{10}K/V_p(1 - D)^2 \gg 1$ and $\omega < u_{10}K\omega_p/V_p(1 - D)^2$, the input impedance to the basic boost regulator is $-R(1 - D)^2$, which is negative as we would expect. Assuming for the moment that the poles and zeros of Eq. (7.12) are in this low frequency range of $Z_1(s)$, the equation $1 + Z_s(s)/Z_1(s) = 0$ yields the straightforward stability criterion

$$\frac{R_d}{L_1} > \frac{1}{RC_1(1 - D)^2} \tag{7.14}$$

From Fig. 4.11, it can be seen that the low-frequency input power to the basic boost regulator is $u_1^2/R(1 - D)^2$. Recognizing that the u_1 in Fig. 4.11 corresponds to the x_2 of Fig. 7.2, we see that the stability criteria of Eqs. (7.2) and (7.14) are identical. This confirms that for frequencies within the regulating bandwidth of the switching regulator, the constant-power model may be used to determine system stability of the EMI filter and the basic switching regulator. By nature, power-line-conducted interference is of more concern for buck and buck-boost topologies than it is for boost topologies.

7.3 Derivation of Feed-Forward State Control Laws

In Sec. 7.2, it was observed that a more elegant analytical approach to the problem of switching regulators with input EMI filters is to treat the entire updated regulator as an integral multiorder system. Although this approach may be more cumbersome algebraically, it provides direct visibility of the additional state variables that are associated with the input EMI filter, as well as the original switching regulator state variables. In accordance with the teachings of optimal control theory, it should now be possible to use these new state variables to implement an improved control law. In this section, we derive such a control law, after Lee,[4] that minimizes the influence of the input EMI filter without relying on the brute-force power circuit design criterion $Z_s(s) \ll Z_1(s)$.

Consider the switching regulator system of Fig. 7.7, consisting of a general second-order switching regulator with state variables x_3 and x_4 preceded by a simplified damped EMI filter with state variables x_1 and x_2: x_3 is the current through the switching regulator inductor L_2, and x_4 is the voltage across the switching regulator capacitor C_2. The EMI filter is simplified in the sense that, in practice, when additional damping resistance is required beyond that inherent to the input power line and the EMI filter components, it would be ac-coupled instead of dc-coupled, as explained in the previous section. In fact, the input EMI filter may consist of multiple stages and be very messy indeed from an algebraic standpoint. Nevertheless, this simplified model will serve to illustrate the basic principles involved and will permit us to draw conclusions about more complicated EMI filter structures.

For maximum potential controllability, the control-law state vector coefficient matrix $\mathbf{F}^T(s)$ consists of four terms in accordance with Eq. (7.15).

$$\mathbf{F}^T(s) = [F_1(s) \quad F_2(s) \quad F_3(s) \quad F_4(s)] \tag{7.15}$$

$F_4(s)$ is the element that represents the familiar output voltage feedback control, $F_3(s)$ is the element that represents current feedback control, and $F_1(s)$ and $F_2(s)$ are the new control elements whose possible benefit we shall now assess. Because of the physical location of the input EMI filter, control associated with x_1 and x_2 might be termed "feed-forward control." However, in a mathematical sense, this new control is simply additional feedback control, and we would like to reserve the term feed-forward control for control that is associated with the sources. On the other hand, it may be useful to distinguish the control associated with the input EMI filter state variables from the conventional feedback control. Thus, we shall term this new control "feed-forward state control."

The EMI filter state equations can be written as

$$\dot{x}_1 = -\frac{R_d}{L_1} x_1 - \frac{1}{L_1} x_2 + \frac{1}{L_1} u_1 \tag{7.16}$$

and

$$\dot{x}_2 = \frac{1}{C_1} x_1 - \frac{1}{C_1} y_1 \tag{7.17}$$

It is easily shown that the linearized output variable y_1 is equal to $x_3 D + x_{30} \hat{d}$ for the buck and buck-boost converters and is simply equal to x_3 for the boost converter. Thus, for the linearized open-loop state equations that apply to Fig. 7.7, $\dot{x}_1$ is not a function of x_3 or x_4, and $\dot{x}_2$ is not a function of x_2 or x_4. Furthermore, for the three basic second-

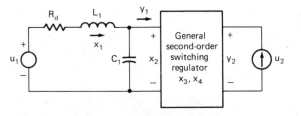

Figure 7.7   Model of general second-order switching regulator with simplified input EMI filter.

order voltage converter topologies, $\dot{x}_3$ is not a function of x_1, and $\dot{x}_4$ is not a function of x_1 or x_2. Thus, the following updated general state coefficient matrix $\mathbf{A}_0$ applies:

$$\mathbf{A}_0 = \begin{bmatrix} \dfrac{-R_d}{L_1} & \dfrac{-1}{L_1} & 0 & 0 \\[2mm] \dfrac{1}{C_1} & 0 & a_{23} & 0 \\[2mm] 0 & a_{32} & a_{33} & a_{34} \\[2mm] 0 & 0 & a_{43} & a_{44} \end{bmatrix} \tag{7.18}$$

The corresponding general $\hat{d}$ coefficient matrix $\mathbf{E}$ is

$$\mathbf{E} = [0 \quad e_2 \quad e_3 \quad e_4]^T \tag{7.19}$$

An apparent necessary condition for minimizing the interaction between the original second-order switching regulator and its input EMI filter, using an improved control law, is that the characteristic polynomial of the updated fourth-order switching regulator be factorable into two polynomials, one containing only original switching regulator terms and the other containing only EMI filter terms. In this way, the possibility of pole-zero cancellation exists, so the resultant transfer function may be dependent upon either the EMI filter or the original switching regulator, but not both. For example, it may be possible to develop a control strategy that eliminates the resonant peak in the output impedance transfer function due to the input EMI filter. If so, this would have very important implications for switching regulators with modulating loads, such as power amplifiers, for example. To examine this possibility, we solve for the characteristic polynomial $\det [s\mathbf{I} - \mathbf{A}_0 - \mathbf{E}\mathbf{F}^T(s)]$ of the updated switching regulator where $\mathbf{F}^T(s)$, $\mathbf{A}_0$, and $\mathbf{E}$ are as defined in Eqs. (7.15), (7.18), and (7.19), respectively.

Defining $[s\mathbf{I} - \mathbf{A}_0 - \mathbf{E}\mathbf{F}^T(s)]$ as the matrix $\boldsymbol{\alpha}$, we have

$$\boldsymbol{\alpha}(s) =$$

$$\begin{bmatrix} s + \dfrac{R_d}{L_1} & \dfrac{1}{L_1} & 0 & 0 \\[3mm] -\dfrac{1}{C_1} - e_2 F_1(s) & s - e_2 F_2(s) & -a_{23} - e_2 F_3(s) & -e_2 F_4(s) \\[3mm] -e_3 F_1(s) & -a_{32} - e_3 F_2(s) & s - a_{33} - e_3 F_3(s) & -a_{34} - e_3 F_4(s) \\[3mm] -e_4 F_1(s) & -e_4 F_2(s) & -a_{43} - e_4 F_3(s) & s - a_{44} e_4 F_4(s) \end{bmatrix}$$

$$\tag{7.20}$$

in which case det $\alpha(s)$ can be expressed as

det $\alpha(s) =$

$$\left\{ \left(s + \frac{R_d}{L_1} \right) [s - e_2 F_2(s)] + \frac{1}{L_1} \left[\frac{1}{C_1} + e_2 F_1(s) \right] \right\}$$

$$\cdot \begin{vmatrix} s - a_{33} - e_3 F_3(s) & -a_{34} - e_3 F_4(s) \\ -a_{43} - e_4 F_3(s) & s - a_{44} - e_4 F_4(s) \end{vmatrix}$$

$$+ \left\{ \left(s + \frac{R_d}{L_1} \right) [a_{32} + e_3 F_2(s)] - \frac{e_3 F_1(s)}{L_1} \right\}$$

$$\cdot \begin{vmatrix} -a_{23} - e_2 F_3(s) & -e_2 F_4(s) \\ -a_{43} - e_4 F_3(s) & s - a_{44} - e_4 F_4(s) \end{vmatrix}$$

$$+ \left[\frac{e_4 F_1(s)}{L_1} - \left(s + \frac{R_d}{L_1} \right) e_4 F_2(s) \right]$$

$$\cdot \begin{vmatrix} -a_{23} - e_2 F_3(s) & -e_2 F_4(s) \\ s - a_{33} - e_3 F_3(s) & -a_{34} - e_3 F_4(s) \end{vmatrix}$$

$$(7.21)$$

Equation (7.21) can be divided into three parts: top, middle, and bottom. The top part consists of two major factors. The first factor is expressed as a polynomial and has only terms related to the EMI filter. We know this because all numbered subscripts are 1 or 2. The second factor is expressed as a determinant and has only terms related to the original switching regulator. We know this because all numbered subscripts are 3 or 4. This represents the desired situation. The major factors of the middle and bottom parts of Eq. (7.21) all have terms related to both the EMI filter and the original switching regulator, which is what we are trying to avoid. The goal, therefore, is to devise a feed-forward state control law that reduces these two parts of Eq. (7.21) to zero.

This goal could be accomplished if the following two expressions were true:

$$\frac{e_3 F_1(s)}{L_1} = \left(s + \frac{R_d}{L_1} \right) [a_{32} + e_3 F_2(s)] \qquad (7.22)$$

and

$$\frac{e_4 F_1(s)}{L_1} = \left(s + \frac{R_d}{L_1} \right) e_4 F_2(s) \qquad (7.23)$$

Unfortunately, Eqs. (7.22) and (7.23) are not independent and cannot both be true. This can be seen clearly by dividing Eq. (7.22) by e_3 and

Eq. (7.23) by e_4. If we choose $F_1(s)$ in accordance with Eq. (7.22), then the middle part of Eq. (7.21) becomes zero, but the bottom part becomes

$$\frac{a_{32}e_4}{e_3}\left(s + \frac{R_d}{L_1}\right)\begin{vmatrix} -a_{23} - e_2F_3(s) & -e_2F_4(s) \\ s - a_{33} - e_3F_3(s) & -a_{34} - e_3F_4(s) \end{vmatrix}$$

If we choose $F_1(s)$ in accordance with Eq. (7.23), the bottom part of Eq. (7.21) becomes zero but the middle part becomes

$$a_{32}\left(s + \frac{R_d}{L_1}\right)\begin{vmatrix} -a_{23} - e_2F_3(s) & -e_2F_4(s) \\ -a_{43} - e_4F_3(s) & s - a_{44} - e_4F_4(s) \end{vmatrix}$$

Thus, although the net effect of the cross products can evidently be significantly reduced with this control strategy, their effect cannot generally be eliminated altogether.

A degenerate case is the buck converter, whose $\dot{x}_4$ equation does not depend upon d. As a result, e_4 is zero, so the bottom part of Eq. (7.21) is also zero. This permits us to choose $F_1(s)$ and $F_2(s)$ strictly in accordance with Eq. (7.22). The solutions for this case are

$$F_1(s) = 0 \tag{7.24}$$

and
$$F_2(s) = \frac{-a_{32}}{e_3} \tag{7.25}$$

It is easily shown that the $\mathbf{A}_0$ and $\mathbf{E}$ matrices for the updated buck converter are

$$\mathbf{A}_0 = \begin{bmatrix} \dfrac{-R_d}{L_1} & \dfrac{-1}{L_1} & 0 & 0 \\ \dfrac{1}{C_1} & 0 & \dfrac{-D}{C_1} & 0 \\ 0 & \dfrac{D}{L_2} & 0 & -\dfrac{1}{L_2} \\ 0 & 0 & \dfrac{1}{C_2} & -\dfrac{1}{RC_2} \end{bmatrix} \tag{7.26}$$

and
$$\mathbf{E} = \begin{bmatrix} 0 & \dfrac{-u_{10}D}{RC_1} & \dfrac{u_{10}}{L_2} & 0 \end{bmatrix}^T \tag{7.27}$$

where L_2 and C_2 are the original switching regulator energy storage elements and R is the load resistance (the ESR of C_2 is, again, neglected without loss of generality for algebraic simplicity). From Eq. (7.26), we see that a_{32} is D/L_2, and from Eq. (7.27), we see that e_3 is u_{10}/L_2. Substituting these values into Eq. (7.25) results in

$$F_2(s) = \frac{-D}{u_{10}} \qquad (7.28)$$

7.4 Improvements with Feed-Forward State Control

A quantitative assessment of the potential improvements in the performance of boost and buck-boost regulators using feed-forward state control is beyond the scope of this book. The potential performance improvement of the updated basic buck regulator of Fig. 7.8 is determined by considering the source-to-output transfer functions

$$T_{11}(s) = \frac{\hat{Y}_1(s)}{\hat{U}_1(s)} = \text{input admittance} \qquad (7.29a)$$

$$T_{12}(s) = \frac{\hat{Y}_1(s)}{\hat{U}_2(s)} = \text{output current susceptibility} \qquad (7.29b)$$

$$T_{21}(s) = \frac{\hat{Y}_2(s)}{\hat{U}_1(s)} = \text{input voltage susceptibility} \qquad (7.29c)$$

and $\qquad T_{22}(s) = \frac{\hat{Y}_2(s)}{\hat{U}_2(s)} = \text{output impedance} \qquad (7.29d)$

in accordance with Fig. 5.1 and Eq. (5.13).

Since the output variables of interest in Fig. 7.8 correspond to state variables, namely, $y_1 = x_1$ and $y_2 = x_4$, it is sufficient to deal with the source-to-state transfer function matrix $[s\mathbf{I} - \mathbf{A}_0 - \mathbf{E}\mathbf{F}^T(s)]^{-1}\mathbf{B}_0$, or

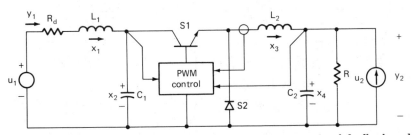

Figure 7.8 Updated basic buck regulator showing both conventional feedback and feed-forward state control.

$\alpha^{-1}\mathbf{B}_0$. It is easily shown that the source coefficient matrix $\mathbf{B}_0$ for Fig. 7.8 is

$$\mathbf{B}_0 = \begin{bmatrix} \dfrac{1}{L_1} & 0 \\ 0 & 0 \\ 0 & 0 \\ 0 & \dfrac{1}{C_2} \end{bmatrix} \tag{7.30}$$

in which case we have

$$\begin{bmatrix} \hat{X}_1(s) \\ \hat{X}_2(s) \\ \hat{X}_3(s) \\ \hat{X}_4(s) \end{bmatrix} = \begin{array}{c} \begin{bmatrix} \dfrac{\text{cof }\alpha_{11}}{L_1} & \dfrac{\text{cof }\alpha_{41}}{C_2} \\ \dfrac{\text{cof }\alpha_{12}}{L_1} & \dfrac{\text{cof }\alpha_{42}}{C_2} \\ \dfrac{\text{cof }\alpha_{13}}{L_1} & \dfrac{\text{cof }\alpha_{43}}{C_2} \\ \dfrac{\text{cof }\alpha_{14}}{L_1} & \dfrac{\text{cof }\alpha_{44}}{C_2} \end{bmatrix} \begin{bmatrix} \hat{U}_1(s) \\ \hat{U}_2(s) \end{bmatrix} \\ \hline \det \alpha \end{array} \tag{7.31}$$

where cof α_{jk} is the cofactor of the matrix element α_{jk}. Combining equations and assuming that $R_d \ll R$, we arrive at the following results:

$$T_{11}(s) = \frac{\dfrac{1}{L_1}\left(s - \dfrac{D^2}{RC_1}\right)}{s^2 + s\left(\dfrac{R_d}{L_1} - \dfrac{D^2}{RC_1}\right) + \dfrac{1}{L_1C_1}} \tag{7.32}$$

$$T_{12}(s) = \frac{-D}{L_1C_1L_2C_2}\left[1 + \frac{u_{10}}{R}F_3(s) - u_{10}F_4(s) - \frac{su_{10}L_2}{R}\right] \Bigg/$$

$$\left(\left[s^2 + s\left(\frac{R_d}{L_1} - \frac{D^2}{RC_1}\right) + \frac{1}{L_1C_1}\right]\left\{s^2 + s\left[\frac{1}{RC_2} - \frac{u_{10}}{L_2}F_3(s)\right]\right.\right.$$

$$\left.\left. + \frac{1}{L_2C_2}[1 - u_{10}F_4(s)]\right\}\right) \tag{7.33}$$

$$T_{41}(s) = 0 \tag{7.34}$$

$$T_{42}(s) = \frac{\dfrac{1}{C_2}\left[s - \dfrac{u_{10}}{L_2}F_3(s)\right]}{s^2 + s\left[\dfrac{1}{RC_2} - \dfrac{u_{10}}{L_2}F_3(s)\right] + \dfrac{1}{L_2C_2}[1 - u_{10}F_4(s)]} \qquad (7.35)$$

Note that det α is comprised of two factors

$$\Delta_1 = s^2 + s\left(\frac{R_d}{L_1} - \frac{D^2}{RC_1}\right) + \frac{1}{L_1C_1} \qquad (7.36)$$

and $\quad \Delta_2 = s^2 + s\left[\dfrac{1}{RC_2} - \dfrac{u_{10}}{L_2}F_3(s)\right] + \dfrac{1}{L_2C_2}[1 - u_{10}F_4(s)] \quad (7.37)$

which correspond, respectively, to the determinant of the input EMI filter with an equivalent load resistance $-R/D^2$ and to the determinant of the original second-order basic buck regulator. The factor Δ_2 cancels in Eq. (7.32), so the input admittance is a function of the input EMI filter only. The factor Δ_1 cancels in Eq. (7.35), so the output impedance is a function of the original switching regulator only. As a result of feed-forward state control, the input voltage susceptibility is nulled out. As implemented, only the output current susceptibility remains dependent on both the input EMI filter and the original switching regulator.

Assuming that the original buck regulator is stable, stability of the updated regulator is assured if

$$\frac{R_d}{L_1} > \frac{D^2}{RC_1} \qquad (7.38)$$

Since only $F_2(s)$ is used for feed-forward state control of the buck regulator, the configuration of the input EMI filter ahead of the capacitor C_1 evidently does not matter, although there would be corresponding changes to Δ_1 and to the stability criterion of Eq. (7.38). The circuit implementation of the control law of Eq. (7.28) can be relatively straightforward if the dc operating range of the input voltage is sufficiently narrow. For regulators that must accommodate wide input voltage variations, the circuit implementation of the control law may be rather complex.[5] Cost-effective enhancements to PWM control circuitry for improved switching regulator performance in the face of increasingly stringent EMI requirements are subjects of continuing study in the power electronics community.

7.5   Illustrative Problems

7.1   An electronics module includes a 100-kHz flyback regulator that draws 100 W from a 28-V dc distribution system in which the power-line-conducted interference specification at 100 kHz is 1 mA rms. How much attenuation must the input EMI filter provide if $D = 0.5$ and $L = L_c$ at the nominal 28-V dc input voltage?

SOLUTION: For $L = L_c$ and $D = 0.5$, the input current waveform of Fig. S7.1 applies.

$$i_{1(\text{avg})} = \frac{100 \text{ W}}{28 \text{ V}} = 3.57 \text{ A} = \frac{I_p}{4}$$

$$\therefore \; I_p = 14.28 \text{ A}$$

$$i_{1\,(\text{fund})} = a_1 \sin 2\pi f_s t + b_1 \cos 2\pi f_s t$$

$$a_1 = 2f_s \int_0^{1/f_s} i_1(t) \sin 2\pi f_s t \; dt$$

$$b_1 = 2f_s \int_0^{1/f_s} i_1(t) \cos 2\pi f_s t \; dt$$

$$a_1 = 2f_s \int_0^{1/2f_s} 2f_s t I_p \sin 2\pi f_s t \; dt$$

$$b_1 = 2f_s \int_0^{1/2f_s} 2f_s t I_p \cos 2\pi f_s t \; dt$$

$$a_1 = 4f_s^2 I_p \left(\frac{1}{4\pi^2 f_s^2} \sin 2\pi f_s t - \frac{t}{2\pi f_s} \cos 2\pi f_s t \right)_0^{1/2f_s}$$

$$b_1 = 4f_s^2 I_p \left(\frac{1}{4\pi^2 f_s^2} \cos 2\pi f_s t + \frac{t}{2\pi f_s} \sin 2\pi f_s t \right)_0^{1/2f_s}$$

$$a_1 = 4f_s^2 I_p \frac{1}{4\pi f_s^2} = \frac{I_p}{\pi}$$

$$b_1 = 4f_s^2 I_p \left(-\frac{1}{4\pi^2 f_s^2} - \frac{1}{4\pi^2 f_s^2} \right) = \frac{-2I_p}{\pi^2}$$

$$i_{1(\text{fund,rms})} = \sqrt{\frac{(a_1^2 + b_1^2)}{2}} = \sqrt{\frac{I_p^2}{2\pi^2} + \frac{2I_p^2}{\pi^4}}$$

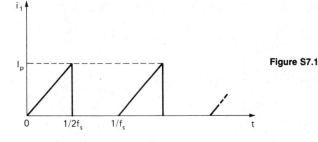

for $I_p = 14.28$,

$$i_{1(fund,rms)} = 3.89 \text{ A}$$

The required attenuation is $10^{-3} \div 3.89$, or

$$-71.8 \text{ dB at } 100 \text{ kHz}$$

7.2   For the damped EMI filter topology of Fig. P7.2, what are the necessary conditions for stability, assuming that the switching regulator can be modeled as a constant power device?

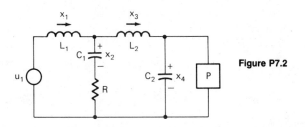

Figure P7.2

SOLUTION: The strategy is to write the system equations according to the format $\dot{x} = \mathbf{A}x + \mathbf{B}u$, linearize as necessary, form the characteristic polynomial $\det [s\mathbf{I} - \mathbf{A}_0]$, and apply the necessary condition that all coefficients must be positive. The Routh-Hurwitz criterion could then be applied to determine any additional stability constraints.

$$u_1 = L_1\dot{x}_1 + x_2 + RC_1\dot{x}_2$$

$$C_1\dot{x}_2 = x_1 - x_3$$

$$x_2 + RC_1\dot{x}_2 = L_2\dot{x}_3 + x_4$$

$$C_2\dot{x}_4 = x_3 - \frac{P}{x_4}$$

Substituting the second equation into the first and rearranging results in

$$\dot{x}_1 = -\frac{R}{L_1} x_1 - \frac{1}{L_1} x_2 + \frac{R}{L_1} x_3 + \frac{1}{L_1} u_1$$

$$\dot{x}_2 = \frac{1}{C_1} x_1 - \frac{1}{C_1} x_3$$

$$\dot{x}_3 = \frac{R}{L_2} x_1 + \frac{1}{L_2} x_2 - \frac{R}{L_2} x_3 - \frac{1}{L_2} x_4$$

$$\dot{x}_4 = \frac{1}{C_2} x_3 - \frac{P}{C_2 x_4}$$

We now linearize the term $P/C_2 x_4$.

$$x_4 = x_{40} + \hat{x}_4$$

$$\frac{1}{x_4} = \frac{1}{x_{40}(1 + \hat{x}_4/x_{40})} \approx \frac{1}{x_{40}} \left(1 - \frac{\hat{x}_4}{x_{40}} \right)$$

Substituting this expression into the $\dot{x}_4$ equation above and considering the ac equations throughout gives us

$$\mathbf{A}_0 = \begin{bmatrix} \dfrac{-R}{L_1} & \dfrac{-1}{L_1} & \dfrac{R}{L_1} & 0 \\[2mm] \dfrac{1}{C_1} & 0 & \dfrac{-1}{C_1} & 0 \\[2mm] \dfrac{R}{L_2} & \dfrac{1}{L_2} & \dfrac{-R}{L_2} & \dfrac{-1}{L_2} \\[2mm] 0 & 0 & \dfrac{1}{C_2} & \dfrac{P}{C_2 u_{10}{}^2} \end{bmatrix}$$

where it is recognized that $x_{40} = u_{10}$.

$$(s\mathbf{I} - \mathbf{A}_0) = \begin{bmatrix} s + \dfrac{R}{L_1} & \dfrac{1}{L_1} & \dfrac{-R}{L_1} & 0 \\[2mm] \dfrac{-1}{C_1} & s & \dfrac{1}{C_1} & 0 \\[2mm] \dfrac{-R}{L_2} & \dfrac{-1}{L_2} & s + \dfrac{R}{L_2} & \dfrac{1}{L_2} \\[2mm] 0 & 0 & \dfrac{-1}{C_2} & s - \dfrac{P}{C_2 u_{10}{}^2} \end{bmatrix}$$

Using the bottom row as a basis for expansion, we have

$$\det(s\mathbf{I} - \mathbf{A}_0) = \Delta$$

$$= \frac{1}{C_2} \frac{1}{L_2} \left[s \left(s + \frac{R}{L_1} \right) + \frac{1}{L_1 C_1} \right] + \left(s - \frac{P}{C_2 u_{10}{}^2} \right) \Delta_1$$

where Δ_1 is defined as the upper-left 3×3 cofactor as given below.

$$\Delta_1 = \left(s + \frac{R}{L_1}\right)\left[s\left(s + \frac{R}{L_2}\right) + \frac{1}{L_2 C_1}\right]$$

$$- \frac{1}{L_1}\left[\frac{-1}{C_1}\left(s + \frac{R}{L_2}\right) + \frac{R}{L_2 C_1}\right] - \frac{R}{L_1}\left(\frac{1}{L_2 C_1} + \frac{sR}{L_2}\right)$$

Using the expression

$$\Delta = a_4 s^4 + a_3 s^3 + a_2 s^2 + a_1 s + a_0$$

we have

$$a_4 = 1$$

$$a_3 = \frac{R}{L_1} + \frac{R}{L_2} - \frac{P}{C_2 u_{10}^2}$$

$$a_2 = \frac{1}{L_1 C_1} + \frac{1}{L_2 C_1} + \frac{1}{L_2 C_2} - \frac{P}{C_2 u_{10}^2}\left(\frac{R}{L_1} + \frac{R}{L_2}\right)$$

$$a_1 = \frac{R}{L_1 L_2 C_2} - \frac{P}{C_2 u_{10}^2}\left(\frac{1}{L_2 C_1} + \frac{1}{L_1 C_1}\right)$$

$$a_0 = \frac{1}{L_1 L_2 C_1 C_2}$$

Necessary condition 1: $a_3 > 0$.

$$R\left(\frac{1}{L_1} + \frac{1}{L_2}\right) > \frac{P}{C_2 u_{10}^2}$$

Necessary condition 2: $a_2 > 0$.

$$\frac{1}{L_1 C_1} + \frac{1}{L_2 C_1} + \frac{1}{L_2 C_2} > \frac{PR}{C_2 u_{10}^2}\left(\frac{1}{L_1} + \frac{1}{L_2}\right)$$

Necessary condition 3: $a_1 > 0$.

$$\frac{R}{L_1 L_2} > \frac{P}{C_1 u_{10}^2}\left(\frac{1}{L_1} + \frac{1}{L_2}\right)$$

Although these conditions, by themselves, do not suggest a particular design algorithm (at least to the author), it can be observed that there is both an upper and a lower bound on the value of R. This may argue against depending on only the ESR of C_1 in military applications where a wide temperature range can be encountered and, hence, where a wide variation in ESR is possible.

7.3 Your task is to design a 28-V dc power-line EMI filter for a lead-compensated 40-kHz push-pull switching regulator that, at nominal line voltage, can be modeled as the switching current source shown in Fig. P7.3. The input voltage range is 20 to 32 V dc. You are asked to use a family of 40-V dc aluminum electrolytic capacitors whose product of C in microfarads and ESR in ohms is approximately 400, and whose product of rms ripple current rating (based on maximum allowed component power dissipation) and ESR in ohms is approximately ⅓. The dc resistance (DCR) of the inductor(s) can be approximated as $10\sqrt{L/I}$ for a conservative component temperature rise. The power-line-conducted emissions specification at the effective switching frequency of 80 kHz is 3 mA rms.

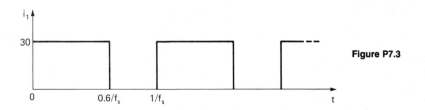

Figure P7.3

SOLUTION: The strategy is to start with a single-section LC filter. If the associated values of ESR and DCR result in stability, then the design is complete. Otherwise, more complicated structures need to be investigated. The first step is to calculate the respective ac and dc components of the switching current waveform.

$$i_{1(rms)} = 30\sqrt{0.6} = 23.24 \text{ A}$$

$$i_{1(dc)} = 30 \times 0.6 = 18 \text{ A}$$

$$i_{1,ac(rms)} = \sqrt{(23.24)^2 - (18)^2} = 14.7 \text{ A}$$

$$\text{Ripple current rating} > 14.7 \text{ A} = 15 \text{ A}$$

The second step is to choose a capacitor based on the assumption that it must accommodate all the ripple current.

$$15 \times \text{ESR} = ⅓$$

$$\text{ESR} = 0.022$$

$$C = \frac{400}{0.022} = 18{,}182 \text{ }\mu\text{F}$$

A standard catalogue item has the following parameters:

$$C = 19{,}000 \text{ }\mu\text{F}$$

$$\text{ESR} = 0.02 \text{ }\Omega$$

$$\text{Current rating} = 15.8 \text{ A rms}$$

A third step is to determine the fundamental component of the ac current waveform. By choosing the origin at $t = 0.3/(80 \times 10^3)$, we have a symmetrical waveform that can only have a cosine component. From Prob. 7.1, we have,

$$b_1 = 2f_s \int_{-0.3/f_s}^{0.3/f_s} 30 \cos 2\pi f_s t \, dt$$

$$= \frac{30}{\pi} [\sin 0.6\pi - \sin(-0.6\pi)]$$

$$= 18.16 \text{ A}$$

$$\frac{b_1}{\sqrt{2}} = 12.84 \text{ A rms}$$

The fourth step is to determine the fundamental voltage drop v_1 across the capacitor, assuming that it absorbs all the ripple current.

$$v_1 = \frac{b_1}{\sqrt{2}} \sqrt{(ESR)^2 + \left(\frac{1}{X_{C1}}\right)^2}$$

where X_{C1} is the capacitive impedance at the fundamental frequency of 80 kHz.

$$X_{C1} = 1/(2\pi \times 80 \times 10^3 \times 19{,}000 \times 10^{-6}) = 0.0001 \ \Omega \ll ESR$$

$$\therefore \quad v_1 \approx 12.84 \times 0.02 = 0.257 \text{ V rms}$$

The fifth step is to determine the value of L that is necessary to prevent the equivalent voltage source v_1 from producing line current in excess of 3 mA rms.

$$\frac{0.257}{2\pi \times 80 \times 10^3 \times L} < 3 \times 10^{-3}$$

$$L > 170 \ \mu\text{H} \rightarrow 200 \ \mu\text{H}$$

$$DCR = \frac{10\sqrt{200 \times 10^{-6}}}{18} = 7.9 \text{ m}\Omega$$

The sixth step is to determine whether or not the single-section filter is stable. The EMI filter resonant frequency f_0 is

$$f_0 = \frac{1}{2\pi\sqrt{200 \times 10^{-6} \times 19{,}000 \times 10^{-6}}} = 81.6 \text{ Hz}$$

which is well within the passband of a lead-compensated switching regulator whose effective switching frequency is 80 kHz. Thus, the equivalent circuit of Fig. S7.3 applies, where the equivalent switching regulator load is determined at the 20-V dc low-line voltage for worst case.

$$R_3 = \frac{P}{(20)^2} = \frac{(20)(18)}{(20)^2} = -0.9 \ \Omega$$

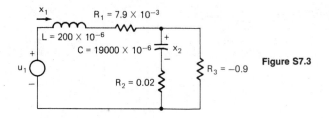

Figure S7.3

The corresponding state equations are

$$u_1 = L\dot{x}_1 + R_1 x_1 + R_2 C \dot{x}_2 + x_2$$

$$C\dot{x}_2 = x_1 - \frac{R_2 C \dot{x}_2 + x_2}{R_3}$$

Combining, rearranging, and assuming $R_1/R_3 \ll 1$ and $R_2/R_3 \ll 1$,

$$\dot{x}_1 = \frac{-(R_1 + R_2)}{L} x_1 - \frac{1}{L} x_2 + \frac{1}{L} u_1$$

$$\dot{x}_2 = \frac{1}{C} x_1 - \frac{1}{R_3 C} x_2$$

$$\mathbf{A} = \begin{bmatrix} \dfrac{-(R_1 + R_2)}{L} & \dfrac{-1}{L} \\ \dfrac{1}{C} & \dfrac{-1}{R_3 C} \end{bmatrix}$$

$$s\mathbf{I} - \mathbf{A} = \begin{bmatrix} s + \dfrac{R_1 + R_2}{L} & -\dfrac{1}{L} \\ \dfrac{1}{C} & s + \dfrac{1}{R_3 C} \end{bmatrix}$$

$$\det(s\mathbf{I} - \mathbf{A}) \approx s^2 + \left(\frac{R_1 + R_2}{L} + \frac{1}{R_3 C} \right) s + \frac{1}{LC}$$

The stability criterion is

$$\frac{R_1 + R_2}{L} + \frac{1}{R_3 C} > 0$$

$$\frac{7.9 \times 10^{-3} + 0.02}{200 \times 10^{-6}} > \frac{1}{0.9 \times 19{,}000 \times 10^{-6}} \,?$$

$$139.5 > 58.5 \text{ ? Yes.}$$

Caution: Aluminum electrolytic capacitors are typically specified in terms of maximum ESR, not minimum ESR. Therefore, special tests may be necessary if ESR is to be depended upon for stability. Note that R_1 by itself is not sufficient. Also note that the resulting filter, while stable, is well underdamped, which may have adverse system repercussions. Feed-forward state control and/ or a third-order EMI filter with greater stability margin may be appropriate here, if the power supply designer can negotiate for the additional volume. Note also that the initial tolerance and temperature variation capacitor values, which have been ignored in this problem for simplicity, are generally not negligible.

References

1. N. O. Sokal and D. E. Nelson, "Preventing Input-Filter Oscillation in Switching Regulators," *Proceedings of Powercon 2,* Oct. 1975, pp. 293–294.
2. R. D. Middlebrook, "Input Filter Considerations in Design and Application of Switching Regulators," *IEEE Power Electronics Specialists Conference Record,* June 1977, pp. 36–57.
3. D. M. Mitchell, "Damped EMI Filters for Switching Regulators," *IEEE Transactions on Electromagnetic Compatibility,* vol. EMC-20, no. 3, Aug. 1978, pp. 457–459.
4. S. S. Kelkar and F. C. Lee, "A Novel Feedforward Compensation Canceling Input Filter-Regulator Interaction," *IEEE Transactions on Aerospace and Electronic Systems,* vol. AES-19, no. 2, Mar. 1983.
5. F. C. Lee, "Input Filter Compensation for Switching Regulators," *NASA Report* N84-24975, VPI&SU, June 1984.

Index

AC link, 3
Active filtering, 2

Bandwidth (*see* Open-loop gain)
Bode plot, 60, 90, 143
  (*See also* Boost converter; Buck
    converter; Open-loop gain)
Boost converter (regulator):
  as CIC control law example, 111–114
  as CIC open-loop gain example, 118–
    122
  as dc solution example, 99, 100
  as EMI filtering example, 143, 144
  as linearization example, 65–68
  with simplified current-injected control
    circuit, 40
  as source-to-state transfer function
    example, 84–86
  steady-state equations for, 8–9
  topological development of, 6–10
  as voltage-mode vs. CIC comparison
    example, 122–129
  voltage-mode open-loop gain Bode plots
    of, 96
  voltage-mode open-loop gain equation
    of, 92
  as voltage-mode open-loop gain
    example, 91–93
  as voltage-mode output impedance
    example, 88–90, 97
  (*See also* Converters)
Buck-boost converter (regulator):
  steady-state equations for, 8–9
  topological development of, 6–10
  voltage-mode open-loop gain equation
    of, 92
  (*See also* Converters)

Buck converter (regulator):
  as feed-forward state control example,
    148–151
  with simple PWM controller, 38
  as state-space averaging example, 60,
    61, 86, 87
  steady-state equations for, 8–9
  topological development of, 6–10
  voltage-mode open-loop gain Bode plots
    of, 94, 98
  voltage-mode open-loop gain equation
    of, 92
  (*See also* Converters)

Capacitance, critical, criterion for, 18–19
Capacitor, practical considerations of, 23,
  53, 139
Characteristic equation (polynomial), 90,
  121, 122, 128, 143, 146
Compensation techniques (*see* Open-loop
  gain)
Computer-aided design (analysis), 44, 51,
  52, 56, 64, 140
Continuity approximation (*see* State-
  space averaging)
Control, PWM (*see* Pulse-width
  modulated control)
Control circuitry, 24, 27
  (*See also* Pulse-width modulated
    control)
Control law, 68, 83
  for CIC converters, 111–114, 118
  for feed-forward state control, 139,
    144–149
  for voltage-mode converters, 84, 89, 91
  (*See also* Feedback control)
Conversion, types of, 1–3

Converters:
  boost-derived, 26, 39, 41
  bridge and half-bridge, 24–26
  buck-boost-derived, 39, 41
  buck-derived, 24, 26, 41, 93
  control of (*see* Pulse-width modulated
      control)
  current, 14–18
  current-fed, 26
  flyback, 27
    (*See also* Buck-boost converter)
  forward, 24–25
  power, definition of, 6
  push-pull, 24–25
  resonant, 27, 28
  SCR, 27
  voltage: fourth-order: with power-line
        EMI filter, 146–151
      topological development of, 19–22
      (*See also* Ćuk converter; SEPIC
        converter)
    second-order: steady-state equations
        for, 8–9
      topological development of, 6–10
      (*See also* Boost converter; Buck-
        boost converter; Buck converter)
  transformer isolated, 23–28
Critical capacitance, criterion for, 18–19
Critical damping, 128, 129
Critical inductance:
  buck converter waveforms for, 11
  criterion for, 10–12
  Ćuk converter, 19, 20, 22, 27
Current-injected (current-mode) control
    (CIC), 39–41, 97, 109–129
  control-law derivation, 111–114
  switching stability criterion, 114, 118
  voltage-mode performance comparison,
    122–129
Current limiting, 112, 114
Current sharing, 112
Cycloconverter, 2

Damping factor, 97, 120, 125, 126, 139
DC characteristics:
  of boost converter, 99, 100
  general discussion of, 97–100
DC link, 2
Diode:
  free-wheeling, 24
  practical considerations of, 23, 45, 95,
    96

Discontinuous conduction mode (DCM),
    12–13, 61–64
Duty factor:
  continuous expression of, 38
  control of, 10
  definition of, 35
  effective, 24, 35
  introduction to, 6
  modulation of, 36
    (*See also* Pulse-width modulated
      control)

Efficiency, practical limitations on, 23
Electromagnetic compatibility (EMC), 36
Electromagnetic interference (EMI), 36,
    37, 90, 95, 110
EMI filtering, effects of, 137–151
  feed-forward state control law, 144–
    151
  performance considerations, 140–144
  stability considerations, 138–140, 143,
    144
Equivalent series inductance (ESL),
    definition of, 23
Equivalent series resistance (ESR),
    definition of, 23
European Space Agency Technology
    Center, 109

Feed-forward control, 39, 84, 93
Feed-forward state control laws, 144–151
Feedback control, 13, 55, 59, 84, 90, 145
  (*See also* Control law; Stability;
    Transfer functions)
Flyback converter, 27
  (*See also* Buck-boost converter)
Frequency response, 97

Gain (*see* Open-loop gain)
Gain margin, definition of, 93
  (*See also* Open-loop gain)

Inductance, critical (*see* Critical
    inductance)
Inductor:
  coupled, 23
  practical considerations of, 23, 53, 88,
    139

Input admittance (impedance):
  of buck converter with feed-forward
    state control, 151
  definition of, 87
  effect on EMI filter design, 138, 140,
    143, 144
Input voltage susceptibility:
  of buck converter with feed-forward
    state control, 151
  definition of, 88
  voltage-mode vs. CIC comparison, 122–
    129
Integrated magnetics, 27
Interference, switching, 6, 7, 37, 45, 57,
    95, 138, 140, 144
Inversion, definition of, 2
Inverters for motor control, 3
Isolation, 24
  (*See also* Transformer)

Lag compensation, 93–97, 122, 125, 126,
    143
Laplace transform, 60, 83, 87, 113
Lead compensation, 93–97, 112, 121,
    127–129
L'Hospital's rule, 13
Limit-cycle controllers, 109, 110
Line regulation, 39, 90, 97, 98
Linear regulator, 5, 6
Linear systems analysis, modern, review
    of, 52–56
Linearization:
  boost converter example of, 65–68
  of CIC control law, 113
  of feed-forward control law, 84
  mathematical treatment of, 51–73
Load regulation, 39, 90, 97, 98
Losses, component, 23

Magnetic amplifiers (*see* Saturable
    reactors)
Mercury-arc tubes, 1
Minimum-phase system, definition of, 93
Modulation, pulse-width (*see* Pulse-width
    modulated control)

Noise, switching (*see* Interference,
    switching)
Nyquist plot, 90

Open-loop gain:
  of CIC boost converter, 118–122
  compensation techniques, voltage-
    mode, 93–97
  for critical damping, 127–129
  dc, of buck converter, 39
  general definition of, 91
  second-order converter equations of, 92
  of voltage-mode boost converter, 91–93
  (*See also* Stability)
Optical couplers, 24
Output current susceptibility:
  of buck converter with feed-forward
    state control, 151
  definition of, 87
Output impedance:
  of buck converter with feed-forward
    state control, 151
  definition of, 88
  voltage-mode vs. CIC comparison, 122–
    129

Parallel supplies, 112
Phase control, SCR, 2, 3
Phase lag (lead) (*see* Open-loop gain)
Phase margin, definition of, 95
  (*See also* Open-loop gain)
Phase variables, 52
Pole cancellation, definition of, 95
  (*See also* Open-loop gain)
Postregulators, 13
Power factor, improvements to, 2
Power-line-conducted interference (*see*
    Interference, switching)
Pulse-width modulated (PWM) control:
  circuit implementation, 37–41, 151
  current-mode (current-injected) control
    (*see* Current-injected control)
  fixed frequency, 37–41
  technique, definition of, 36
  variable frequency, 36, 37, 109, 110
  voltage-mode: vs. CIC comparison,
    122–129
    definition of, 39
  waveform, spectral analysis of, 41–45
  (*See also* Control law)

Rectification:
  definition of, 2
  off-line, 26
Regulation, line (load), 39, 90, 97, 98

Regulator, switching:
  control of (*see* Pulse-width modulated
    control)
  definition of, 6
  equivalent linear circuits of, 71–73
  transfer functions for (*see* Transfer
    functions)
  (*See also* Boost converter; Buck-boost
    converter; Buck converter;
    Converters)
Resonant converters, 27, 28
Right-half-plane (RHP) zero, 93, 97, 118,
  119, 125
Ripple, definition of, 7
Routh–Hurwitz criterion, 90, 140, 143

Sample-and-hold PWM system, 42
Sampling, real-time, 42
Saturable reactors, 1, 27
Scaling, voltage (*see* Transformer)
Semiconductors, power, 1
  (*See also* Diode; Transistor)
SEPIC converter, 21, 22
Silicon-controlled rectifier (SCR) (*see*
  Converters; Phase control, SCR)
Small-signal approximation (*see*
  Linearization)
Stability:
  of buck converter with feed-forward
    state control, 151
  current-mode switching, 114–118
  general considerations, 90–93
  operational amplifier, effect of, 39
  subharmonic, 45, 95, 96, 114, 122, 129
  of switching regulator with EMI filter,
    138–140, 143, 144
  transport lag, effect of, 42
  (*See also* Open-loop gain)
State-space averaging:
  buck converter example of, 60, 61, 86,
    87

State-space averaging (*Con't.*):
  mathematical treatment of, 51–73
State variables, definition of, 52
Subharmonic instability (*see* Stability,
  subharmonic)
Switching regulator (*see* Regulator,
  switching)

Tail chasing (*see* Stability, subharmonic)
Thevenin equivalent circuit, 141, 143
Transfer functions:
  of buck converter with feed-forward
    state control, 149–151
  current-mode (*see* Current-injected
    control)
  of switching regulator with EMI filter,
    141, 142
  voltage mode, 83–100
    source-to-output, 86–90
    source-to-state, 84–86
Transformer:
  B-H characteristic, 24
  current, 39
  dc, 71–73
  flyback, 27
  imbalance, effects of, 45, 95, 96, 112
  for isolation and voltage scaling, 3,
    23–27
  magnetizing current, 24, 27
Transistor, practical considerations of,
  23, 45, 95, 96
Transport lag, 42, 93

Voltage-mode control (*see* Pulse-width
  modulated control)

Waveshaping, 2, 3

ABOUT THE AUTHOR

Daniel M. Mitchell was born in Denver, Colorado, in 1938. He received his B.S.E.E. degree from Massachusetts Institute of Technology in 1960 and his M.S.E.E. degree from Iowa State University in 1966.

From 1960 to 1963 he was with the Westinghouse Research and Development Laboratories, where he assisted in the development of variable-frequency solid-state drives for induction motors. From 1963 to 1967 he was associated with the Collins Radio Company, where he designed signal conditioning equipment for the Apollo program and was a power supply design engineer. In 1967 he joined the Hallicrafters Company, where he designed prototype high-power switching regulators and pulse modulators. In 1968 he returned to Collins Radio as a power supply project engineer. In 1974 Collins Radio became part of the Rockwell International Corporation. Since 1976 the author has been a member of the Advanced Technology and Engineering Department of Collins Defense Communications. From 1976 to 1980 he was responsible for power conversion IR&D projects specializing in miniaturized power supplies operating in the 200- to 600-kHz range. In 1982 he was promoted to Manager, Synthesizers and Circuit Technology, where he is responsible for advanced design and development in the areas of frequency synthesis, LSI components, and power conversion.

Mr. Mitchell has published over 33 internal working papers and magazine articles, five IEEE papers, and has been issued ten patents. He is an Adjunct Instructor at the University of Iowa.